Return to the Land of the Head Hunters

NATIVE ART OF THE PACIFIC NORTHWEST
A Bill Holm Center Series

The mission of this publication series is to foster appreciation
and understanding of Pacific Northwest Native art and culture.

In the Spirit of the Ancestors:
Contemporary Northwest Coast Art at the Burke Museum
edited by Robin Wright and Kathryn Bunn-Marcuse

Return to the Land of the Head Hunters:
Edward S. Curtis, The Kwakwa̱ka̱'wakw,
and the Making of Modern Cinema
edited by Brad Evans and Aaron Glass

RETURN TO THE LAND OF THE HEAD HUNTERS

EDWARD S. CURTIS, THE KWAKWAKA'WAKW, AND THE MAKING OF MODERN CINEMA

EDITED BY

BRAD EVANS

AND

AARON GLASS

BILL HOLM CENTER FOR THE STUDY
OF NORTHWEST COAST ART
Burke Museum, Seattle

in association with

UNIVERSITY OF WASHINGTON PRESS
Seattle and London

Bill Holm Center
for the Study of Northwest Coast Art
BURKE MUSEUM

The publication of *Return to the Land of the Head Hunters*
was made possible in part by a generous gift from
ROBERT & JUDITH WINQUIST
and a grant from the
QUEST FOR TRUTH FOUNDATION

Bill Holm Center for the Study of Northwest Coast Art
Burke Museum of Natural History and Culture
University of Washington, Box 353010
Seattle, WA 98195, USA
www.burkemuseum.org/bhc

University of Washington Press
PO Box 50096
Seattle, WA 98145, USA
www.washington.edu/uwpress

Cataloging-in-Publication Data is on file with
the Library of Congress. ISBN 978-0-295-99344-7

The paper used in this publication is acid-free and meets the
minimum requirements of American National Standard for
Information Sciences—Permanence of Paper for Printed Library
Materials, ANSI Z39.48–1984. ∞

*A portion of the royalties earned from this book will be donated to the
U'mista Cultural Centre to benefit Kwakwaka'wakw communities.*

We were terribly saddened in the summer of 2010 by the loss of our dear friend and close colleague, Andrea Sanborn (Pudłas), executive director of the U'mista Cultural Centre from 2002 to 2010, who played an absolutely central role in the conceptualization and realization of the Curtis film project. For over a decade, in her official capacity and out of personal commitment, Andrea devoted herself tirelessly to the preservation and promotion of Kwakwa̱ka'wakw language and culture. Without her limitless stores of energy, her resourcefulness, and her redoubtable personality, the project could not have been completed as envisioned.

We dedicate this volume to her efforts and to her memory.

CONTENTS

U'MISTA CULTURAL SOCIETY
STATEMENT OF PARTICIPATION

La̱'misa̱n's Kwakwa̱ka̱'wakw la̱x̱an's gweła'asi la̱x̱ux̱ da U'mista̱x̱ olak̕ala a̱mya'x̱ala i'ax̱'ine'yas Edward Curtis la'e sa̱badza̱we'gila x̱an's k̕wa̱lsk̕wa̱l'yakwi la̱x̱a ḵwisała 'nala. La̱'ma'as ika'mas x̱an's ni'noka̱'yi le'ga̱n's 'na̱max̱a̱s dłu' duḵwa̱mxda'x̱wax̱. La̱'misa̱n's ugwa̱ka̱ ko̱dła'nakwa̱la le'ga̱n's duḵwala̱x̱ ya̱x̱wała'ina'yasa̱n's k̕wa̱lsk̕wa̱l'yakwi dłu'wi da ik six̱wa la̱x̱a x̱wak̕wa̱na. Yu'a̱m i'a̱l'stsa ḵwa̱lsk̕wa̱l'yakwi ya̱x̱us ga̱x̱ex̱ x̱its̱a̱x̱alasu'wa. La̱'misux̱ 'na̱max̱a̱s ga̱xs ła̱xwe'yasa̱n's k̕wa̱lsk̕wa̱l'yakwi la̱'ex̱ 'wi'la dłidła̱gad la̱x̱an's gwaya̱ya̱'elasi. Ga̱'walida Kwakwa̱ka̱'wakw la'e sa̱badza̱we'gili Curtis la̱x̱ 1914, it̕ida ga̱'wala la̱x̱ 1973 la̱'ex̱ hiłasu'wux̱da a̱x̱adza̱we' yasa sa̱badza̱'weyu. Ika̱nu'x̱w ni'noka̱yi le'ga̱nu'x̱w gige'x̱ux̱da i'a̱x̱ala̱x̱ ka'ux̱da sa̱badza̱'weyux̱w ka ugwa̱ḵama̱xs dała̱x̱ gweła̱sesa̱nu'x̱w 'nala.

The Kwak̕wala speaking peoples—the Kwakwa̱ka̱'wakw, represented by the U'mista Cultural Society—are indeed indebted to Edward Curtis for his work in documenting some of our traditions in this early film. To see our old people as they looked in those early days is very special. We continue to learn by watching the dance movements and the expert paddling in the film. The young people who participated in the live performance as part of this project are descendents of the people you see in the film. Because they have all been initiated and named in our ceremonies, they bring a true spiritual connection with them in their singing and dancing. The Kwakwa̱ka̱'wakw people helped make Curtis's film in 1914 and then helped again in 1973 when it was remade. We are proud to have been involved in the current project, as this film is part of our history.

CHIEF WILLIAM T. CRANMER
Chair, U'mista Cultural Society

FOREWORD

BILL HOLM

It is now just a bit less than a century ago that Edward S. Curtis, in the midst of his monumental project of recording the cultures of the Native peoples of western North America in photographs and text, embarked on an ambitious project to produce a motion picture based on the culture of one of those tribes. Although he apparently planned to make other such films, this one, on the Kwakwa̲ka'wakw people of the central British Columbia coast, was the only one that he completed. That he chose this one Native group as the subject of his venture into cinematography is probably easily explained. Curtis found the Kwakwa̲ka'wakw to have a still-living, highly dramatic, and photogenic traditional culture lurking just below a veneer of acculturation, and an able, experienced, and willing Native guide to help him toward his goal. George Hunt, the son of an English Hudson's Bay Company employee and a Tlingit noblewoman from Alaska, worked for museum collector Johan Adrian Jacobsen in the early 1880s and for Franz Boas from 1888 until the end of Hunt's life in 1932. Without George Hunt's expertise and help, Curtis would likely have been unable to successfully make the motion picture he planned, and volume 10 of *The North American Indian* would not have *twice* as many pages (printed on thinner paper for uniformity) as the average of the preceding volumes. Hunt furnished Curtis with information on all aspects of Kwakwa̲ka'wakw life and traditions, history, warfare, shamanism, social organization, language, ceremonial activities, and more. He commissioned masks, totem poles, and regalia, and hired and directed carvers and weavers, actors and dancers. Although Curtis, or perhaps William Myers, his able ethnologist/scribe, worked with other Kwakwa̲ka'wakw people as well, George Hunt's presence pervades the Kwakiutl volume and the film *In the Land of the Head Hunters*.

It is common today to think that Curtis manipulated his Indian subjects, dressed them in costumes, directed their actions, and generally applied his

Fig. F.1. Edward S. Curtis, *Twin Child Healer (b)*, 1914. (*NAI,* vol. 10.) Photograph depicts George and Francine Hunt enacting a shamanic curing rite of the G̱usgi'mukw people. Charles Deering McCormick Library of Special Collections, Northwestern University Library.

romantic notions. For example, a recent commentary on a well-known Curtis photograph of a Kwakwa̱ka'wakw woman in a cedar-bark skirt and cape, wearing a spruce-root hat, and harvesting abalone from rocks on the beach, suggested that the anonymous woman was merely following Curtis's idea of what she should look like (see photo essay 2, fig. E.2.9). That she was anonymous in the photograph's original caption was certainly true, but she was

Fig. F.2. George and Francine Hunt, Ft. Rupert, 1930. Photo by J. B. Scott.
American Museum of Natural History Library, 328734.

far from an unknown Native actress directed by Curtis. Familiarly known as
Tsak̕wani she was George Hunt's second wife Francine, a noblewoman of the
'Nak̕waxda'x̱w tribe (figs. F.1 and F.2). The story of her life, her many noble
names and marriages, and her last traditional marriage as T̓łat̓łaḻawidzamga
to George Hunt, occupies forty-five bilingual pages in Franz Boas's "Ethnnol-
ogy of the Kwakiutl" (Boas 1921:1028–73). Tsak̕wani made needed cedar-bark
(and substitute raffia) robes for the film, advised on details, and played several roles in Curtis's drama. She was a prime example of the rich sources of
information utilized by Curtis in 1914.

In everyday life at Fort Rupert in the early twentieth century, Tsak̕wani
dressed much as her Euro-Canadian counterparts did. But Fort Rupert was an
old village where "Big Houses" still predominated over the new, framed individual family homes. Travel to other villages and to Alert Bay, the metropo-
lis of the area, was usually by planked gill-net fishing boats powered by
gasoline engines, although traditional canoes still had a place in transporta-

Bill Holm

tion. Kwaḱwala was the common language. Missionaries and government agents were trying hard to wean the people away from their language and Native customs, mostly concentrating on the children. Ceremonial activity was unlawful but alive, often surreptitiously. Ancient concepts of rank and privilege were as strong as ever, although under constant attack by the authorities.

In the 1950s and '60s things had changed, and ceremonial life was beginning to pick up with the removal of the antipotlatch provisions of the 1884 Canadian Indian Act. Kwaḱwala was still spoken. In Alert Bay, taxi cabs shuttled back and forth on the long street paralleling the beach. It was just too far to carry your purchases from the grocery store to the Nimpkish Reserve at the west end. But the taxi drivers and the dispatcher spoke in Kwaḱwala. Kwakwaka'wakw fishermen, communicating by radio with one another from their seiners, spoke it, to the consternation of non-Native competitors. Chiefs would never presume to use dance privileges or prerogatives belonging to others, nor fail to pay all the witnesses in the Big House when their inherited privileges were publically presented. That is just as true today as it was then or in Curtis's time. Even when a public dance performance today is given at, for example, a museum opening in some distant city, only dances that can be properly claimed by a member of the troupe will typically be included, and often a symbolic payment of a Native carving or some suitable memento is presented to an official of the sponsoring institution. Potlatches are frequent today. The new Big Houses are huge by ancient standards, holding up to a thousand guests, all to be paid according to protocol.

I remember when, some seventy years ago, I first became really aware of the work of Edward S. Curtis. It was in the library of the junior high school I attended in Seattle, when I pulled from the shelf a little brown book titled *In the Land of the Head-Hunters*. Since moving to Seattle from my boyhood home in Montana, I had gradually become interested in the cultures of the Native peoples of the Northwest Coast, mostly from frequent trips to the Washington State Museum on the University of Washington campus. Some time later, when that interest increased to include serious research and frequent interaction with the very people who inspired Curtis's story, the significance of the first sentence in the foreword of that little volume began to stand out—"This book had its inception in an outline or scenario for a motion picture drama dealing with the hardy Indians inhabiting northern British Columbia" (Curtis 1915:viii). Had Curtis really carried out his plan to make a "motion picture drama" based on the life of the Kwakwa̲ka'wakw people of the British Columbia coast? No one I knew among Northwest Coast scholars had heard of it. But when I asked my friend, the Kwagu'ł chief and traditionalist Mungo Martin, he was quick to assure me that "Mr. Curtis" had indeed made such a movie at and around his home village of Fort Rupert, on the north end of Vancouver Island, but neither he nor anyone of his people, as far as he knew, had ever seen the finished film. I began to ask about it among older Kwakwa̱ka'wakw friends and was regaled with stories of the adventure of recreating the life of their parents and grandparents, the drama of war and potlatching, and even witchcraft! I began a serious search for any trace of the film, and after following one blind alley after another, on a visit to Chicago's Field Museum, curator George Quimby stunned me when he said, "We have a copy!"

The story of what Quimby and I did with the Field Museum's somewhat fragmented copy has been told in detail in our book, *Edward S. Curtis in the Land of the War Canoes* (Holm and Quimby 1980). In the summer of 1968 my wife and I, with our two young girls, traveled in our little sailboat from village to village in the Kwakwa̱ka'wakw country, laden with a projector and a big reel of unedited and somewhat shuffled film. The trip was an adventure in itself. The harbor at Fort Rupert, for example, has a long sloping bottom and no dock or float, so we anchored and piled our projector and the four of us into our little dinghy to row ashore, and then back again in the middle of the night! Each village had its own adventures. Those who attended the showings had never seen the movie before, but they were full of stories about the time when Edward Curtis came with his camera and crew. A few of the actors, including siblings Margaret Wilson Frank, Robert Wilson, and Helen Wilson Knox (all grandchildren of George Hunt), were still alive and had vivid memories of the project. The audiences often responded with ad-lib dialogue and song, leading me to believe that a soundtrack could be developed to fit the film.

In the summer of 1972, we arranged for a crew of film students from Houston's Rice University, led by David Gerth, to record sound, which we were finally able to do in the auditorium of the British Columbia Provincial Museum in Victoria when a large group of Kwakwa̱ka'wakw friends came down-island for a funeral. All of them had seen the footage when we had carried it around the villages. We projected each scene several times, the audience conferred and decided who was to speak or sing, and then we recorded as the scene was projected once again. There was no script; it was all extemporaneous. Our sound crew, back in Houston, matched the dialogue and song, along with other background recordings (sounds of canoe paddling, surf, and so forth) to the film. The effect in one scene was particularly

Bill Holm

xvi

impressive to me. The hero's father brings the heads of a sorcerer and his assistants, who had attempted to bewitch his son, to the father of the son's prospective bride. The dynamic, forceful, and rhythmic formal speech of the 1914 Kwakwaka'wakw actors was exactly matched by their 1972 counterparts. It is hard to imagine that the sound had not been recorded on the spot.

From time to time, after our completed version of the movie was shown, we were criticized by some viewers for including demeaning scenes of head-hunting and war against unsuspecting neighbors, but none of the Native audiences ever complained. Their old people had described just such scenes from their youth. George Hunt, the source of much of Curtis's information and arguably his partner in making the film, was eleven years old in 1865 when the last revenge party returned to Fort Rupert, bringing heads and a slave from the Salish country to the south. Nakapankam's War Song against the Sanetch is still sung today! And there were others older than Hunt who had participated in making *In the Land of the Head Hunters*, and for whom such customs were personal memories. In 1914, in spite of the efforts of government agencies and churches to eradicate traditional customs, Kwak'wala predominated over English, traditional Big Houses were still the norm, concepts of rank and privilege were strong, and potlatching and traditional dance and ceremony had never ceased although they were against the law in Canada for thirty years. In 1922, eight years after Edward Curtis filmed images of those customs, the law was even more rigidly enforced when twenty-two Kwakwaka'wakw people went to jail for participating in a potlatch in violation of the antipotlatching provisions of the law.

In 1972, fifty-eight years after the release of *In the Land of the Head Hunters*, Quimby and I, a pair of enthusiasts new to film making and working on a shoestring, released a reconstructed version, *In the Land of the War Canoes*. Now, forty-one years later, Edward Curtis's epic melodrama of the precontact Kwakwaka'wakw world has been given a new life, with the advantages of the discovery of a surviving bit of original film, the revival of the orchestral score originally composed for the motion picture, the expertise of film historians and musicians, and the use of advanced film-reconstruction technology and modern concepts of restoration. It is a new chapter in the story of Edward S. Curtis in the land of the headhunters.

PREFACE

BRAD EVANS AND AARON GLASS

Like the century-old film that is its subject, this volume is the result of numerous collaborative efforts. At its core, the book is an interdisciplinary and multivocal exploration of *In The Land of the Head Hunters,* the landmark motion picture that photographer Edward S. Curtis produced along with the Kwakwaka'wakw (Kwakiutl) people of British Columbia between 1913 and 1914. It provides a kind of sequel to the 1980 book *Edward S. Curtis in the Land of the War Canoes* by Bill Holm and George Quimby, which described in detail, for the first time, the history of the film in the context of the authors' own efforts to restore and reedit it in the early 1970s in consultation with some of the indigenous people who had worked on the film. Their version, renamed *In the Land of the War Canoes* and released in 1973, has been the only one available to film scholars, anthropologists, and the Kwakwaka'wakw alike. In recent years, the two of us, along with many of the authors included in this volume, have uncovered additional archival material related to the original film that Holm and Quimby did not have access to. As a result, we joined forces with the U'mista Cultural Centre, a Kwakwaka'wakw community organization and museum in Alert Bay, British Columbia, to return to the film once again in light of these new discoveries. This volume examines the entire history of the film and the multiple moments of collaborative effort that have resulted in its various iterations. The authors examine Curtis's relationship to the Kwakwaka'wakw as well as larger issues raised by a shared history of intercultural exchange, ethnographic representation, and colonial modernity.

As editors of this volume and co-coordinators of the most recent restoration effort, we—Brad Evans, a professor of English at Rutgers University, and Aaron Glass, a professor of anthropology at the Bard Graduate Center—begin with a few words about the genesis of the project itself. We first met and discussed the Curtis film in 2003, sharing the archival discoveries we made independently during our respective graduate research. In Chicago, Evans had examined the only known sixteen-millimeter print of *Head Hunters* at The Field Museum, which he had analyzed for the narrative content of its intertitle cards as they differed from those later included in *War Canoes* (Evans 1998). A few years later, Glass located the manuscript for the film's original musical score by John J. Braham at the Getty Research Institute in Los Angeles. It had been acquired along with a large collection of Curtis photographs and ephemera, including multiple boxes of musical scores related to another of Curtis's projects—his 1911–12 picture opera or musicale; the film score manuscript, titled simply "Head Hunters," was among these other boxes and had never been identified. Glass also consulted copies of Curtis's wax-cylinder recordings of Kwakw<u>a</u>ka'wakw music, on which the score was purportedly based, at the Archive of Traditional Music (University of Indiana at Bloomington).

We agreed that although both were still fragmentary, the original film and the score ought to be reunited and made publically available for the first time since 1914, so that they could supplement *War Canoes,* the only version most people had ever seen. Working together since 2006, we made further, highly significant finds. Most dramatically and unexpectedly, in the UCLA Film & Television Archive, we located a few original, uncatalogued, extensively tinted and toned nitrate reels containing footage missing from The Field Museum's print. In a private collection, we discovered original film ephemera, including full-color posters, playbills, and even an eight-by-twenty-foot billboard (see appendix 1). From newspaper and film company archives, we pieced together details about the film's wider distribution throughout the United States after its 1914 premier. And meeting with the collector who donated his copy to The Field Museum in 1947, we learned more about the fate of the picture once it left Curtis's control. All of these materials and discoveries provided the means for a thorough reevaluation of the film in the context of cinema history.

It was clear to us from the start that, as with Curtis's original filmmaking and Holm and Quimby's initial restoration effort, we would want to partner with the Kwakw<u>a</u>ka'wakw once again in order to fully contextualize the film and its complicated, intercultural history of production and reception. When Glass mentioned our archival discoveries to the late Andrea Sanborn, executive director of the U'mista Cultural Centre, she told him that she and a number of local Kwakw<u>a</u>ka'wakw dancers had thought for a long time about putting together a traditional cultural presentation to accompany a screening of Curtis's film. She contracted with the <u>G</u>wa'wina Dancers, a semiprofessional, community-based dance group in Alert Bay that specializes in cultural presentations and is known for the caliber of their singing, dancing, masked regalia, and public interpretation. It was important to all of us to couple the academic goal of historical film reconstruction to that of maintaining Kwakwa̱ka̱'wakw cultural dialogue with a film that they rightfully consider a part of their own history.

We decided to work together to join these goals under the mantle of a nonprofit project we called "Edward Curtis Meets the Kwakwa̱ka̱'wakw *In the Land of the Head Hunters.*" The aim of the project was twofold: to provide a scholarly recovery of the original melodramatic contexts and content of the film and musical score; and to establish an indigenous reframing of this material given unique Kwakwa̱ka̱'wakw perspectives on the original film, its specific cultural content, and its historical context of production. Partnering initially with the Getty Research Institute, the UCLA Film & Television Archive, and The Field Museum—the three institutions holding key components of the film and score—we eventually expanded the project to include a number of other venues, sponsors, and partners, including art and natural history museums as well as universities and performing arts centers. We also drew on the expertise of anthropologists, historians, musicologists and experts from the Kwakwa̱ka̱'wakw community, many of whom are represented by chapters in this volume. The diversity of institutions and voices contributing to the project reflects the multidimensional nature of Curtis's ambitious film as well as its long history of repackaging and reinterpretation.

As a result of our archival research, the original film title and intertitles were restored, color tinting was recreated to match what was known of the original, scenes from UCLA's rediscovered footage and still photographs from the Library of Congress copyright office were used to fill out missing scenes, and the 1914 score was reactivated and heard for the first time since the film premiered. Over the course of 2008, we produced a six-city tour of public events that featured a screening of the restored film with live musical accompaniment of the score, followed by a cultural presentation by the G̱wa'wina Dancers, who also discussed the film with audiences. In addition, we and our partners launched a comprehensive website (www.curtisfilm. rutgers.edu), put together photography exhibits (one of which is represented in photo essay 2 in this volume), and organized public conferences, symposia, and panel discussions to complement the screening events. Around the same time as this book was published in 2014, Milestone Films released the reconstructed *In the Land of the Head Hunters* with Braham's musical score

Brad Evans and Aaron Glass

on a DVD, packaged together with *In the Land of the War Canoes* so that both versions can be studied side by side.

It is our hope that these materials and events will encourage renewed interest in the complexity of cross-cultural encounter exemplified by the film and by the history of its reception. Produced at a moment of intense colonial imposition, *In the Land of the Head Hunters* nonetheless offers a remarkable model for understanding both the tenacity of cultural heritage and its compatibility with the modern world—a model, in other words, for thinking about indigenous people and the motion-picture medium within a shared rather than exclusionary experience of modernity.

ACKNOWLEDGMENTS

It is a daunting task to begin to acknowledge and thank the scores of individuals and institutions that have collaborated to bring this project and volume to fruition. The project involved a large number of major institutional sponsors, whose coordinated effort made both the reconstruction and the 2008 screening series possible. The restoration of the film was completed by the UCLA Film & Television Archive, with funding from the National Film Preservation Foundation and the Stanford Theatre Foundation. The Getty Research Institute funded the creation of a performance edition of John J. Braham's original musical score. In addition to the major sponsoring institutions already mentioned, we would particularly like to thank the venues that screened the series: the Getty Center (Los Angeles; June 5–6, 2008); the Moore Theatre (Seattle; June 10, 2008); the Chan Centre for the Performing Arts (Vancouver; June 22, 2008); the National Gallery of Art (Washington, DC; November 9, 2008); the American Museum of Natural History (New York; November 14, 2008); and the Field Museum (Chicago; November 16–17, 2008).

Additional funding and support for the screening series was provided by the following organizations: the UCLA Film & Television Archive, the Autry National Center, Marlene Share, Judson Mock, Bruce Whizin, Ann A. Morris, John and Judy Glass, and anonymous donors (Los Angeles); the Seattle Theatre Group, the Burke Museum of Natural History and Culture, the Seattle International Film Festival, the Bill Holm Center for the Study of Northwest Coast Art, the Canadian Studies Center, Henry M. Jackson School of International Studies, the University of Washington, ShadowCatcher Entertainment, David Skinner and Catherine Eaton Skinner, Mike and Lynn Garvey, the Hugh and Jane Ferguson Foundation (Seattle); the Canada Council for the Arts, the BC Arts Council, the AV Trust Feature Film Education and Access Fund, the Vancouver Foundation, the UBC Museum of Anthropology, the UBC First Nations Studies Program, the UBC Centenary Fund, the

UBC Department of Anthropology, Killam Trusts, Hudson's Bay Company, the Leon Blackmore Foundation, the McLean Foundation, and Chase Office Interiors (Vancouver); the Smithsonian's National Museum of the American Indian (Washington, DC); the Margaret Mead Film and Video Festival, the American Museum of Natural History Division of Anthropology, the Smithsonian's National Museum of the American Indian, the NYU Native People's Forum, the NYU Center for Multicultural Education and Programs, the Bard Graduate Center, Foreign Affairs Canada, Rutgers University (New York); and the National Endowment for the Arts (Chicago). For additional fund raising assistance and advice, we acknowledge John and Judy Glass, Harriet Glickman, Sharon Grainger, Dave Hunsaker, Lou-Ann Neel, and David Skinner.

We would like to thank the Getty Research Institute, and in particular Karen Stokes and Katja Zelljadt, for bringing together an impressive range of scholars, historians, and cultural representatives to discuss and develop the project, both prior to the film and score restoration and then again upon its completion. At the Getty, Gail Feigenbaum, Charles Salas, Rebecca Peabody, Evelyn Sen, and Beth Brett were all supportive at various stages of the process. The work represented by the restored film and the scholarship in this volume could not have been accomplished without the contributions of those participating in conferences and panels held in conjunction with the screening events. The Getty Research Institute initially hosted a working "Research Lab" (October 25–26, 2007) to discuss the prospects for the restoration project, which was attended by Melissa Anderson, Colin Browne, Laurance Cushman, Brad Evans, David Farneth, David Gilbert, Aaron Glass, Jere Guldin, Bill Holm, Rebecca Peabody, Michael Pisani, Andrea Sanborn, Rani Singh, Norman Stanfield, Jannon Stein, Karen Stokes, Rob Stone, Neal Stulberg, and Katja Zelljadt. Around the film premiere, the Getty then hosted a two-day symposium, "Documents of an Encounter" (June 5–6, 2008), with the following participants: Dorothy "Pewi" Alfred, Melissa Anderson, Paul Apodaca, Mique'l Askren, Colin Browne, Dana Claxton, William Cranmer, Laurance Cushman, Brad Evans, Gail Feigenbaum, Mick Gidley, David Gilbert, Aaron Glass, Jere Guldin, Klisala Harrison, Ira Jacknis, Anne Makepeace, George Miles, Rebecca Peabody, Michael Pisani, Neal Stulberg, Hulleah Tsinhnahjinnie, Kim Walters, and Katja Zelljadt. In Vancouver, the UBC Museum of Anthropology hosted a post-screening panel discussion entitled "AfterWords: Responses to 'Edward Curtis Meets the Kwakwa̲ka̲'wakw'" (June 24, 2008), featuring Mique'l Askren, Dana Claxton, Barbara Cranmer, and Aaron Glass. A smaller conference, "Moving Pictures: The Celluloid Archive, Indigenous Agency, and the Work of Edward S. Curtis" (November 13, 2008) was held at

Rutgers University coincident to screenings of the film in Washington, DC, and New York, with presentations by Brad Evans, Kate Flint, Aaron Glass, Alison Griffiths, Jolene Rickard, Alan Trachtenberg, and Shamoon Zamir. We would like to thank the support provided at Rutgers by John Belton, Curtis Dunn, Ann Fabian, Jeff Friedman, Richard Koszarski, Fran Mascia-Lees, Matt Matsuda, Barry Qualls, Tanya Sheehan, Susan Sidlauskas, Virginia Yans, the Center for Cultural Analysis, the School of Arts and Sciences, and the Departments of Anthropology, Art History, Dance, English, and History.

Crucial support for the screening series was provided by individuals at the venues and cosponsoring institutions who were committed to the goals of the project. In addition to those already mentioned from the Getty, we gratefully acknowledge the support of Rob Stone, Kelly Graml, and Chris Horak at the UCLA Film & Television Archive; and of Melissa Anderson, Armand Esai, Michael Godow, and Elizabeth Babcock at The Field Museum. Additionally, we would like to thank Donna Tuggle, Kim Walters, Rich Deely, and Paul Edelman of the Autry National Center; Vicky Lee, Vicki Infinito, and Robert Margoshes at the Moore Theatre/Seattle Theatre Group; Carl Sander, Robin Wright, Becky Andrews, Erin Younger, and Ruth Pelz at the Burke Museum of Natural History and Culture; Cindy Behrmann, Audrey Chan, Joyce Hinton, Donna Caedo, Cameron McGill, and Christine Offer of the Chan Centre for the Performing Arts; Anthony Shelton, Roberta Kremer, Jennifer Webb, Jill Baird, Anjuli Solanki, Krisztina Lazlo, Skooker Broome, and Joanne White at the UBC Museum of Anthropology; Linc Kesler from the UBC First Nations Studies Program; Nancy Mortifee and Sid Katz at the UBC Public Affairs/ Centenary 2008 Committee; Bruce Miller in the UBC Department of Anthropology; Jeremy Berkman and Karen Pledger of the Turning Point Ensemble; Stephen Ackert and Margaret Parsons at the National Gallery of Art; Howard Bass, Melissa Bisagni, Michelle Svenson, Elizabeth Weatherford, and Margaret Sagan at the Smithsonian's National Museum of the American Indian; Elaine Charnov, Monique Scott, Ariella Ben-Dov, Roberto Borrero, Natalie Tschechaniuk, Lily Szajnberg, Peter Whiteley, Charles Spencer, Steve Reichl, and Lynn Hassett at the American Museum of Natural History; T. James Matthews at the NYU Native People's Forum; Richard Chavolla and C. C. Suarez at the NYU Center for Multicultural Education and Programs; and Peter Miller, Elena Pinto Simon, Graham White, Ben Rosenthal, and Deborah Tint at the Bard Graduate Center. A very special note of thanks goes to Faye Ginsburg at New York University, who was visionary in understanding the scope of the project and in helping organize the East Coast screenings. We also appreciate the following people for assisting with videography of the public events as well as rehearsals: the staff of the Getty Research Institute (Los Angeles); Daniel Hart and the students of Native Voices at the University of Washington (Seattle); Tony Massil and Colin Browne (Vancouver and Alert Bay); and Heather Weyrick, Anoosh Tertzakian, and Nina Krstic (New York).

The restoration project and screenings drew on a remarkable range of talent and creative energies. Credit for the high quality of the reconstructed film goes to Jere Guldin at the UCLA Film & Television Archive. David Gilbert, of the UCLA Music Library, edited and created a performing edition of the score from the original sources. To date, four different orchestras have performed the score. The premiere in Los Angeles by the UCLA Philharmonia was conducted by Neal Stulberg, whom we would like to thank not only for a great performance but for his enthusiastic embrace of the challenges posed by this curious piece of historical music. Owen Underhill took the lead in interpreting the score with the Turning Point Ensemble in Vancouver and an assorted group of local musicians in Seattle. Laura Ortman deserves a great deal of credit for pulling together for the first time the Coast Orchestra, an all Native-American classically trained ensemble, to perform the score in Washington, DC, and New York City. Conducted by Timothy Long, the Coast Orchestra put on a fascinating performance that started with the Braham score but took liberties by "reclaiming" the music through the addition of Native American musical elements.

Accompanying the screenings, and occupying a central place on the project website, were two photographic exhibits bringing Curtis's photography into conversation with the present life of First Nations on the Northwest Coast. The first of these, *Old Images/New Views,* is partially reproduced in this volume, and we would like to thank the contributors for their thoughts about Curtis, as well as the UBC Museum of Anthropology and the UBC First Nations Studies Program for coordinating their efforts. The second exhibit, *Staging Edward Curtis,* paired portraits of the Kwakwaka'wakw by Curtis with contemporary ones by Sharon Grainger, and was projected onscreen at all of the events before the commencement of the film. Our great thanks to Sharon, both for allowing us to exhibit her photographs and for valuable consultation in all aspects of the production. In addition, she led the project's photo documentation at the West Coast venues.

The participation of the Gwa'wina Dancers was central to our thinking about the public presentation of this project, and we would like in particular to thank William Wasden Jr. and Dorothy "Pewi" Alfred for the creative energies they brought to sharing their culture and cultural perspectives with audiences. Many of the dancers are direct descendents of actors or crew members in the film, which made the presentations particularly meaningful for both the dancers and for audiences. The G̲wa'wina Dancers were Dorothy "Pewi" Alfred (G̲wal'sa̲'las), Edgar Cranmer ('Ma̲lidi), Eli Cranmer (U'maga̲lis), Kevin Cranmer (Ṫła̲tłakwu'ła̲ma'yi), Tyler Cranmer (Gayutła̲las), Gilbert Dawson (G̲wa'yam), Andy Everson (Na̲gedzi), Ḵodi Nelson (Wawigustolaga̲litsugwi'lakw), Ian Reid (Nusi), Dustin Rivers (Ṫła̲kwa), Caroline Rufus (Dła̲dza̲wegi'lakw), Jacob Smith (Ṫsa̲ndiga̲mgi'lakw), Lauren Smith (G̲wa̲nti'lakw), Norman Wadhams (Ye̲ka̲widi), Maria Wadhams (Pudłas), and William Wasden Jr. (Wax̲awidi). Their regalia was designed and created by Wayne Alfred, Beau Dick, Calvin Hunt, John Livingston, Don Svanvik, William Wasden Jr., and Sean Whonnock. Our thanks to Maxine Matilpi, who accompanied the regalia to events on both the West and East Coasts and was a master of improvisation when it did not arrive on time. We are very grateful to Dave Hunsaker for artistic advice on staging and lighting the performance, and to Art Brickman for production assistance on the West Coast. Jim Simard, Lucas Hoiland, Toby Corbett, Azadeh Yaraghi, and the UBC Department of Theatre and Film offered additional staging advice and design assistance.

In many ways, this project is built upon the foundation of previous work by George Quimby and Bill Holm. Although Quimby has passed away, we are exceptionally grateful for Holm's guidance and support throughout the course of our work, from beginning to end. In addition to invaluable assistance with research and development, Holm generously lent his personal regalia collection to the G̲wa'wina Dancers for use in the Seattle event. Additional timely research advice on the film was offered by Peter Macnair, Colin Browne, Ira Jacknis, and Deanna and Jerry Costanzo, and advice on the music by Jim Littleford, Michael Bushnell, and Norman Stanfield. We are particularly grateful to have had the opportunity to speak with Hugo Zeiter, collector of Curtis's film.

At the University of Washington Press, we would like to thank our editors, Ranjit Arab, Mary Ribesky, and Tim Zimmerman, as well as our copyeditor, Kerrie Maynes, and the two anonymous readers for the press. Kathryn Bunn-Marcuse, managing editor of the Bill Holm Center for the Study of Northwest Coast Art, shepherded the project through at every stage and offered exceptionally useful and detailed suggestions. Ashley Verplank McClelland at the Burke Museum of Natural History and Culture was instrumental in facilitating image procurement and permissions, and in the production of the prop list in appendix 3.

Finally, there is the personal assistance without which neither the events nor elements of this book would have managed to come together. Glass would like to thank his research assistants Mei-Ling Israel, Hadley Jensen, Erin Allaire-Graham, Jaime Luria and Adam Solomonian; Laura Friesan and Phil Dion for design advice; his wife Helen Polson, who labored diligently behind the scenes—even behind the dance curtain—to help make the events a dramatic success and the book a well-edited endeavor; and his daughter Eva for providing joyful distraction. For Evans, the list includes especially Jenna Lewis, Jessica Cain, and Weis Baher, who tracked down numerous stray references to both *Head Hunters* and Native Americans in early motion pictures; and, as always, the support of his family, Sophie, Simon, and Théo.

Return to the Land of the Head Hunters

INTRODUCTION

Edward Curtis Meets the Kwakw<u>a</u>ka'wakw:
Cultural Encounter and Indigenous Agency
In the Land of the Head Hunters

AARON GLASS AND BRAD EVANS

"No ethnographic film is merely a record
of another society: it is always a record of the
meeting between a filmmaker and that society."

—David MacDougal (1995:125)

A few years after initiating his ambitious project to document Native American life in pictures and text, commercial photographer Edward S. Curtis (1868–1952) turned his attention to the indigenous inhabitants of the north Pacific coast. Curtis famously—and infamously—took it upon himself to produce a comprehensive visual record of the American Indian, popularly claimed at the turn of the twentieth century to be vanishing due to demographic decline, territorial restriction, and political pressure to assimilate into North American society. Fashioning himself a photographic Audubon of sorts, and influenced by George Catlin's "Indian Gallery" and the salvage anthropology that he would come to emulate, Curtis declared in an early lecture, "Every phase of their life must be noted and, as far as possible, pictured, and the gathering of this lore, logic and myth must go hand-in-hand with the picture making, as without the knowledge of their life, ceremony, domestic, political and religious, one cannot do the picture work well."[1] Backed by powerful interests—the initial financial patronage of J. Pierpont Morgan, the political support of Theodore Roosevelt, and the encouragement and editorial services of Frederick W. Hodge at the Bureau of American Ethnology—Curtis produced, between 1907 and 1930, his massive, limited-edition series *The North American Indian* (hereafter *NAI*), twenty volumes of illustrated text along with twenty oversized portfolios of fine photographic prints. Especially since the so-called Curtis revival of the 1960s and 1970s, the sepia-toned photographs of Native North Americans drawn from those volumes, long a favorite in museum displays and bookstores and increasingly available from commercial fine arts galleries and on the Internet, have come to embody the quintessential Indian in the global imagination.

The images are beautiful and deeply affecting, but, as has long been understood, they also are based on a stereotypical idea about Native Americans as a "vanishing race," as Curtis himself titled his famous image of a line of Navajo warriors riding on horseback into the setting sun of history (see fig. E.2.5). Curtis was committed to imaging and describing Native life for posterity, but he shared with more academic ethnographers of the era a tendency to privilege the purportedly authentic—the last vestiges of precontact aboriginal life free, relatively speaking, of the taint of acculturative influence and obvious signs of modernity.[2] Where this was not possible, he partook of methods common to photographic portraiture of the period, including careful lighting and framing, providing clothing and props while controlling backdrops, and staging reconstructions and reenactments. Curtis's early interest in the pictorialist movement lent his images an air of aesthetic sophistication and soft-focus romanticism, an artistic effect that permeated the early volumes of the *NAI* in particular, and which is characteristic of many of the prints that are reproduced popularly today. Now largely separated from the volumes in which they first appeared, Curtis's photographs can seem more than ever before to represent his Native subjects as inhabiting a timeless world—a world far removed not only from the exigencies of modern life on Indian reservations but also from the contingencies of philanthropic and political patronage, ethnographic and artistic prestige, and mass marketing and cultural production.

Even though the pictorial content of much of Curtis's work privileges an image of Native Americans removed from modernity, the historical fact of the work itself is in many respects representative of an intercultural participation in and collaborative production of the modern condition. This story is less frequently told, and the quickest way to sketch its contours may be to recall the wide variety of Curtis's lesser-known popular and commercial endeavors, undertaken in order to raise funds for his field trips and publishing ambitions, all of which gained him and his images considerable

Aaron Glass and Brad Evans

4

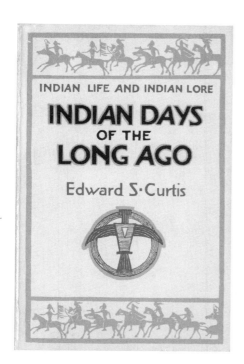

Figs. I.1a and I.1b. Book covers of (a) *Indian Days of the Long Ago* (1914), and
(b) *In the Land of the Head-Hunters* (1915) by Edward S. Curtis. Courtesy of Aaron Glass.

notoriety outside the small list of his book series subscribers. Curtis sold post-cards and limited edition portfolios; he gave interviews and slide lectures; he mounted exhibits in natural history and art museums; he published articles and popular books (figs. I.1a and I.1b; Flint, this volume); and he produced a multimedia musicale or picture opera combining magic lantern slides with an original musical score (fig. I.2; Gidley and Jacknis, this volume). Far from being restricted to the high-culture circuit, Curtis was very much involved in the production of Native American images for popular audiences. And though these images were in many ways flawed, they likely appealed not only to white Americans but also to the ambitions of Native intellectuals and reformers with whom he worked or with whom he might now be associated from our own historical perspective (Zamir, this volume). Such figures did not always rebuke these images, but often used them to carefully refashion themselves in ways aimed at obtaining stronger recognition in both cultural and political spheres for Native survival and persistence—what Gerald Vizenor (1994) calls "survivance."[3]

At the top of the list of Curtis's commercial endeavors is his direction of what many consider to be the first feature-length, narrative, ethnographic

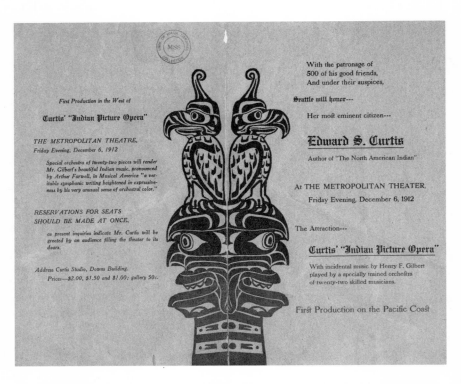

Fig. I.2. Promotional program for Curtis's musicale or Indian picture opera, 1912.
University of Washington Libraries, Special Collections, UW 33540.

film with an all-indigenous cast, *In the Land of the Head Hunters* (1914).[4] The film is now recognized as a seminal forerunner to the documentary genre, and was at the time one of the most ambitious, independent, modernist (if also primitivist) spectacle films ever produced. Though unspecified by name in the film and its promotional materials, *Head Hunters* featured the Kwakwaka'wakw (Kwakiutl) of British Columbia, who were to be the subject of the tenth volume of the *NAI*, published in 1915.[5] By that time, the Kwakwaka'wakw already had a long history of theatrical self-representation to anthropologists, tourists, missionaries, and colonial agents—an aggressive and strategic form of cultural brokerage that in effect adjusted and reshaped customary practices during a period of intense colonial encroachment (Glass, this volume). Materials collected on the Northwest Coast, from massive totem poles to ceremonial masks, formed the hub of Native American collections in museums around the world. These in turn found their way into the popular imagination of the ethnographic "other," as well as into modernist art by the likes of Marsden Hartley and Max Weber, who visited the collections for primitivist inspiration (Rushing 1995:43–58). *In the Land of the Head Hunters*

Aaron Glass and Brad Evans

6

entered into what was already by 1914 a dense historical web of representation and self-representation of Kwakwaka'wakw cultural heritage. As we suggest throughout this volume, it is important to understand that what is represented by the film is not merely Curtis's sensationalist exploitation of indigenous people but also a meeting of Curtis and the Kwakwaka'wakw in the shared enterprise of making a modern motion picture. *Head Hunters* was one of the most ambitious of many such attempts undertaken by Kwakwaka'wakw—and by other First Nations, in other forms, across Canada and the United States—to use the emerging market for culturally inscribed goods as a form of self-preservation in a moment made precarious by colonialist expansion.

The fuller history of *In the Land of the Head Hunters* that this collection of essays elaborates helps us to recognize the quintessential modernity of Curtis's project when taken as a whole, as well as the ways in which his indigenous collaborators were also integrated into modern life—the way that their cultural identity was itself a modernist formation under specific political conditions. The stories told in this volume describe the ongoing political and economic demands made upon indigenous people for such things as land, labor, and assimilation. But even more, they document the manner in which indigenous communities negotiated such demands by drawing upon and reacting against the complex representational nexus of "the Indian" exemplified by Curtis's forays into popular culture (see especially Deloria 1998 and 2004; Hutchinson 2009; Smith 2009). By the turn of the twentieth century, under converging pressures by settlers, government agents, industrialists, and missionaries, indigenous cultural practices and beliefs were no longer something that most Native people could take for granted. Rather, "traditional culture" became something consciously reflected upon and strategically abandoned, adapted, or asserted in diverse modern contexts of self-presentation and political outreach. To that extent, revisiting Curtis's massive undertaking from aesthetic, commercial, and political vantages can help us reevaluate not only the subject matter of his images but also the nature and agency of representation in the production of cultural identities and cultural value as we have come to understand such things today.

The arguments that coalesce in this volume respond to what we have often felt to be a dead end in the academic and popular understanding of Curtis's entire body of work—an understanding that rarely seems to have room for consideration of the Native American subject's place in its production, or, for that matter, in its reception. As we discuss below, Curtis is often situated as either a frontier artist devoting his life to picturing and thus honoring the historic image of the noble Indian, or as the most pernicious contributor to the racist and colonialist stereotypes that Native people today still labor under given the fact that they did not vanish after all. Both of these positions tend to bracket a number of factors crucial for a more complete evaluation of Curtis's photographic and filmic output, including his own representational ambitions within scientific and popular culture at the time; the actual historical experience of his indigenous models and subjects as they adapted to life in the settler nations of Canada and the United States; and the multitude of ways his images, placed in circulation over the last century, have been received and resignified by both indigenous and non–indigenous audiences.

When resituated within the history of cultural production in the early twentieth century and framed by current indigenous perspectives, Curtis's work—in all its variety, but especially as suggested by his landmark motion picture—can be recast as visible evidence of intercultural exchange and ongoing Native survival under shifting historical and political conditions. To resituate Curtis in this fashion changes not only our understanding of the specific subject matter of his work but also the way we conceptualize the representation of indigenous populations in popular artistic and commercial media. Curtis's images are not timeless documents of the neutrally historical past but objects around which future cultural configurations have taken shape and continue to do so. In attending to the diverse histories of production and subsequent circulation of images, ethnographies, souvenirs, spectacles, and film associated with Curtis's enterprise, the chapters of this book draw attention to a new way of thinking about Curtis, the nature of his collaboration with indigenous subjects, and the reshaping of cultural identities and values that has occurred since their images entered the global marketplace. For nearly a century and counting, *In the Land of the Head Hunters* has constituted a filmic lens through which to reframe and re–imagine the changing terms of colonial representation, cultural memory, and intercultural encounter.

From Representation to Encounter:
Agency, Genre, Modernity

Before considering the specific historical contingencies related to the filming and reception of *In the Land of the Head Hunters*, we would like to review in a more general way three perspectives on Curtis's work—themes that run throughout this volume—that have been particularly overlooked in scholarship on him, whether adulatory or critical: a recognition of indig-

Aaron Glass and Brad Evans

8

enous agency; the generic classification of his photographs and film; and the relationship of so-called traditional cultures to modernity. The goal is to rebalance attention away from what Curtis did (or meant to do) and toward indigenous intentionalities at the time, as well as the ongoing effect of Curtis's various projects once they were placed in circulation. Curtis's work, coauthored to a significant degree by his Native models, was key in establishing the representational nexus out of which contemporary cultural identities have been constructed, contested, affirmed, reinvented, marketed, and selectively deployed.

Indigenous Agency

We begin with the challenge of recognizing shared agency. This volume reacts to two dominant and overlapping trends in photographic and film analysis regarding Native people. The first seeks to evaluate historic images for their ethnographic components, either in the anthropological sense of accounting for their empirical accuracy, or in the technical sense of exploring their production values. In the most basic form, such studies attempt to figure out if the person behind the camera got it right or wrong according to some more or less clearly defined criteria of documentary accuracy, while in more interesting versions the question turns to the complex theoretical challenges of ethnographic image making itself (e.g., Holm 1983a; Russell 1999; Ruby 2000; Edwards 2001; Griffiths 2002; Sandweiss 2002; Bunn-Marcuse 2005). The second trend, which of course often retains elements of the first, seeks to lay bare the colonialist ideologies behind much frontier image making; that is, to reveal the hegemonic formations—racist, sexist, capitalist, imperialist—underlying majority representations and signifying practices (e.g., Lyman 1982; Dippie 1991; Faris 1996; Rony 1996; Wakeham 2008). What this volume takes to be the lesson of prior approaches to the subject are the important insights yielded by way of deep microhistories of image reception and dissemination: studies designed to contextualize the images and films in their own historical period, and from within the specific genre conventions—aesthetic or scientific—in which they were made. Doing so, we believe, offers the best opportunity to avoid the risk of occluding the active participation and intentionality of the Native subjects who helped to create the filmic records in the first place, an occlusion that comes about by focusing exclusively on dominant modes of production and reception. We are deeply suspicious of accounts that would leave indigenous people at the margins of a colonial modernity entirely imposed upon them—passive victims of representational violence and not active collaborators in the production of popular images of themselves, agents in the dissemination of such images, and party in unique ways to their consumption.

Acknowledging the fundamentally collaborative nature of ethnographic knowledge creation is not only a way to open up notions of authorship—a long-standard insight from poststructuralism—but also to shift our evaluation of the texts or images *as representations*. Many factors familiar to textual or visual analysis still apply: the unique materialities and temporalities of various expressive media; the cultural specificities of the players involved; the historical contingencies and imbalance of colonial power relations. But the chapters in this volume suggest a refocusing of attention away from "ethnographic authority"—especially as it has been defined and critiqued over the past thirty years as the sole locus of the scholar, writer, curator, or imager (Said 1978; Clifford and Marcus 1986; Bennett 1995)—and toward an acknowledgment of collaborative production, even if under strained and unstable political conditions. A recovery and recognition of indigenous agency within colonial contexts of exchange opens up new modes of interpreting historic visual, literary, and musical texts. Rather than approaching Curtis's images as mere products of colonialist fantasy or imperialist nostalgia, we argue that they should be treated as complex documents of an encounter to which both photographer and photographic subject brought particular interests, resources, and agendas, whether those proved to be commensurate or conflicting (see Holman 1996).[6]

What motivations—personal, communal, financial, political—might Native Americans and Canadian First Nations have had to pose for Curtis's camera, to reenact their own past, to stage their culture for foreign consumption? What happens when we ask descendants of Curtis's photographic subjects what *they* think of his work? How does our understanding of his pictures change when we understand them to be family portraits and not merely colonial stereotypes (Barbara Cranmer, this volume)? In the particular case of *Head Hunters*, we know that the film was made at a time that the potlatch and its rituals were against the law in Canada, prohibited by federal edict in the effort to convert and assimilate First Nations people (see below). What did it mean for the stars of the film to perform dances for the camera, for a white man, for money, that they might have been arrested for had they been performing for themselves? Perhaps their decision to adapt the dances for the film—and for other contemporaneous contexts such as world's fairs, anthropological exhibits, tourism, and museum display—contributed to the survival of visual art and ritual as embodied knowledge during this prohibition period (Glass 2004a, 2006a). Likewise, what if we see some of the cultural inaccuracies in the Curtis film and pictures not only as a result of *his* misunderstanding and misrepresentation, but also (in some cases at least) as a result of decisions by his subjects about what they would and wouldn't do for the camera, how they did and did not want to be portrayed? To imagine that Curtis had total control over his actors or models—that he had the freedom or the power to dress them in costumes or force them into poses of his own choosing, against their will—strikes us as historically implausible. Changing our understanding of the contexts in which the images were produced demands a shift in our assessment of their status, value, and reception as historical as well as artistic or ethnographic documents.

Genre Errors

Another substantive argument behind our project to recreate and revisit *In the Land of the Head Hunters* is that much of the criticism of Curtis based on the supposed inaccuracy or inauthenticity of his images commits a crucial category error. It has been assumed that the primary mode in which Curtis worked was "documentary," and that his conscious intention was to create images meant to reproduce reality with minimal intervention or overt manipulation. Instead, we argue that Curtis practiced somewhere along the artistic continuum between this documentary mode and what A. D. Coleman (1979) calls the "directorial mode," in which photographers make a concerted effort to manipulate, interpret, and comment upon reality by creating images that viewers (ideally, at least) recognize as staged. Critics, however, have tended to project presumptions about the criteria for ethnographic documentary backward in time. To call *Head Hunters* a "documentary" is, of course, an anachronism, one made all the more striking when recognizing the extent to which it draws upon the historical and cinematic conventions of love stories, Westerns, and travel films, borrowing narrative elements from classical and modern literature as well as emerging pop-culture clichés, such as those about savage headhunting and exotic "fire dances" like those performed at world's fairs and carnival sideshows.[7] In addition, Curtis capitalized on recent interest in Eskimos, Inuit, and Arctic exploration by framing his film as an "Epic Drama of the Northern Seas," perhaps in an attempt to distinguish it (as a "Northern") from typical Westerns depicting Plains Indians (Evans, this volume); Alaska was frequently and mistakenly invoked in reviews as the film's location. Despite his efforts to authenticate aspects of his film—the posters promoted the all-Native cast and the "Native music symphonized" (false advertising, as we now know)—Curtis never suggested that it was a glimpse of Native life in 1914 (appendix 1). It was set in the past, with

Kwakwa̲ka'wakw playing their own ancestors. Today we might be tempted to call it something like a "historical docudrama," in which outright reenactment might commingle (sometimes imperceptibly) with current commentary and archival footage.

That said, the film surely "documents" some aspects of Kwakwa̲ka'wakw culture with considerable accuracy—the handling of the magnificent canoes, the staging of dramatic ceremonials, the reconstructed dress and architecture of daily life in the eighteenth and early nineteenth centuries. The Kwakwa̲ka'wakw had then and have now a very elaborate theatrical approach to ritual, in which performance gives voice to the spirits and embodied manifestation to ancestral rights and responsibilities. Curtis was attracted to them for this reason (as Holm mentions in the foreword to this volume), and his filmic vision was married to their ceremonial style of visual display. But the film also imports neighboring practices (such as whaling—in a scene filmed with a rented whale carcass), fabricates some aspects of the culture (such as a spectacular round dance), and traffics in stereotypes of the American Indian (such as the evil sorcerer and spiritual vision-quester). Rather than seeing the film—and by extension, Curtis's large body of photographs—as *either* an aesthetic masterpiece *or* a failed attempt at ethnographic truth, we approach the film as a creative coproduction that brought Edward Curtis together with the Kwakwa̲ka'wakw to join distinctive yet complementary dramatic traditions, to help create a new and altogether modern form of entertainment—the movies. Curtis himself admitted as much in a promotional article for the film published in 1915 in the *Strand Magazine*: "I had pretty well formed my [Native] 'company' in the rough, and started their minds to work along the lines of the story I had fashioned with their help" (in Holm and Quimby 1980:122).[8]

Tradition and Modernity

This brings us to the lasting tension between tradition and modernity in the evaluation of Native American cultural and artistic productions and representations. For too long now, these two terms have been presented as mutually exclusive: one anchored in the past and the other in the present (or future); one suggesting the lack of change and the other, its active achievement; the first committing First Nations to the halls of ethnology and natural history museums, and the second allowing them entry into fine art galleries and the corridors of government (Glass, this volume). In many of his photos, Curtis actively erased signs of modernity to give the impression that his Native subjects were still living in some "traditional" past, indexed not so much by existing knowledge or cultural practice but by the superficial trappings of clothing, hairstyle, and physiology. Yet his photographic subjects and film actors were participants in the modernity of 1904 or 1914 or 1924. They may have agreed to dress up in the daily wear of their ancestors or the ceremonial regalia of their ritual practices, active or moribund, but they were also on other occasions photographed in their Sunday best at weddings and other important evens, both in urban studios and on reserves or reservations (see figs. F.1 and F.2). It is just that these latter pictures did not end up in glossy coffee table books, only in family albums or historical archives that are rarely made public.

The very fact that *Head Hunters* was made at all, not to mention that its production involved the self-conscious performance of indigenous pastness, is an index of an emergent Native modernity at the time, regardless of the fact that its pictorial and narrative content—its staged ethnographic fantasy—erased the visible signs of modern life in the early twentieth century. This is true of much of Curtis's photography as well. As argued throughout this volume, Curtis's film and photography constitute historical documents of social and intercultural practice, not merely vehicles of representation or misrepresentation. It is not, moreover, a practice whose locus can be assigned solely to the historical past. The dynamics of image production are certainly important, but just as important is an understanding of circulation and reception, which opens up the possibility of understanding the changing status of images over time—their strategic deployment in the marketplace not only by whites but also, over the years, by indigenous populations. Attending to the three issues of genre, agency, and modernity, we want to reassess Edward Curtis's work in particular, not as failed attempts at documentary realism—inauthentic portraits of the presumably vanishing races—but as visual evidence for the social relations of image coproduction, as authentic documents of ongoing intercultural encounter even if under conditions of political inequality.

The Kwakwa̱ka'wakw and Edward Curtis

Between 1910 and 1914, Curtis turned his primary attention to the Native people of Vancouver Island, British Columbia. Intrigued by his exposure to the anthropology of Franz Boas, Curtis was attracted to the Kwakwa̱ka'wakw in particular for the same reason that Boas and other ethnographers, photographers, and museums collectors were (Makepeace 2002:126).[9] By the late nineteenth century, they had garnered the reputation among local missionaries and Indian Agents for being "incorrigible" and highly resistant to assimilation—"a most difficult lot to civilize," in the opinion of one regional administrator (Cole and Chaikin 1990:62). Attracted to their vigorous art forms and highly dramatic ceremonial performances, Curtis found in Kwakwaka'wakw territory a perfect combination of picturesque natural scenery and visual culture among people whose stubborn maintenance of customary practices was matched by the occasional willingness to participate in photographic reenactment.

In fundraising letters, Curtis drew on these long-held assumptions about the Kwakwaka'wakw, describing them as closer to their "precontact" state than any other Native North Americans (Gidley 2003b:99, 105). For instance, during his first summer in Alert Bay in 1910, Curtis excitedly (if hyperbolically) wrote to one of his patrons:

> The season has been largely spent in the north Pacific country, among tribes of which we possess little intimate knowledge. These tribes who were universally head-hunters, and largely cannibalistic, furnish such a wealth of material that one is almost encouraged with the thought of an adequate treatment in the available space ... of this vast harvest of extraordinary pictures and material. (Gidley 2003b:99)

Published five years later, the introduction to the *NAI*'s tenth volume distinguished the Kwakwaka'wakw from their coastal neighbors by suggesting that "theirs are the only villages where primitive life can still be observed" (Curtis 1907–30, vol. 10:xi). Other than the Hopi, the Kwakwaka'wakw were the only nation to receive a dedicated volume, one of the longest in the book series.

Though Curtis celebrated the Kwakwaka'wakw for their attachment to ancient customs, their daily lives in the early twentieth century were deeply conditioned by the realities of colonial modernity. During the previous century, the Kwakwaka'wakw had been variably and increasingly exposed to the institutions, technologies, and sensibilities of Euro–North American life and labor (Knight 1978; Lutz 2008). While some villages on the outer coast of Vancouver Island had been engaged in the maritime fur trade since the late eighteenth century, settlement came much later to most Kwakwaka'wakw territories than to other areas of the north and south coast. Nonetheless, by the 1880s permanent settlements had cropped up around the Hudson's Bay Company trading post at Fort Rupert and around a fish cannery in Alert Bay, attracting missionaries, Indian Agents, provincial police, customs officers, and other colonial officials while at the same time encouraging disparate

Fig. I.3. Edward S. Curtis, *Carved Posts at Alert Bay*, 1914. (*NAI,* portfolio 10.)
Charles Deering McCormick Library of Special Collections, Northwestern University Library.

Kwakw<u>a</u>ka'wakw bands to amalgamate at these sites to take advantage of mercantile and educational opportunities. Their modern material reality is visible through the veneer of Curtis's romantic primitivism in the presence of milled lumber, glass windows, and European cloth adjacent to totem poles and masks (fig. I.3; see also Zamir, this volume). Moreover, many Kwakw<u>a</u>ka'wakw (again, particularly those in Alert Bay and Fort Rupert, where Curtis made his base) were quite used to attention from outsiders interested in observing, recording, and collecting their cultural practices and products, even as settlers, missionaries, and government agents were committed to eradicating those same elements. Since the 1880s, a steady stream of explorers and steamship tourists, anthropologists and ethnographic photographers, and amateur and professional museum collectors spent time (mostly during summer months) hoping to cash in on the Kwakw<u>a</u>ka'wakw's reputation for living an unacculturated lifestyle.[10]

Some, but by no means all, Kwakw<u>a</u>ka'wakw accommodated these modern conditions by willingly and perhaps strategically putting themselves and their traditions on display as a form of wage labor as well as a means of recording valuable cultural knowledge, whether or not they fully subscribed to the salvage paradigm that presumed this knowledge to be vanishing. Key cultural brokers emerged to help facilitate ethnographic fieldwork and museum collection, the most famous and important being George Hunt (1854–1933), the son of an English Hudson's Bay Company factor and a Tlingit noblewoman from Alaska.[11] Hunt grew up at Fort Rupert, became literate in both English and Kwak̓wala, and married into Kwakwa̱ka̱'wakw families (first among the local Kwagu'ł and then among the 'Nak̓waxda'x̱w from Blunden Harbour) from whom he received ceremonial prerogatives and official standing in the potlatch system. Most significantly in terms of intercultural exchange, Hunt worked as a guide, translator, interpreter, collector, photographer, and ethnographer for Franz Boas and others for over forty years. With Boas, Hunt also coordinated a troupe of fifteen Kwakwa̱ka̱'wakw to live and perform at the 1893 Chicago World's Fair (a decade later, two more Kwakwa̱ka̱'wakw attended the 1904 St. Louis World's Fair). Hunt proved invaluable to the production of Curtis's photographs, text, and film, as we shall see throughout this book.[12]

While the Kwakwa̱ka̱'wakw were engaged with those elements of Euro-American society that appreciated and encouraged their traditional culture, in many cases by commoditizing it, they were also busy negotiating the modern (and modernizing) regime of colonial assimilation and its multiple agents: merchants looking for a reliable labor force; Indian administrators who monitored Native movements and activities on newly established reserves; missionaries out to save souls by eradicating indigenous cosmologies and ceremony; and teachers running the day and residential schools that forced children into Euro-American habits of mind, body, and language. Partly in response to missionary and Indian Agent appeals for federal assistance in assimilation efforts, the Canadian government amended the Indian Act in 1884 to outlaw the potlatch and accompanying dances. Few initial convictions were made based on this statute, largely due to the vague wording of the law and the lack of clear terminological definitions. The Indian Act was amended further in 1895 in an effort to clarify the outlawed practices, perhaps in response to Canadian government consternation over sensational press coverage of violent dances performed at the 1893 Chicago World's Fair. The Kwakwa̱ka̱'wakw responded to the expanding potlatch ban with a variety of strategies that included capitulation but also outright defiance (holding illegal ceremonies, either clandestinely or in public), legal protest (submitting petitions and hiring lawyers), and adaptation (spreading dancing, speech making, and other ritual acts onto different occasions, or distributing pot-

Aaron Glass and Brad Evans

16

latch gifts on Christian holidays) (Sewid-Smith 1979; Cole and Chaikin 1990; Webster 1992; Loo 1992; Bracken 1997; Glass 2004a).

During the specific four-year period that Curtis spent among the Kwakwa̱ka̱'wakw, many aspects of their uniquely modern condition dramatically coalesced, although most were assiduously occluded in Curtis's romantic reenactments. In the hopes of demonstrating the harmlessness of their performances, the Kwakwa̱ka̱'wakw consistently invited members of the provincial and federal governments to witness their dance displays. In 1912, people from Alert Bay were photographed dancing for Prince Arthur, the Duke of Connaught and acting governor-general of Canada (fig. I.4). Nonetheless, potlatch participants Ned Harris and John Bagwany were arrested and found guilty in 1914 in one of the first successful convictions under the amended 1895 Indian Act.[13] Later that year—the same year that Curtis's film premiered in Seattle and New York—the Indian Act was revised again to further limit dancing outside of one's home reserve and the wearing of ceremonial regalia in any "show, exhibition, performance, stampede or pageant." Some chiefs responded by submitting a petition to the government stating, "God created us here and it was the Almighty that put us here, and it is our fashion [that] each nation has dances of their own, and no one stops them. The Indian dance is our native dance, which has been followed up from time immorial [sic] up to this present time" (Cole and Chaikin 1990:129). Around the first two weeks of June 1914, people gathered in regalia in Alert Bay to welcome the Royal (or McKenna-McBride) Commission on Indian Affairs, which was charged with resolving the "Indian Land Question" in British Columbia (fig. I.5), while making a further gesture by donating money to the Canadian war effort.[14] In the same years that the Kwakwa̱ka̱'wakw were employed by Curtis to stage their own cultural past, they were also deeply engaged in battles with the provincial and federal authorities to ensure their cultural survival into the future.

Of course, Curtis and Boas were not the only interested parties aiming their preservationist gazes and modern instruments at the Kwakwa̱ka̱'wakw. Tourists with Kodak Brownie cameras wandered Alert Bay, one of the major stops on steamships bound for Alaska (fig. I.6). In fact, a few years before Curtis arrived, George Eastman himself disembarked in Alert Bay, where he was reported to have taught some local 'Na̱mgis to use his portable cameras (Williams 2003:171), perhaps fueling a nascent interest among them in recording their own appearance for posterity, whether wearing customary or modern clothing.[15] In 1912, while Curtis was staging his dramatic, Northwest Coast–themed picture opera, the British Columbia painter Emily Carr toured

INDIAN DANCERS. ALERT BAY B.C.

Top: Fig. I.4. Kwakwa̱ka'wakw dancing for Prince Arthur, the Duke of Connaught, in Alert Bay, 1912. Royal BC Museum, BC Archives, PN1872.

Bottom: Fig. I.5. Kwakwa̱ka'wakw chiefs in regalia welcoming the Royal Commission on Indian Affairs in Alert Bay, 1914. Royal BC Museum, BC Archives, PN12531.

Fig. I.6. A tourist's photograph of Alert Bay, ca. 1900.
National Anthropological Archives, Smithsonian Institution, INV 00075800.

Kwakwa̲ka̲'wakw villages in her own effort to record Native cultures in oils before the totem poles and war canoes fell into obscurity. For the past four years, Carr had been picturing many of the specific houses, poles, and canoes that Curtis photographed and filmed (figs. I.7 and I.8). Carr would go on to become deeply influenced by the Group of Seven, nationalist artists from eastern Canada who adapted European modernism—in the form of abstraction and romantic primitivism—to the cause of defining a uniquely Canadian aesthetic, primarily by depicting the country's landscapes and aboriginal populations in a common colonial mode of artistic appreciation through national appropriation.[16]

So while Curtis gravitated toward the Kwakwa̲ka̲'wakw due to their reputation for unvarnished cultural authenticity and resistance to colonial authority, they were deeply engaged with the parameters of modern institutions

Fig. I.7. *(above)* Emily Carr (Canadian, 1871–1945), *Indian Village, Alert Bay*, ca. 1912. Oil on canvas, 25 x 32 in. Gift of Lord Beaverbrook. Beaverbrook Art Gallery, 59.30.

Fig. I.8. *(below)* Emily Carr (Canadian, 1871–1945), *War Canoe, Alert Bay,* 1908. Watercolor on board, 10 5/8 x 15 in. This is an image of one of the dugout canoes used for the filming of *Head Hunters.* Private Collection. Photo by Brian Goble, Heffel Fine Art Auction House.

and the practitioners of modern representation. That they managed to hold on to many aspects of their ceremonial culture despite these pressures is a testament to their tenacity and adaptability in the face of great pressure to fully assimilate. Curtis took it upon himself to engage their modern consciousness while erasing overt signs of their contemporary lives and technologies in order to reconstruct a previous moment of their history. As evidenced by the existence of the film itself, his Kwakwa̱ka'wakw collaborators were game.[17]

In the Land of the Head Hunters

Curtis planned to make a series of full-length Indian pictures, of which the one on the Kwakwa̱ka'wakw was to be the first (Holm and Quimby 1980:113; Gidley 1998a:237). In 1912 he sought support from the Smithsonian Institution for an ethnographically detailed, scientific film documenting Kwakwa̱ka'wakw daily life and industry (Holm and Quimby 1980:32). Yet the eventual film was a blatantly commercial endeavor, much like his popular books and musicale, borrowing the main plot lines not from Kwakwa̱ka'wakw ceremony or lore but from Homer, Shakespeare, Longfellow, Fennimore Cooper, and the cinematic melodramas of the time. After the death of his primary patron J. P. Morgan, in 1913, raising funds for his book series became even more urgent. *In the Land of the Head Hunters*, billed on publicity posters as an "Indian Epic Drama" and in one playbill as an "Indian Trojan War," tells a romantic story of love and rivalry set amid the tumult of jealous sorcery and blood feuds between warring bands just before the time of European contact (an alternate title during its formulation was "In the Days of Vancouver"). The film juxtaposes ethnographically accurate scenes with staged contrivance, appropriation of neighboring practices, and pure invention. Holm and Quimby (1980) have presented a very detailed account of the film's origin, plot, and production, and here we only summarize these stories as relevant to the current restoration project and the new research that has accompanied it (see also Gidley 1998a).

As with Curtis's photographic work with the Kwakwa̱ka'wakw, the film's production relied extensively on the brokerage of George Hunt and his social and kin networks among the Kwagu'ł and 'Nak̓waxda'x̱w (Holm and Quimby 1980:57–61). One telling image, taken by Curtis's cameraman Edmund Schwinke (1888–1977), shows Hunt holding a megaphone on the set in the role of an assistant dixrector (see fig. 1.5). Hunt's youngest son Stanley played the hero, Motana, likely named after a famous A̱wik̓inux̱w Hamaṫsa or "Cannibal Dancer" called Mudana ("Four Man Eater"), who is identified in Hamaťsa songs and narratives recorded by both Curtis and Boas (many of the film characters' names are Anglicizations of Kwak̓wala ones).[18] Other extended kin played both major and supporting roles (see appendix 2 for a complete list). Apparently the main actors—drawn primarily from high-status families—demanded that their ceremonial enactments conform to hereditary privilege; that is, only people with recognized claim to certain masks and dances would perform them in the film (Makepeace 2002:136). For instance, we know that three different actresses ended up playing the heroine, Naida, as some scenes called for behavior inappropriate for people of a certain social rank (e.g., a highly ranked woman was not to paddle her own canoe, so it seems that a "stunt double" replaced the primary actress, Margaret Frank, in one scene). This is but one indication that the cast and crew asserted a good degree of control over certain aspects of the production. It also suggests possible explanations for other peculiar or culturally inappropriate features of the storyline. While the main narrative was certainly devised by Curtis, it is likely that his Kwakwaka'wakw collaborators helped him flesh out the action with culturally relevant—and acceptable—performances. For example, perhaps the ethnographically inaccurate round dance was a way for the film stars to display dramatic masks and performances without violating hereditary proscriptions about doing certain dances (see Glass 2009b).[19]

Curtis commissioned locals, especially Francine Hunt, to manufacture customary regalia for use in the film shoot (appendix 3); some of the regalia and clothing was made rather quickly out of raffia, which reads much like cedar bark on screen (Holm and Quimby 1980:44–55).[20] Curtis also supplied the actors with long black wigs and nose ornaments, as the Kwakwaka'wakw were in the process of abandoning many of their previous modes of daily adornment. George Hunt coordinated the purchase or fabrication of masks and canoes as well as the building of village sets, including one totem pole he may have carved himself (now at the University of British Columbia Museum of Anthropology). Anthropologist Peter Macnair suggests that the *hamsamł* (Hamaťsa masks) in particular may have been made for the filming, as chiefs may have been reluctant to bring out their most prized ceremonial regalia (in Jacknis 2002a:400n87). Extant, although increasingly obsolete, massive dugout war canoes were rented, repaired, and repainted (figs. I.9a and I.9b). In a number of cases the same props were reused for scenes featuring both the heroes and villains, which likely contributed to the narrative confusion of audiences. For instance, the same canoes are paddled by both village communities, with the designs repainted when used by one group, and the

Aaron Glass and Brad Evans

Figs. I.9a and I.9b. Dugout canoes, both of which were later used in *Head Hunters*, in Alert Bay, 1909 (the canoe in I.9b is the same one painted by Emily Carr in 1908). Photos by Harlan Smith. American Museum of Natural History Library, 46030 and 46031.

same dance masks and full-body costumes are performed in scenes taking place in both rival villages. As for the set, Curtis used the same open-faced Big House interior with its two winged totem poles to represent two different locations: the house of the good Chief Waket and the evil warrior Yaklus.[21] Appropriately, perhaps, both men were played by the same actor (Holm and Quimby 1980:59). Thus, in the case of Naida, multiple actresses played the same character, and in this case, the same actor played multiple characters.

Unlike the scores of short "Indian pictures" at the time, *Head Hunters* is notable for many of its gestures toward an authentic representation of Native life (Browne, Evans, this volume). It featured an entirely Kwakwaka'wakw cast at a time when many early studio films used white actors in redface; it was shot on location, not on a set in New Jersey or in the hills of Los Angeles; and it told a story set before the coming of Europeans with no cowboys or settlers in sight. The six-reel (about 90- to 100-minute-long) film was also highly ambitious artistically; at its release in 1914, it was reported to have cost Curtis $75,000 to make (*Motography* Vol. 12, No. 20:658)—a considerable sum for films in those days. Its production prints were extensively tinted and toned (Guldin, this volume).[22] The intertitle designs (fig. I.10) were created by Dugald Walker, an art nouveau book illustrator, based on totem pole motifs similar to those used by Curtis on his elaborate billboard.[23] Promotional posters were printed by the H. C. Miner Litho Company, a New York lithography company known at the time for promoting vaudeville, Broadway theater, and motion pictures, including D. W. Griffith's *Birth of a Nation* (1915) (see figs. 7.1a and 7.1b; appendix 1).[24] In at least some screening venues, the film was accompanied by "cyclorama" stage sets designed by Frank Cambria, a theater designer trained by David Belasco and a regular on the New York vaudeville circuit.[25] Most notably, premier screenings featured an original orchestral score composed by John J. Braham, based (reportedly) on wax cylinder recordings of tribal music made by Curtis on the Northwest Coast (Jacknis, Gilbert, and Harrison, this volume).[26] Braham was known at the time for his American performances of Gilbert and Sullivan operas, and he was also the composer of popular songs. The film was produced by the World Film Corporation, an important side project of the Shubert brothers' early twentieth-century theatrical empire; among many other ventures, they managed and produced events for New York's Casino Theatre, where the film premiered with full orchestral accompaniment.

Despite Curtis's ambitions, *In the Land of the Head Hunters* did not have a lasting effect on the emerging feature film industry. It received glowing reviews by critics when it premiered simultaneously at the Casino in New

Fig. I.10. Dugald Walker (American, 1883–1937), design used on original *Head Hunters* intertile cards. UCLA Film & Television Archive, The Field Museum, and Milestone Films.

York and the Moore Theatre in Seattle in December 1914 (Glass and Evans, this volume), but it received only limited distribution thereafter and was a disappointment to Curtis financially. The film's influence is most directly traceable in the history of documentary (Browne, this volume). In April 1915, filmmaker Robert Flaherty (1884–1951) and his wife visited Curtis's office in New York, where he screened the film for them (Holm and Quimby 1980:30; Ruby 2000:72–74). Flaherty must have had elements of *Head Hunters* in mind when he made *Nanook of the North* (1922), an immediate worldwide hit and now widely hailed as the first ethnographic documentary, despite Holm and Quimby's effort to assert Curtis's claim to this title (Holm and Quimby 1980:5; Quimby 1990; see also Winston 1988).

Some insight into Curtis's feeling about the poor reception of the film might be gleaned from his correspondence with the American Museum of Natural History from 1923 to 1924. By this time Curtis was living in Los Angeles, where he had found employment as a photographer for major Hollywood studios, shooting stills for Cecil B. DeMille's *The Ten Commandments*

(Davis 1985:70–72, 238–43). After extended negotiations, which involved the museum finding a trustee interested in financing the purchase of moving pictures, Curtis sold his negative of the film to the museum, relinquishing all copyright to it. The film by that time was in pieces, having been taken apart and reedited on numerous occasions, and Curtis apparently sent the museum all of the film he had—the negative, his master positive, and a thousand feet of extra negative.[27] An internal memo notes that the negative was heavily damaged and the positive print stained such as to make it impossible to duplicate.[28] Pliny Goddard, curator of ethnology at the museum, had the film screened for Franz Boas, who apparently dismissed the story but recommended that they acquire the ceremonial footage and scenes of industry. Goddard himself was interested in extracting a ten-minute sequence featuring the dances and boats—not coincidentally, the same features that Holm and Quimby would emphasize decades later (Gidley 1998a:243–44). A month after sending it to New York, Curtis telegraphed the museum asking if a check had been sent, a telegraph that ends ominously "am anxious as need is urgent."[29] An undated telegram from Goddard, presumably sent a few days later, assures Curtis that "payment is being made sorry for delay." Curtis had originally asked for fifteen hundred dollars, but the final price was only one thousand. The museum apparently did nothing with the print once it was in their possession. To this day, we have no record of its ultimate disposition.[30]

The Moving Archive and Further Collaborations

The experience with the American Museum of Natural History presages one of the great ironies of the history of *Head Hunters*. Although Curtis's photographic career was built on the mythology of the "vanishing race," it was largely Curtis who vanished from the history of the film. The preservation of the film ended up depending neither on Curtis's reputation nor on the romantic melodrama he concocted but rather on the interest people had in the ethnographic documentation of the world-famous Northwest Coast Indians (the Kwakwa̱ka'wakw in particular). The film would likely have been lost to history were it not for an eccentric collector, Hugo Zeiter, who donated a copy of it to The Field Museum in 1947. Evans spoke to Zeiter about the film in 2006, shortly before he passed away, at which time Zeiter recalled that he had a friend who regularly sent him discarded films recovered from a dumpster behind a movie house in Chicago. Zeiter had filled not only his home in Danville, Illinois, with the films but two small garages as well, where he also housed his extensive collection of circus memorabilia and American

Indian artifacts. A stray copy of *In the Land of the Head Hunters* was among the thousands of films he had collected by the mid 1940s.

Of particular interest is the fact that Zeiter had little idea of what it was he had donated to the Field—or, rather, little idea of it under the category of its more recent fame, as the long-lost silent feature film by Edward S. Curtis. The film's first scenes were missing, and no title or credits were attached. When Zeiter first approached The Field Museum, he promoted the film's value in terms of its apparent documentary footage of ceremonies from the Northwest Coast. In his correspondence, he suggested that the material reminded him of Flaherty's *Nanook of the North* and of photographs that he had seen published in a 1945 issue of *National Geographic*, and thus he thought the natural history museum might be interested in having it.[31] Zeiter made no mention of Curtis at the time (nor did he when speaking on the phone with Evans those many years later). Rather, he offered his thirty-five-millimeter nitrate copy to the museum under the name "The Vigil of Motana," the title of part 1, which shows up in the first title frame of The Field Museum's extant footage. It was under this title, with no reference to Curtis, that the film was archived at The Field Museum until the late 1960s. Preservation of the film in this setting came to depend almost entirely on anthropological classificatory schemes, not artistic or mass cultural ones; that is to say, it came to depend not on Curtis's artistry but on a conceptualization of the film as a largely unmediated representation of its historical, Northwest Coast Indian subject (see Holm and Quimby 1980:15n2).[32]

This story of the "vanishing" Curtis marks the second of four periods in the film's history, the first being that of its initial distribution (Glass and Evans, this volume). The third period is that of its recovery by Holm and Quimby in the 1960s. In their work on the film, the documentary impulse initiated by the museum continued, but it gained two significant new elements by being reunited with Curtis's name and by granting the Kwakwa̲ka'wakw descendants of its cast and crew the opportunity to shape its 1973 rerelease as *In the Land of the War Canoes*. It is particularly telling that it was Holm's Kwakwa̲ka'wakw friends who encouraged him to look for the movie that they remembered making with Curtis in the old days, leading Holm on an archival hunt that serendipitously ended one day at The Field Museum (Holm, this volume; Holm and Quimby 1980:16). It may have been unintentional, but many of the changes Holm and Quimby made to *Head Hunters* speak to concerns that have come to be known under the rubrics of postmodern anthropology and the so-called Native American literary and artistic renaissance. Holm and Quimby's work on the film in the 1960s and 1970s corresponds not only with the rise of the American Indian Movement but also with the first wave of the "crisis of representation" and political realignment of anthropology as a discipline.[33] It also followed the end of the official potlatch prohibition, which facilitated a revival of public potlatches in British Columbia, and an effort to repatriate ceremonial regalia that had been confiscated by the Canadian government and dispersed to museums in the 1920s (just as Curtis's film entered the museum archives). At the same time that work on *War Canoes* was completed, the U'mista Cultural Society, the current cosponsors of our own reconstruction effort, was incorporated under the British Columbia Societies Act in order to develop a museum and cultural center to house the repatriated regalia (Webster 1990).

Although groundbreaking for facilitating an indigenous intervention into Curtis's filmic vision, the editorial decisions made by Holm and Quimby pose significant problems for cultural historians interested in understanding *War Canoes/Head Hunters* as an intercultural document of its original time (Glass and Evans, and Browne, this volume).[34] They faced a number of challenges, of course, foremost among them being the fact that the film they discovered in The Field Museum had been reduced to about two-thirds of its original length. Zeiter had shipped four reels of nitrate to The Field Museum in 1947, but we know from Curtis's letters to the American Museum of Natural History that it had been a six-reel film in 1914, plus we know that some of the Field's copy had been further damaged in transferring it to safety stock. Holm and Quimby, confronted with what they took to be an incoherent narrative, and also struck by the potentially offensive qualities of the film, decided to make significant alterations. On the textual front, they changed the film's title, making it less sensational, and they rewrote all of the intertitles to cover holes in the plot left by damaged or missing film. Reduced drastically in number, the new intertitles condensed the narrative descriptions of the action sequences and cast the film in an ethnographic light by playing up the Kwakwaka'wakw cultural context and playing down the melodramatic storyline and florid prose of Curtis's cards (Evans 1998, and this volume).

Most significantly, in collaboration with the Kwakwaka'wakw, Holm and Quimby produced a new soundtrack for the film featuring both naturalistic sound effects, such as splashing waves and screeching seagulls, and dialogue and song recorded in the Kwak̓wala language. Some of the participants in this process had worked on the film as children, and all saw it for the first time when Holm screened it for them (Holm and Quimby 1980:17). Characteristically, the new music is appropriate to the ceremonial scenes depicted, although approximations were made where the content was not definitively identified by the Native collaborators (Harrison, this volume). The overall effect simulates a synch-sound film, as if the audio had been recorded with the image, implying the kind of naturalistic, observational documentary film common by the time the two were doing this work in the 1960s. Indeed, as Holm states in his forward to this volume, "It is hard to imagine that the sound had not been recorded on the spot."

While Holm is referring to the admirable fact that much Kwakwa̲ka̲'wakw oratory and cultural practice has survived the decades since the film's production, he also captures the challenge of interpreting *War Canoes* as a film in its own right. Even though the reconstructed film included an opening disclaimer about its editorial changes, it has been our observation that audiences tend to experience the audio as synchronous rather than anachronistic, which introduces real problems for interpretation. The naturalism of the audio is clearly at odds with the exaggerated acting style of silent films, which thus comes across as being particularly amateur and stagey. The remnants of Curtis's imposed story make little sense alongside the accurate ethnographic framing, and each tends to subvert rather than complement the other. And while *War Canoes* is innovative in its attempt to give literal voice back to the previously silent Native actors, the lack of subtitles for the new Kwak̓wala dialogue makes it inaccessible as narration, functioning instead—for English speakers at least—as background sound to signal an authentic aboriginality at the expense of narrative legibility.[35] The temporal rupture between the simulated synch-sound of 1973 and the filmed image of 1913/14 further compounds the already anachronistic chasm between the 1914 production and the film's historical setting, which, if extrapolated, would date to sometime in the late 1700s.

For the past four decades, everyone—from Curtis scholars to film historians to the Kwakwa̲ka̲'wakw themselves—have evaluated Curtis's film through the filter of Holm and Quimby's editorial decisions. Yet it has not been our intention to replace *War Canoes* with a supposedly "authentic" and thus improved document. In fact, for the Kwakwa̲ka̲'wakw at least, *War Canoes* is likely to remain the preferred version due to the multigenerational presence of their ancestors—faces from the 1910s with voices from the 1960s. Rather, we hope to supplement it given new archival discoveries that allow us to glimpse more clearly the film that Curtis and the Kwakwa̲ka̲'wakw made together in 1914. With an extensive website, photography exhibits, and public symposia, we aimed to use the collaborative restoration project to raise new questions about how Curtis worked in 1914—especially how he might have worked *with* rather than *on* his Native subjects—and how we might interpret his film and photographs in light of this historical perspective. As historian Paul Apodaca noted with some additional irony at one of our symposia, in a curious way we have tried to reverse the degree of *War Canoes'* significant and innovative intervention by returning the film to its own aesthetic and cultural origins. To put it somewhat schematically: Curtis erased the sense of lived indigenous modernity when he asked his Native partners to stage their own premodern past; Holm and Quimby restored the contemporary voices and cultural knowledge of *their* Native partners in the 1960s by obscuring Curtis's problematic vision of their ancestors; and we have tried to restore Curtis's own modernist project (in part by replacing the voices from the 1960s with the music from 1914) while emphasizing with *our* Native partners the ways in which traditional culture and intercultural exchange have continued to be integral to their experience of modernity for over a century now.

From the beginning of our work on the latest reconstruction, we had two major objectives.[36] The first was to restore *Head Hunters* to its place in cinematic and cultural history, and to give audiences today a sense of what audiences in 1914 would have seen and heard in theaters. This entailed restoring to the film its original title, intertitles, missing scenes, musical score, color tinting, and advertising ephemera, in all their romantic sensationalism, spectacular framing, and promotional overstatement. Second, it was important to us to examine the relevance of the film to today's multiple audiences, to put the film into dialogue with contemporary Kwakwa̲ka'wakw and other indigenous peoples as well as scholarly communities in order to better understand it as a historical, intercultural artifact with lasting effect and resonance. It is neither our intention to celebrate Curtis for his cinematic vision, nor to continuously chastise him for dressing up his actors in wigs and cedar-bark clothing to make them appear centuries older than they were in 1914. Both of these perspectives convey a degree of truth, but they are also conversation-stoppers, discursive dead-ends that tell us little about Curtis, his images, or the people he imaged. With the film reconstruction project, as with this volume, our goal has been to complicate this stalemate by shifting attention away from Curtis's iconic pictures and personal intentions, and toward the social, historical, cultural, and political contexts of his image production.

Themes of the Book

The chapters in this volume cover disparate aspects of Curtis's body of work and of the history of *Head Hunters* in particular. The first part of the book,

Aaron Glass and Brad Evans

"Mediating Indians/Complicating Curtis," establishes some of the broader cultural contexts for the production and consumption of Curtis's images of Native Americans—historically and today, by Natives and non-Natives alike—insisting in particular on the idea that Curtis was the instigator of much more than the photographs for which he is best known today. The second part, *Head Hunters* across Two Centuries," turns more directly to the historical and theoretical issues that arise when the film (in multiple versions) is highlighted in terms of its circulation among various publics after the moment of its first release—a circulation that, almost immediately, was out of the control of both Curtis and his Kwakwa̱ka'wakw collaborators. The final part, "Reimagining Curtis Today," focuses on technical, historical, and cultural issues highlighted by the current film reconstruction and screening project. Together, the chapters offer not only an extended historical exploration of one of the seminal instances of visual and ethnographic representation of Native Americans in the early twentieth century, but also a comprehensive theoretical basis for understanding the intercultural dynamics of the ongoing production and consumption of these materials by both indigenous and nonindigenous audiences.

In the foreword, Bill Holm recounts how working on *War Canoes* evidenced for him the remarkable cultural continuity of the Kwakwa̱ka'wakw people and the integrity of their songs and dances, which had survived the severe impositions of the colonial economies of the twentieth century—and which were, in fact, much more intact in 1968 than the fragile and fragmented print of Curtis's film that Holm and Quimby were trying to reconstruct. Holm's narrative sets up a dynamic explored throughout this volume, for while the continuity of tradition is certainly one of the stories revealed by the ongoing interest in *Head Hunters*, another is that of the continuity of the Kwakwa̱ka'wakw's engagement with public performance and self-representation as modern strategies for survival. This point is made in different ways in part 1 of this volume. Mick Gidley qualifies and historicizes the idea of "documentary" in order to suggest that *Head Hunters* was a collective and collaborative effort typical not only of the *NAI* project but also of the elaborate musicale or picture opera that Curtis put on just before undertaking the motion picture. Next, Shamoon Zamir provides a new reading of indigenous agency in Curtis's photography, refuting the now-familiar critique that the photographs literally froze indigenous peoples in time. Kate Flint and Ira Jacknis focus on the variety of genres and media in which Curtis worked. Flint turns our attention to the literature of Native representation at this time by contrasting different visions of "Indianness," Native history, and relations to the land in Curtis's 1915 novelization of his film and the volumes of Native legends assembled by Pauline Johnson. Jacknis explores yet another "new media" in which Curtis worked—wax cylinder recordings—providing a detailed breakdown of the Curtis team's pattern of recording, transcribing, publishing, and otherwise disseminating songs across the entire *NAI* book series.

Part 2 directly assesses *Head Hunters* as both a film project and a historical object around which multiple audiences have fashioned new versions of their cultural selves. Aaron Glass and Brad Evans begin by offering a historical survey of the reception of the film in its various guises over the last hundred years given different audiences and theoretical or cultural predilections. In the next two chapters, Colin Browne and Evans consider cinematic contexts for the production of *Head Hunters* and their varied relationship to film history. Browne locates *Head Hunters* within the history of documentary film while underscoring some of the possible explanations for Curtis's anxiety about modernity, which led in part to his proclivity for "antiquing" his images of Indians. Evans's chapter returns *Head Hunters* to its cultural context as a fictional feature film. He argues for understanding the significance of Indian spectatorship of early cinema, situating the film and its Native audiences as a part of the "vernacular of modernism," and concludes with a reading of the film's successes and failures as a fictional narrative. The final two chapters of this section address the issue of how the film continues to be an object around which Native identities are challenged and constructed. Klisala Harrison's essay takes up a paradox at the core of *Head Hunters*, asking what it means politically for the multiple iterations of a silent film to depend so heavily upon the representation and mediation of indigenous music and song. Barbara Cranmer, a contemporary Kwakwaka'wakw documentary filmmaker, reflects on her engagement with Curtis's movie and photographs in her own filmmaking and according to her own ancestry.

Part 3, "Reimagining Curtis Today," details multiple aspects of the current restoration work. The first chapter is by Jere Guldin, who oversaw reconstruction of the film at the UCLA Film & Television Archive, and who describes the interesting and complicated process of reassembling the film. David Gilbert, who undertook the effort to revitalize John Braham's original musical score, offers a thorough account of the original score in the context of emerging genres of silent film music and the New York theatre scene, including a sense of the challenge of matching the film score to the reconstructed film. Next is an interview with Neal Stulberg, Owen Underhill, Timothy Long, and Laura Ortman, who were all involved either in conducting or playing the score at the live screening series in 2008. The conversation suggests the challenges of working with an incomplete film and a score not perfectly matched to the film, the need to adapt the music to fit their particular orchestras, and the creative work of realizing a musical component to a film that is admittedly problematic for contemporary audiences.

The volume concludes with a number of chapters that bring contemporary indigenous and intercultural perspectives to the Curtis project and to larger issues in performance as a mode of self-representation. In his interview with Evans and Glass, William Wasden Jr., creative director of the Gwa'wina Dancers, whose members represent many of the Kwakwaka'wakw bands, reflects on their experience traveling with the film and sharing some of the culture represented in it with today's audiences. Dave Hunsaker, who was an artistic adviser to the production, suggests the compromises and negotiations involved in balancing public performance and interpretation with Native protocols surrounding proprietary knowledge and restrictions on access—a dynamic that certainly occurred in the making of Curtis's film itself. Glass's chapter offers an ethnography of the Gwa'wina Dancers' presentations as exemplifying what he calls a Kwakwaka'wakw "culture of display," a tendency to adapt performative and declarative aspects of the potlatch to the contexts of intercultural and colonial exchange that have long defined the conditions of an indigenous modernity. In his afterword, Paul Chaat Smith concludes that, for good or bad, no one did more to shape the world's ideas about American Indians, including Indians' ideas about themselves, than Edward Curtis. Like others in this volume, Smith argues that cultural understanding depends upon a savvy respect for the complexity of media forms and the varying desires and expectations of their multiple audiences.

In addition to the chapters, the book features two photo essays that bring word and image into closer dialogue. In the first, urban-Iroquois visual artist Jeff Thomas engages in an imagined conversation with Curtis. He wrestles with the images, and the work Curtis did, taking him to task for creating romantic stereotypes while also acknowledging that there is more subtlety, history, and individuality in the larger *NAI* project than one might suppose from its commercial mass-marketing today. Thomas juxtaposes his own images of powwow dancers in order to reflect on the lessons he learned from Curtis—what to do and what not to do in staging the photographic encounter—and to open questions about how Curtis might have approached his own subjects, who were in Thomas's view active participants in photo making. The second photo essay presents selections from an exhibition originally developed for the touring series of film screenings. It features the

Fig. I.11. G̲wa'wina Dancers under the Moore Theatre marquee, Seattle, June 10, 2008.
Photo by Sharon Grainger. U'mista Cultural Centre.

reflections of ten indigenous artists, scholars, and community leaders in the Pacific Northwest, each responding to an Edward Curtis photograph he or she selected. In the diversity of perspectives—from declarations of kinship to postcolonial critique—we find considerable nuance regarding Curtis's images and their complex relationship to First Nations today.

* * *

At the public events surrounding our restoration project, audiences saw fully modern, contemporary Kwakwa̲ka'wakw presenting what they consider traditional dance in traditional regalia, much like their fully modern ancestors did when they dressed up and staged the past for Edward Curtis (fig. I.11). The presenters told stories about how their grandparents worked on the film during the potlatch prohibition, identified their own genealogical rights to the dances they performed, and educated audiences about current efforts to battle fish farms and to negotiate treaties and land claims; that is to say, they laid bare the larger cultural and political contexts in which both their ancestors and they themselves choose to stage intercultural presentations.

Aaron Glass and Brad Evans

If you looked carefully, Adidas track pants were visible under their button blankets; this was not an attempt on their part to erase the current trappings of modernity, like Curtis is accused of doing, but rather to emphasize that traditional culture was and is a key component of modernity—at least *their* indigenous version of it. Might we say the same for Curtis's models and film stars almost a century ago?

After watching and presenting *Head Hunters* with the Kwakwa̠ka'wakw, it is impossible for us to see it simply as a colonialist fantasy, a nostalgic eulogy for a colorful and safely vanished impediment to civilization. Nor, however, is it an expression of unmitigated—or unmediated—Kwakwa̠ka'wakw self-fashioning. Rather, it shares something with both of these visions, not so much as a measure of Curtis's own aesthetic sensibility or cultural propensities, but due to its very particular and collaborative history of both production and reception. With this volume, we challenge readers to think about other kinds of archival or familiar filmic documents as results of similar decisions made within the nexus of multiple agencies, genres, and modernities; as artifacts of very specific historical, social, and political conjunctures; as documents of complex and often extraordinary intercultural encounters.

1   Edmund Meany Papers (#106-70-12), box 83, folder 18, University of Washington Special Collections.
2   Certainly, Curtis's powerful political and industrialist patrons had more than a scientific or nostalgic investment in convincing the American public of the reality of Native disappearance (Gidley 2003b:13–15; Trachtenberg 2004).
3   As noted at numerous points in this volume and elsewhere, George Hunt was of particular importance for the dissemination of Northwest Coast materials. But similar figures abounded, such as Simon Pokagon (Potawatomi), Daniel La France (Mohawk), Gertrude Simmons Bonnin (Yankton Dakota), Charles Alexander Eastman (Santee Sioux), Angel DeCora (Winnebago), Francis La Flesche (Omaha), Arthur Parker (Seneca), and Luther Standing Bear (Lakota). For more on this subject, see Gidley (1994); Deloria (1998, 2004); Hoxie (2001); Maddox (2005); and Hutchinson (2009).
4   Curtis's film title lacked a hyphen in "head hunters," although his 1915 book of the same name hyphenated the term as "head-hunters."
5   Although the film and its promotional material fail to identify the Kwakwa̠ka'wakw, a couple of newspaper reviews mention "The Kwakiutl" by name, suggesting that Curtis related this identification directly to reporters on occasion (e.g., *Seattle Sunday Times,* December 6, 1914; *New York Times,* December 8, 1915).The term *Kwakwa̠ka'wakw* (pronounced KWA-kwuh-kyuh [glottal stop] wahkw) means "those who speak Kwak̓wala" and is used to describe sixteen to eighteen independent bands, each with their own local terms of address (some of which are used in this book). This term is increasingly used to replace the famous misnomer "Kwakiutl," an Anglicized form of *Kwagu'ł,* the band living at Fort Rupert with whom Edward Curtis and Franz Boas did most of their work. The orthography used in this book for writing Kwak̓wala was developed by the U'mista Cultural Society. *First Nations,* along with *Inuit* and *Métis,* are the preferred categorical terms of address for indigenous peoples in Canada, although we also use the term *Native* as a general descriptor.

6   In this respect the volume builds on work that has acknowledged, at least in passing, indigenous agency with regard to Curtis's work, including Lippard (1992); Northern and Brown (1993); Horse Capture (1993); Gidley (1994); Coleman (1972, 1979, and 1998); Rushing (2003); Trachtenberg (2004); Zamir (2007); and Glass (2009b). More broadly, the approach we are proposing finds theoretical analogues in work by Edwards (2001); Ginsburg (1995); Myers (2002); Evans (2005); Comaroff and Comaroff (2009); and Smith (2009).

7   In the years just prior to Curtis's film, many other similarly titled productions appeared, from Frederick Monsen's ca. 1910 photographic pamphlet *With a Kodak in the Land of the Navajo* (Dilworth 1996:116) to the 1911/12 libretto for L. O. Armstrong's pageant *Hiawatha in the Land of the Ojibwe* (McNally 2006). In 1912 and 1913, the Méliès Company undertook a highly publicized world tour, making "ethnographic" films for both entertainment and education (Hoffman 1913); in New Zealand, for instance, they focused on filming Maori legends (of lovers from opposing tribes) and tales of warfare, sorcery, and cannibalism, all themes of Curtis's own film. On the popularity of ethnographic films focused on hunting in the years around Curtis's film, see Griffiths (2002:264–65, 270–76). Loïe Fuller's Orientalist burlesque "Fire Dance of Salome" was an international sensation of the 1900 Paris World's Fair and immortalized by Mallarmé and his circle (Reynolds 1998), and fire-eating or fire-walking entertainments were popular sideshow fare in the early twentieth century (Harry Houdini mentions a Navajo Fire Dance among others in his 1920 *The Miracle Mongers and Their Methods*).

8   This is not to say that they were *equal* contributors—Curtis did maintain editorial control and would have reaped the financial benefits, had there been any. After the filming, the distribution of *Head Hunters* (including its extensive advertising campaign) appears to have been largely out of the hands of the Kwakwaka'wakw participants. However, we must take seriously the fact that Curtis could not have made his film or his photographs without the active cooperation of his actors and models.

9   In fact, Curtis relied on Boas's published material while in the field (Gidley 1998a:139) and later acknowledged the utility of it in the preface to volume 10 (Curtis 1907–30, vol. 10:xii).

10 The most important ethnological and administrative visitors to the Kwakwaka'wakw during the decades around 1900 were Johan Adrian Jacobsen, George Dawson, Israel Powell, Franz Boas, Charles Newcombe, and George T. Emmons (see Cole 1985; Jacknis 2002a).

11 Edward Curtis, in the introduction to volume 10 (1907–30, vol. 10:xii), mistakenly identifies Hunt as having a Scottish father and Tsimshian mother, an error repeated frequently in the subsequent literature. On George Hunt, see Cannizzo (1983); Jacknis (1991, 1992); Gidley (1994); Berman (1994, 1996); Glass (2009b).

12 Hunt went on to work on other motion pictures after Curtis's: a film made by Pliny Goddard in 1922 that no longer survives; *Totem Land*, produced by Montreal's Associated Screen News in 1927; and the film footage shot but never edited by Franz Boas in Fort Rupert in 1930 (see Bunn-Marcuse 2005; Savard 2010).

13 Halliday to McLean, May 12, 1914; McLean to Halliday, June 17, 1914. National Archives of Canada.

14 *Annual Report of the Canadian Department of Indian Affairs for 1914,* xxviii.

15 Many Native peoples on the Northwest Coast adopted photography in the late nineteenth century, not only reproducing Euro-American uses of it but also adapting it to their own ceremonial and memorializing needs (Askren 2007; Gmelch 2008).

16 There is a vast literature on Carr; see especially National Gallery of Canada (2006). On the colonial dynamic of national appropriation through aboriginal artistic appreciation, see Thomas (1999).

Aaron Glass and Brad Evans

17   The two main villages in which *Head Hunters* was made, Fort Rupert and Blunden Harbour, later hosted additional ethnographic and travelogue filmmakers in the 1920s, 1930s, and 1950s, including Franz Boas, William Heick, and Robert Gardner (see Jacknis 1987, 2000; Morris 1994; Bunn-Marcuse 2005).

18   Curtis (1907–30, vol. 10:234–39) relates the story and song of "Mótana," and Boas (1921:1292) includes a mourning song for him. Tom "Mackenzie" Willie, a Kwakwaka'wakw singer, composer, and song leader, recorded a song and information about Mudana in 1991 (Song #8, pp. 9–11, File #3080.7.2, U'mista Cultural Centre).

19   Additionally, Stanley Hunt (playing Motana) dances clockwise around the fire in the first of his three prayer vigil scenes (Harrison, this volume), which is the opposite direction of travel from dance in Kwakwaka'wakw ceremony. Likewise, the Navajo were said to perform dances incompletely or in the improper direction, thereby purposely delegitimizing them so that Curtis could film them in 1904 (Lyman 1982:69; Gidley 1998a:101; Makepeace 2002:55, 182). Faris (1993:383–84) qualifies this interpretation, suggesting that Curtis's Navajo footage was printed laterally reversed, although he does acknowledge that the dancers pictured are awkward and not performing as they would in ceremony.

20   Many of the props were acquired in 1927 by Seattle's Washington State Museum, now the Burke Museum of Natural History and Culture (accession #2162). Further items from Curtis's collections ended up in other museums (see Jacknis 2002a:398n14). In 2008, the Burke Museum acquired additional film props, including the set of distinctive Hamaṫsa masks, which are now on permanent display (see appendix 3 and fig. 15.11).

21   To suggest the foreboding dwelling of Yaklus, a *hạmspek* ("cannibal pole") and a *mawił* (dance screen) were added to the set, as if the Hamaṫsa-related equipment distinguished it as a place of sinister malfeasance. Additionally, figures of Dzunuḵ'wa, the man-eating giantess, were added to the poles (Holm and Quimby 1980:52–54). On the poles used in these scenes, see also Wasden, photo essay 2, this volume.

22   Curtis suggested to the press that, working with a chemist, he invented the "Hochstetter-Curtis" process, "a new system of color photography as applied to moving picture films" (*New York Times* December 2, 1914), but this appears to have been yet another exaggerated claim on his part (Jere Guldin, personal communication; see Guldin, this volume).

23   Dugald Walker (1883–1937) was a young Virginia-born illustrator and member of the Art Student's League living in New York City at the time Curtis made his film. Walker specialized in fables and fairytales and was known for his early book *Stories for Pictures* (1912). It is not clear why he was selected by Curtis, but he may have been producing *Fairy Tales from Hans Christian Anderson* (1914) while he worked on the *Head Hunters* intertitle design.

24   H. C. Miner Litho Company was started in 1896 and was operated by H. C. Miner and his son H. C. Miner Jr. It was reorganized in 1908 under a new president, artist Hugo Ziegfeld, and continued operation until 1935, associated primarily with United Artists and Fox. Perhaps coincidentally, the company had also produced film posters for an unrelated 1913 film entitled simply *Head Hunters*. See Rhodes (2007:236) and http://www.learnaboutmovieposters.com/newsite/index/countries/US/HISTORY/LITHOS/HCMiner/Miner.asp (accessed January 22, 2012).

25   Frank Cambria (1883–1966), an Italian American theater designer, studied at the National Academy of Design in New York City and became known for his local creation of elaborate stage scenery and vaudeville theatrics (Marsh 1985; Gomery 2002). One of his first jobs in the United States was creating a painted cyclorama of a yachting scene in 1912 at Madison Square Garden, which may have provided

one context for gaining Curtis's attention. He moved to Chicago in the 1920s, where he worked for Balaban and Katz expanding on the vaudeville model of combining cinema with live stage entertainment. Although not documented as early as 1914, Cambria later innovated by staging elaborate theatrical "prologues" to films (Koszarski 1990:51); the Curtis film score does feature an extended musical "prelude" or overture, although there is no indication that a live performance accompanied it. It is not clear what Cambria's "cyclorama stage set" for the *Head Hunters* screenings would have looked like. It may have consisted of a painted and possibly curved backdrop behind or around the film screen itself (David Mayer and Richard Koszarski, personal correspondence). According to the *New York Clipper* (December 5, 1914:12), "Special scenery, derived from photographs of the totem pole country" was planned for the Casino engagement, but no reviews that we've found describe it in any detail.

26 Both John Braham's original 1914 manuscript score for *Head Hunters* and David Gilbert's 2008 transcription are available in complete form through the Getty Research Institute's online library at http://www.getty.edu/research/library/.

27 Edward Curtis to Pliny E. Goddard, Curator of Ethnology, October 16, 1924. Division of Anthropology Archives, American Museum of Natural History.

28 One wonders if the "staining" referred to Curtis's extensive tinting and toning. As such, it helps support the notion that the museum's interest in the film was for its ethnographic footage and not its potential commercial appeal.

29 Curtis to Goddard, November 17, 1924, Division of Anthropology Archives, American Museum of Natural History.

30 The American Museum of Natural History destroyed or deaccessioned much of its film collection in the 1950s out of concern for safety given the volatility of nitrate stock, and it is possible that Curtis's film was lost at this time (Alison Griffiths, personal communication).

31 Zeiter to Field Museum, February 17 and March 5, 1947, Field Museum Archives. Zeiter cited two articles in his letter to Clifford Gregg of March 5, both from the January 1945 edition of *National Geographic*: Matthew W. Stirling, "Indians of Our North Pacific Coast," and W. Landon Kihr [*sic;* W. Langdon Kihn], "Totem Pole Builders." He also cites a July 1946 issue of *Coronet* with an article entitled "Strange Indians of the North West," illustrated with paintings by John Clymer.

32 We say "almost" because it is clear from his correspondence with the Field that Zeiter, unlike the museum's anthropological curators, appreciated the film *as a* film: he asked, for example, that they preserve the thirty-five-millimeter nitrate for its colored toning, which would be lost if transferred to sixteen-millimeter safety stock (Guldin, this volume). That request was ignored, largely due to the volatility of the original nitrate. Holm and Quimby (1980:14) relate how the film was once projected in order to identify it and quickly caught fire, resulting in further loss of extant footage. In the wake of this accident, it was immediately transferred to safety film.

33 Three of the seminal texts motivating and contributing to this realignment were published in the years that Holm and Quimby were working on the Curtis film: Vine Deloria Jr.'s *Custer Died for Your Sins* (1969), Dell Hymes's edited book *Reinventing Anthropology* (1972), and Talal Asad's volume *Anthropology and the Colonial Encounter* (1973).

34 Holm and Quimby (1980:126) detailed the specific changes they made to the film in converting *Head Hunters* to *War Canoes*.

35 The lack of English subtitles for the Kwak̓wala in *War Canoes* is an added shame given the seriousness (as well as humor) with which its Kwakwaka'wakw recording artists approached their charge. To our ears, the "spooky" sounds made on the soundtrack to the sorcery scenes speak volumes to the pleasure that the actors had in intervening with the text of the original film. In working on the current project, Glass asked the late Lorraine Hunt, a descendant of George Hunt and a fluent Kwak̓wala

speaker, to translate the dialogue in *War Canoes*, and the resulting transcription confirms Holm's report (in Holm and Quimby 1980:17) that they really imagined what the characters might be saying, often by interpreting physical gestures as well as narrative context. It is currently intended that the Milestone Films DVD release of *Head Hunters* and *War Canoes* will feature an optional subtitle track for *War Canoes* to make the Kwak̓wala dialogue accessible to English speakers for the first time.

36 Given the significant amount of damage to the extant film reels, we speak more often of "reconstruction" than "restoration" in characterizing the current print of *Head Hunters* (Guldin, this volume).

PART ONE

Mediating Indians / Complicating Curtis

1

EDWARD CURTIS AND
IN THE LAND OF THE HEAD HUNTERS

Four Contexts

MICK GIDLEY

Edward S. Curtis's Kwakwa̱ka̱'wakw movie *In the Land of the Head Hunters* was first screened, after germinating for several years, in 1914.[1] Major claims can be made—and have been made—for its significance as a groundbreaking venture: that it was the very first narrative documentary, preceding Robert Flaherty's *Nanook of the North* (1922), the film usually credited with that role, by several years; that it was one of the earliest full-length feature films to secure the willing participation of an indigenous community; and that, as it combined spectacle with story, it was especially successful in its use of visual effects that would come to be recognized as specifically cinematic. The contention of this essay is that such "firsts" were not accidental but a logical outcome of previous efforts by Curtis—and also by his collective project—to produce *The North American Indian* (1907–30; hereafter *NAI*), the huge serial work that in 1915, with the publication of the tenth volume, also devoted to the Kwakwa̱ka̱'wakw people, would reach its halfway point.[2]

The Curtis project was the largest American anthropological venture ever undertaken. My study of it, *Edward S. Curtis and the North American Indian, Incorporated* (Gidley 1998a), examined and critiqued its vision in some detail, arguing that there were political, economic, ideological, and aesthetic determinants of its representation of Native Americans. The *NAI*—twenty volumes of illustrated text accompanied by twenty portfolios of photogravures—was monumental and had profound effects. The project to produce it was extraordinary and, in some respects, unique. Yet both the project and its product were also, perhaps paradoxically, typical of their phase of American history. Most obviously, the elegiac note for Indians as a "vanishing race," so frequently struck by the project, resounded through the very air in the United States at the time.[3] There were, in other words, cultural constraints and contexts to the project's representation of Native Americans.

Curtis himself did not see it this way. For the most part, he presented the *NAI* as a straightforward "record." In a 1911 speech he said, "It is an effort to make a broad picture and word record of the Indians,"[4] and in 1914, at the height of his fame, during the very year of the movie's release, he published in the *American Museum Journal* his "Plea for Haste in Making Documentary Records of the American Indian." In this article, as if there were nothing problematic about what he was saying, he claimed, "We want the documentary picture of the people and their homeland—a picture that will show the soul of the people" (Curtis 1914a:165). By contrast, I believe that there were marked tensions in such an aim. Paying due respect to the historical complexity with which the *NAI* enterprise confronts us, this essay sketches four contexts for *In the Land of the Head Hunters*.

1. Curtis as Photographer

Curtis was out and out, first and foremost, a photographer. He had begun to take photographs at least as early as 1890, was a partner in a professional printing and portrait studio before he was twenty-five, and achieved almost immediate local recognition in Seattle, his adopted hometown, first for his practice, then also as an authority on the medium. Much of his early work, whether made in his own portrait studio, done for local businesses, or created in the context of his leisure as a mountain climber, constituted what at the time was often termed "record photography." In these pioneering days Curtis talked constantly to his one-time assistant William Wellington Phillips of his ambition to create "cracker jack pictures" (Phillips memoir reproduced in Gidley 1998a:51), for a while he contributed a column of photographic aesthetic-cum-technical advice to a Seattle magazine, and his own work won prizes. He got his grounding partly in the studio, but also *en plein air* : making portraits, landscapes, and genre scenes, all of which, translated into motion picture footage, would be features of *In the Land of the Head Hunters*. He was a *photo*grapher before he ever became an *ethno*grapher or a *cinemato*grapher, and his photography fed into both his text making and his film making.

J. C. Strauss, a St. Louis pictorialist and member of Alfred Stieglitz's Photo Secession movement, as part of his 1904 display for the world's fair in his

Fig. 1.1. Edward S. Curtis
as Frans Hals, 1904.
Photo by J. C. Strauss.
Courtesy of Mick Gidley.

adopted city, took a little-known portrait of Curtis that depicts him in the guise of a Frans Hals lookalike (fig. 1.1). To those able to discern Curtis as the subject behind the costume of a seventeenth-century Dutch painter, Strauss was here making a double reference: Hals and Curtis were both known for their portraiture, of course, but both also made picturesque genre studies, scenes of ordinary, everyday life. It was as a winner of prizes for these studies of local Coastal Salish Indians in the Seattle area that Curtis first achieved national recognition. The Library of Congress file of Curtis images includes one of his slightly later picturesque genre studies: done in 1904, it shows young Quentin, the son of President Theodore Roosevelt, trying to catch June bugs. We can see it replicated in the depiction of a Sioux child tellingly titled *Nature's Blossom* (n.d.).[5]

In *Edward S. Curtis and the North American Indian, Incorporated*, I pointed out that the kind of picturesque genre study Curtis produced was indebted to Peter Henry Emerson's representation of the landscapes and disappearing folk life of England's Norfolk Broads, both in general style and in the composition of specific images (Gidley 1998a:72, 75). Emerson abjured the studio-based (sometimes composite) studies of his predecessor Henry Peach Robinson as too manipulated to be "natural"—and, indeed, it is sometimes forgotten that, while Emerson also bemoaned the pursuit of photographic "sharpness" as an end in itself, he revered the "record" as much as Curtis later claimed to do. "Photographic pictures," he wrote, "may have one merit that no other pictures can ever have, they can be relied upon as historical records" (Emerson 1980:103). Emerson's "naturalism"—as he and others in photographic circles of that time called it—was complex. In some ways, it is comparable in its seeming contrarieties to American literary naturalism as practiced by, say, Stephen Crane during the same period. Just as we know that Crane's naturalism was able to display elements of symbolism and even what some critics have called "impressionism," the photographic naturalism that Curtis inherited from Emerson was similarly a mixed mode. "Impressionism," for example, was a designation Emerson also associated with his kind of naturalism. Thus, even though Curtis deployed the term "documentary," his naturalism was never meant to be documentary in a mid-twentieth-century sense, and for this reason strident castigations of its "failure" to meet such documentary standards are misplaced (see also Browne, this volume).[6] As photography critic A. D. Coleman has suggested, we need to work toward a fuller understanding of the special kind of realism that Curtis practiced (Coleman 1998).

In many of Curtis's comments there is implicit advocacy of a symbolic interpretation of his photographs. "In the study of primitive man," he said in his *Museum Journal* essay, "the interest is more in his psychology than in his economics, more in his songs and prayers than in his implements. In fact, we study his implements that we may get light upon his mental processes" (Curtis 1914a:164).[7] This could merely express a preference for the mental over the material, but it is also a claim that the mental may be apprehended *through* the material. We sometimes observe this being substantiated not only by images, but by their captions. In *The Scout—Atsina* (1907–30, vol. 5), for example, we notice the blade of grass standing up from the subject's hair, and the caption informs us that it is a symbolic remnant of the mass of grass such a scout would traditionally have put on his head to camouflage himself in looking out over a hunting ground or at potential enemies. The very title of a picture of some Southern Yokuts pots laid out beside a gnarled tree is symbolically indicative: *Art Old as the Tree* (1907–30, vol. 14). The portrait *Nakoaktok Chief's Daughter* (1907–30, vol. 10), paralleled in the movie, has more subtlety: her high status in Kwakwaka'wakw society is indicated by her platform seat's elevation by two carved figures, which, in turn, represent the lower servant caste (fig. 1.2).[8] Simultaneously, though, Curtis's particular and perceptive framing of this scene makes it clear that he has discerned another relationship, an almost purely visual one, between the chief's daughter and the carved figures: their positioning in such a way as to replicate her posture and sour expression seems to suggest that they mock her pose and pretensions.

Fig. 1.2. Edward S. Curtis, *A Nakoaktok Chief's Daughter*, 1914. (*NAI*, portfolio 10.) Charles Deering McCormick Library of Special Collections, Northwestern University Library.

When we examine pictures actually depicting "songs and prayers," a symbolic reading is virtually inevitable. Our principal initial impression is that they are images of stasis, frozen moments: the supplicant is arrested at a midpoint in his devotions, as in *The Sun Dancer* (1907–30, vol. 3) or (to choose from Kwakwaka'wakw culture) *Hamatsa Emerging from the Woods—Koskimo* (1907–30, vol. 10). A kind of *tableau vivant* is created. An element of the purity

Mick Gidley

46

of this tableau aesthetic was transferred, as we will see, to the movie. But some still images have another purpose: they imply a larger narrative, and frequently in the *NAI* that narrative is supplied by the written text; a photograph of an eagle catcher, for example, could be made to complement an account of the Plains-culture eagle-catching process. The *NAI* also contains several sequences of images, usually numbered to provide a visual narrative akin to one that is—or could be—supplied in words. In the third volume, for example, the Sioux Hunkalowanpi ceremony is evoked in a sequence of five pictures, and, of course, in the tenth volume there are several images of masked dancers that presage and parallel the *Head Hunters* film footage in which Wasp, Thunderbird, and Grizzly dance in the prows of canoes. Similarly, *Hamatsa Emerging from the Woods*, as one image in a long series of images, might be thought of as equivalent in some sense to a single movie frame (which the Curtis musicale, to be discussed later in this essay, may in practice have literalized with dissolving views; Glass 2009b).

But when we get an emphasis on arrested motion, the image also suggests that the process of vanishment already referred to, could—at least in representation—be stopped in its tracks. Yet, paradoxically, these prayer pictures, such as the Sioux *Prayer to the Mystery* (1907–30, vol. 3), with its statuesque figure seemingly sculpted by light above a similarly lighted buffalo skull that the caption declares is "symbolic," are also instants out of time, as it were (on themes of temporality, see Zamir, this volume). In *Offering to the Sun—San Ildefonso* (1907–30, vol. 17), attention is drawn to a very particular point in the sun's passage, yet the shape of the man's chest tessellates with the contour of the nearby rock as if he had been cut from it; thus patterned, he has always stood there. These are mystical, transcendental moments captured with noticeable reverence. They constitute images that, in a manner akin to Christian religious art throughout Western history, invite a kind of devotion. The invocatory nature of some of the Kwakwaka'wakw still photographs, such as *Twin Child Healer (b)—Koskimo* (1907–30, vol. 10), with its frame sufficiently broadened to take in arranged ritual objects and its portrayal of the formality of the healer's outstretched arms, seem similarly devotional (see fig. F.1). *Twin Child Healer (b)* is, of course, also a sequential view, but this kind of aura translates only occasionally to the cinema screen. In viewing the movie, I think we are most aware of it when the camera takes in, and lingers over, a "scenic" moment, such as a canoe receding into the sunset.

The attitudes evoked here, with their internal contradictions and consequent stylistic variation, were literally embodied by the visual tropes that carried them into the *Head Hunters* movie. An indicative feature of the

Fig. 1.3. Edward S. Curtis, *A Chief's Party—Qagyuhl*, 1914. (*NAI,* portfolio 10.) Charles Deering McCormick Library of Special Collections, Northwestern University Library.

Strauss portrait of Curtis is the attention drawn to Curtis's hand, which in turn is reflected in the sheen of the polished table beneath his arm. Practitioners of pictorialism were particularly interested in lighting effects of this sort, and for their own sake. Curtis is no exception. His still image *A Chief's Party—Qagyuhl* (1907–30, vol. 10), in which the dappled light on water so calls attention to itself as to occlude any "informational" aspect of the image, is typical of this interest (fig. 1.3). The picture was taken during the making of *Head Hunters,* and in content and style it exhibits parallels with some of film's motion picture footage.

The movie's first reviewers noted its purely visual effects, and some early commentators, such as the poet Vachel Lindsay in 1915, saw them as cinematic extensions of still photography (Glass and Evans, this volume). In grappling to capture the aesthetics of the new medium, Lindsay envisioned motion pictures as able to activate graphic and plastic forms; calling Curtis "the super-photographer," he claimed that the *NAI* shows "the native as a figure in bronze" and that *In the Land of the Head Hunters* "abounds in noble bronzes" (Lindsay 1915:114). (In general, "photoplays," as movies were often termed at this time, were thought of as closer by nature to photography than

Mick Gidley

would be the case today.) Gutzon Borglum, the sculptor of Mount Rushmore, on seeing the film, like Lindsay, discerned a three-dimensional element that he related to metal, this time gold—perhaps because he also had Curtis's orotones in mind.[9] He wrote to congratulate Curtis, speaking of the "Kodak … freezing [the] strange, evanescent gold, which I call the soul of any subject," and declaring that Curtis's "moving picture" carried this "thread of gold" from the Plains stills on into the movie (quoted in Gidley 1998a:255).

2. The Demands of *The North American Indian* Project

When, in 1906, Curtis secured funding from J. Pierpont Morgan to create the *NAI*, he committed himself to a particular product. The multivolume set as a whole, its photogravures printed on tissue or vellum, was to be a luxurious example of the bookmaker's craft, and original fieldwork was to be conducted, not only to secure fine pictures but to track down what were thought to be disappearing lifeways. The general introduction to the set, published in the first volume the following year, emphasized that the work would supply a "broad and luminous picture" and that it would primarily be interested in those peoples "that still retain to a considerable degree their primitive customs and traditions" (Curtis 1907–1930, vol. 1:xv, iii). That is, alongside pictorialism, the project was dedicated to a version of primitivism.

The opening pages and illustrations of that first volume, with their bare-skinned Apache subjects setting the tone for the book as a whole, emphasize an appeal to the "natural" and the "traditional," notes to be heard frequently thereafter. Such an emphasis meant that, as in Franz Boas's salvage ethnology, there was a concomitant commitment to reconstruction of the "natural" and the "primitive" when it was considered that they were no longer to be had. The very title of *The Spirit of the Past* (Curtis 1907–1930, vol. 4), depicting Crow scouts on the lookout, informs us that such scouting parties were no longer dispatched; the scouting in it was being staged for the camera. Larger mounted "war parties" also performed for Curtis's still camera just as they were to do for the movie cameras of countless Hollywood directors. In Kwakw<u>a</u>ka'wakw territory, in parallel with a scene in the movie, an unidentified Koskimo man posed for *The Fire-Drill* (Curtis 1907–1930, vol. 10), purporting to light tinder by striking sparks through friction between the drill and hard wood—when, in fact, by that time Hudson's Bay Company safety matches had long been in regular use.

Similarly, for the movie, buildings—lacking roofs, so as provide sufficient light for filming—were erected. Complete rows of false house fronts were

Fig. 1.4. Carvings on display with unidentified figure, 1913.
Photo by Edmund Schwinke. Courtesy of Mick Gidley.

thrown up, just as they were for Hollywood Westerns. The Raven housefront, as is clear from the film itself, was capable of swallowing a man whole (see fig. A.1.12). Edmund August Schwinke, who had joined the project in 1910 as a stenographer before learning to wield a camera on the job, took pictures of these reconstructed sets. He also captured the canoes newly painted especially for the movie, and it is possible that another of his images—of an unidentified man standing in a doorway, surrounded by carvings that appear to be on display—depicts a carver, his workshop, and the new ceremonial props he had made especially for the movie (fig. 1.4).

The reconstruction element of the film connects to a significant thematic aspect: scripts for *In the Land of the Head Hunters* indicate that it was to be set "in the days of Vancouver," and in one early script Vancouver himself is to land and explore the aboriginal village (partly reproduced in Gidley 1998a:250–51; see also Holm and Quimby 1980: appendix 2). But predominantly its action was to take place, in the words of one of the titles of a later Curtis still image, "before the white man came." That is, there was a determined effort to retrieve for the viewer a depiction of pre-Columbian, or at least precontact, Indian lifeways. Needless to say, such an effort accords with the much-touted critique of Curtis's work referred to above, that it failed to recognize First Nations cultures as dynamic, and represented them as outside, or above and beyond, history. As I have argued elsewhere, this critique is a gross oversimplification, but it does hold some water (see, for

Mick Gidley

example, Gidley 2001 and 2003a; see also the introduction to this volume). We should also acknowledge that the precontact setting means that, unlike in the "sham battles" often featured at world's fairs or as part of Wild West shows, and unlike more conventional Westerns, whether made at the time or decades later, the archetypal conflict between "good" and "evil," in being made wholly indigenous, is not racialized in Curtis's movie.

On the title page, each volume of the *NAI* affirms that it was "written, illustrated and published by Edward S. Curtis," but—in light of the necessarily communal nature of film making—I cannot stress enough that the project to produce the *NAI* was itself collective and, as such, provided more than adequate preparation for the movie. Curtis had already furnished his studio with Native American artifacts and pictures, and the Morgan funding permitted him to brand it as "the home of the North American Indian" and to take on extra photographic support staff.[10] The Morgan Bank–based business company The North American Indian, Inc., opened a sales office in New York City. Most importantly, the company was able to dispatch a team, sometimes two, to the field, including not just ethnologists, such as William Edward Myers, the principal ethnologist who reserached and wrote most of the text of the *NAI*, but also a cook and other assistants. Crucially, in the field, Native American helpers, interpreters and informants were also engaged.

In the Land of the Head Hunters, with its complex financing, as described elsewhere in this book, was also a corporate venture that was both a part of, and a parallel to, the larger *North American Indian* project. It was essentially the most elaborate, and the most communal, aspect of the overall enterprise. As well as involving moneymen and, later, sales people, it engaged such creative figures as a composer, musicians, and, of course, indigenous artists and actors. Schwinke, like his "chief," Curtis, got behind a movie camera as an operator, and George Hunt, as translator and general broker, joined them on the set with a megaphone through which he communicated Curtis's directions (fig. 1.5).

3. The Musicale

The *NAI*, as a set of richly bound books, was sold—very expensively, and on a subscription basis—to such major libraries as Harvard and the American Museum of Natural History, and, more significantly, to very wealthy individuals, including transportation tycoons Edward Harriman and Henry Huntington. Some of these individual grandees would, in turn, donate subscriptions to libraries; Gifford Pinchot, Theodore Roosevelt's forestry commissioner

Fig. 1.5. George Hunt (with megaphone), Edward S. Curtis, and actors filming
In the Land of the Head Hunters, 1914. Photo by Edmund Schwinke.
Burke Museum of Natural History and Culture, 1988-78/135.

and a future governor of Pennsylvania, for instance, gave a subscription to Yale. The sales campaign for the *NAI*—but also, in effect, the actual publication—was directed at elites.

At the same time, Curtis wanted to reach a much larger public. Individual Indian images were released separately as inexpensive postcards. Curtis and his friends, Edmond S. Meany for example, wrote popular accounts of the project's "adventures" in the field for newspapers and middlebrow magazines.[11] Exhibitions of the pictures were mounted in museums and expensive hotels, but also in popular venues, including department stores. Curtis produced illustrated short and readable accounts of indigenous life, such as *Indian Days of the Long Ago* (1914b) and *In the Land of the Head-Hunters* (1915), which tells the same story as the film (see figs. I.1a and I.1b), making use of the research that was going into the *NAI*. These ventures were meant to make money, to broaden the market for Curtis's pictures, and, of course, to publicize the major work. The most important endeavor of this kind in the period before the movie—which was itself, of course, part of this overriding publicity effort—was the musicale or "picture opera" staged nationwide in 1911.

The musicale was essentially a very grand magic lantern slide show, featuring monochrome and tinted slides (fig. 1.6), clever transitions, occasional rapid sequencing, and atmospheric dissolves. Curtis was spotlighted onstage speaking alongside a huge tipi (loaned by the American Museum of Natural

Mick Gidley

Fig. 1.6. Edward S. Curtis or Edmund Schwinke, ca. 1914.
Hand colored lantern slide depicting a scene from *Head Hunters*,
similar to those used by Curtis in his 1911–13 musicale.
Burke Museum of Natural History and Culture.

History) and real trees. The projection of images provided what Curtis called
"a picture within a picture" and was accompanied by a small orchestra playing music especially composed by Henry F. Gilbert to mesh with the visuals.
The music, like that produced for the later movie, was (at least supposedly)
based on transcriptions of actual Indian music the Curtis team had recorded
in the field (Jacknis, this volume). I say "supposedly" because it is in reality
very much in the classic Western musical tradition.

It is important to realize that the musicale both included movie footage—mainly of Hopi and Navajo scenes, footage that Curtis had made as
early as 1904—and touted the presence of this movie footage as a selling
point. The section on the Hopi in one of the program notes for a version
of the musicale known as "The Intimate Story of Indian Tribal Life" reads,
"The story of the Snake Dance. Many separate pictures of the most sacred
incidents of the Snake rite. Motion pictures of the dance, accompanied by
the orchestra" (reproduced in Gidley 1998a:217). Significantly, the musicale
included Kwakw<u>a</u>ka'wakw footage, too, probably made in 1910 or 1911, and
one program note reads as follows:

The Tribes of British Columbia, and their remarkable ceremonial life. Pictures showing the general life and manners. "The Kominaka Dance," or dance of the skulls. The Whaler. The Whale Ceremony. Motion picture, "Dance of the Mummy." "On the shores of the North Pacific," a dissolving composition depicting life by the moonlit ocean. This series of pictures … contains some of the most remarkable ever taken of the secret rites of the Indians. (reproduced in Gidley 1998a:236)

Viewers of *In the Land of the Head Hunters* will appreciate that certain of the sequences enumerated in this program note—like so many of the purely still photographs devoted to "ceremonial life"—were in fact later filmed for, and appeared in, the movie.[12] The musicale was a spectacular extravaganza, and it filled Carnegie Hall and other venues (fig. 1.7; see also fig. I.2).

The musicale was also appreciated by museum directors and others with a potential interest in subscribing to the *NAI*. Curtis himself reported that Franklin W. Hooper, after a full-house showing at the Brooklyn Institute, which he directed, praised "the entertainment" as "a message of more than national importance … it should be heard in every town in the United States … by the adults [and] school children" (quoted in Gidley 1998a:216). The musicale marked the acme of Curtis's fame, and it did reach a broad public. Even where the audience was small, as at a Philadelphia showing, there was appreciation; another of Curtis's letters recalls an incident afterward:

As my son, Harold, and I were walking towards the hotel, one of the house policeman … came up and put his arm round my shoulder, and with considerable feeling wished that they might have that sort of thing four times a week, and as he was leaving us he called out, "Come again, and we will give you a house so full that we will have to turn them away." It is a great deal of satisfaction to be able to please even a policeman. (quoted in Gidley 1998a:209)

The picture opera was successful in every respect—except financially. It is important to realize that the later movie was projected as *the* modern way—through greater verisimilitude, more spectacular effects, and a full-blown story—of achieving the financial profit that had eluded the musicale, not to mention the fusion of art, science, and entertainment that Curtis sought.

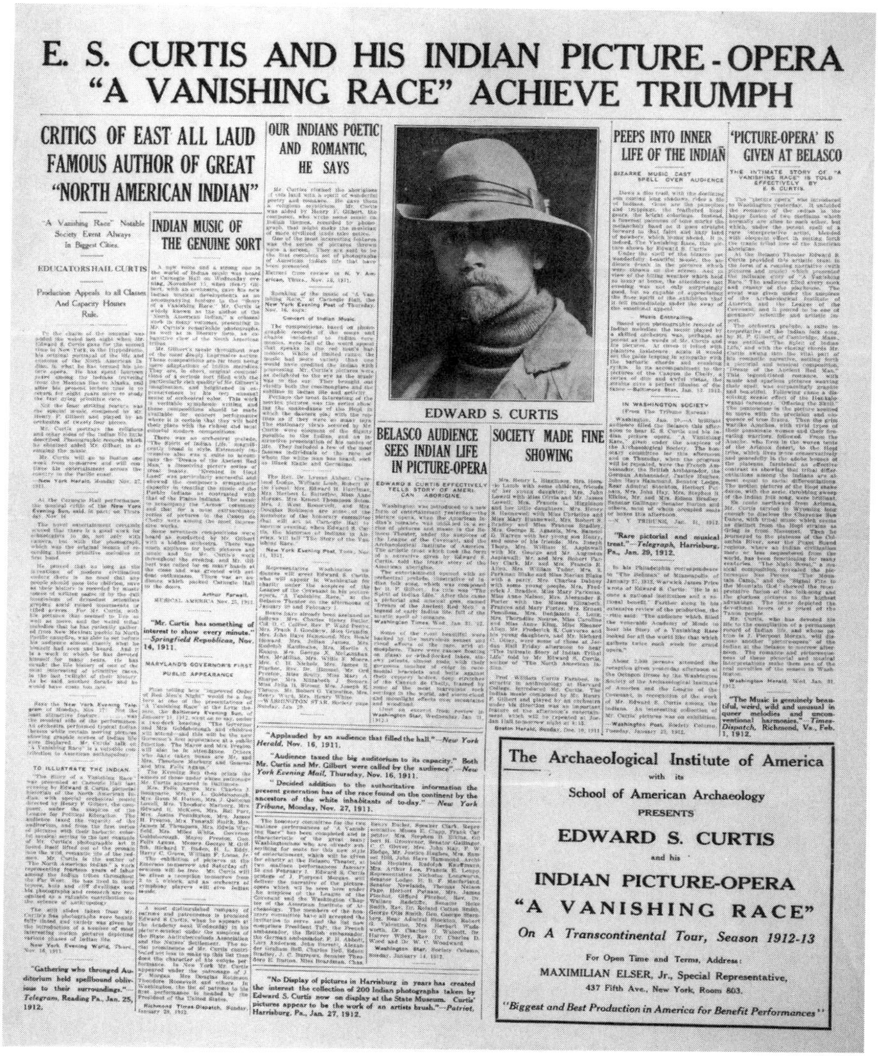
E. S. CURTIS AND HIS INDIAN PICTURE-OPERA "A VANISHING RACE" ACHIEVE TRIUMPH

CRITICS OF EAST ALL LAUD FAMOUS AUTHOR OF GREAT "NORTH AMERICAN INDIAN"

"A Vanishing Race" Notable Society Event Always in Biggest Cities.

EDUCATORS HAIL CURTIS

Production Appeals to all Classes And Capacity Houses Rule.

INDIAN MUSIC OF THE GENUINE SORT

"Mr. Curtis has something of interest to show every minute." —*Springfield Republican*, Nov. 14, 1911.

MARYLAND'S GOVERNOR'S FIRST PUBLIC APPEARANCE

OUR INDIANS POETIC AND ROMANTIC, HE SAYS

Concert of Indian Music

EDWARD S. CURTIS

BELASCO AUDIENCE SEES INDIAN LIFE IN PICTURE-OPERA

EDWARD S. CURTIS EFFECTIVELY TELLS STORY OF AMERICAN ABORIGINE

SOCIETY MADE FINE SHOWING

PEEPS INTO INNER LIFE OF THE INDIAÑ

BIZARRE MUSIC CAST SPELL OVER AUDIENCE

'PICTURE-OPERA' IS GIVEN AT BELASCO

THE INTIMATE STORY OF "A VANISHING RACE" IS TOLD EFFECTIVELY BY E. S. CURTIS

"Rare pictorial and musical treat."—*Telegraph*, Harrisburg, Pa., Jan. 29, 1912.

"The Music is genuinely beautiful, weird, wild and unusual in queer melodies and unconventional harmonies."—*Times-Dispatch*, Richmond, Va., Feb. 1, 1912.

"Gathering who thronged Auditorium held spellbound oblivious to their surroundings."—*Telegram*, Reading Pa., Jan. 25, 1912.

"Applauded by an audience that filled the hall."—*New York Herald*, Nov. 16, 1911.

"Audience taxed the big auditorium to its capacity." Both Mr. Curtis and Mr. Gilbert were called by the audience".—*New York Evening Mail*, Thursday, Nov. 16, 1911.

"Decided addition to the authoritative information the present generation has of the race found on the continent by the ancestors of the white inhabitants of to-day."—*New York Tribune*, Monday, Nov. 27, 1911.

"No Display of pictures in Harrisburg in years has created the interest the collection of 200 Indian photographs taken by Edward S. Curtis now on display at the State Museum. Curtis' pictures appear to be the work of an artists brush."—*Patriot*, Harrisburg, Pa., Jan. 27, 1912.

The Archaeological Institute of America

with its

School of American Archaeology

PRESENTS

EDWARD S. CURTIS

and his

INDIAN PICTURE-OPERA

"A VANISHING RACE"

On A Transcontinental Tour, Season 1912-13

For Open Time and Terms, Address:

MAXIMILIAN ELSER, Jr., Special Representative,

437 Fifth Ave., New York, Room 803.

"Biggest and Best Production in America for Benefit Performances"

Fig. 1.7. Simulated newspaper publicity brochure for the 1912 musicale, with inset portrait of Curtis made in 1899. Courtesy of Mick Gidley.

4. Active Indigenous Participation

This section, on indigenous participation, is about a social context, but also about the element, the physical performance, that ultimately constitutes the basis for the text itself.

In a sense, it is surprising that such willing involvement in the making of the movie was achieved. The precedent set by world's fairs and by Wild West shows, in which Indians were frequently demeaned—objectified as mere exhibits or made to perform in a manner not characteristic of their cultures—was not a happy one (see Rydell 1984 and Russell 1970). Also, as we have seen, the project subscribed to the widespread notion that Native peoples were doomed to die out. Sometimes Curtis himself expressed regret, even anger, that they faced this fate, but he seems to have accepted that it was inevitable. This was in part because, like many others at the time, he thought that white settlement was advancing at such a pace that it simply couldn't be resisted. But also, again like many others, the project saw Indians as inherently inferior, in that they were said to subscribe to all sorts of "superstitions" and other "primitive" beliefs and lifeways. Even his chief ethnologist, William E. Myers, more of a dispassionate anthropologist than Curtis himself, spoke frequently of the "primitive," even "dangerous," beliefs of the Pueblo peoples.[13] On one occasion, in a private letter, Curtis went so far as to give himself a pat on the back for dispelling supposed superstition among the Navajo people:

> As to the harmful effects of my work there, I am of the opinion that in breaking their old superstitions sufficiently to get the pictures which I did, I did more to disintegrate the same superstitions than any other one ever has. The fathers at St Michael say my work in one season did more to break down old superstitions [than] all the years of their missionary work. (quoted in Gidley 1998a:100)

And when we look at the volume of the *NAI* devoted to the Kwakwaka'wakw we see that even here there are attitudes that might well have prevented cooperation. In the opening remarks, the habitat of the people is presented as "forbidding" and "dark," and the people themselves are "no less inhospitable." In fact this opening description, moving through a variety of ways in which the people are castigated for being wholly "savage" (and thus culturally authentic; see the introduction to this volume), ends on a truly damning note: "It is scarcely exaggeration to say that no single noble trait redeems the Kwakiutl character" (Curtis 1907–1930, vol. 10:4).

Yet, as several of the snapshots made by Schwinke show, the project must in fact have had an easygoing relationship with these supposedly ignoble people. In one photograph, far from being "gloomy," the Natives positively fall about with laughter (fig. 1.8). Whatever the stated beliefs of the project, the truth is that by the time it reached the Northwest Coast, it had acquired all of the training and preparation necessary for the daunting task of winning over the major part of a community. Without such community endorsement,

Fig. 1.8. Actors relaxing during the making of
In the Land of the Head Hunters, 1914. Photo by Edmund Schwinke.
Burke Museum of Natural History and Culture, 1988–78/149.

the huge "Kwakiutl" volume of the *NAI* could not have been compiled and the film could not have been made.

From the first portraits onward, indigenous people had been so open to Curtis's camera that, even today, what I have elsewhere termed their "ontological presence" in such still images makes a claim upon the viewer's attention (Gidley 2007:44; see also Zamir, this volume). That claim may be at its most profound when—however much also the subject of prying anthropological examination—they were actually *performing* for the camera, as in *Hamatsa Emerging from the Woods* and *The Fire-Drill*. But it is also apparent when, as in the *Nakoaktok Chief's Daughter,* they simply sat for portraits. They were *giving* themselves to the photograph in a manner reminiscent of Walter Benjamin's observation—which is not ultimately a technical one— about the subjects of other early photographs: "During the long exposure they grew, as it were, *into* the image" (Benjamin 1980:204). And such interaction was not due solely to Curtis's superior artistic gifts as a photographer: it reveals, too, the involvement and agency of the subjects.

As we have seen, as early as 1904, both the Navajos and a relatively "conservative" people, the Hopis, had been persuaded to perform ceremonial dances for Curtis's motion picture camera. On the Plains, several times, as the surviving pictures in the *NAI* testify, people had reenacted for the camera war parties and other practices that had otherwise ceased. A factor in such involvement was undoubtedly material need. The project regularly paid its informants and photographic subjects, sometimes in food, often in cash, and it did so at a higher rate than other anthropologists and artists.

But another factor, more nebulous and harder to pin down, was that the project opened up possibilities for individuals. In many of the images of Native artists, as in *Painting a Hat—Nakoaktok* (1907–30, vol. 10), for example, we sense that the person depicted presents the work with pride. Those who acted as what are often termed "cultural brokers," including A. B. Upshaw among the northern Plains peoples and, of course, George Hunt among the Kwakwaka'wakw, especially benefited (see Gidley 1994 and Zamir 2007). The film broadened such possibilities, not only involving artists in wood and dancers in masks, as we have seen, but also individual figures able to take on leading roles as actors. It provided Stanley Hunt, for instance, with the opportunity for individual self-expression as the heroic protagonist Motana (fig. 1.9).

Most crucial, in ways that are further elaborated elsewhere in this book, the film—in permitting and encouraging the performance of collective ceremonial dances and other rites—was a vehicle for the *community's* self-expres-

Mick Gidley

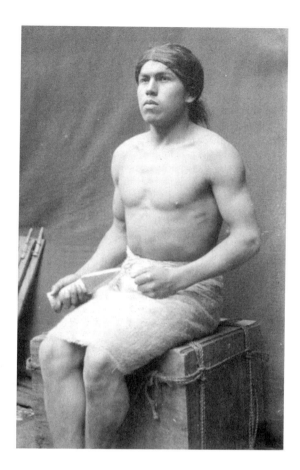

Fig. 1.9. Stanley Hunt in the role of Motana, 1914. Photo by Edmund Schwinke. Courtesy of Mick Gidley.

sion. To me, perhaps the most extraordinary thing about the *War Canoes* version of the film, released in 1973, is the utter concordance between the dance movements filmed some sixty years earlier and the sound rhythms produced for the 1973 movie by the then present-day relatives of those original performers. The more recent powerful performances of the G̲wa'wina Dancers at the various events held to announce and celebrate the new epic reconstruction of *In the Land of the Head Hunters* also echo—in gesture and aurally, step by step, vocable by vocable—the actions of their ancestors. These literal reverberations, in themselves, testify to the power and, just as important, the continuing viability for a new generation of the wholly indigenous aspects of Kwakwa̲ka̲'wakw culture, a century after Curtis shot his film.

1   There has been some dispute as to whether Curtis's middle name was spelled "Sherriff" or "Sheriff." I am aware that "Sheriff" is the usual form—I have used it myself in numerous publications—but the name derives from a maternal family name, and Curtis's grandson Jim Graybill has explained that the spelling of that family name is, in fact, Sherriff.

2　The portfolio photogravures from *NAI* are all reprinted, together with a selection of images from the text volumes, in Curtis (1997). The text and pictures of the *NAI* also appear on the Web at http://curtis.library.northwestern.edu/. The fullest treatment to date of *In the Land of the Head Hunters* is Holm and Quimby (1980).

3　Subsequent uncited data is taken from Gidley (1998a). On the ideology of the vanishing race, see Dippie (1991) and Gidley (1998b).

4　Edward S. Curtis speech from unpublished 1911 "script" for the musicale, not all pages numbered. Private collection; photocopy in Mick Gidley collection.

5　Strauss's portrait of Curtis is reproduced in Gernsheim (1962:131); Gernsheim, however, did not realize the identity of Strauss's fellow photographer. *Nature's Blossom* is reproduced in Curtis (2000). In both images of infancy a kinship between childhood and nature is stressed, but the Indian child is actually called a blossom *of* nature. This point originally appeared, differently put, in Gidley (2003a).

6　For Emerson, see Newhall (1978) and Taylor (2007). The scholarship on Crane's visuality is too extensive to cite here. A much-referenced castigation of Curtis is Lyman (1982).

7　In this essay I stick close to the photographs themselves, but it is important to realize that their status as avowedly symbolic entities connects Curtis's practice to broader trends in modernism (both aesthetic and, in such cases as Boas, scientific), which hoped to reveal underlying larger realities behind surface forms; see Hutchinson (2009). For discussion of Curtis's photographic responses to Modernism, see Egan (2006).

8　See fig. 9.2 for an alternate image of this woman, Francine Hunt, and see Barbara Cranmer (this volume) for a commentary by her descendant. See also the foreword and introduction for a discussion of Francine Hunt's role in the making of *Head Hunters*.

9　Curtis sold many of his images as striking and shimmering "Curt-tones," gold-toned prints on glass. For suggestive commentary on Curtis's pursuit of both metaphorical and actual gold, see Trachtenberg (2004:170–210).

10　Curtis's studio manager, Adolf Muhr, himself a photographer, wrote a publicity piece in which he spoke of the studio as "the home of Mr. Curtis and of the Curtis Indian" (Muhr 1907), and the phrase "the home of the American Indian" appeared in *NAI* advertisements and on notices on the verso of framed Curtis Indian photographs sold by the studio.

11　Typical such accounts of "adventures" are Curtis (1907) and Meany (1908).

12　Although the movie does not contain footage precisely equivalent to that already shown in the picture opera as "Dance of the Mummy," Motana's vigil dance in the house of the skulls, where a mummy sits visibly on the floor, maintained the thematic aspects and the imagery (Glass 2009b).

13　For Myers's views, see chapter 5 of Gidley (1998a). As per items cited in note 2 above, these notions of Native demise were fraught and complex.

Mick Gidley

2

IMAGES OF TIME

Portraiture in *The North American Indian*

SHAMOON ZAMIR

Critical accounts of *The North American Indian (NAI)* very often single out a sense of timelessness as *the* defining characteristic of Edward Curtis's image work. Curtis's lush and sensuous photogravures, it is argued, deploy a set of visual conventions that immobilize his Native American subjects in time, and within sentimental fictions of "traditional culture" that reflect the realities of neither the past nor the work's own time. The images are said, then, to reveal ethical and political compromises or failures because their form is inextricably bound to colonial ideology. The reading presented here comes at Curtis's work differently. It proposes that rather than being drained of time, the images from the *NAI* are in fact filled with multiple temporalities, and that nowhere is the human experience of time made more visible than in the portraits. It is proposed further that we cannot grasp this complexity unless we revise our understanding of the form of Curtis's work: instead of looking at isolated images, we need to examine image ensembles and their interactions with the texts that accompany them because Curtis conceived the *NAI* as an integrated combination of the visual and the written—as a photobook. This approach to Curtis opens up a new understanding of the ethical and political aspects of his major work, which we might extend to his overtly commercial endeavors such as his film *In the Land of the Head Hunters*, which has been subject to criticism similar to that of his still images. While these similarities are everywhere suggested in the discussion that follows, they are not pursued at length or theoretically.

Fig. 2.1. Edward S. Curtis, *In a Piegan Lodge,* 1910. (*NAI,* portfolio 6.) Charles Deering McCormick Library of Special Collections, Northwestern University Library.

The Missing Clock

One image more than any other has been called to witness the excision of the time of modernity, which is to say of history itself, from the *NAI.* The photograph *In a Piegan Lodge* (fig 2.1) shows two men seated inside a tipi surrounded by an array of traditional tribal artifacts. The Piegan were and are members of the Blackfoot Confederacy. The photograph was taken in northern Montana, most likely in 1909, and published in 1911 as one of the photogravures in the sixth portfolio. The printed caption names the two men but is concerned primarily with identifying the objects around them and with describing the structural features of the lodge itself:

> Little Plume with his son Yellow Kidney occupies the position of honor, the space at the rear opposite the entrance. The picture is full of suggestion of the various Indian activities. In a prominent place lie the ever-present pipe and its accessories on the tobacco cutting-board. From the lodge-poles hang the buffalo-skin shield, the long medicine bundle, an eagle-wing fan,

and deer-skin articles for accoutering the horse. The upper end of the rope is attached to the intersection of the lodge-poles, and in stormy weather the lower end is made fast to a stake near the centre of the floor space. (Curtis 1907– 30, vol. 6: portfolio title and caption page)

The composition of *In a Piegan Lodge* is not entirely persuasive. The men appear a little stiff in their poses, and the spatial void that opens up between them seems to push each to the opposite edges of the frame. The medicine pipe and the accessories on the cutting board lying between the two men are meant to fill this void and to center the image. These objects carry a cultural weight as a consequence of the ritual uses to which they are put and the religious beliefs that attach to them—the great importance of pipes within Piegan culture is acknowledged by the preoccupation with their individual histories and uses throughout the ethnography of the Piegan chapter. But, at least for non-Piegan viewers, the objects are unable by themselves to generate a center of gravity visually proportionate to their cultural meanings; Curtis relies instead on the caption to direct our attention. But as our eyes follow this direction, we notice a strange circular area of light and shadow just above the upper edge of the cutting board and immediately to the left of Little Plume's right elbow. As Christopher Lyman (1982:106–7) pointed out many years ago, this small disturbance in the photogravure's surface is the ghostly trace of an object of industrial manufacture, which has been dexterously removed by Curtis and his dark-room assistant during the printing process. In the original glass negative the object is clearly identifiable as a medium-sized metal clock of the kind that might have been found in many white middle-class households in America at the turn of the century (fig. 2.2).

Curtis first visited the Piegan of Montana in 1898 and spent his last and most extensive period with the tribe in 1909. The clock pictured in the original negative dates from this same period. It is a nickel drum clock of a type manufactured by a number of companies in the United States, mostly in New England, in the late nineteenth and early twentieth centuries.[1] Even though what seemed affordable for a middle-income white family may still have been relatively expensive for most Native Americans, it appears that clocks were relatively common among the Blackfeet once the tribe had become settled on reservations.[2] Cultural historians have acknowledged the contribution that the design and production of firearms, ammunition, locomotives, agricultural machinery, and sewing machines made to the development of the American system of manufacture in the nineteenth century, but "the assembly of standardized interchangeable parts, and continuous process

Fig. 2.2. Edward S. Curtis, original version of *In a Piegan Lodge*.
Library of Congress Prints and Photographs Division.

manufacture" were carried farthest and to new levels of precision in the production of clocks and watches (Church 1975:616–17). However, the clock we see in Curtis's image represents more than the proliferation of the bourgeois commodity and the rise of the efficiency and strength of the American industrial system; it embodies also the increasing regulation of time within both the domestic and public spheres characteristic of modernity.

The picture of Little Plume and Yellow Kidney was made during a period when time itself had become an arena in which the forms of daily life and the structures of economy that have come to define modernity were being created and shaped. The regulation of labor and time keeping under industrial capitalism was well under way, but more immediately time itself was being standardized. It was only in 1883 that the railroad companies, then the largest and most powerful corporate entities in North America, finally recognized the economic advantage to be gained from a uniform regulation of time and, at noon on November 18, divided the United States and Canada into four standardized time zones. Until then the United States had been a crazy patchwork of hundreds of temporal domains, with each city, town, village, and locale using one form or another of diurnal calculation and relying for time

Shamoon Zamir

keeping on well-known clocks in public spaces—on church steeples and town halls or in shop windows.[3] The increasing presence of clocks in homes, while not directly a result of this contemporaneous standardization, nevertheless helped tie the time of the domestic sphere to the time of corporate and public life across the nation. However, this process of adjustment and incorporation was a slow one. Standard time was not established in law until the passage of the Standard Time Act in March 1918, seven years after the publication of the sixth volume and portfolio of the *NAI*. And if American cities, towns, and villages became integrated into the newly restructured national network of time only gradually, this process of integration must have been even slower on Native American reservations that were not only geographically but also culturally on the peripheries of this network of communication and the circulation of goods. What we see then in Curtis's original image is the coming of modernity into a cultural space that can be conceived of as the home of modernity's other. But are we seeing the incorporation of the Piegan world into the world of modernity, or are we witness to a different and altogether more complex and mobile accommodation between cultures?

Curtis's erasure of the clock appears to banish time itself from the image and to deny Little Plume and Yellow Kidney their contemporaneity with the viewer and their participation in a modernity characterized not only by industrial manufacture and the commodity but also by a regulation of time different to the experience of time within Piegan culture (Thomas, this volume). The Anisshinaabeg (Chippewa) writer Gerald Vizenor ties this excision of time to the collapse of portraiture into primitivist cliché in the *NAI*. "Curtis invented and then possessed tribal images," he writes, "while at the same time he denied the tribal people in one photograph the simple instrument of chronological time. The photographer and the clock, at last, appear more interesting now than the two tribal men posed with their ubiquitous peacepipes" (Vizenor 1990:85).[4] Here, it is taken for granted that the clock as an instrument for telling time can, by extension, be said to speak history, and that this speech, in turn, is in some sense also the speech of Little Plume and Yellow Kidney. As a visual eruption within the pictorial mise-en-scène of the image, the clock exposes Curtis's representation of Native cultures as a historical falsehood. Since the presence of the clock is clearly a sign of an intentionality on the part of one or both of the men in the picture (they placed the clock there, not Curtis), the clock's disruptive and revelatory effects could be read (as they appear to be by Vizenor) as evidence of a certain resistance, however ambiguous and elusive, on the part of the Piegan men to the fiction created by the photographer. In erasing the clock Curtis not only violates the agency of the two Native American men, he violates also the imperative of documentary verity upon which the ethnographic project rests, thus revealing his work to be not a work of science or a record but above all a work of mythography.

But *In a Piegan Lodge* is better read as a palimpsest that brings into view the aesthetic and ethical dimensions of Curtis's work as a complex set of visual, as well as textual, permutations and negotiations produced by the meeting between Curtis's photographic practice and the agency of his sitters, and between the requirements of scientific record and the preoccupations of art that exceed these requirements. It is precisely because it is a not-quite-achieved image, an image that falls short of the artistic accomplishment of Curtis's best work, that it lets us see the achievement of Curtis's visual work in the making.

The clock is working. We can tell this by comparing *In a Piegan Lodge* with the original negative of another image, *Lodge Interior* (fig. 2.3), in which Little Plume and Yellow Kidney appear alongside Yellow Kidney's wife, Hairy Face, and from which the clock was also removed in the published version. Five minutes have elapsed between the making of this earlier image and *In a Piegan Lodge*.[5] But the clock is still in its box. As seen in these particular images, its function of marking "chronological time" has, in a sense, been suspended or incorporated into another order of signification; even though it continues to tell the time, to be its ordinary self, the clock appears also as a special object among other special objects, placed on display as they have been and absorbed into their community. The "pipe and its accessories," the "medicine bundle," the "articles for accoutering the horse"—these are ceremonial objects; if the clock is not itself an object of this kind, it nevertheless, in being associated with them in the manner of its presentation and placed center-stage with the pipe, goes beyond its instrumental uses and takes on a talismanic quality. The retention of the box suggests that the possession and display of the clock can be read as a declaration of status, though certainly less so than is the case with the traditional objects, which, as the ethnography informs us, are of very considerable cultural and spiritual value to both the tribe and to the families and individuals who possess them. If anything, it is precisely in its association with these other objects that the presence of the clock within the image suggests a configuration beyond obvious social forms.

What *In a Piegan Lodge* pictures is a deep and multiple temporality. As Paul Ricoeur puts it in his work on time and narrative, "Chronology—or chronography—does not have just one contrary, the a-chronology of laws or

Fig. 2.3. Edward S. Curtis, original version of *Lodge Interior—Piegan*.
A retouched copy of the photograph appears in *NAI*, vol. 6.
Library of Congress Prints and Photographs Division.

models. Its true contrary is temporality itself" (Ricoeur 1984:30). The plac-
ing of the clock beside the medicine pipe and its accessories creates a visual
structure of mirroring and reciprocity that appears to signal the ability to
simultaneously inhabit culturally different temporalities, but precisely as a
balanced accommodation rather than as a kind of cultural schizophrenia.
The lodge exists within or, better, contains within itself, at least two distinct regimes of time, the time of a non-Native American modernity and the
time of Piegan culture. Too often the cultural authenticity of indigenous
peoples has been figured as timelessness. But, as Cheryl Wells notes, "Native
Americans, like Euro Americans and African Americans, functioned within
multiple, conflicting, competing, uneven, slippery, cyclical, linear, gendered,
religious, personal [and] natural times … amongst others." Clock time was
an addition to these times, often in the form of the mission bell rather than
through the presence of actual clocks or watches. But "Native American temporalities did not collapse with the addition of clock time"; rather "Indian
temporal consciousness, like European temporal consciousness, changed
over time to include clock time while maintaining older temporal ways."[6]

It should be noted here that the clock is not the only instrument of time pictured by Curtis. All of the Piegan ritual objects we see, including the pipe, are also objects that embody time, a slow and formal ceremonial time. As Curtis himself notes, in the past at least the Piegan "did not confine their religious observances to a fixed time or place, but rather were constantly in act or thought supplicating the Infinite." The "excessive use of the pipe" was "a noteworthy phase of such form in their daily and hourly life." It was precisely the Piegan refusal to accommodate the time of the pipe to the time of a mercantile economy that appears to have been a source of irritation for some whites. According to Curtis, for example, one trader "bemoaned the fact of [the Piegans'] constant formal smoking, as it interfered with expeditious trading" (Curtis 1907– 30, vol. 6:11).

The composition of Curtis's original image suggests that we see the coexistence of Native and non-Native times not as a parallel juxtaposition but as a dynamic relation. The way in which the clock is isolated within the scene of the picture, its encirclement within the lodge interior and Piegan paraphernalia, seems to signal not merely a temporal duality but, perhaps a little more forcefully, the absorption of "our" time into "their" time, a harnessing of the time of modernity into which Native American cultures were thrust with such violence to the imperatives and logic of the life forms of the Piegan world. But in their intertwining, the "time of modernity" and "Piegan time"—I use the problematic distinction only as a heuristic to reflect the stylized demarcations suggested by the image itself—produce something more than a doubled time; their dynamic interaction constructs a hybrid temporality, a third regime of time in effect. This time is a form of what Heidegger refers to in his phenomenology as "within-time-ness." Ricoeur glosses the concept as follows: "Within-time-ness is defined by a basic characteristic of [what Heidegger termed] Care, our being thrown among things, which tends to make our description of temporality dependent on the description of the things about which we care" (Ricoeur 1984:62). The solicitous manner in which all the objects, including clothes, are displayed in Curtis's image figures this care; care transforms time from the abstraction of being merely "intervals between limit-instants" into "the present of preoccupation, which is a 'making present,' inseparable from 'awaiting' and 'retaining'" (Ricoeur 1984:2, 63).

If our attitude toward the world of objects around us can give us our experience of time, then we can read the stage machinery and props that make up the mise-en-scène of *In a Piegan Lodge* as a representation of the way in which Little Plume and Yellow Kidney inhabit time. Furthermore, this representation can and should be read as a self-representation as much as an acting out of someone else's script. We can only take the inclusion of the clock in the mise-en-scène of Curtis's image as a willed and unambiguous insistence on their contemporaneity by Little Plume and Yellow Kidney, an insistence apparently set against the othering of time that underwrites salvage ethnography and that is said to underwrite Curtis's pictorialism, if we associate the intentionality and agency of the two Piegan men exclusively or primarily with the clock and only the clock. But the other objects in the photograph, these are also theirs, as are the clothes they wear and the lodge within which they sit. And the willingness to be there before Curtis's camera, their willingness to set out the display and to make themselves available as actors within Curtis's photographic tableau vivant—these decisions and actions are also their own.

If we need to explain the presence of the clock in the image, we need equally, and perhaps more, to explain the presence within it of everything but the clock. The clock does not have clear dominion within the scene of the picture. To "our" eyes, the clock, in its incongruity, may dominate the scene and obliterate the other objects around it. But if Little Plume and Yellow Kidney had stood behind the camera and viewed the scene they had helped to create, it is more than likely that they would have perceived things differently. It is most unlikely that in *their* eyes, formed by an entirely different cultural history to ours, the pipe and the other Piegan objects could so easily have been outweighed by the clock. The prominent display of the clock suggests that it is certainly a valued object and a marker of status, but relative to the Piegan ritual objects it is surely also an object of fairly incidental value. In a sense it is the furniture of Piegan daily life that is more striking than the clock because, at a time when so many tribal ceremonies and the social institutions that supported them had atrophied, disappeared, or been outlawed by the government, and when tribal objects such as the ones we see were regularly being sold to museums or collectors, the Piegan objects in the picture do not reveal only the quotidian; they evidence a forcefully willed retention, a sense of value to self staged in the time of the clock but also against it.

In other words, in displaying not only the tribal objects but also themselves in front of Curtis's camera, Little Plume and Yellow Kidney do not reduce themselves to objects among other objects but declare their agency as modern custodians of a culture treated as its other by modernity itself. In order to open up the meanings of *In a Piegan Lodge,* we need to try to see the image that Little Plume and Yellow Kidney attempted to compose before Curtis's camera and not the image we register at first sight. I believe that it is, to some extent at least, because Curtis understood that such an effort on the part of his white viewers would most likely be forestalled by the startling presence of the clock, and not because he wanted desperately to maintain a fiction, that he removed the clock from the published version of the image. And if we accept that Little Plume and Yellow Kidney—and by extension Curtis's other Native models and film actors—bring to the making of the picture in all its aspects a meaningful level of agency, then it is also necessary to read the image as something more than a declaration of their simple acceptance of chronological time set against a desire on Curtis's part to ignore this intent by securing the men within a simulation of a time before modernity. It is the complex accommodation which the Piegan men have made and the labor by which they have achieved it, rather than some timeless and mythical "Indian" past, which are threatened by the forms of institutional, cultural, and physical violence that come to them under the name of history. This is the time they display in the image, a time of their own making—a time, in effect, of their precarious cultural survival.

The Shirt and the Tipis

I have of course so far been reflecting on the original version of *In a Piegan Lodge* and not on the image that was eventually published under this title. Whatever the range of meanings that can be sustained by the unpublished version of *In a Piegan Lodge,* Curtis's decision to remove the clock from the published version does appear to close down these possibilities. It is easy to read it as an attempt to banish ambiguity and to maintain an immaculate and timeless fiction. But the clock has proved to be as distracting in its absence as it might have been in its presence. The fixation on the clock and its removal has made it the sole signifier of modernity within the domain of Curtis's image when in fact it is only the most startling one. Yellow Kidney, the younger man sitting to the left, is clearly wearing a shirt of industrial manufacture, a fact that has, as far as I am aware, received no comment at all. If the clock is integral to the speech of the two Piegan men, then the shirt makes it clear that this integrity has not so much been violated as registered in a quieter form.

Curtis did not leave the shirt in only because it was altogether more difficult to remove than the clock. Nor did he simply hope that, as a more fugitive sign than the clock, and one that was pushed to the periphery of the image, it would go unnoticed, even though this appears to have been its fate. Both possibilities become patently implausible as soon as we examine Curtis's image not in isolation but as it was meant to be seen and understood, in the company of the other images. In the Piegan chapter and portfolio there are a number of images in which individuals appear in modern clothing. Crow Eagle, seated on the bare ground, is dressed in shirt and trousers, only his footwear indicating Native American manufacture (*NAI* portfolio 6, plate 201). In his full-length portfolio portrait, Iron Breast is richly attired "in the costume of the members of the Bulls," but as the caption also indicates, this "age society" has been "for many years obsolete"—what remains of the present and what is signalled by the caption as the young man's actual day-to-day clothing is the bright floral shirt worn by him in his assertive pose (*NAI* portfolio 6, plate 206).

The most intriguing and also the most poignant juxtaposition of indigenous and nonindigenous (what Curtis's white audience might have articulated as "traditional" and "modern") material cultures among the Piegan images occurs in Curtis's portfolio portrait of New Chest (fig. 2.4). The tightly buttoned collar of a commercially produced and somewhat scruffy shirt is clearly visible beneath the Piegan sleeved tunic in which New Chest presents himself in a pose of slightly exaggerated and melancholy dignity, the gravitas of the pose sharply sculpted by the slanting light. But the detail that holds our eyes once we come upon it is the safety pin hanging across the lower left ribs to the right in the image. There are only six other images in the whole of the *NAI* in which safety pins can be seen clearly. In these images, all of which appear after the Piegan volume, the pins are entirely functional; they hold in place either blankets of industrial manufacture or traditional fur or cedar-bark robes, which have been wrapped around the individuals pictured.[7] In New Chest's portrait, by comparison, not only is the pin more prominently displayed, it appears to an outsider's eyes at least to be also entirely and therefore enigmatically decorative, a sort of fashion accessory, so to speak.

Invented in 1849 and industrially manufactured and mass marketed from the late 1870s onward, the modern safety pin, like the metal clock, was a relatively new object.[8] And yet safety pins appear in fact to have been fairly commonplace among the Blackfeet at the turn of the century. According to Adolf Hungry-Wolf, a cultural historian and archivist of the tribe, "Everyone had one or more of these, to hold a robe together at the front, or for emergency repairs to clothing."[9] But to non-Native viewers, then as well as now, the pin, like the clock, inevitably appears as a disjuncture, a kind of enigma or question. The viewer is equally invited to perceive the safety pin as a novelty rather than as a commonplace by the name of the man pictured. New

Fig. 2.4. Edward S. Curtis, *New Chest—Piegan,* 1910.
(*NAI,* portfolio 6.) Charles Deering McCormick Library of
Special Collections, Northwestern University Library.

Chest (more often translated as New Breast) is not an unusual name among
the Blackfeet. But the highlighted presence of the pin across the left breast in
this picture encourages us to register the image as a visual pun, found rather
than engineered, on the name. New Chest's newness resides, of course, not
in the pin per se but in the cultural history signalled by the relationship of
pin and Piegan clothing.

But not all of the signs of modernity in the *NAI* are as fleeting or marginal
as Yellow Kidney's or Iron Breast's shirts or New Chest's pin. In one Piegan
image, at least, the startling juxtaposition of the clock and the medicine pipe
and other tribal paraphernalia is presented in even more explicit form and
made the sole subject of the image. *A Piegan Home* (fig. 2.5), from the volume
rather than the portfolio, shows a neatly constructed log cabin next to a tipi.

Shamoon Zamir

The title is intentionally ambiguous since it does not make clear which of the two structures is best considered a representative "Piegan home." The transformation of Piegan culture between past and future is left as an open question. So while Curtis removes the clock from *In a Piegan Lodge,* he does not in fact erase the dramatic demand it makes on our attention; he merely displaces this demand in its most insistent form to another image. If the pin is there because Curtis decided to leave it there, the modern log cabin is there not only because Curtis decided to include the image in the *NAI* but because he actively sought out the temporal and cultural disjuncture it pictures.

We feel the full force with which *A Piegan Home* raises the question of futurity only if we see that it summarizes a preoccupation with time and history that has been present in the Piegan chapter from the very beginning. And this preoccupation unfolds around the image of the tipi. In the "General Description" which forms the first section of the chapter on the Piegan, Curtis describes how he "first saw the Piegan during the summer of 1898 at the season of their medicine-lodge ceremony": "They were in camp on a depressed stretch of prairie, entirely concealing them from the sight of any one approaching. Suddenly one rode out in full view of their encampment and beheld a truly thrilling sight. The camp was a combined one of the Piegan and many visitors from the Piegan of the north, the Bloods, and the Blackfeet, in all some two hundred and thirty lodges" (Curtis 1907–30, vol. 6:12–13). This almost cinematic description stretches across two pages, and as we turn from page twelve to thirteen we encounter an image of a Piegan camp inserted between the pages which captures in medium long shot precisely the view described of tipis scattered across a prairie (fig. 2.6). We appear to have here a perfect example of image and text working in synergy to create a characteristic Curtis effect, what Alan Trachtenberg describes as "an enchanted world—and perhaps an unspoken motive, to reenchant a world the white Americans had stripped of charm, magic, and mystery." It is then up to the critic "to disenchant the images" and "to free the pictures from their illusion of stillness" by taking the "measure of the ideology that holds them in place" (Trachtenberg 2004:206, 207). And yet the remainder of Curtis's account of his first view of the Piegan encampment itself pushes us suddenly and without interruption toward a rude awakening. Having noted his own first impression of a populous gathering, Curtis immediately converts the plenitude registered by both his text and seemingly by his image into a sign of tragic diminishment: "If this poor remnant of a once so powerful tribe proved such an inspiring sight," he continues, "what must it have been at the height of their existence!" (Curtis 1907–30, vol. 6:13).

Top: Fig. 2.5. Edward S. Curtis, *A Piegan Home*, 1910. (*NAI*, vol. 6.) Charles Deering McCormick Library of Special Collections, Northwestern University Library.

Bottom: Fig. 2.6. Edward S. Curtis, *A Prairie Camp—Piegan*, 1910. (*NAI*, vol. 6.) Charles Deering McCormick Library of Special Collections, Northwestern University Library.

The description of the encampment has been immediately preceded by a disturbing account of the dramatic decline in the Piegan population since the eighteenth century. "Disease was the white man's first bequest to [the Piegan], and smallpox spread in advance of the traders and trappers," notes Curtis. He adds, "Quickly following, as fit ally in the distribution of death, came the whiskey sellers, whose chief object was so to debauch the natives that their furs and other trafficable property could be secured as cheaply as possible." Having listed a number of smallpox epidemics over the preceding century, and the shortage of food during the winter of 1883–84 (which was "the result of official stupidity" and which led to the deaths of "more than one-fourth" of the remaining Piegan), Curtis brings his survey of the fate of the Piegan, "the most harmless of tribes" and one "associated with massacre, outrage and treachery … without justification," to a dramatic conclusion with a brief account of "the attack on Red Horn's camp in January, 1870, in which one hundred and seventy-three (three fourths of whom were women and children) were massacred." The massacre "was officially only a 'killing,'" and Curtis observes drily that "had the incident been reversed and Red Horn and his people made an early morning attack on a Montana village of three hundred inhabitants and killed one hundred and seventy three of them, regardless of sex or age, every member of the attacking party who could have been caught would have been hanged on the spot." But Curtis not only registers the horror of the killing and his own sympathetic indignation, he also pursues some explanation of "the causes which led to this regrettable affair," focusing in particular on the exploitation of intertribal divisions by external agents, the greed of new white settlers, the failures of the United States government to honor the terms of its own treaties, and the gross mis-representations of Piegan aggression against the white population (Curtis 1907–30, vol. 6:6–8).

Accounts such as this one of Piegan historical experience do not occur in every volume of the *NAI*, but nor is it the case that the Piegan example is only an isolated instance. It seems, therefore, too blunt and categorical to speak of Curtis and his team as having "*naturalized* the predicament faced by indigenous North American peoples," as Mick Gidley suggests, or to accept that their work disguised the "almost endless series of damaging political and economic decisions made by human individuals and agencies" (Gidley 1998a:73–75). Curtis's practice may be inconsistent, but this inconsistency has been too readily drained of its imaginative achievement and converted into a largely consistent colonialist and racialist stance. What is most important to the present argument is that what is given explicitly to us by the text is also given, albeit less directly, by Curtis's images; the history of change surveyed by Curtis comes also, in an elusive and transformed figuration, to inhabit his pictures.

All in all the sixth volume and portfolio of the *NAI*, which deal not only with the Piegan but also with the Cheyenne and the Arapaho, contain twenty-seven images in which some sign of modernity is visible, and this distribution is entirely representative of the project as a whole. Roughly a quarter of all of the images included in the *NAI* contain some sign of modernity, very often no more than the equivalent of Yellow Kidney's shirt, but sometimes at least as accentuated as the modern log or lumber cabin, or as startling as the clock and the safety pin. And it is not the case, as has sometimes been claimed, that such images are more prevalent in later volumes because Curtis was by then unable to hold at bay the encroachments of modern material culture into his visual field. The very last volume and portfolio, published in 1930 and focused on Alaskan tribes, have only five images between them that signal contemporaneity in any way, the lowest number out of the twenty volume and portfolio pairs which make up the project. The nineteenth pairing, on the other hand, dedicated to the tribes of Oklahoma and also published in 1930, contains fifty-four images in which some sign of modern material culture is visible. This is the highest distribution of all in the *NAI*. There is in fact no volume or portfolio which does not include such images, and the earliest volumes include relatively high numbers: there are twenty in the first volume and portfolio pair, published in 1907, and thirty-eight and nineteen, respectively, in the second and third pairs from 1908.

It is certainly true that in some cases Curtis would have had to go to extreme lengths to exclude the modern from view, as he did in having his collaborators recreate premodern styles of clothing for use in his film. He could not, for example, have easily photographed the Kwakwaka'wakw totem poles for the tenth volume and portfolio without including the modern houses behind them (see fig. I.3). But in a very large number of images throughout the *NAI*, Curtis could easily have obscured such disruptive intrusions either in the setting up of the image or in the printing process. Or he could just as easily have omitted the images or substituted others in their place without unduly damaging the visual component of his work (after all, he took something like 40,000 images over three decades, from which he included only around 2,200 in the finished project). That Curtis did not do this evidences not an incapacity on his part in the face of cultural transformation and deterioration, but a process of composition and design integral to the meanings of the *NAI* and distributed consistently across its image and text combina-

Shamoon Zamir

tions. "Process" here signals a certain visual predilection, a form of visual thought, in Curtis's work rather than an intention or rationale consciously and verbally articulated.

Portraiture

The exaggerated dignity of New Chest's pose declares an effort. The face labors to rise above and beyond the cultural contradiction and division signaled by his worn commercial shirt, his pin and his Piegan tunic. This rising is not a transcendence but the work of mastering a disparate reality. The safety pin is both a sign of the cultural division that affects the face and a symbolic suture that holds the division together, if only just. St. Augustine speaks of the distended mind as a mind torn asunder: "I ... have been disarticulated into time," he writes, "I cannot put the times together in my mind, my thoughts are shredded, my soul unstrung" (Saint Augustine 2006:281). In New Chest's portrait, and in effect in every portrait of an adult in the *NAI*, what we see is a resilience, an effort to hold the self together inside a divided, or culturally multiple, temporality. New Chest's eyes do not look upon space but upon time and interiority. The "newness" announced by New Chest's name resides in his effort to negotiate the novelty of the cultural situation in which he finds himself. It is for this reason that, within the visual rhetoric of Curtis's picture, the safety pin appears almost to be worn as a badge that acknowledges and declares this effort. What remains most gripping in New Chest's portrait is that it is the cultural hybridity signaled by the integration of tunic and pin, as well as the individual will, which fuses Piegan culture and modernity, rather than an essentialized "tradition," that are proposed as the forms of a true individual and collective identity over and against the more quotidian reality and historical process symbolized by the shirt. If we cannot say what exactly Curtis himself made of the incongruous safety pin, we can at least be reasonably sure that he registered the anomaly, that he was to a degree transfixed by it, and that he wanted his audience to share this experience.

To understand the achievement of portraiture in the *NAI* we need to understand the ways in which what I have referred to as deep temporality comes to occupy the face. The temporal multiplicity that is given externally through Curtis's particular form of photographic alienation effect becomes an internal property of the face. The removal of the clock allows the element of portraiture in the Piegan image to come more clearly to the fore; it enhances conditions conducive to identification. The leaving in place of the shirt as a contradictory effect marks out the difference of time and history which must be accepted as the condition of its work by this process of identification. The Native American face emerges in Curtis's work out of a doubled, disjunctive temporality, the portrait becomes a site on which subjectivity, time, and history meet. Unless this relation is grasped, the achievement of portraiture in the *NAI*, both the achievement of Curtis's art and the work this art achieves within his project, remains out of focus.

By removing the clock from his portfolio portrait of Little Plume and Yellow Kidney, Curtis liberates the eyes from distraction. The difference between the published and the unpublished versions of *In a Piegan Lodge* is the difference between the loud insistence of immediate effect and the quiet, slow revelation of surprise that arises in contemplation. What the viewer makes of the shirt and the faces, of the clash of temporalities and of Native subjectivity in these images depends, in other words, on the different speeds at which the two versions of the image engage and structure the viewer's attention. An understanding of the different times in which the two images are experienced is essential to an understanding of the representation of time within them.

The ability of the viewer to engage with the rich temporalities that belong to the scene depicted is, then, dependent on the varieties of time made available by the compositional and formal possibilities of photography and photogravure. These are possibilities not available readily, if at all, in *Head Hunters*. Both the *NAI* and Curtis's Kwakwaka'wakw film attempt to bring into view cultural "pasts," in either surviving or recreated forms, through the modern media of photography and film. Some in Curtis's audience no doubt were and are aware of a potential clash between the "modern" and the "premodern." But this is not the kind of temporal disjuncture I am attempting to articulate. I am arguing for a visual praxis in the *NAI* that brings disjuncture into view; I am not describing an inadvertent exposure of cultural and historical contradictions or paradoxes the work seeks to disguise. The linear unfolding and undifferentiated speed of film coupled with the narrative conventions that drive *Head Hunters* keep the temporal palimpsest I am exploring largely out of sight. Curtis's mastery of photogravure as a vehicle for contemplative pause can do the very opposite and invite the viewer to dwell among the simultaneities of times and histories. Nowhere are these layered configurations more powerfully visible than in Curtis's lingering over the human face.

For Vizenor, the clock may offer testimony for the contemporaneity of the Native sitters against Curtis's nostalgia, but its compositional effect is, paradoxically, partly to obliterate the subjects on whose behalf it is said to bear witness. The eyes, transfixed by the shining and incongruous object, try to rise up to the faces but are pulled back down again and again. The inclusion of the clock in the image creates a centrifugal force field, which produces a divided attention, a more restless and staccato perceptual movement than that which is constructed by the image in which the clock has been removed. With the clock touched out of the image, the eyes are free to pursue an altogether slower and more even pace of attentiveness. They come to rest first and foremost on the faces of the two Native American men who, no longer triangulated with the clock, now provide two points of relative stillness. The eyes still move from one face to another and back again but now without the interference of the clock between them.

Although identified as father and son, the two men were in fact brothers. To be more precise, they were half brothers: they shared the same father but had different mothers. Their father, a noted warrior named Wounded Mouth, died in 1877 when Yellow Kidney was only four years old. Yellow Kidney was thereafter brought up by his brother, who was twenty years his senior (Hungry-Wolf 2006:1473, 463). The relationship was then as much a parental and filial one as it was a fraternal one. This may be why Curtis mistook the brothers for father and son. What is most important for the present reading of *In a Piegan Lodge* is not the precise nature of the kin relationship between the two men but the way in which the image creates a generational narrative.

Since we clearly see the difference in age between Little Plume and Yellow Kidney, and since the angled composition of the picture places the younger man a little "behind" the older one, the image inevitably invites a reading of the movement from left to right, from background to foreground, as a visually compressed representation of the slow transition from youth to old age. By identifying them as father and son the caption underscores this particular temporal dimension of the picture. But the universal narrative of generations also takes on, thanks to the presence of the shirt, a culturally specific signification. The young man in his modern, commercial shirt beneath his traditional clothes and the old man entirely in tribal costume can be read as marking different attitudes to modernity. The movement from "son" to "father," from left back to right foreground, is a kind of reversed movement in time, from the present to the past—but also from a present which is culturally hybrid, and accepted as such by youth, to a past which, within the logic of the picture at least, is altogether less acculturated and divided. We are in Yellow Kidney's and Hairy Face's lodge; it must therefore also be the case that the clock belongs to them and not to the older man, a fact that only reinforces the association of the younger man with modernity suggested by his shirt. With the clock left in the picture, it is easier to associate the two men with a single attitude to the time of modernity, to tie their intentions and dispositions jointly and equally to the clock that lies between them. With the clock removed, the image lends itself to a more differentiated and narrative reading. The void at the center of the picture can now be read not so much as a compositional anomaly or lapse but as an integral part of the design. In creating a dialectical counterpoint with the diagonal dynamics of the image, it allows the image to suggest the bonds of kinship that hold the men together but also the generational gap that appears to separate them in their different, though by no means opposed, attitudes toward the historical transformations of their culture.

If Curtis's recomposition of *Lodge Interior* into *In a Piegan Lodge* and his removal of the clock tell us anything, they tell us that he recognized the presence of this more complex and elusive picture as an imminent possibility within his own visual work and sought to bring it out—much like a sculptor who sees his sculpture as a potentiality within the stone. Curtis's erasure of the clock does not expose his wanton disregard for the intentions and attitudes of his Native American sitters; it merely suggests that he may have been a better photographic artist than Yellow Kidney or Little Plume, able to honour the meanings these men brought to the making of the picture while also developing these meanings in independent though complementary ways.

1   I am grateful to Robert Crosswell, who is a member of the National Association of Watch and Clock Collectors, and to Dr. Samuel Licata, library volunteer researcher with the association, for helping to identify the type of clock pictured, the date of its manufacture, and its retail cost. Email correspondence with author, February 27, 2010, and March 2, 2010.

2   My thanks to Adolf Hungry-Wolf , author and editor of *The Blackfeet Papers* (2006), for this information. Email correspondence with author, May 7, 2010.

3   On the history of time in the United States, see O'Malley (1990); Stephens (1983); and Earle (1983).

4   It should be noted that such manipulations are rare in the *NAI* —according to Mick Gidley there are only a dozen or so examples among the more than two thousand published images (personal communication; see also Holm 1983a). But this does not blunt the force of the criticism directed against Curtis since the extreme or exceptional nature of *In a Piegan Lodge* brings into view only a general attitude that is said to pervade Curtis's project and his image work as a whole.

5   For the identification of Hairy Face, see Hungry-Wolf (2006:463).

6   I am grateful to Cheryl Wells (2005) for permission to quote from the introduction to her work in progress, *Suns, Moons, Clocks, and Bells: Native Americans and Time,* and for generously sharing her research. An earlier draft of the introduction

is available at http://www-bcf.usc.edu/~philipje/USC_History_Seminar/Wells/
Wells_SUNS_MOONS_reading.pdf (accessed March 16, 2013).

7   The other images with visible safety pins are *Kutenai Female Type* and *A Young Kutenai* (vol. 7, facing 136 and 140); *Quinault Female Type* in frontal and profile poses (portfolio 9, plates 294 and 295); and *Tsawatenok Girl* and *Mask of Octopus Hunter—Qagyuhl* (vol. 10, facing 90 and 246).

8   See Wulffian (1981); Petroski (1993); Kane (1997); and Michael H. Burchett, "Safety Pin," at http://technologyencyclopedia.web.officelive.com/Documents/SAMPLE_ARTICLE.pdf (accessed April 19, 2010).

9   Personal email communication, April 24, 2010.

3

INDIAN LANDSCAPES

Pauline Johnson and Edward Curtis

KATE FLINT

In the preface to E. Pauline Johnson's *Legends of Vancouver* (1911), poet and critic Bernard McEvoy positions the author between two worlds, two environments. "It may be permissible," he writes, "to record one's glad satisfaction that a poet has arisen to cast over the shoulders of our grey mountains, our trail-threaded forests, our tide-swept waters, and the streets and skyscrapers of our hurrying city, a gracious mantle of romance. Pauline Johnson has linked the vivid present with the immemorial past" (Johnson 1911:8). Native engagements with modernity—or, more accurately, with different modernities—and with what Simon Gikandi has called the "mutual imbrication" of cross-cultural encounters (Gikandi 1996:xviii) have received a good deal of consideration in recent critical and historical work on American Indian cultures. Such scholarship traces particular negotiations of practices and values, raises broader conceptual issues about the simultaneous yet different ways in which social and cultural change takes place, and interrogates what, precisely, may be understood by the term "modernity" itself. Such encounters can be found, say, between missionaries and those they sought to convert and teach; between those who boarded at Indian schools and their educators; between Native trackers and British sportsmen; between trappers and traders and fishermen; between those who traveled off their tribal lands to find work in cities or, temporarily, with Wild West shows, and those who employed them and worked alongside them; and, of course, between those who were involved in the transmission and recording of traditions, legends, and cultural practices.

It is in relation to this last type of interaction that I want to juxtapose Pauline Johnson's *Legends of Vancouver*, which draws together a number of tales from the Pacific Northwest, with both Edward Curtis's melodramatic silent film *In the Land of the Head Hunters* (1914) and his related, photo-illustrated volume of 1915 that bears the same title. I will be doing this in large part through considering their treatment of landscape: landscape as it is mediated through the lens of the film or still camera, in accordance with Western representational conventions; and landscape as it is understood as a lived environment that functions as a repository of history, myth, and a people's understanding of its relationship to the land. Both Curtis and Johnson intended their productions for an audience more familiar with the first of these two categories, but Johnson, as I will show, was far more purposeful in her attempt to convey that Native people's knowledge and understanding of the landscapes they inhabited rendered these habitats something far more complex than scenery or backdrop. To do this, she in fact establishes common ground—some shared experience of modernity, some shared allusions—between contemporary First Nations peoples and the probable reader of her text. By contrast, Curtis, with an eye to what he considered to be his film's likely commercial appeal, played up the "primitive" qualities that he claimed to find among his subjects. This distinction is further brought home by their contrasting styles, with Johnson writing in a conversational, almost intimate register, and, in the book that accompanied the film, Curtis's deliberate adoption of a rhetoric that, to him, signified "bard-like" formal oratory.

Johnson (1861–1913), also known by her Mohawk name Tekahionwake (see fig. 3.4), was the daughter of a British mother and a Mohawk leader (to whom she pays tribute at the end of the volume). She had already gained an established name as poet, performer, and journalist before she moved to Vancouver in 1909 after retiring from the stage. In the details of her career, and in the carefully constructed persona that she projected, Johnson exemplifies the ability to move flexibly between traditional First Nations culture and colonial, urban, and commercial life on both sides of the Atlantic, as well as on both sides of the Canada/US border. In this brokering position, she might usefully be compared to George Hunt (also of mixed ancestry), who was at times selectively presented as either Indian or white by Franz Boas (as well as by himself) depending on whether an authentic "participant" or neutral "observer" was required to establish ethnographic authority.

Johnson took pleasure in a deliberately shifting self-presentation, replying half-jokingly to a question about consistency: "Oh *consistency*! ... How can one be consistent until the world ceases to change with the changing days?" (Mackay 1913:274). Her suspension between two cultures is well illustrated by the photographic portrait that is published opposite the title page of *Legends of Vancouver*. In this, Johnson wears a necklace of bear claws, a bodice that seems to be made of little furry pelts, and what look to be feathers or elaborate braiding materials in her hair. And yet she also sports a fashionable front of curls—possibly false. This portrait is, moreover, signed, in the style of a fashionable celebrity.

Pauline Johnson originally published the stories that were collected together as *Legends of Vancouver* in the Sunday magazine of the *Vancouver Daily Province* and the *Mother's Magazine*. Fifteen of these twenty-two stories were compiled into a volume that could be sold—as the preface informs us—for her benefit since her health had broken down. Indeed, a number of the stories that appeared in the *Province* had been dictated to the magazine's editor, Lionel Makovski, when Johnson no longer had the strength to write, adding a new twist to oral transmission. The language of the biographical notice that preceded the *Legends* presents Johnson as a hero—"only a woman of remarkable powers of endurance could have borne up under the hardships necessarily encountered in travelling through North-western Canada in pioneer days … and shortly after settling down in Vancouver the exposure and hardship she had endured began to tell on her" (Johnson 1911:xii). Johnson was in fact suffering from breast cancer, and had considerable medical and care expenses: if the reference to "in pioneer days" seems to mark her as white, rather than Indian, this must be balanced against the fact that this was in effect a benefit volume, published by her friends, and doubtless aimed at the sympathies and pockets of a white readership (Johnson 1911:16–17).

But the volume's contents draw attention to Johnson's self-identification as half Indian. A companion volume of "boys' stories," *The Shagganappi,* which appeared after her death in 1913, and which brought together material that she had published in the *Boys' World* between 1906 and 1913, also contains folklore from the Pacific Northwest, mingled with contemporary adventure stories that foreground the symbolic national advantages of being of mixed blood. This blending of heritages finds its literary analogue in Johnson's self-consciously bicultural storytelling, which mingles, in all her later work, contemporary Western styles of narrative with elements of ritual, repetition, and rhetorical turns that have their basis in various indigenous oral formulations.

The traditional narratives of *Legends of Vancouver* were, for the most part, given to Johnson by Chief Su-á-pu-luck—Joe Capilano—chief of the

Squamish band of the Central Coast Salish Indians, and his wife, Líxwelut (Mary Agnes). Johnson had met Capilano when she was performing in London in 1906. He, together with two other British Columbian chiefs, was there petitioning King Edward VII to challenge new restrictions that had recently been placed on where the Central Coast Salish could hunt, and to protest against the fact that there were railroad surveys passing through their ancestral burial grounds. The experiences of these First Nations men are alluded to not just in *Legends* but—slightly awkwardly—in *The Shagganappi*. In the latter book, Five Feathers tells the boy Jerry that "over the great salt water, in your white man's big camping ground named London, in far-off England, the medicine man hangs before his tepee door a scarlet lamp, so that all who are sick may see it, even in the darkness" (Johnson 1913:149). As though she is determinedly making a point about Indian cosmopolitanism, Johnson then adds an asterisk and a note: "Some of the Indian tribes of the Canadian North-West are familiar with the fact that in London, England, the sight of a physician's office is a scarlet lamp suspended outside the street door" (Johnson 1913:149). Even if Five Feathers's language follows the defamiliarizing convention, used as a matter of course by Johnson in her journalism, of translating Indian terms directly into English—which could be seen as being somewhat quaint and belittling—the effect is also an educational reminder, in a text aimed at young people, that different cultures respond to social phenomena in their own preexisting conceptual frameworks, which are, in turn, formulated through language. What is true for First Nations storytellers, presenting things through their own linguistic and interpretive tools, must therefore also be true for the Anglo observer, who sees and expresses things differently—but not necessarily more correctly. One can see Johnson, I think, as a literary advocate for the cultural relativism that Boas and his students were advocating, at this time, within anthropology.

Most of the tales in *Legends of Vancouver* center, however, around places, not things—the Capilano River, Deadman's Island, the Lost Salmon Run, the Tulameen Trail, the trees in Stanley Park, Point Grey, Deer Lake, the Siwash Rock. The tales relate how these places came by their names, embedding legend into the stony forms of the landscape. Thus the Siwash Rock is a man who, "'thousands of years ago' (all Indian legends begin in extremely remote times)," had been swimming in the narrows as his son was being born, to ensure that he was spotlessly clean at the moment of his new fatherhood (Johnson 1911:13). A canoe bearing four giant men bore down upon him, and he refused to get out of their way. In the end, on hearing the cry of the newborn, the giant men turn the man, and his wife and new son, into stone, so that he might in fact live forever "as an indestructible monument to Clean Fatherhood" (19). Capilano's rendition is, says Johnson, "the only treatise on the nobility of 'clean fatherhood' that I have yet unearthed," despite her recent reading of "numberless articles in yet numberless magazines, all dealing with the recent 'fad' of motherhood" (13–14). This kind of an aside is crucial to Johnson's mediation: she grants herself the power and authority that comes with cosmopolitan knowledge and experience, and appeals to an Anglo reader's concern with contemporary social debate at the same time as she plays on the "otherness" of Indian life in the Pacific Northwest. Despite her interest in the local, and her sensitivity to Capilano's emotional and historical commitment to his land, Johnson's ultimate frame of reference is always outward, to the broader world of her readers.

This is also an aside, however, that allies Johnson, as narrator, with non-domesticity. It is as though she is being cautious about the implications of associating herself too closely with this side of women's lives—or, perhaps, that she is anxious about having her own literary commodity too readily classified as appealing to women alone. In turn, this points to the degree to which Johnson was selective in aspects of her retelling. In *Paddling Her Own Canoe*, Veronica Strong-Boag and Carole Gerson present an excellent discussion of the relationship of *Legends of Vancouver* to Johnson's role as a translator of oral history into the written form; her status as a privileged outsider to Squamish culture and the implications of this for the direction that anthropology more generally was taking; and the implications of her publishing Capilano's narratives in a magazine that had shown itself as "distinctly hostile to the Aboriginal cause" (Strong-Boag and Gerson 2000:177). But through a comparison of the stories in the *Vancouver Province Magazine* with such earlier versions as appeared in the *Mother's Magazine*, Strong-Boag and Gerson also demonstrate how, in unifying the tales through Capilano's voice, the role of his wife as a bearer not just of stories but also of women's preoccupations in general is greatly diminished. However, I would suggest that by making this choice, Johnson not only helps draw attention to her own singularity, but also, that by aligning herself with the forms of strength that she presents as inhabiting the scenery around her, her own preference for a rugged form of heroism—at a time when her own body was destroying her from within—is implicitly stressed. The mediation that takes place is one that goes beyond the transmission of oral into written, and beyond the interpolation of points of reference for an Anglo reader: it is one in which the mediator's personal, physically weakening circumstances are symbolically countered.

Kate Flint

Pauline Johnson is wholly alert to the fact that the legends that she relays are, for their tellers, a means of reading tribal history through natural formations in the landscape surrounding Vancouver. In order to gain confidence and access to these histories she relies, moreover, on her own legibility as Indian. In "The Grey Archway" she gives a Chinook salutation to an elderly man on a steamer, and he decides to tell her about the story belonging to a small island out among the channels and narrows: "He gave a swift glance at my dark skin, then nodded. 'You are one of us,' he said, with evidently no thought of a possible contradiction. 'And you will understand, or I should not tell you. You will not smile at the story, for you are one of us'" (Johnson 1911:101). In another tale, "The Sea-Serpent," Johnson speaks of how "all my association with the Pale-faces has never yet robbed me of my birthright to believe strange traditions" (62). She continually positions herself as a double intermediary: not just as an interpreter for an Anglo audience but as someone who can help other Native people put in context what they have themselves seen of the world outside the Northwest.

This is the way in which, in the volume's opening piece, "The Two Sisters," Johnson talks about the twin peaks that rise above the city and that are "known throughout the British Empire as 'the Lions of Vancouver'" (Johnson 1911:1; fig. 3.1). But the Indians are not familiar with this label. Capilano, she recounts, "seemed so surprised at the name that I mentioned the reason it had been applied to them, asking if he recalled the Landseer Lions in Trafalgar Square. Yes, he remembered those splendid sculptures, and his quick eye saw the resemblance instantly. It appeared to please him, and his fine face expressed the haunting memories of the far-away roar of Old London. But the 'call of the blood' was stronger" (2–3). He went on to tell Johnson the Indian name—or at least its anglicized form, "the Two Sisters"—and the tale of the two chief's daughters who were immortalized on the mountain's crest. Johnson's task, in other words, was to show how Native legends and experience of the modern, urban world are not incompatible: different belief systems, and different temporalities, can coexist (Zamir, this volume). This, for Johnson, became a cultural expression, bold for its time, of a refusal to buy in to the conventional notion that the only option for Native futures lay in assimilation or extinction.

Edward Curtis's film *In the Land of the Head Hunters* is, on the face of it, a very different sort of production from *Legends of Vancouver*. Set in a past that ignores the temporal patterns of Western history, it refuses even the briefest glimpse of the changing world of the Kwakwa̱ka'wakw—the presence of the community's missionary, for example; or the school with its bell, signaling

PAULINE JOHNSON AND EDWARD CURTIS

Fig. 3.1. Bishop & Christie, *The Lions (The Two Sisters)*. From E. Pauline Johnson, *Legends of Vancouver*, Vancouver, BC: David Spencer, 1911.

a new kind of timekeeping; or the introduction of small-framed houses and milled timber and windows that indicated the Kwakwaka'wakw's involvement with a broader timber industry (see fig. I.3). It deliberately excludes exactly the kind of detail that Curtis himself incorporated into his description of "Kwakiutl" ceremonial dancers in the tenth volume of *The North American Indian* (*NAI*), indicating the currency of contemporary technology and manufactured goods:[1]

> After the initiates have danced, dishes, previously arranged on scaffolds in piles duly apportioned among the people, are distributed. The second and the third night are passed in the same manner, except that such articles as button blankets and shawls are given on the second night, and sewing-machines, tables, clocks, and household utensils on the third. (Curtis 1903–30, vol. 10:243–44)

In the Land of the Head Hunters is—for the Anglo spectator at least—elaborately set up as a glimpse into a world in which factual records of cultural practices, legends, and history are as one. It suggests the appearance of unmediated Native life, and hence produces the effect of a supposed timelessness—or rather, it relies for its effect on a tacit assumption that the cinemagoer (and, by extension, the filmmaker) exists in a different temporal dimension and

Kate Flint

possesses a different temporal understanding from the people depicted. This is the "allochronism" that Johannes Fabian famously critiqued as bedeviling contemporary anthropology in *Time and the Other* (Fabian 1983:33) and of which Curtis has been, understandably, accused of adopting in all except his late work. Its presence is particularly pronounced here, since not only does Curtis's film appear to obliterate traces of Western modernity, but it conflates elements that were an active part of current Kwakwaka'wakw life with those that were already very much on their way out (such as cedar-bark clothing and the magnificently painted dug-out canoes); with those that came from an earlier period of their culture (such as headhunting itself); and with practices that were appropriated from other, nearby societies (such as whaling).

The modernity of *In the Land of the Head Hunters* does not announce itself in its filmic content but has to be inferred from its context: from the fact of cinematography having taken place at all; from the studio stylization of the frames that contain the narrative commentary; from the cadences and instruments of John J. Braham's orchestral score; and, of course, from the accounts of the film's shooting. As Curtis scholars have made clear, there are plenty of ways in which the contact history of the Pacific Northwest is inseparable from the making of *Head Hunters*. For a start, there is the role played by George Hunt, son of a Tlingit woman and a British Hudson's Bay Company employee, whose extensive knowledge of the Kwakwaka'wakw, and whose interpretive skills, were essential to Curtis's enterprise. Hunt's ledger, together with written records left by Curtis and others, plus the production photographs taken by the cinematographer, Edmund August Schwinke, allow one to see the extensive degree of community involvement not just when it came to acting but in the making of, say, costumes, carved figures, masks, cedar-bark regalia, and whale-rib clubs (see figs. 1.4 and 1.5; Holm and Quimby 1980). Other material items incorporated into the film, such as feast dishes and ladles and basketry hats, were ones that were already in daily use. As Mique'l Icesis Dangeli has noted, such craft labor was paid for, albeit in "an alien currency," yet the products masked "evidence of our adaptation to our colonial oppressors" (Dangeli in photo essay 2, this volume)—the kind of evidence that, as I note above, Curtis was scrupulous about recording in his anthropological writing.

Research by Philip Deloria and Nicolas G. Rosenthal has done much to illuminate the presence of Indians within the nascent, pre–first world war movie industry—employment and direction that often built on the assumption, already inherent within Wild West show performances, that the Indians were not so much acting as reenacting: playing their historical selves

(Deloria 2004:67). Such figures as Luther Standing Bear, James Young Deer, and Princess Red Wing could capitalize on their authenticity.[2] But they were acting away from home—coming to Hollywood out of a mixture of economic opportunity and adventure. Some of these Indian-featuring movies took up the cowboys-and-Indians theme of Buffalo Bill's spectacular shows; others pivoted on cross-racial romance; still others dramatized "Indians and social relations in the contemporary world" (Deloria 2004:89). What clearly distinguishes *Head Hunters* from films shot in Hollywood or New Jersey is that the Kwakwaka'wakw are both acting (the stereotyped love story/captivity story) and reenacting (their dances and ceremonies) on their own lands and waters.

However, this (re)enactment has an uneasy relationship to its location. The Kwakwaka'wakw animate their tribal activities through an invented tale that has the aura of legend, but that in fact carries far less claim to a traditional relationship to the scenery in which it is performed than do the tales, set in the landscape around Vancouver, that Johnson repackaged for her Anglo readership. More than that, the shore's landscape—already, of course, bearing the marks of Western settlement—was further overwritten by artifice masquerading as indigeneity. A year after filming, the wooden structures that had supported the false house fronts were left standing, memorializing the collaborative artifice that went into the make-believe of this film.[3]

The production history of *In the Land of the Head Hunters* and the records of behind-the-scenes work on this movie reveal the Kwakwaka'wakw's highly complex engagement, and participation, in the processes of modernity despite Curtis's avowed intent (expressed to potential backers) to "go back as close to the primal life as possible" (quoted in Holm and Quimby 1980:32). This included the production and articulation of Indian culture and identity, agency rarely given them on "Hollywood's frontier" (Rosenthal 2005:331). These were processes that, in turn, allowed the history *of* modernity, and of the production's effect on their community, to be written *onto* their landscape, a process that has been revisited much more recently by Sharon Eva Grainger's project "Staging Edward Curtis," in which, in collaboration with the U'mista Cultural Centre in Alert Bay, British Columbia, she has rephotographed Curtis's images using Native models who, themselves, have discussed and posed exactly how they wish to be represented.[4]

And yet, in Curtis's own images, the land appears as backdrop, however picturesque, as objectified through the camera, as available to the eye of the spectator—as, in other words, *landscape*. As Lucy Lippard has pointed out, however, there is "no such word in indigenous languages and no such retrospective, passive concept of the land" (Lippard 1997:73). American Indian land imagery, Lippard explains, may itself frequently be based on a ritualistic understanding of what is sensed and what is seen: its understanding of place is one not based on ownership or aestheticism but on a far less divisible relationship between self and earth, being and land. To be sure, the Indian obviously *uses* the land and its resources, but, as Kiowa N. Scott Momaday has written, "The point is that *use* does not indicate in any real way his idea of the land. 'Use' is neither his word nor his idea. As an Indian I think: 'You say that I *use* the land,' and I reply, yes, it is true; but it is not the first truth. The first truth is that I *love* the land; I see that it is beautiful; I delight in it; I am alive in it" (Momaday 2008:580). From this, Momaday extrapolates the idea that the Native American's regard for earth and sky is a deeply ethical one, "a reverence for the natural world that is antipodal to that strange tenet of modern civilization that seemingly has it that man must destroy his environment" (Momaday 1976:580). At the same time, to read the landscape on the Northwest Coast along these lines would be to impose a wishful, Western idea of some kind of homogenous "ecological Indian" onto it. Then and now, proprietary claims to specific pieces of land are a cultural fact, whether constructed by lineages tied to hereditary rights, or, increasingly, made by bands, tribes, or nations in the modern context of land claims and treaties. Indeed, Capilano's mission to London reflects just such a legalized claim to ownership.

A row of rickety wooden facades is hardly performing the same kind of environmental wreckage as open-pit uranium mining at Laguna Pueblo or the Peabody Coal Mine at Black Mesa, which overlaps both Navajo and Hopi lands. But it does, nonetheless, stand for an engagement with the landscape that foregrounds and privileges white agency when it comes to the collaborative enterprise that was the filming of *Head Hunters*, and that left its mark upon the Kwakwaka'wakw lands. By contrast, the text of *Legends of Vancouver* appears to offer something more complex in its mediation—an understanding that written onto an environment are overlapping layers of history, of association, and of meaning.

Yet when one considers Johnson's volume as a whole, the landscape is quite clearly rendered as something to be admired by a visitor—or by a nonlocal reader of the volume. It is illustrated by photographs: a distant view of The Lions, which at least allows one to imagine two leonine profiles; the Siwash Rock; the dark, narrow cleft of Capilano Canyon; the flatter, fast-running expanse of the Capilano River; the entrance to the narrows; Vancouver, illuminated by a dramatic sunset; Kitsilano Beach—another sunset scene; and the tall redwood trees, known as the Seven Sisters, in Vancouver's Stan-

Fig. 3.2. Bishop & Christie, *Entrance to the Narrows, Vancouver*.
From E. Pauline Johnson, *Legends of Vancouver*, Vancouver, BC: David Spencer, 1911.

ley Park (fig. 3.2). These photographs are by the commercial photographers Bishop & Christie, who operated the Kodak House at 431 Granville Street, Vancouver, which, although primarily a supply house, employed a number of staff photographers. Only the contextualization provided by Johnson's prose differentiates these particular images from standard tourist-souvenir fare (one might, of course, make the same point about the circulation of Curtis's images once separated from the *NAI* books; see Zamir and Thomas, this volume).

In many ways, the counterpart to *Legends of Vancouver* is not so much Curtis's film but an accompanying book, also entitled *In the Land of the Head-Hunters*, published in 1915, and illustrated with photographs. As Curtis explains in the foreword, the book "had its inception in an outline or scenario for a motion picture drama dealing with the hardy Indians inhabiting northern British Columbia"—a description that strongly suggests that it was intended to act as a stand-alone volume rather than moviegoers' memorabilia. Curtis submitted the idea to his friend and collaborator Robert Stuart Pigott, "who urged that it be put into book form and that the declamatory style of the tribal bards be followed" (Curtis 1915:vii). The language, as a result, is extremely overblown—quite different from Johnson's confiding and confidently contemporary diction. As the *New York Times* (March 28, 1915)

Kate Flint

reviewer of the Curtis book remarked, "Possibly many will think it better if the work had been done in a more historical and less declamatory manner."

From the start, the prose emphasizes the remoteness of the inhabitants of the Pacific Northwest from Curtis's contemporary readers and viewers—a distance established in the preface, where he says that despite the slight differences between the film and the text, "both give a glimpse of the primitive Americans as they lived in the Stone Age and as they were still living when the hardy explorers Perez, Heceta, Quadra, Cook, Meares, and Vancouver touched the shores of the Pacific between 1774 and 1791" (Curtis 1915:vii). Indeed, the printed volume ratchets up this sense of remoteness, stating bluntly what is only assumed in the film. "In warfare," Curtis writes in the prologue, the "native dwellers in this land … are head-hunters with small regard for life, and ceremonial cannibalism is not unknown. Their mentality is to the Caucasian difficult of comprehension, and their conclusions are similarly inverse" (5). In other words, Curtis is doing in the book what, in the film, he performs with a range of cinematographic tools, whether intertitles, visuals, props, or the plot itself.

This protestation of primitivism established the setting for the romance of Motana and Naida that follows, set against a landscape that, in the opening pages, is constituted through some predictably exaggerated adjectives. Here "a somber, gloomy forest meets a forbidding sea"; the cliffs "throw back the ever-beating, roaring surf"; while "near and far, snow-capped peaks thrust their rugged, cloud-wrapt forms from the forest green to the sky" (1). No attempt is made to read this environment through the eyes, let alone the legends, of its inhabitants, unless one counts the description, in the final dramatic scene that ends with the destruction of the canoe-carrying Yaklus and his "howling pack" in the waters of the "boiling gorge" of Hyal, where the natural energies are anthropomorphized: "To lure their victim on, the waters first flow with low and subtle murmur like the whispering breeze across the forest tops, but all too soon the gorge shows its vicious, all-consuming greed and anger" (106). It is nothing but backdrop (see also Evans, this volume). This is in contrast, one might note, to the way in which landscape and inhabitants are drawn symbiotically together at the opening of the tenth volume of *NAI*, where we are told, "It is an inhospitable, mysterious country, with its forbidding, rock-bound coasts, its dark, tangled, mysterious forests, its beetling mountains, its long, gloomy season of rains and fogs. No less inhospitable. Mysterious, and gloomy, to the casual observer, is the character of its inhabitants. They seem constantly lost in dark broodings" (Curtis 1907–30, vol. 10:4).

Backdrop, too, is the role that the landscape plays in the many photographs that accompany the *Head-Hunters* book. This is very different from the role that it plays within the film itself, where the camera repeatedly lingers on picturesque scenery and natural phenomena: the sun setting over the sea and sending up sparkly reflections, the life of the sea lions on the rock, the tide rolling in at the very end and the seabirds flying. All of these were elements that greatly appealed to East Coast reviewers, even if the Seattle press seemed less struck by their familiar landscape.[5] But within the book, after an early image, taken from the sea, of clouds swirling around the cliffs that rise straight up from the water, the dramatic scenery takes second place to its inhabitants, with a couple of exceptions showing its other occupants: a tiny rocky island covered in sea lions, and a ragged octopus washed up on the beach, which is peculiarly literal and ineffective as an illustration of Motana's confident declaration, as he recruits men to go and rescue Naida, "Great is my knowledge of the monster that writhes in the ocean's depths and destroys the luckless ones" (Curtis 1915:101). In the remainder of the photographic illustrations, the height of a cliff serves to accentuate a warrior's noble grandeur as he stands at its peak, praying to the "Spirits of the Wind"; the sun's reflections sparkle back from the waves that are traversed by the elaborate war canoes; Motana and his father sit on lichen-covered rocks with thick, out-of-focus forest behind them. In yet other pictures, the emphasis falls almost entirely on individual humans, where the only visual context is given by the Kwakwa̱ka'wakw's elaborate carvings. These include portraits in the style that Curtis favored that followed the conventions of late-nineteenth-century studio photography while emphasizing physical type, dress, and adornment; shots of dancers, including an effectively fearsome "Eclipse Dance" opposite the foreword, with its talk of primitivism (an image that also appears as plate 355 in vol. 10 of *NAI*); and one rather awkwardly posed picture, purporting to show Motana and Naida courting, yet in fact looking decidedly self-conscious in fur pelts, shawl, and chunky jewelry.

Conspicuously absent is any image of the white people who arrive, trade, and depart in the course of the narrative: nothing accompanying, for example, the episode in which the marveling Kwakwa̱ka'wakw wonder to themselves, "Were the men of white skins and hair of every color spirit creatures? Or were they men with red blood and white skins?" (Curtis 1915:69–70). For the white men's part, they see the "looks of cunning and distrust" and decide to awe the Natives by shooting a seagull out of the sky, killing "by the magic of thunder" (70) and ensuring that they receive hospitality. This allows for a midstory interlude that forcibly reminds one of the difference between

Kate Flint

Native and Western cultures by inserting a pointed comparison with classical mythology that situates the guests—and the reader—completely outside the Kwakw<u>a</u>ka'wakw frame of reference: "The beaks, wings, eyes, and jaws on the graven posts flapped, rolled, and growled automaton-like. Within them hollow, bellowing voices bade the guests welcome. The guests felt as if they had entered Hades and the Keeper of the Unfortunates had in mockery called a welcome" (73). Small wonder that after receiving food and entertainment, and trading unspecified goods for fur pelts, the visitors depart.

It would be easy to create a neat contrast between Curtis's deliberate archaism on the page, as well as in his film, and Pauline Johnson's deliberate mediation between past and present, drawing her authority from her Indian blood. In doing so, of course, she is essentially figuring herself as a kind of pan-Indian spokesperson, avoiding analysis of the differences between the Iroquois and the Squamish, except in so far as she acknowledges her position as an outsider listening to legends. Such a juxtaposition would figure Curtis—not entirely unjustly—as someone whose drive was toward a style of photographic record making that deliberately emphasized a version of "authenticity" that placed true Indianness firmly in a precontact past. Against this, one can set Johnson's sustained desire to interpret one culture to another through highly contemporary analogies, while retaining the integrity of Squamish legends. If the photographs that illustrate *In the Land of the Head-Hunters* treat woods and water as generic, ambient qualities, the combination of text and image in Johnson's text brings firmly home the point that what might look like pleasant, picturesque views to one set of eyes may be completely imbued with history and association to another.

And yet, the publication history of Pauline Johnson's volume tells a slightly different story as it moves away from Johnson's own control—as, for that matter, Curtis's own images came to circulate independently of the rich cultural and historical context provided by *NAI* (even if he could, through his own marketing, be said to have been at least complicit in this decontextualization). The book was published as *Legends of Vancouver*, yet Johnson's own wish had been for it to be entitled *Legends of the Capilano*—vesting ownership with the family who communicated these legends to her. The eventual title signaled the commercial appeal of the less obscure—to a white reader—proper name. Furthermore, different editions featured covers that emphasized a stylized signification of Indianness. The cover printed in 1911 for the Trust Fund by the Saturday Sunset Presses bore a Pacific Northwest–style bird, in blocks of blue and black, suspended beneath a geometrically designed bar (fig. 3.3). But this is the only design that, combined with stark, blockish lettering, seems to remain true to the aesthetics of the First Nations people whose heritage forms the rationale for the book's existence. Another 1911 edition brought out by the Pauline Johnson Trust showed, incongruously, the volume's title arched over the profiled head of a Plains Indian in feathered headdress; an edition published by David Spencer, also in 1911, bore Johnson's signature, and a little sketch of a vaguely Indian bowl, spade, and pick; a privately printed 1911 edition sports a culturally unspecific ornamental dagger. When the Toronto firm of McClelland, Stewart, and Goodchild brought out a so-called new edition in 1912, the cover was by a founding artist of the Group of Seven, J. E. H. MacDonald. Dark brown on a tawny background, this graphically accomplished, stylized design shows fir trees and totem poles against a background of dark woods and snow-capped peaks, granting the volume a certain geographical specificity through its subject matter, yet, through the prominent Arts and Crafts lettering, directing the consumer to appreciate the volume in a far broader aesthetic context (fig. 3.4). Similarly, the elaborately ornamented intertitles that introduce each episode of Curtis's film signal a desire to speak the visual language of contemporary cinema design, even as Dugald Walker's stylized totem pole–like designs suggest the aesthetics of the film's protagonists (see fig. I.10).

As Curtis and Pauline Johnson's friends and well-wishers knew, and as a developing tourist industry had very much taken to heart: Indianness sells. It sells to those who are already primed to recognize its dominant stereotypes, and who want to believe in its "authenticity"—that is, in a form of purity, adorned, in both these cases, with up-to-the-minute Western aesthetics. *Legends of Vancouver*, like Curtis's movie and accompanying volume, relied on a packaging and promotion that displayed its dependence on preconceived notions of Indianness. Yet, once drawn in, Johnson's reader is offered a much more nuanced account of what it means to be a part of First Nations culture in the 1910s than either Curtis's movie or the accompanying book ever come close to hinting. Curtis turns away from the implications of modernity; Johnson, however strongly she might have felt (and on occasion exploited) a romantic version of "Indianness," knew very well the dangers of ignoring the pressures of a changing world. The irony in this, of course, is that in format, the opposite is true: Johnson relies on classic oral tradition and textual storytelling, while Curtis is far more innovative in choosing to work with the motion picture form.

In each case, landscape—and the relationship of people to landscape—is pressed into service as a way of consolidating these very different points of view. What emerges from this is a demonstration of the shaping role that

Kate Flint

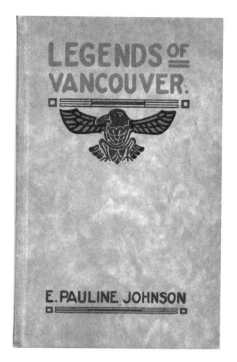

Fig. 3.3. Cover to E. Pauline Johnson, *Legends of Vancouver*, Vancouver, BC: Saturday Sunset Presses, 1913.

Fig. 3.4. J. E. H. MacDonald, cover to E. Pauline Johnson (Tekahionwake), *Legends of Vancouver*, Toronto: McClelland and Stewart, 1922.

cultural productions have to play in displaying and interpreting landscape. However much Curtis might wish landscape to be an unchanging backdrop from which his Native subjects draw strength, identity, and authenticity, his selectivity in choosing and filming particular views under particular atmospheric conditions ultimately emphasizes the interpretive part played by filmmaker and photographer. To be sure, the photographs that accompany *Legends of Vancouver* likewise have little to distinguish them from contemporary tourist fare. But they are precisely that—accompanying illustrations; they are not as numerous as the photographs that play a central part in *In the Land of the Head-Hunters,* nor, of course, are they as visually dominant as the film's spectacular scenery. Johnson's text, her shifts in style, and her acknowledgment that there are different ways of relating to natural landmarks and to their cultural history, work ultimately to create a far more complex presentation of the mediated, hybrid forms that constituted Native life in the Pacific Northwest in the second decade of the twentieth century than do Curtis's more dramatic, nostalgia-infused productions.

PAULINE JOHNSON AND EDWARD CURTIS

1   Shamoon Zamir (this volume) has made a similar point about Curtis's description and images of modern technologies in other volumes of the *NAI* series.

2   The word "authenticity" is a particularly apposite and troubling one to use in the case of James Young Deer. As Philip Deloria discussed on a BBC Radio 3 program, "James Young Deer: A Winnebago Movie Maker" (produced by Matthew Sweet; broadcast September 26, 2010), there are some doubts about Young Deer's actual Indian heritage. See also Aleiss (2005:176n2), and chapter 5, note 4, this volume.

3   One of the shallowly carved totem poles accompanying this village set was later collected for the University of British Columbia Museum of Anthropology as an artifact of aboriginal craftsmanship without apparent knowledge of its inception as a movie prop said to have been carved by George Hunt himself (introduction, this volume).

4   Sharon Grainger's photo series "Staging Edward Curtis," can be viewed at www.curtisfilm.rutgers.edu/ (accessed August 12, 2012).

5   As Teresa Scandiffio (2001) has shown, the movie thus has a good deal in common with filmic travelogues from the period.

4

A CHAMBER OF ECHOING SONGS

Edward Curtis as a Musical Ethnographer

IRA JACKNIS

Edward Curtis is now so firmly identified as a photographer that we tend to forget he was one of the few ethnographers of his day to adopt a multimedia approach to cultural documentation, employing still photography, film, sound recording, artifact production and collection, Native text transcription, and written ethnography. While some contemporary anthropologists, such as Franz Boas and Alfred Kroeber, used these multiple modes of recording, Curtis was quite distinctive in trying to combine several media streams in public presentations. In his effort to preserve "the vanishing Indian" (Gidley 1998a:33), Curtis always characterized his goal as the creation of beauty and artistry (Curtis 1907–30, vol. 1:xiii). At the same time, however, he felt that his work was fundamentally documentary and inclusive. In a well-known comment, Curtis spoke of his interest in the complete range of Native culture: "While primarily a photographer, I do not see or think photographically; hence the story of Indian life will not be told in microscopic detail, but rather will be presented as a broad and luminous picture" (Curtis 1907–30, vol. 1:xv). Here Curtis seems to regard "photography" not as visual documentation but as the presentation of detailed facts, of which sound could be a part. Yet, while he often contrasted the written to the pictorial record—the verbal lore compared with the "picture work," as he called it (Gidley 1998a:78–79, cf. 169)—Curtis rarely spoke of sound or music. This avoidance may have resulted from the fact that the prime actor here was not Curtis but his more aurally talented assistant, William Myers.

As an ethnographer, Curtis faced the same problems of cultural holism and objectification with sound as with other things (Jacknis 1996). First, a Native cultural reality was fragmented and captured by various tools of Western inscription: written texts, photographs, film, sound recordings, and plaster casts, in addition to the collection of original Native indices such as artifacts and body parts. Each ethnographic inscription then became part of a continual stream of refracted versions. Field notes were copied, reworked, and expanded. Sound recordings could be transcribed, published, copied to alternate media (disc, tape, digital file), or freely adapted to creative compositions. Each version would have a different purpose and audience. These ethnographic objects then survive, or not, to be confronted—across time, place, and culture—in archives, museums, and other collections. For the nascent discipline of Native American musicology, sound recording and notated transcriptions were the necessary preconditions for knowledge production, a process parallel to the role of museum collections and photography for art history.

This essay offers an overview of Edward Curtis's inscriptions of Native American music—focusing on the Kwakwaka'wakw—from their initial field inscription on wax cylinders, to their transcription and publication, their use in orchestral versions during his musicale lectures and *Head Hunters* film screenings, and to their final preservation in sound archives. Unlike Curtis's visual documentation of the Kwakwaka'wakw, there is little that is distinctive about his sound recording among these people (Harrison, this volume).

Why, then, consider his sound recording at all? There are several reasons. As noted, his sound recording was only part of a total documentary strategy. His *Head Hunters* film has to be understood alongside his sound recordings and written texts as well as photographs, all of which comprised his complete project. Curtis's multimedia approach to public presentation—embodied most clearly in *Head Hunters*—was anticipated by his work with Henry F. Gilbert, who transcribed the original recordings in order to prepare a score to accompany the 1911–12 musicale. Next, it is important to consider the extent to which the recordings were used as a source for the film's musical score (Gilbert, this volume). This analysis can also serve as a historical background to the reconstructive work of Bill Holm and George Quimby in devising the soundtrack for their 1973 version. Finally, despite its obvious importance to Curtis and his contemporaries, as well as to us today, the subject of Curtis's sound recordings has never been thoroughly studied, and, in fact, has been widely obscured by repeated errors and misunderstandings.

Ira Jacknis

Precursors for Curtis's Sound Recording

Most likely Curtis was exposed to the idea of recording Indian music by the same person who suggested that he systematically photograph the North American Indian: his friend the conservationist George Bird Grinnell. During 1897 and 1898, Grinnell had made his own cylinder recordings of the Blackfoot and the Cheyenne; and both men were together on the 1899 Harriman Expedition, in which Curtis participated as the official photographer and which carried a phonograph to record the Alaskan Indians.[1] The following year, Grinnell's invitation to witness the Blackfoot Sun Dance in Montana led to Curtis's career-changing mission.

When Curtis began his work in the early 1900s, there were already hundreds of recordings of Native American music (Lee 1993), even though the first such recordings had been made only in 1890. In March of that year, Jesse W. Fewkes made the world's first field recordings among the Passamaquoddy of Maine, followed with the Zuni later in the year and the Hopi the year after (Brady 1999:53–55). In the first decade of the 1900s, the three main American institutions with systematic recording programs were, in roughly chronological order, the Smithsonian's Bureau of American Ethnology, the American Museum of Natural History, and the University of California at Berkeley. In Washington, DC, the leading recorders were Alice Fletcher, Washington Matthews, James A. Mooney, John P. Harrington, and, most important, Frances Densmore. The most ambitious program, however, existed at the American Museum of Natural History, led by Franz Boas, director of the Jesup Expedition to the Northwest Coast and Siberia (Keeling 2001), followed soon by Clark Wissler, who supervised a program of Plains research. The anthropology museum at the University of California, founded in 1901, naturally focused on the Natives of the state. Led by Alfred L. Kroeber, recording was especially active during the institution's first decade (Keeling 1991; Jacknis 2003b). In fact, most of the principal anthropological museums had some sort of sound recording program.[2]

Almost all of this museum-based recording was carried out by teams of individuals as part of their general collecting and ethnography. And, as in the wider world of artifact collection, these institutions tended to practice geographical specialization. Frances Densmore was unique as a museum-sponsored musical specialist. She was also the only one who resembled Curtis in her continental survey: between 1907 and the early 1940s, Densmore recorded more than 2,500 wax cylinders, and over 3,500 recordings in all, from forty tribes (Hofmann 1968:113; Levine 2002:xxv).

But not all recordings were institutional. Some were produced by enthusiastic amateur ethnographers such as Grinnell among the Cheyenne and Walter McClintock among the Blackfoot. One of the more important, although somewhat distinct, was Natalie Curtis Burlin (no relation), a trained musician who began recording the Hopi in 1903. Others came from a group of composers called "Indianists," who creatively incorporated Native American music into their compositions. Among those who also made their own sound recordings were Frederick R. Burton, Charles Wakefield Cadman, and Thurlow Lieurance. With his private funding and role as a commercial photographer, Curtis was more or less unique, but he clearly fits into this more personal, rather than institutional, mode.

Having just referred to Curtis as a personal collector, it is important to remember that the body of field data across multiple media that we attribute to "Edward S. Curtis" was more accurately produced by a team of talented individuals, supervised by Curtis (Gidley 1998a:135). The entire North American Indian, Incorporated, project was more like a multimedia film project, with Curtis as the producer, director, and photographer. The sound recording, in fact, was done by others. When Curtis was beginning his work in the early years of the twentieth century, there were already several important models of such ethnographic expedition teams, two of which employed sound recording: the Jesup North Pacific Expedition from the American Museum of Natural History, 1897–1902 (Keeling 2001), and the Torres Strait Expedition from Cambridge University, 1898 (Herle and Rouse 1998). Like these teams, Curtis's collaboration was a primary reason that his project could be so large, complex, and multimedia.

Curtis's Cylinder Recordings: An Overview

Given the vagaries of the historical record, we shall probably never be able to fully reconstruct the scope and content of Curtis's sound recording practice.[3] Yet, from the extant sources, we can piece together a reasonably good sense of his efforts: 600 to 700 wax cylinders recorded between 1907 and 1913 from over thirty tribes, spread throughout most regions of western North America.

While we cannot be certain of who among his multiparty team was the recordist, the likely candidate—for most if not all of the recording—was William E. Myers (1877–1949). A former journalist, Myers joined the crew in 1906. He went on to play an extremely active role in the research and writing, leaving to Curtis the actual photographic work. We do know that Myers, who was especially good at linguistics, had some responsibility for the songs: "Myers even had the gift, according to Curtis, of being able to sing accurately by ear Indian songs he had recorded, even though he did not understand their literal meaning" (Gidley 1998a:136). We also know that at least some of the recording was done by others; another likely candidate was Edmund Schwinke, who assisted from 1910 to 1915.[4] For some of the cylinders the team used a pitch pipe to ensure that the playback speed, and thus the pitch, would match that used in the recording. This method, which would ensure an accurate transcription, indicated that some members of Curtis's team—probably composer Edgar Fischer, who was in the field in the early years—had some kind of musical sophistication.[5]

Generally, there is little surviving documentation on the recording sessions or the reactions of Native participants. What we do have is the oft-repeated expression of amazement at the machine's mimetic abilities (Brady 1999:31). According to Curtis, "The singers and fellow tribesman were awe-struck on hearing the songs as repeated from what they called the magic box" (Graybill and Boesen 1976:30). It is significant that such reflexive comments were rare in Curtis's writing, and none were included in *The North American Indian* (*NAI*) itself. In general, Curtis obscured the pragmatics of his ethnographic process, and when he did comment on it, in his popular lectures and articles, he invariably cast himself as the heroic explorer who had to overcome Native resistance to his recording efforts (30).

The Curtis cylinders are extraordinarily wide in geographical scope, covering most of the regions in which Curtis worked—Northwest Coast, Plateau, Great Basin, Southwest, and Plains.[6] This diverse spread of culture areas would have been relatively rare for most recordists, but, as already noted, it was comparable to the work of a musical specialist such as Densmore. While some tribes are more thoroughly represented than others (for example, Hidatsa, Piegan, and Blackfoot), by and large all of the tribes were recorded equally, indicating the survey approach of the Curtis team. Not surprisingly, this audio strategy paralleled that of the photographic and textual documentation.[7]

The dating of Curtis's sound recording is somewhat less clear. According to the Indiana archives, their entire Curtis collection was recorded between 1907 and 1913 (Lee 1979:55–58).[8] Judging from the evidence of the publications, these dates are probably accurate, for, with a few minor exceptions (Hopi and Oto), all of the published transcriptions were based on fieldwork from essentially this period. Moreover, Curtis's work fits squarely into what one could call the "classic" age of Native American sound recording, with relatively little before 1900 and a gap between the end of the cylinder period

EDWARD CURTIS AS A MUSICAL ETHNOGRAPHER

(ca. 1930) and the revival of field recording with tape recorders in the 1950s (Myers 1993:405).[9]

While we have no firm documentation of when Curtis began to use the phonograph, circumstantial evidence points to the 1906 season. First, this was the year that Myers joined the team. As a still photographer, it seems natural that Curtis would have begun to use a movie camera before turning to sound. He appears to have first used film in 1904, during his spring field season among the Navajo, followed by his work among the Hopi in 1906 (Makepeace 2002:51; cf. Gidley 1998a:234–35). By the time of a lecture in early 1907, describing the previous year's work, Curtis lists a phonograph as part of his field equipment (Gidley 1998a:78).[10] He might have been encouraged to expand his armamentarium in 1906, the year that J. Pierpont Morgan began to fund the project (cf. Graybill and Boesen 1976:20). On the other hand, it is possible that Curtis used a phonograph even earlier. Cylinder machines were not especially difficult field equipment: some of the machines were powered by hand or foot, others by portable batteries, but no electrical amplification was required for the sound production (fig. 4.1). Obtaining and shipping the fragile wax cylinders were much more of a problem than any expense. Although stored in cardboard boxes, these wax tubes were highly susceptible to heat, insects, mold, and breakage.

Fig. 4.1. Cylinder recording machine: Edison Standard Phonograph with recording horn, ca. 1900. Photo by Carl Fleischhauer. American Folklife Center, Library of Congress.

It is harder to determine the ending of Curtis's recording period. By and large, his Northwest Coast fieldwork (Haida/Nootka) seems to have marked the effective conclusion. At least those are the last documented recordings we have. However, Curtis later mentioned recordings for the Hopi (whose final fieldwork came in 1919, but which had started as early as 1900) and for several Oklahoma tribes. Curtis did the latter fieldwork late in his project (1926), with the assistance of Stewart Eastwood, after the resignation of Myers (Gidley 1998a:155). Although there are no surviving cylinders from this region, Curtis indicated that they were made.[11] These would have certainly marked the end, representing a kind of "outlier," after a recording gap of many years. And we know that Curtis did not take a phonograph with him on his last, challenging trip to Alaska in 1927.

The biggest mystery, however, concerns the number of cylinders that Curtis recorded. The most common estimate—in fact, the only one—is around 10,000 items.[12] Evidently filmmaker and author Teri McLuhan was the first to suggest this figure: "It is reported that Curtis recorded over 10,000 songs, over 700 of which are still intact today at the University of Indiana" (McLuhan 1972:x; cf. McLuhan 1974 [film]). This statement raises a host of ambiguities. First, it is not clear what source she was invoking, as no earlier written source is known; she may have been guided by family folklore. Furthermore, in the only known collection of surviving Curtis recordings—the Archives of Traditional Music at Indiana University—there are only 276 cylinders, holding about 10.5 hours of music. According to the archives, "several thousand more are scattered" (Seeger and Spear 1987:83), but to date, no others have been located.

One way of determining the corpus of recordings is by matching published transcriptions to existing cylinders, for most of the transcriptions were based on recordings.[13] Some of the cylinders have undoubtedly been lost, since we have printed transcriptions for songs with no extant cylinders, and since Curtis reported recordings whose cylinders are now missing.[14] For the "Kwakiutl," for example, we have more transcriptions (for example, twenty-three) than surviving cylinders (six). Another clue is the numbering of the cylinders. Around 1912, at a time when Curtis had completed most of the field recording for which we have any evidence, the highest number in Gilbert's correspondence with Myers and Curtis is recording number 576.[15]

This raises another critical issue: what are we counting—cylinders or songs? McLuhan cited 10,000 original "songs," and one would assume that the 700 intact number refers also to songs. However, according to the Indiana archives, there are a total of 463 "strips" (bands) for the set of 276 cylinders. During these years, in fact, cylinders varied a good bit in their size and recording duration. While most lasted between two and three minutes, there was no reason that several shorter performances could not have been recorded on a single cylinder, simply by starting and stopping the machine between renditions. Most of Curtis's cylinders, in fact, contain multiple songs, sometimes as many as five. In this, his practice differed from ethnographers such as Alfred Kroeber, who pioneered the recording of a single song or narrative over multiple cylinders (Jacknis 2003b:245–46). This meant that Curtis was able to capture only a fragment of a much longer musical entity. The reasons for Curtis's practice are obscure, but most likely he wanted to use his cylinders frugally, due to difficulties in obtaining or shipping them. Yet it also seems to be another expression of his survey approach, choosing broad sampling over intensive documentation.

So, allowing for lost or unidentified recordings and even counting multiple songs rather than cylinders, the extant total is substantially less than McLuhan's reference to the Indiana corpus, and orders of magnitude less than her oft-quoted 10,000 estimate. An institutional comparison puts this into perspective. All of the principal contemporary collections, produced over decades by multiple recordists, contain a good bit fewer.[16] Even Densmore, perhaps the largest single recordist, recorded less than 3,000. A likely estimate is that Curtis recorded about 600 to 700 wax cylinders, with about half of them remaining at Indiana. Most likely, the gross exaggeration of the cylinder corpus is another expression of the mythology that we find all too commonly in the Curtis story, compounded by the difficulty that historians have had in locating and accessing his original ethnohistorical documentation.

The Uses of Curtis's Cylinders

What did Curtis expect to do with these recordings? Like all ethnographic data, they were created first for purposes of cultural documentation. Curtis likely considered sound recording as a part of his general mission to preserve what he regarded as a vanishing culture. Beyond this, however, the cylinders could selectively be made public. Today, we commonly expect to listen to such recordings, but at the turn of the last century, many considered cylinders to be an intermediate stage before musical transcriptions, which could then be published and widely shared. While some of the cylinders were so transcribed and published, most were not. Judging from the related publication history of his photographs, Curtis clearly viewed his project as the creation of a large corpus, which would be selectively mined for public dissemination. Trained as a commercial photographer rather than a scientist, Curtis wanted to control his field materials for as long as possible, so that he could derive financial benefit from them.

For mechanical recording media such as the phonograph, or even the camera, the inscription of cultural reality in the field could be separated from the transcription or analysis in the study. Not only could the time and place be displaced, but so could the agent. This separation explains why so many recordists could make so many recordings that they assumed would be valuable to other scholars in the future. Some ethnographers—such as

Fletcher, Boas, and Densmore—were musically competent enough to actually transcribe Indian music in the field with Western notation, but most—including Curtis and his usual team—were not. Despite his astounding auditory sensitivity and linguistic skills, Myers evidently was not musically literate.

Publication was important at the time due to the common belief that sound recordings were a means to an end, especially for scholarship (Brady 1999:62). The actual sounds were of little commercial value, for, unlike African American or Euro-American ethnic music, Native American music was not listened to for entertainment and had very little popular appeal. Instead, the music was transcribed and analyzed by scholars (Cohen and Wells 1982; cf. Jacknis 2003b:237) or creatively transformed by Indianist composers. And certainly the transcriptions would have been more broadly appreciated at a time when musical literacy was more widespread than it is today. Curtis was keenly aware of the distinction between the production of raw field materials and his edited public presentations. As he was forced to support himself by public appeals, he needed to select what he believed would be most popular (Lyman 1982:78). We really do not know Curtis's reasoning in selecting his sound recordings or their publication, but he once implied that the decisions were fairly circumstantial: "In many instances I made a large number of records. From these were selected such as we had room for in the book."[17]

Music in *The North American Indian* (1907–30)

Like all other aspects of Native American culture, music was amply treated in Curtis's published ethnography. The "author"—nominally Curtis—often discusses musical behavior in the text, particularly singing, but also instrumental music and dance. Almost every volume has index entries for these topics. Occasionally, the illustrations include photos of musical instruments: drums are perhaps the most common, but there are also a number of rattles (especially on the Northwest Coast). As with the field research itself, the published volumes of the *NAI* were a collaborative product, despite Curtis's sole credit on the title pages. While the editorship of Frederick W. Hodge, anthropologist for the Smithsonian and for George Heye's Museum of the American Indian, was acknowledged by Curtis himself, Myers's primary authorship was never made clear (Gidley 1998a:137). From passing references as well as internal evidence, the text appears to be a palimpsest, composed of multiple layers from more than one author. Since we know that Myers did most of the recording and wrote most of the text, it is likely that he was responsible for most of the musical descriptions, incorporating transcriptions and commentary from one of the three musicians whom Curtis acknowledged: Edgar S. Fischer, Henry F. Gilbert, and Carl A. Weber.

For some of his cylinders, at least, Curtis had transcriptions made, which he published in the *NAI*. Yet, of the twenty volumes, only eleven included transcriptions, for a total of 197 songs; transcriptions were presented only for the Plains, Plateau, and Northwest Coast tribes, and, with some token exceptions, not for any Eastern, Southwestern, Californian, Subarctic, or Arctic peoples (see note 9). Although these gaps may have been intentional, they seem more likely to have been circumstantial. We do know that the extant cylinder collection closely matches the published corpus—the major discrepancy being the eastern Pueblos (Acoma, Nambe, San Ildefonso, San Juan, Santo Domingo, and Tesuque), which were recorded but not transcribed. Most likely, the prime reason for a shift in Curtis's procedure was his financial reversal after 1915. It may have become too cumbersome and expensive to make the recordings in the first place, and it was even more expensive to pay a trained musician to make the transcriptions. Then again, there were changes in his team; especially the departure of Myers in April, 1926, but also the successive deaths of Fischer in 1922 and Weber in 1929.

Like most contemporary recordists, Curtis needed to find a trained musician to make transcriptions from the cylinders. In 1905, Theodore Roosevelt had recommended Natalie Curtis Burlin for such work (Gidley 1998a:203). While not all of the published transcriptions are credited, we know that the Sioux and Assiniboine songs in the third volume were made by Fischer. The founding conductor of the Walla Walla Symphony Orchestra, Fischer was a German-trained violinist who could reportedly speak eight languages.[18] Based on fieldwork from 1905 to 1908, when he was teaching music at Whitman College, Fischer worked "both from his personal field notes and from phonographic records" made by the Curtis team (Curtis 1907–30, vol. 3:xiii). Thus he was the only one of Curtis's field team competent enough to make transcriptions by ear.

The principal transcriber for the set was the composer Gilbert, who worked on the sixth through the ninth volumes (Gidley 1998a:202–3, from Curtis 1907–30, vol. 10:xii; Gilbert 1921; Levine 2002, 42–43). Known also for his work with African American music, Gilbert was one of the leading Indianist composers, having studied with Edward MacDowell and collaborated with Arthur Farwell. Significantly, perhaps, it was Myers who usually sent the cylinders to Gilbert, who lived in Cambridge, Massachusetts (Gidley 1998a:204). In 1910, Gilbert transcribed at least sixty cylinders. The following year he composed and conducted the score for Curtis's musicale lecture tour, before returning to the transcriptions for the ninth volume (in 1912) and the tenth (in 1913 and, perhaps, 1914) (Gidley, this volume; Gidley 1998a:210–11).

The transcriptions in the tenth volume (1915), the Kwakiutl volume, were done partly by Gilbert and partly by Weber, a Seattle-based musician, composer, and arranger (Curtis 1907–30, vol. 10:xii). The German-born Weber played French horn in the Seattle Symphony and taught music.[19] Undoubtedly, he was chosen because Gilbert left the volume's work in midstream. Weber may have also done the transcriptions for the eleventh volume, also on the Northwest Coast (nine for the Nootka; five for the Haida), which was published the following year. In fact, although we cannot be certain, most likely Weber produced Curtis's final published transcriptions (three for the Hopi, and six for the Oto and Ponca).

Two of Curtis's three musical collaborators contributed written commentaries on Indian music, dealing especially with problems of transcription (Fischer 1908; Gilbert 1976). Like Native American music in general, most of the transcriptions are of vocals only. Some include musical accompaniment, such as drums (for example, a Chinook song, Curtis 1907–30, vol. 8:96–98). A few are solely instrumental melodies—flute music used for courting. The songs themselves are presented by means of three separate yet related components: musical notation, the text in the Native language, and an English translation. Sometimes all three are given; other times just one or the other.

Curtis carefully considered the proper rhetorical style for his musical transcriptions. Writing to editor Frederick Hodge in early 1908, as he was considering the first volumes to include music, Curtis mused,

> In the future, I want to show enough of the music to give a general idea of it and its application to their ceremonial life. I had thought of printing the engraved staff of music in the body of the text in its exact position as far as the description of the ceremony is concerned. In discussing this with Mr. Myers, he seems to feel that it will hopelessly mar the page, and suggested all music be printed in the Appendix.... I shall also discuss the matter with Orcutt, the printer, and perhaps with others, and it might be worthwhile to have a sample page made up in this way and see how it does affect its appearance. Another thought had been to run such music as was used in the way of a footnote, which would come in that case almost as a tail piece for the page. We have ample time to consider it, but tell me what you think. (Graybill and Boesen 1976:41, 44)

In the end, Curtis compromised between the two positions. In most of the volumes, some of the transcriptions were presented in the text, while others were saved for an appendix.

In other words, music was not treated the same throughout the set. In some volumes, it is not present, while in others it comes only in the appendix. These appendices function somewhat like the portfolios associated with each volume: as a place for Curtis to include condensed tribal summaries, mythic texts, and other extensive factual "deposits." (While the portfolios may have been intended for art collectors, the appendices—including the transcriptions—were definitely meant for scholars). Most of the songs in the appendices were presented without commentary, although sometimes there was a brief introduction. As Curtis suggested, the music is usually described as it relates to some ongoing cultural event. Often, the song is simply placed at a point in the narrative where it would have been sung. More rarely, the music itself was described, analyzed, or even evaluated aesthetically.

This raises the broader issue of the objective boundedness of the songs, and their relation to a holistic cultural context. Curtis's practice is ambivalent. Most of the time, he basically "dumps" his transcriptions, especially those in the appendices, with little commentary. Occasionally, however, he links the transcription to some social context, usually when and how the song was performed. Unlike an analysis of the music, which Gilbert could supply from Cambridge, this would depend on some kind of fieldwork. Myers's linguistic abilities clearly enabled Curtis to supplement a purely observational method with access to an inner world of meaning, accessible through words and thus the interview method (for the Boasian critique of materialism, see Jacknis 1996).[20]

Of all of the aspects of musical analysis, Curtis and his team clearly emphasized some over others. They focused on recording and transcription; song genres and the relations of words and music; performance practice; the social and cultural context of music; and organology (the study of musical instruments). While not a major concern, there were occasional discussions of regional relations, as well as of history and acculturation. Some of the most extensive commentaries on song come in the Plateau volumes (7 and 8); they largely disappear after that. They combine notes on performance practice, which could only have come from a field observer such as Myers, and aesthetic commentary, which must have been contributed by a musician such as Gilbert (Curtis 1907–30, vol. 8:54–61). Most of the comments are contextual. Curtis writes of how people learn songs, how they inherit them, and which social actions they are associated with. Even more, the discussions of music are largely observational. That is, they are mostly visual descriptions, for example, of the postures and actions of the singers, dancers, or musicians. Occasionally, Curtis will mention the quality of the voice or a sound, features that can be heard. While such an observational approach is to be expected from a nonmusician, it also resonates with Curtis's earlier career as a photographer and Myers's as a journalist. This observational style, in which the level of verbal detail resembles a filmic description, was unmatched by most of Curtis's contemporaries, particularly those dependent on recordings.

As in his photography, in his musical descriptions Curtis often resorts to the reconstruction of musical behavior. Such reconstruction—a vital feature of the *Head Hunters* film—is a major topic in Curtis studies (Holm and Quimby 1980:23, 31–32; Faris 1996). Like many anthropologists of his day, Curtis employs an "ethnographic present." For instance, after a very detailed and compelling description of a Haida ceremonial comes the admission that the ceremony had not been given since 1888 (Curtis 1907–30, vol. 11:143). Thus the entire report must have been reconstructed, although this is not noticeable unless one reads carefully. Clearly, such reconstructions are the verbal correlate of Curtis's photographic reconstruction of costuming and props, coupled with the avoidance of acculturative evidence.

While we lack evidence on how the musical analysis was formulated, one comment by Gilbert is quite revealing. He explained how he once "edited out" indications of acculturative influences in the music, just as Curtis himself had done photographically (although there is no evidence that Curtis asked him to do this):

> The majority of melodies collected by Mr. Curtis's field staff were genuine tribal melodies. But owing to the Indian's contact with the white man I occasionally, in the course of my transcribing work, came across a melody which was plainly a garbled version of some familiar tune which the Indian had picked up from his white associates. Thus one of the tunes which I transcribed was so plainly an Indian version of "The Wearin' of the Green" that I did not dare to allow it to be printed as a genuine Indian melody. (Gilbert 1921:91)

On the other hand, both Gilbert and Curtis admitted in print that such influence had occurred (Curtis 1907–30, vol. 8:75, 166).

Judged as scholarship of Indian music (Lee 1993; Keeling 1997), the *NAI* is quite significant, primarily for its 197 transcriptions and its musical ethnography. It was published only about two decades after the pioneering work of Theodore Baker (1882) and Alice C. Fletcher (with Francis La Flesche,

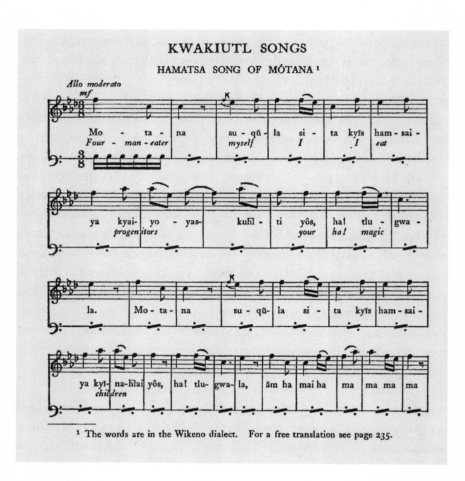

KWAKIUTL SONGS

HAMATSA SONG OF MÓTANA [1]

Allo moderato

Mo - ta - na   su - qŭ - la   si - ta   kyĭs   ham - sai -
Four - man - eater   myself   I   I   eat

ya   kyai- yo - yas-   kuhl - ti   yôs,   hal   tlu - gwa -
progenitors   your   hal   magic

la.   Mo - ta - na   su - qŭ - la   si - ta   kyĭs   ham - sai -

ya kyĭ- na-hlai yôs,   hal   tlu- gwa- la,   ăm ha   mai ha   ma   ma ma   ma
children

[1] The words are in the Wikeno dialect.   For a free translation see page 235.

Fig. 4.2. Example of a transcription by Henry F. Gilbert. "Hamatsa Song of Motana."
(*NAI,* vol. 10:311.) Charles Deering McCormick Library of Special Collections,
Northwestern University Library.

1893), who combined contextual and musicological analysis from John C.
Fillmore. Curtis's set began to appear not long after Benjamin Ives Gilman,
in 1891, became the first to publish a transcription derived from a recording
(Levine 2002:54–55). Unlike the path-breaking work of German scholars Otto
Abraham and Erich M. von Hornbostel (1906), who offered only a formal
analysis, Curtis's publication is quite holistic and contextual. Unlike some
contemporary musicologists, such as Fillmore, his analyses are not particularly evolutionist or even addressed to diachronic issues. The *NAI,* Boasian
in approach (Keeling 1997:xviii), most resembles the work of Densmore,
although with much less musical analysis. In the same way that the bril-
liance of Curtis's photographs has blinded us to the significance of the text,

Ira Jacknis

the *NAI* was actually one of the most extensive and significant publications of American Indian music of its day, although it is little-remembered for this in disciplinary histories.

The Kwakwa̲ka'wakw Recordings on Cylinders and the Page

Curtis's fascination with the Kwakwa̲ka'wakw led to a greater emphasis on this group than on just about any other. His team visited them, usually during the summer season, between June 1910 and the summer of 1914 (Holm and Quimby 1980:26–30).[21] In fact, the surviving six Kwakwa̲ka'wakw cylinders were all recorded on July 24 and 26 of 1910, thus coming at the very beginning of the fieldwork. As this would have most likely been well before Curtis had conceived the idea for the *Head Hunters* film, any use of the cylinders as source material for a musical accompaniment would have been retroactive. In a 1914 letter on equipment needed for the field season, Myers reported to Schwinke, "Hunt has the phonograph here, but we shall need records" (Gidley 1998a:139), implying that they were still recording Kwakwa̲ka'wakw music (if recorded, these cylinders have not survived).

Myers's statement suggests that George Hunt played an active role in the sound recording. This would be expected, as Hunt had participated in some of the earliest recordings of Indian music—and the first among the Kwakwa̲ka'wakw—by Boas, Fillmore, and Gilman during the 1893 Chicago World's Fair (Jacknis 2003a). While Hunt continued to take his own photographs and worked with subsequent filmmakers, we know of no sound recordings associated with him other than his collaboration on Boas's last trip in 1930–31.[22] All of the surviving Curtis cylinders were recorded in Fort Rupert, British Columbia, Hunt's home and the base for the future film project.

These six Kwakwa̲ka'wakw cylinders, ranging from two to three minutes each, contain eleven songs. Several male singers were recorded, but none were identified. All of the recordings are solos, there was no group singing, and most of the solos were accompanied by the beating of a wooden baton on a board. The subjects of the songs are given by Curtis (1907–30, vol. 10) as devilfish (octopus) mask (298–99); wild man of the woods, a "Paqusilahl" song (319); song of "Nuhbimahla" for winter ceremony (157, 215–16); bear song for winter ceremony (320); love song (324–25?); mourning [?] song (313); nursery song (325–26?); Hamaťsa song (313–14?); Hamaťsa song of Motana (311–13); and two "Pahala" or healer's songs (323–24).[23] As is apparent, most of the songs are ceremonial, matching the focus of the Kwakiutl volume as well as the content of the film. In terms of the extant archival documentation, some have Kwak̓wala texts, with an English translation, undoubtedly supplied by Hunt. Beyond the texts, only one has a contextual note. A nursery song bears the comment, "The song represents a conversation between an infant song and the father, who rocks the child in his arms and sings."

In addition to the *Head Hunters* film, the Kwakwa̲ka'wakw received the longest volume in the series, and, accordingly, had the largest number of published transcriptions from any individual tribe (twenty-three, as opposed to the next largest, the Crow, with seventeen). Eight songs were presented as in-text transcriptions. Another fifteen were printed in the appendix, under "Kwakiutl Songs" (fig. 4.2). In addition, two songs were given without musical notation. According to Curtis (1907–30, vol. 10:xii), Gilbert transcribed six of the songs (beginning on 187, 195, 311, 313, 315, and 325), and Weber did the seventeen others. For the Kwakiutl volume, Myers had wanted Gilbert to do an analysis of Kwakwa̲ka'wakw time beating, what he called "baton rhythms" or "the relation of the beats to the rhythm of the voice" (Gidley 1998a:211–12).[24] He stressed, however, that the transcriptions had priority, and, in the end, Gilbert did not supply any analysis. In 1914 Curtis asked for more transcriptions from Gilbert, but to no avail. The Kwakiutl volume was transitional, marking the last of the Gilbert transcriptions.

There is little that is distinctive about the treatment of music in the Kwakiutl volume as compared to the rest of the *NAI* set. Again, the emphasis is heavily on the social and cultural context of the music, rather than its formal qualities. In fact, there is perhaps less attention to music within the text than in previous volumes, due to Gilbert's reduced role. The first transcription is presented more than halfway into the text. Among the topics considered are serial mourning songs (Curtis 1907–30, vol. 10:56–57), the use of a shaman's rattle (82), shaman songs (83–85), composition (171–72), vocal production (172), song learning (172–73), and ceremonial performance style (180). The lengthy account of song composition and learning is certainly one of the highlights of the volume, and even of the entire series. Curtis offers details on the specialized roles of composers and "lyricists" (word passers), the sources of their inspiration, and the payment for and usage of songs in the Hama̓tsa repertory. In a contemporary news account, Curtis says that while making his *Head Hunters* movie, he had watched an Indian song maker at work (Gidley 2003b:104–5), but he may have derived some of this fine description from George Hunt or another consultant.

One interesting feature of this volume are the references, perhaps the only in the series, to phonographs. One Native consultant, speaking of the reaction of a young Hamatsa initiate to a ritual encounter, said, "His hamatsa was new, and it was just like a person having a phonograph for the first time: the boy was such a wonderfully fine dancer that the people often spoke of his ability, and besides being fond of dancing he was proud of the attention he attracted" (Curtis 1907–30, vol. 10:194). One chief included twenty-five phonographs as part of a promised potlatch gift (131). By the time of Curtis's fieldwork, phonographs were fairly common among the small Kwakwaka'wakw community—numbering 1,161 in 1915—and they are frequently mentioned as potlatch gifts (Codere 1961:471). All of which shows that the facile complaint about Curtis shunning signs of acculturation is a bit overdone (Zamir and Flint, this volume).

Only two photos of overtly musical subjects were published in the Kwakiutl volume. The main one (a scene repeated in *Head Hunters*) shows a hand game with a line of drummers, their batons on the board, and a man beating a skin hand drum (fig. 4.3), and the other is of a box drum in the rear of an image of a Grizzly-Bear dancer (Curtis 1907–30, vol. 10:opposite 202).

While the Kwakiutl volume remains one of the fullest accounts of Kwakwaka'wakw musical behavior, by 1915 many Indian songs and dances had already been published by Boas. Curtis himself (1915a:xii) acknowledged the priority of Boas's 1897 monograph on the secret societies and social organization of the Kwakiutl, which had been heavily illustrated with musical transcriptions (made by Boas and John C. Fillmore, cf. Jacknis 2003a; Keeling 2001). On the whole, Curtis's work complements Boas rather than competes with him.

Curtis's Musicale (1911–12) as a Precursor for *In the Land of the Head Hunters*

Today, we might think it natural for Curtis to have played his cylinders during his many public lectures, thus pioneering the public presentation of field-recorded Indian music. By this time, in fact, public phonographic concerts were common (Altman 2004:51).[25] They were especially popular for travelogues, which often combined a lecture with lantern slides and sound recordings (Feaster and Smith 2009:313). One such venue for playing ethnographic recordings was the scientific meeting. Fewkes shared some of his cylinders during lectures in 1891 (Brady 1999:61), and Boas organized a panel of American Indian recordists at the 1898 annual meeting of the American Folklore Society in New York. An even closer comparison to Curtis's practice was photographer and lecturer Joseph K. Dixon, who was clearly inspired

Fig. 4.3. Edward S. Curtis, *The Hand-Game—Qagyuhl*, 1914. (*NAI*, vol. 10.)
Charles Deering McCormick Library of Special Collections,
Northwestern University Library.

by Curtis and his work. On his 1909 trip to the Crow reservation, to record the "Last Great Indian Council," Dixon also resorted to a multimedia strategy—making still photographs, motion film, and sound recordings—which he presented in subsequent public lectures with an instrumental musical arrangement (Krouse 1990:222; Graf 1991).[26]

Given the state of contemporary acoustic technology, primarily the phonograph's low volume and limited pitch range, Curtis could not easily play back the three-minute cylinders during his presentations. In fact, there is no evidence that Curtis played any of his cylinders in public, although he did begin to show film footage. As with their scholarly analysis, the cylinders needed to be transposed to another medium in order to be shared.

The first Native music, therefore, that Curtis was able to present publicly came in the form of the score to what he called his "musicale" or "picture opera," presented during two national tours over the 1911–12 and 1912–13 seasons (Gidley 1998a:202–3; Gidley, this volume). Employing a multimedia approach, the musicale—often entitled *The Vanishing Race*—consisted of a lecture (read from a script), accompanied by a dissolving series of projected hand-colored lantern slides, with some film footage, an orchestral score (at least on the 1911–12 tour), and scenery. Such musical accompaniment to lantern slide shows had been common since the late nineteenth century (Cooke 2008:7).[27] Instead of using the actual field recordings, Curtis commissioned Gilbert to prepare an orchestral score of twenty-six selections. He did, however, send Gilbert some of the cylinders as aural inspirations. Some of Gilbert's score was generic mood music, while in other passages he more closely followed the Native music (Pisani 2005:211–12, 235–39). Gilbert, who accompanied the first tour as musical contractor and conductor, carefully marked in the score the points of synchronization between the music, the changing images, and the narration (Gilbert 1921:91). The coordination of all of these elements—the sequence of narration, dissolving lantern slides, as well as some actual film footage—with the musical performance was clearly a precursor for a score to accompany a feature-length motion picture such as *Head Hunters*.[28]

The Columbia Record Company released a record with two selections from the musicale, arranged by Gilbert, but none of the original field recordings were ever distributed during Curtis's lifetime.[29] The lack of credit for these arrangements was just one of the reasons Gilbert fell out with Curtis following the first season of the musicale. The composer was also upset because he had not been paid for his work as musical manager or conductor (Gidley 1998a:208–15). While Gilbert gave up his transcriptions of Curtis's cylinders, he continued to make use of his work with Curtis in later compositions. When he proposed one project to Curtis in 1912, the photographer was concerned, fearing that it would compete with his own use of the music. However, Curtis came to accept this, and that year Gilbert published a piano version of five of his musicale pieces titled *Indian Sketches*, which the Boston Symphony Orchestra presented in an orchestrated version in 1921.

There was great popular acclaim for Curtis's musicale, despite some anthropological hostility and its financial failure due to costly expenses. Curtis was already responding to an impulse of ethnographic holism, one that beckoned to many of his anthropological colleagues (Jacknis 1996). Having experienced a once coherent and conjoined cultural expression in the field, he had been forced to document it by separate recording devices. The musicale was an attempt to reunite these sensory strands (Gidley 1998a:215). The playing of the actual wax cylinders—possible, if not practical—would have brought a New York audience closer to British Columbia, taking them back from the screen to the field.

John J. Braham and the
Head Hunters Score (1914)

In understanding the original *Head Hunters* "sound track" experienced by Curtis's audience in 1914, we must take ourselves out of a century of alternate practices, especially in the talkie era. While not completely valid, there is much truth to the oft-repeated observation that silent movies were never silent. In fact, even at the invention of film, there were attempts to accompany the moving image with recorded sound (Cooke 2008:7–8). In the 1890s, Thomas Edison specifically developed his Kinetoscope film process to supply synchronized visual illustrations for his already successful phonograph. While experiments using prerecorded sound continued throughout the first decade of the century, needless to say, they were not successful (Altman 2004:158–66).

During these early years, however, there were at least two ethnographic experiments that we know about. During the 1902 meeting of the International Congress of Americanists in New York, archaeologist Edward H. Thompson demonstrated his "synchronous" wax cylinder recordings and film footage of Yucatec Mayan dances (Thompson 1932:47–50). Although not presented in public, on his last field trip in 1930–31, Boas recorded Kwakwaka'wakw songs on wax cylinders while filming dances in Fort Rupert, British Columbia. Since he never edited or otherwise presented these field materials, we cannot know his intentions, but his efforts were suggestive (Ruby 2000:58–59).[30]

Curtis's cylinders could have been used in this way. Given the technology at the time, however, cylinders still raised two principal problems: their volume was not loud enough to be heard in large halls, and they still could not be precisely synchronized with the images. Thus, like other films, the sonic accompaniment would have been performed live by an orchestra or pianist/organist, depending on the size and elaborateness of the theater or occasion. These scores were almost always stock cues; only rarely was music custom written for a given film, as it was for the Curtis film.

Undoubtedly, Curtis was thinking of Gilbert's compositions as he commissioned a custom score for his *Head Hunters* film from John J. Braham (Gilbert, this volume).[31] According to the playbill for the Seattle showing of the film, the score was "Interpretive Music Composed by John J. Braham from Phonographic Records of Indian Music" (Holm and Quimby 1980:15). While Curtis probably sent Braham some Kwakwaka'wakw cylinders, there seems to have been no real aural influence (Harrison and Gilbert, this volume). Following musicologist Michael Pisani (2005:228), we can characterize Braham's style here as a kind of primitivist reference to Indianness. The generic nature of Braham's score was most likely due to circumstantial constraints, such as the abilities and interests of the composer and the amount of time he had to prepare the score. As well, Braham was almost a generation older than the other musicians who worked with Curtis. Still, Braham's generic style was quite characteristic of the representation of Indians in silent film music, almost all of which consisted of stereotypical stock compositions (Pisani 2005:295–98). The innovative aural representation possible in the *Head Hunters* film was not to be.

After *Head Hunters*:
The Fate of Curtis's Cylinders

All of Curtis's field materials were subjected to substantial disruption and dispersal, due primarily to his chronically precarious financial situation. Through these numerous upheavals, Curtis was able to keep some assets, and some went to his ex-wife in 1916 as part of their divorce settlement, but most were sold, along with their reproduction rights, to J. P. Morgan's son Jack in 1928. The status of Curtis's sound recordings is uncertain. In 1933, writing to ethnomusicologist George Herzog, Curtis explained, "Such phonographic records as were made in collecting material for the North American Indian are still in my possession—in storage." He went on to note that, unfortunately, "a part of the catalogue of them was destroyed by rats in a former storage house."[32] Curtis's categorical statement poses problems for what we know of the collection's subsequent history.

In 1935, the Morgan Company liquidated all of the assets of the North American Indian, Incorporated, selling them to a Boston book dealer. Some of the cylinders must have been part of this purchase, since the dealer sold them to the Archives of Traditional Music in 1956 (Seeger and Spear 1987: 80–83). Because all of the surviving cylinders came from the Morgan office, one is tempted to conclude that at one point the library may have had them all, losing some or most of them over the years. We do know that the Morgan Library kept many of the glass-plate negatives, but that most were given away or destroyed during World War II (Davis 1985:78). If Curtis had more, or even most, of the cylinders, then that would help explain the wider scope of his original recording, but it would then leave us with the problem of what happened to the rest of the corpus.

It is probably not accidental that none of the extant cylinders found their way to a public collection until after Curtis's death. We do know that during the project itself, Curtis expressed a desire to hold on to his field materials. In 1907, Curtis refused the request of his friend Edmond Meany to deposit his negatives, prints, and collections at the University of Washington (Davis 1985:52). He outlined a number of reasons: he still needed to raise financing for the project; he might need to move his headquarters to New York (as he later did, at least for the *NAI*); his wife would need the assets should he die; he did not trust the regents to preserve the collections intact; and he was unhappy with the lack of support from the Seattle elite.[33] And in 1912, Curtis initially objected to Gilbert's publication of his adaptations of the recordings, arguing, "I fear that the publication of the elaborated music will spoil the value of the material as it now stands. This music, published and available for concert use, would remove all the novelty of the music in connection with the pictures. I do not know whether I will ever make any great use of the music in this way, but my investment in it is still rather heavy."[34]

In the end, the cylinders appear to have been a victim of multiple circumstances. The most critical was Curtis's loss of control over at least some of them by their forfeiture in 1928 to an institution with little understanding or concern for such ethnographic materials. Curtis's cylinders did not fit in with the Morgan Library's institutional priorities: first, because they were Native American in subject matter, and second, because they were sound recordings. Other research libraries, such as the Huntington and the Newberry Libraries, did maintain Native American collections, but they consisted only of manuscripts, books, and artwork. And while the Morgan subsequently did amass a musical collection, it was devoted solely to Euro-American classical manuscripts and editions.

This raises the question of the creation of sound collections in the first place. As Richard Bauman notes (2011), when the technology was introduced, people were not sure whether sound recordings should be preserved by institutions, and if so, whether by libraries (like printed books), archives (like unpublished manuscripts), or museums (like unique artifacts). As it happened, it took much of the first half of the twentieth century for sound collections to be established, and they were incorporated in all three kinds of institutions (Hart and Kostyal 2003:58–61; Sterne 2003:325–33).[35]

For anthropology, the decades after World War II saw the progressive consolidation of ethnographic sound archives. Even the largest collections—at the American Museum of Natural History and the Smithsonian's Bureau of American Ethnology—transferred their wax cylinders to other repositories: respectively, to Indiana University (Archives of Traditional Music, established in 1948, based on an earlier collection begun by George Herzog at

Columbia University in 1936) and the Library of Congress (Archive of Folk Culture of the American Folklife Center, founded in 1928 as the Archive of American Folk Song).

Compounding these institutional factors was the simultaneous shift in recording technology. Curtis's fieldwork coincided with the age of wax cylinders. While these acoustic machines were already being superseded as a commercial medium by the early twentieth century, they were still widely used by amateur recordists—especially ethnographers—until the 1930s because of their portability and ease of use. During that decade, however, they were supplanted by the superior fidelity of electrical recording made possible by microphones and portable disk-cutting machines. While wax cylinders may have been obsolete, there was no technical reason why they could not have been transferred to disks. As early as 1906, the Berlin ethnographic sound archive had developed a mastering process to duplicate cylinders, and by the late 1940s, near the end of Curtis's life, the Library of Congress was copying cylinders onto disks. Nevertheless, these replicating methods were not used much.

This meant that for most purposes Curtis's sound recordings were fundamentally different from his photographs. Like most ethnographic sound recordings of his time, his cylinders were unique originals. Unlike photographs produced from a negative, the same medium that had captured the original performance was used to play it back, on the same kind of machine. It also meant that, unlike photographs, cylinders could not be edited or easily manipulated. This separated the wax cylinders from the commercial market of multiple copies. Thus it is understandable that a large collection of wax cylinders, produced without institutional support, would have been dispersed or destroyed. Few knew what to do with these records.[36] Finally, unlike all of the rest of Curtis's ethnographic productions, there would have been little or no commercial value in the cylinders.

There is still that collection of cylinders that Curtis supposedly had, but it would have suffered the same fate as the rest of his nonphotographic documentation, such as the many unique artifacts he collected (Gidley 1998a:81–82, 298; Holm and Quimby 1980:44–57, 127–28; Jacknis 2002a, 27–28, 54–55). Curtis's main commercial concern, his photographs, could be copied fairly easily, which they were. Yet even these were destroyed, lost, and widely dispersed, due to his bankruptcy and the loss of control of his company's assets. Whatever cylinders remained in Curtis's possession would have been divided among his heirs (his son and three daughters, and then their spouses and descendants). Yet there is one further possibility, suggested by Mick

Gidley (personal communication, 2010): that the cylinders have survived but have been separated from their documentation. They are out there but no one knows that Curtis recorded them, the same fate that had faced *Head Hunters* until Holm and Quimby's rediscovery of it at The Field Museum (introduction, this volume). In fact, such loss of provenance is a common occurrence with wax cylinders.[37]

Coda

As we now know, Curtis was mistaken in his fears about the disappearance of Kwakw<u>a</u>ka'wakw music and culture. Many of the ceremonies have continued and many of the songs that he recorded have been handed down and are still sung. Yet Curtis's ethnographic objects did not really, or completely, document this Native American cultural reality, as he intended. Instead, they recorded a cross-cultural encounter, created between and among Curtis's team and his Native interlocutors. While we may argue about whether Native American cultures have or have not disappeared, more accurately it is the particular moment of cross-cultural encounter that has vanished. It is this moment that survives in bits and pieces, in the primary tangible remains—such as the wax cylinders, photographs, films, and field notes—and the secondary texts derived from them.

As one historian has noted (Sterne 2003:287), the desire of early recordists to preserve sounds for the future was ironically contradicted by the fragility of those very recordings. Wax cylinders are subject to what conservators call "inherent vice." While the wax grooves are fairly stable in themselves, what is destructive is the playback technology: every time a cylinder is played—whether for transcription or public performance—the sonic content is degraded and lost. Although some of the Curtis cylinders remain, they are not the same objects that Curtis brought away from the field. Their fate matches that of the film's own survival, as well as that of Braham's unpublished score (only recently rediscovered, still incomplete).

The enormity of the Curtis project, coupled with his private, noninstitutional funding, compounded by his personal financial problems, meant that its published, public version existed in very few copies, and was practically archival material from the beginning. Subsequently, its own original material was widely scattered and even lost. In the process, the holistic, multimedia mode of Curtis's ethnography, which was so innovative, was largely dispersed or destroyed. It is this sad and obscured history that has contributed to the vastly inflated estimates of the corpus of Curtis's sound recordings. It

Ira Jacknis

has also meant that Curtis's sound ethnography has not become part of the subsequent literature on Kwakwa̱ka̱'wakw music. For whatever reason, Ida Halpern, the leading scholar of the subject in the twentieth century, did not cite Curtis (Cole and Mullins 1993:28). Until recently, the Curtis recordings were not widely distributed or consulted by the Native peoples he recorded, but this has changed substantially with new technologies.[38]

This history prompts us to consider the reproduction of ethnographic objects, reflecting in a hall of mirrors, or rather, in this case, a chamber of echoes. A progressive series of "transcriptions" transforms cultural information from one version to another. In such forms of appropriation and object creation, there is a temptation to view one state as the "authentic" version, but it is more accurate to regard each rendition as having its own status and validity.

The continuing vitality of Kwakwa̱ka̱'wakw music allowed Holm and Quimby to create their replacement score in 1973. While this new soundtrack may have seemed more "authentic," it was, in fact, a recreation of something that never really existed (Harrison, this volume). While it may have seemed more authentic to one cultural reality—that of the Kwakwa̱ka̱'wakw—it falsified the cultural reality of Curtis's own culture and how movie music was created and perceived in 1914 (Gilbert, this volume). The current project has gone far to maintain and restore the integrity of all alternate versions.

We have learned much in this traversal of Curtis's sound recordings, yet, as the cliché goes, mysteries remain. Surely this tale confirms the comment of photography critic A. D. Coleman (1998:133): "It seems the more we learn about Edward Sheriff Curtis, the more we find there is to know; for every answer received new questions arise."[39]

For generous sharing of research materials and information, I would like to thank the volume editors, Aaron Glass and Brad Evans, as well as Richard Bauman, Mick Gidley, Marilyn Graf, and Gina Rappaport. Also helpful were conversations with Klisala Harrison, Thomas R. Miller, and Wendy C. Wickwire.

1   All of George B. Grinnell's surviving recordings are preserved in the Archives of Traditional Music (hereafter referred to as ATM), Indiana University, Bloomington, Indiana.

2   Smaller efforts existed at The Field Museum (George A. Dorsey and James Murie on the Plains), the Southwest Museum (Charles F. Lummis with the Southwest and Native and Hispanic California), the University of Pennsylvania Museum of Archaeology and Anthropology (Frank Speck among eastern Indians), and the Harvard Peabody Museum (Jesse W. Fewkes in the Southwest, and psychologist Benjamin Ives Gilman at the Chicago World's Fair of 1893, both funded by patron Mary Hemenway). In Canada, the National Museum (now the Canadian Museum of Civilization) sponsored a similarly active program of sound recording by Marius Barbeau, James Teit, and Edward Sapir.

3   There are two principal sources on Curtis's sound recordings: the only known extant collection of 276 wax cylinders at the ATM; and the published musical transcriptions in *The North American Indian* (1907–30), which were derived from some of them. Another important source is the Curtis correspondence with composer Henry F. Gilbert, preserved in the Irving S. Gilmore Music Library, Yale University, which also contains some of his transcriptions (MSS 35). There are also two lists in the Edward S. Curtis Papers (GC 1143) in the Seaver Center for Western History Research, Natural History Museum of Los Angeles County: "Phonograph Records," listing seventy-five Plains cylinders (box 4B, folder 11); and "Catalogue of Phonograph Records-Series 200," with fourteen San Ildefonso cylinders (box 17, folder 8).

4   Curtis refers to Myers's role in a letter to Gilbert, April 17, 1912: "I am now writing to Myers to see if he has made a partial selection of his phonographic records to be worked up for the coming volume." This suggests that Myers made the initial recordings as well as the selection of which to publish. But he was evidently not the only recorder, as Myers indicates in another letter to Gilbert on May 14, 1912. Myers was sending Gilbert six records for the ninth volume, with the explanation, "The fewness is caused by a very unsatisfactory lot made by a careless o[p]erator who once worked Curtis while pretending to work for him"; Gilbert Papers (hereafter referred to as GP). According to Makepeace (2002:125), "Schwinke operated the Edison recording machine," while Myers took shorthand notes, when the party was among the Wishram in early 1910. However, she does not specify her exact source. Although it appears to be derived from one of Curtis's unpublished memoirs (in Gidley 2003b:87–91), that account has no reference to the sound recording.

5   Myers to Gilbert, August 26, 1912, GP. Significantly, Fischer had referred to the use of "international pitch" in his note on the music (in Curtis 1907–30, vol. 3:143). The issue of recording versus transcription pitches had been a subject of debate between Fillmore and Gilman (McNutt 1984:68).

6   See the published listing in Lee (1979:54–58). A more up-to-date listing is available on the ATM's catalogue on their website at http://www.indiana.edu/~libarchm/.

7   Curtis's preference for survey over intensive study thus matches the stance of Kroeber in his debate with Franz Boas over ethnographic strategy (Jacknis 2002b:525–26).

8   The documentation of the Curtis cylinder collection at Indiana is minimal, taken almost entirely from inscriptions on the cylinders and their boxes. These notations may include a tribe, a song title/type, sometimes a singer, the existence or tribal source of the texts, and a recording date.

9   As Curtis remembered the tribal coverage in a 1933 letter, without access to a catalogue (which he said had been destroyed), these were "the groups represented in the records": vol. 3 (Sioux, Yanktonai, Assiniboine); vol. 4 (Apsaroke Crow, Hidatsa); vol. 5 (Arikara, Mandan); vol. 6 (Piegan Blackfoot, Cheyenne, Arapaho); vol. 7 (Yakima, Klickitat, Interior Salish, Kutenai); vol. 8 (Nez Perce, Walla Walla, Umatilla, Chinookan tribes); vol. 9 (Salishan tribes of the Coast, Chimakum, Quilliute, Willapa); vol. 10 (Kwakiutl); vol. 11 (Nootka, Haida); vol. 12 (Hopi); vol. 19 (Wichita, Southern Cheyenne, Oto, Comanche). Edward S. Curtis to George Herzog, January 18, 1933; Herzog Papers, ATM.

10 Makepeace (2002:101) claims that Curtis submitted some of his cylinders to the Smithsonian committee investigating him in 1907, but as Gidley notes (1998a:136, 304–5), there is no contemporary evidence for this inquiry. Its first mention seems to have been Graybill and Boesen (1976:28).

11 Curtis recalled that recordings were made among the Wichita, Southern Cheyenne, Oto, and Comanche of Oklahoma. Curtis to Herzog, January 18, 1933, Herzog Papers, ATM.

12 See Graybill and Boesen (1976:13); Davis (1985:16, 253n4); Worswick (2001:14); Egan (2012:310, 322); George Horse Capture on the PBS American Masters website

Ira Jacknis

at http://www.pbs.org/wnet/americanmasters/episodes/edward-curtis/shadow-catcher/568/ (accessed March 28, 2013); and Eric J. Keller, director, Soulcatcher Studio, Santa Fe, New Mexico, at http://www.soulcatcherstudio.com/artists/curtis_cron.html (accessed March 28, 2013); and Wikipedia at http://en.wikipedia.org/wiki/Edward_S._Curtis (accessed March 28, 2013).

13 Fischer seems to have been the only one of Curtis's transcribers whom we know was part of the field party and thus could have taken down transcriptions directly. While Weber might have been present, Gilbert—who did the bulk of this work—certainly was not in the field, and thus would have worked completely from cylinders.

14 Transcribed songs with no extant cylinders: Assiniboine, Oto, Ponca, Hopi, and Chinook. (There are also transcriptions for the Teton and Dakota Sioux, Clallam, and Twana, but the cylinder identifications for these are uncertain in the Indiana catalogue.) Reported recordings with missing cylinders: Assiniboine, Sioux, Yanktonai, Wichita, Oto, Comanche, Hopi, Quilleute [sic]—and perhaps Walla Walla and Umatilla.

15 Gilbert Papers.

16 In his 1936 survey of North American ethnographic and folk music sound collections, George Herzog identified over 15,000 records—most of them cylinders—in almost forty collections, institutional and private (1936:582). Keeling (1997:xiii) conservatively estimates that 17,000 cylinders were recorded in Native American communities, between 1890 and 1940.

17 Curtis to Herzog, February 6, 1933, George Herzog Papers, ATM.

18 Because neither Fischer nor Weber—unlike Gilbert—can be found in accessible biographical sources, I will include some extra detail in these notes. Edgar Simpson Fischer was born in Philadelphia in 1873. His father, William G. Fischer (1835–1912), was a leader of religious choirs and the composer of more than two hundred hymns. Edgar Fischer studied in Berlin with noted violinist and composer Joseph Joachim. Around the turn of the century, he was invited to Whitman College in Walla Walla, Washington, by the university president (Stephen B. L. Penrose, 1894–1934), a friend of his father's. During his time at the Whitman Conservatory of Music, Fischer married Alice Reynolds, a piano teacher at the school. In 1906 the Fischers started a competing institution, the Fischer School of Music, but gave it up the following year, when the newly founded Walla Walla Symphony asked Fischer to serve as its conductor. Fischer held this post until his sudden death on March 18, 1922, at the age of forty-nine (Becker 2007).

19 Carl Alfred Weber, born in Dresden, Germany (January 27, 1863), married Elizabeth Johanna Bubach of Breslau, Germany (October 20, 1894). A student of the Royal Conservatory of Music, Dresden, Germany (1872–80), Weber served as assistant conductor of the Imperial German Marine Band. He immigrated to the United States in 1904 and the following year moved to Seattle, where, from 1905 until near the time of his death, Weber played the French horn in the Seattle Symphony Orchestra. He became a naturalized citizen on August 8, 1913 (Anonymous 1927:230). According to his death record in the Washington State Archives, Weber died on October 2, 1929. Perhaps not surprisingly, both Fischer and Weber lived in Washington State, Curtis's home base.

20 The challenge of transcribing Native American music in Western notation has been an enduring problem, and it was of keen concern for its first analysts during the late nineteenth century (Levine 2002). As Pisani notes, transcription involves an inevitable abstraction and bias, and he likens it to the difference between a photograph and the event itself (2005:227). A composer's creative musical interpretation is then a second-order interpretation, a "portrait of a musical photograph." While focusing on common aspects of vocal style and rhythm, Fischer (1908:142) and Gilbert (1911:166) differed on the matter of transcription practice and on how closely Western notation

systems can capture the subtleties of Native music and song. For example, while Fischer gives tempo markings only (e.g., "moderato," "andante"), Gilbert offers metronome marks (e.g., "mm = 120").

21 Although Gidley (1998a:89) suggests that Myers first visited the Kwakwa̱ka̱'wakw in 1909.

22 Around 1894, just after returning from his recording session at the Chicago World's Fair, Hunt asked Boas to supply him with a phonograph, but there is no evidence that he ever got one (Jacknis 1992:146, 150).

23 Question marks here indicate uncertainty as to whether the corresponding songs discussed in the tenth volume are identical or only similar in type to those recorded on the cylinders. Three of the eleven Kwakwa̱ka̱'wakw songs in the Indiana collection are available on the film project website at www.curtisfilm.rutgers.edu.

24 On baton rhythms, see Myers to Gilbert, November 26, 1912, and January 4, 1913, GP.

25 Despite their popularity, these "concerts" were still severely limited: records were played on machines with oversized horns or were listened to with individual earphones.

26 Most of Joseph Dixon's photographic collection is at the Mathers Museum of World Cultures, while his surviving cylinders are in the ATM, both at Indiana University.

27 By the premiere of the *Head Hunters* film in 1914, there had already been several ambitious music dramas (theater, opera, and film) based on Native American subjects (Pisani 2005:257–67; Gidley 1998a:214).

28 Some of Gilbert's musicale compositions did accompany film footage; cf. Curtis to Gilbert, August 7 and August 12, 1911, GP. A decade later, Gilbert composed a score to accompany an otherwise silent film about Yankee whaling, *Down to the Sea in Ships* (1922).

29 In the years between Curtis's death in 1952 and 2009, the only commercial reproduction of the cylinders came in brief excerpts in the two principal Curtis film biographies (McLuhan 1974 [film]; Makepeace 2000 [film]). In 2009 some of the Curtis musical corpus was released for the first time in disc format, although in a limited edition: twelve of the thirteen Haida recordings (Williams-Davidson 2009, disks 4, 5A, 5B, and 6A).

30 Both Thompson's and Boas's recorded music was thus what film scholars call "diegetic," that is, on the screen we can watch the sound that we are hearing being produced. Since Boas's materials have survived, we know that he actually filmed the cylinder machine and that his assistant changed the cylinders. None of the Braham score was like this, although at times in *Head Hunters* one can see people singing, dancing, and making music (Harrison, this volume).

31 Both John Braham's 1914 manuscript score for *Head Hunters* and David Gilbert's 2008 transcription are available in complete form through the Getty Research Institute's online library at http://www.getty.edu/research/library/.

32 Curtis to Herzog, January 18, 1933, and February 6, 1933; Herzog to Curtis, February 12, 1933; Herzog Papers, ATM.

33 Curtis to Edmond S. Meany, August 25, 1907, Edmond S. Meany Papers, Special Collections, University of Washington Library.

34 Curtis to Gilbert, October 28, 1912, GP.

35 The Phonogrammarchiv der Osterreichischen Akademie der Wissenschaften in Vienna was the first ethnographic sound archives, established in 1899, followed the next year by the Berlin Phonogramm-Archiv, which soon became the leading collection of its kind. By 1940, it had amassed about 11,000 cylinders and discs, before its substantial disruption during World War II (Berlin and Simon 2002).

36 The fate of Curtis's cylinders was by no means unprecedented. By the 1950s, only 47 of John Lomax's 250-plus cylinders of cowboy songs, recorded ca. 1910, had survived (Sterne 2003:325).

Ira Jacknis

37 There is little room on a cylinder itself for any written documentation. Notes were either placed on the tube or box container, which may easily be separated or lost, or spoken at the beginning of the recording.

38 According to Marilyn Graf (personal communication 2010), archivist at the Indiana collection, "General distribution of the Curtis recordings for non-commercial use, particularly to tribes represented in the collection, has been liberal, especially since the 1980s when our holdings went online through what is now Worldcat. Copies are also requested and provided to individuals for personal research, and occasionally museums and galleries. We can expect an order for Curtis cylinders every few months. A query arrived yesterday from a Northwest coast tribe for CD replacements of the cassettes they received several years ago."

39 On the spelling of Curtis's middle name, see chapter 1, note 1, this volume.

PHOTO ESSAY 1

"At the Kitchen Table with Edward Curtis"

JEFF THOMAS

Looking at First Nations peoples' pasts through a frame of photographs, paintings, and films produced by white society has always left me feeling uneasy due to the silences coming from these images. I would wonder what the indigenous sitters were thinking about during their experiences of being photographed, painted, or filmed. How did they see their world in comparison to how their world was being represented through the lenses and paintbrushes of white artists and anthropologists?

With so many questions in mind, I could not simply turn my back on photographic archives of indigenous peoples and let them languish in their stasis. And rather than feeling like another armchair tourist, I was determined to challenge the silences in the archive. I was faced with a complex question: How could I go about moving Eurocentric images from a passive position to an active one? I began by looking to my childhood for a point of departure from which to begin my journey.

I have a childhood memory of my mother hearing me crying and coming into the TV room where I was watching a Hollywood Western movie. She asked what was wrong, and I pointed at the TV and said that the Indians scared me. To settle me down, she said I that was an Indian but that I needn't be afraid, that I wasn't "that kind of Indian." So the question I had to live with was, What kind of Indian am I? I was reminded of this when the director Ali Kazimi was filming a documentary about my work called *Shooting Indians* (1997). Kazimi organized a trip to Seattle and Vancouver Island to interview people associated with the reedited Curtis film *In The Land of the War Canoes,* such as Bill Holm and Maggie Frank. What kind of Indian did Curtis see?

I have another early memory of the first time my father took me to a library. It was at the suggestion of my teacher, because I was having a hard time learning to read. While my father filled out the form for my library card, I wandered around the stacks and saw a book lying open on a table. I began paging through it and came across a portrait of a very distinguished-looking Indian man wearing buckskin clothing and feathers. When my father came over to get me, I looked up at him and saw a similarity between their faces.

These connections would eventually form a foundation for my work in the visual arts, influencing my photographic practice, my research, and my role as an independent curator. Like that young boy in the library, I continue to be fascinated by the past and with the challenge of building a new paradigm that unites the past and the present. The gateway to that past for me would be found in the work of photographer Edward S. Curtis and his monumental social and cultural study of indigenous people, *The North American Indian* (*NAI*).

This twenty-volume series, which records tribal life among indigenous communities throughout the North American west, came about because of Curtis's interest in the plight of Native North American peoples at the dawn of the twentieth century. Although many aspects of cultural tribal life had already ceased to exist in their original state by the time Curtis arrived, he tapped into the memories of elders for his text and their faces for his camera.

My first encounter with a Curtis photograph was in the 1970s. I was in a gift shop and came across a series of large-format cards adorned with faces of Native Americans, faces that had a power and luminance unlike others I had seen before. These were not the ubiquitous stiff and static Indians I was familiar with.

This encounter coincided with my emerging interest in photography and with teaching myself to use a camera. I had been searching for First Nations role models to build my artistic practice upon, but was unable to find any established Native photographers. Was I the only person who felt uncomfortable looking at representations of indigenous peoples from the nineteenth and early twentieth centuries? Where were the discourses challenging the silences put forward by such images? Why was no one else asking these questions? Or, if they were, how come they weren't being heard?

It was this void that influenced my decision to make a career out of photography. From my first encounters with Curtis's images I felt that I had found a potential gateway to the past, to a way to challenge the traditional format for imaging Indians. I was drawn to Curtis's unique framing—to the close physical proximity Curtis had with his sitters. From my perspective, the sitters exerted far more control over the image-making process than they had been given credit for.

This question of indigenous agency emerged from personal experiences with family elders living on the Six Nations reserve in southern Ontario. While staying at Six Nations as a child, I would sit in the kitchen and listen to my elders tell stories about life on the reserve. Topics ranged from politics to everyday gossip to the price of pigs. The best stories took place when visitors stopped by the farm or while driving back and forth between Buffalo and the reserve.

Given my fascination with conversations and storytelling, it is not surprising that I was uncomfortable with the silences I perceived in most photographs of First Nations peoples. But the Curtis photographs hint at conversation. They made me long to hear their subjects' voices. They made me lonely for my elders and reminded me of the powerful influence they had had on me.

One day, one of my elders, Emily General, spoke about an anthropologist from Ottawa who had come to the reserve to see her father when she was a child. She wondered what had happened to the information that the anthropologist collected. As an impressionable young boy, I made a vow that one day I would find out and bring that information back to her. I did, in fact, find that information, at the Canadian Museum of Civilization, and subsequently curated an exhibition—*Emergence from the Shadow: First Peoples' Photographic Perspectives*—based partly on the photographs made by the anthropologist Sir Francis Knowles at Six Nations in 1912. One of the photographs was of Jacob General, Emily's father. Unfortunately, Emily had passed away by this time.

Yet Emily's story of the Ottawa anthropologist influenced the conversation I would eventually pursue with Curtis. I could imagine Curtis stopping by the family homestead on the reserve in 1912 and sitting at the kitchen table and describing his reason for being there. I could imagine Curtis talking about what he had witnessed and experienced—it must have been much more than what the *NAI* gives evidence of. I could imagine how it would have changed the look of his work had he included evidence, for example, of the cross-cultural effects he saw.

The quest for me then, in this photo essay, is to search for these "outtakes" and to use my own work to suggest what they may have looked like. With this in mind, I began my journey into the world of photography with the belief that what I saw in books and magazines was only a small part of the archive. These were photographs that nonindigenous people thought were worth taking. These were photographs that nonindigenous people thought were worth publishing. Perhaps an indigenous person like me would choose to highlight different aspects of the photographic archive. When, in the *NAI*, Curtis says that he doesn't know what was on the "other side" of assimilation (Curtis 1907–30, vol. 3: xii–xiii), he left the gateway open to someone like me to pick up where he left off. Perhaps I could have a conversation with Curtis around the metaphorical kitchen table.[1]

Indian Time

Fig. E.1.1. Jeff Thomas, *Indian Time*, 2005.
Left: Edward S. Curtis, *In a Piegan Lodge [Little Plume and His Son Yellow Kidney]*,
March 11, 1910. Library of Congress, LC-USZ62-61749. *Right:* Jeff Thomas, *Red Indian*,
Queen Street, Toronto, Ontario, 2003. Courtesy of the artist.

Edward Curtis attributes the genesis of his project to a visit he made in 1898—at the invitation of naturalist George Bird Grinnell—to a Piegan summer ceremonial gathering in northern Montana. Curtis was very impressed by the ceremonies that he witnessed, and, due to his belief that such events would inevitably die out because of white society's pressure on indigenous people to assimilate, he decided to gather existing information from tribal elders.

Curtis's experience at the Piegan gathering is one of the possible catalysts for the development of his photographic stagings and strategies that, in many cases, omitted any evidence of contact with white society. Throughout the thirty years that Curtis devoted to the production of the *NAI*, he remarked that he saw himself as a historian first and as a photographer second. This is a significant point, because the restaging and photographing of scenes of tribal life were done mainly to illustrate his text. It is my view that the photographs cannot be separated from the text—they must be seen in the context of the overall publication.

Unfortunately, however, the Curtis images are rarely discussed in conjunction with his text. It is this omitted context that I am continuously searching for in images that catch my attention. In photographs of indigenous

Jeff Thomas

peoples, far too often the absence of such context produces an isolated figure in an imaginary world, much like a museum. I continue to search historical photographs for signs that may give clues to when and where they were made, who the people were, and why they were photographed.

In addition to the insight that the text provides on Curtis's work, looking at unedited photographs provides another layer of information that is critical to my engagement with it. The Library of Congress has several versions of a photograph of Yellow Kidney and his family, one of which includes a clock on the ground between the two men (see also Zamir, this volume). He did not include the clock in the version in the *NAI* in order to remove any signs of modernity. But, from my perspective, the inclusion of the clock is a poignant reminder of how quickly the Piegan world was changing. It prompts me to tell a story about Indian Time:

I am sitting in the research room at Library and Archives Canada and look up to see Edward S. Curtis walking through the large glass doors. Here is my opportunity to ask him all of the questions I had been carrying for many years. I introduce myself as a photographer who is also First Nations and explain how provocative I find his work and how the questions it raises help me develop my own practice.

JT: I am curious about *The Piegan Lodge* image I found on the Library of Congress website—the one that includes the clock. I responded to your image with a photograph of an antique store in Toronto that has the words "Red Indian" on its sign. For me, the name on the store front has photographic value in itself, but it is the large clock that made it far more appealing. You edited the clock out of *In a Piegan Lodge* for the final version in the *NAI*. Why did you do that? Was it symbolic of how you felt pressure to stop time before the traditions and knowledge of the people you were photographing were lost?

EC: The great changes in practically every phase of the Indian's life that have taken place, especially within recent years, have been such that had the time for collecting much of the material, both descriptive and illustrative, herein recorded, been delayed, it would have been lost forever. The passing of every old man or woman means the passing of some tradition, some knowledge of sacred rites possessed by no other; consequently the information that is to be gathered, for the benefit of future generations, respecting the mode of life of one of the great races of mankind, must be collected at once or the opportunity will be lost for all time. (Curtis 1907–30, vol. 1:xvi–xvii)

Culture Revolution

Fig. E.1.2. Jeff Thomas, *Culture Revolution,* 1984.
Queen Street, Toronto, Ontario. Courtesy of the artist.

My conversation with Edward Curtis took an unexpected turn in 1984 while making a portrait of my son, Bear, during a photo walk. I stopped to photograph a brick wall spray painted with the words "Culture Revolution" and decided to pose Bear in front of the wall, thinking it would make a nice memento for him. But when I saw the print in my darkroom, I realized something new had emerged.

I was intrigued by the contrast and juxtaposition of the elements within the frame—over the brim of Bear's baseball cap is a Curtis portrait of Two Moons, a renowned Cheyenne warrior and leader who was also a veteran of the infamous Battle of the Little Big Horn in 1876. The brick wall represented the wall I felt myself running up against as I attempted to address questions

Jeff Thomas

of representation and of who or what makes an "authentic" Indian. I saw my reflection in my son and recalled the feeling of invisibility I felt growing up as an urban Iroquoian person and the absence of photographs showing First Nations people living in cities.

JT: The first time I saw Two Moons was on my son's baseball cap, the same portrait I found in portfolio 6, plate no. 213, of the *NAI*. Can you tell me something about Two Moons?

EC: Two Moons was one of the Cheyenne chiefs at the battle of Little Bighorn in 1876, when Custer's command was annihilated by a force of Sioux and Cheyenne.[2]

JT: What is your impression of the Cheyenne people?

EC: The Cheyenne character instinctively resents imposition. Even to-day the poor fragment of a tribe existing on the Northern Cheyenne reservation in Montana displays individuality and courage worthy of consideration. The majority of Indian tribes, realizing the utter hopelessness of resistance against the wrong done them by individuals and by the Government, accepted such imposition sullenly, perhaps, but without conflict. Not so with the Cheyenne, who ever retaliated even when he must have known his cause to be hopeless. (Curtis 1907–30, vol. 6:91)

JT: It is said that Two Moons belonged to the Kit Fox warrior society. What role did warrior societies play among the Cheyenne?

EC: In addition to their dances and their raids, the warrior societies performed the duties of the so-called soldiers common to all plains peoples. They were the camp police, and they preserved order on the general buffalo hunt. They enforced the orders of the chiefs. But more than that, their wishes were consulted before any matter of public interest was settled. They were in fact the real ruling power, the only body that could compel obedience. (Curtis 1907–30, vol. 6:108)

JT: You might be interested to know that Two Moons was one of three Indian men that designer James E. Fraser used for the Indian head nickel. The other two were Chief Adoeette (Big Tree), who was a Kiowa, and a Cheyenne chief named Chief Iron Tail. The model for the buffalo on the reverse was a bison from the New York City Zoo named Black Diamond.

Returning the Gaze:
Black Eagle and Kevin Haywahe

Fig. E.1.3. Jeff Thomas, *Returning the Gaze: Black Eagle and Kevin Haywahe*, 2005.
Left: Edward S. Curtis, *Black Eagle [Wa"bŭdi-sápa—Assiniboin]*, ca. 1908. Library of Congress,
LC-USZ62-105371. *Right:* Jeff Thomas, *Kevin Haywahe in Powwow Dance Attire, Assiniboine tribe*, Carry-the-Kettle Reserve, Saskatchewan, 1991. Courtesy of the artist.

JT: I am intrigued by two images of Assiniboine men. My image is of powwow dancer Kevin Haywahe, whom I first met at an urban powwow
in Winnipeg in 1990. He is a renowned "traditional" dancer who performed with the American Indian Dance Theater. The traditional dancer
category draws its style from the old-time Plains warrior society. Your
photograph is of Black Eagle. Your daughter, Florence Graybill Curtis,
related a story about your attempt to photograph Black Eagle and his
refusal, his determination not to give the white man any more information. Black Eagle eventually relented when you told him, through an

interpreter, that Black Eagle's descendents would look for him among all of the photographs of prominent men, and would feel a sense of disappointment and loss by not finding him there. People who see your work are often not aware of the extensive information you provide in the *NAI* on the people you photograph. They see a stereotypical generic "Indian" and nothing more. Who was Black Eagle?

EC: [He was] Assiniboin. Born in 1834 on the Missouri below Williston, North Dakota. He was only thirteen years of age when he first went to war, and on this and on the next two occasions he gained no honors. On his fourth war excursion he was more successful, alone capturing six horses of the Yanktonai. While engaged in a fight with the Atsina near Fort Belknap, Montana, he killed a man and a boy. In a battle with the Yanktonai he killed one of the enemy, and in another repeated the former success. Black Eagle led war-parties three times. He had a vision in which it was revealed to him that he would capture horses, and the vision was fulfilled. He had the same experience before he killed the man and the boy. He claims no medicine. Black Eagle married at age of eighteen. (Curtis 1907–30, vol. 3:182–183)

Medicine Crow

Fig. E.1.4. Jeff Thomas, *Medicine Crow*, 2010.
Left: Edward S. Curtis, *Medicine Crow—Apsaroke*, ca. 1908. Library of Congress, LC-USZ62-106886. *Center:* Jeff Thomas, red-tailed hawk photographed at the Alberta Birds of Prey Foundation, Coaldale, Alberta, 2006. Courtesy of the artist. *Right:* Edward S. Curtis, *Medicine Crow*, ca. 1908.Library of Congress, LC-USZ62-98537.

When I saw Medicine Crow's portrait for the first time I was curious about the bird he wore on his head and wished I could see it in greater detail. I was reminded of the way I photographed powwow dancers by first making a full-length portrait—both front and back—and then moving closer and making detailed studies of their outfits. I was intrigued by the transformation dancers made from their everyday lives into dancers, and how it literally transformed each into an ancient personality, one handed down from generation to generation. During this process, a thousand years of cultural development and survival appeared before my eyes.

I searched through volume 4 of the *NAI* for additional information on Medicine Crow and found a short description by Curtis of plate 117: "The hawk fastened on the head is illustrative of the manner of wearing the symbol of one's tutelary spirit."[3]

Jeff Thomas

JT: Although you did not single Medicine Crow out for an extended description of the hawk he is wearing on his head, could you elaborate on your overall impression of North American Indian people and their sense of connection to their world?

EC: Rather than being designed for mere embellishment, the photographs are each an illustration of an Indian character or of some vital phase in his existence. Yet the fact that the Indian and his surroundings lend themselves to artistic treatment has not been lost sight of, for in his country one may treat limitless subjects of an aesthetic character without in any way doing injustice to scientific accuracy or neglecting the homelier phases of aboriginal life. Indeed, in a work of this sort, to overlook those marvellous touches that Nature has given to the Indian country, and for the origin of which the native ever has a wonder-tale to relate, would be to neglect a most important chapter in the story of an environment that made the Indian much of what he is. Therefore, being directly from Nature, the accompanying pictures show what actually exists or has recently existed (for many of the subjects have already passed forever), not what the artist in his studio may presume the Indian and his surroundings to be. (Curtis 1907–30, vol. 1:xiii–xiv)

JT: You highlighted Medicine Crow, of the Mountain Crow band, in the biographical sketch section of volume 4. What were your impressions?

EC: [Medicine Crow was] born [in] 1848. Mountain Crow; member of the Newly Made Lodge clan and of the Lumpwood organization. At eighteen he fasted four days and three nights, and on the morning of the fourth day a spirit resembling a white man appeared and foretold the passing away of the buffalo and the coming of many white men with cattle, horses, and steamboats. His medicine of hawk was purchased from another man. Counted three first coups, captured five guns and two tethered horses, and led ten successful war-parties. In a fight with the Nez Perces he killed a warrior, counted first coup upon him, and captured his gun—two regular honors at one time, besides the distinction of killing an enemy. This act he twice repeated in battles with the Arapaho and the Sioux. Twice he fought on the side of the white men when "their flag was on the ground": once against the Nez Perces in Chief Joseph's retreat, and again under General Crook when the Sioux under Sitting Bull were fleeing across the Canadian border. (Curtis 1907–30, vol. 4:203)

JT: What is the Lumpwood society?

EC: There were four tribal societies—Lumpwood, Fox, Big Dog, and Muddy Hand. While all embodied minor features designed for social entertainment, they were in reality military organizations. Among them existed a spirit of intense rivalry in war, and in the case of the Lumpwood and Fox societies, their members extended this rivalry to affairs of the heart. (Curtis 1907–30, vol. 4:13)

Indian Families

Fig. E.1.5. Jeff Thomas, *Indian Families*, 2010.
Left: Photographer unknown, Jim Abikoki and family in front of the fence surrounding the Anglican Mission on the Blackfoot (Siksika) Reserve, Alberta, ca. 1900. Glenbow Museum Archives, NC-5-8. *Center:* Edward S. Curtis, *Yellow Bone Woman [Arikara tribe]*, ca. 1908, North Dakota. Library of Congress, LC-USZ62-101183. *Right:* Jeff Thomas, *Good Eagle Family*, Bismarck, North Dakota, 1996. Courtesy of the artist.

JT: The undercurrent of pressing issues facing the communities—poverty, government paternalism, restrictions of ceremonies, pressures to assimilate, and a forced program of residential school training for children—are not evident in your images. But once I began to research the *NAI*, I found that you had, in fact, addressed social issues in your texts. For example, you noted the great pressures the Sioux were under. Could you tell me more about that?

EC: The great change that now comes to the Sioux and to other tribes of the plains with the opening of their reservations to settlement and in the consequent increased contact with alien influences will, within the present generation, further demoralize and degenerate. This, however, is one of the stages through which from the beginning the Indians were destined to pass. Those who cannot withstand these trying days of the metamorphosis must succumb, and on the other side of the depressing period will emerge the few sturdy survivors. (Curtis 1907–30, vol. 3:xii–xiii)

JT: During the years you worked in Alberta and Saskatchewan, the Indian residential school system was in place and indigenous children were being forced to leave their families and attend schools that were often far from their communities. In Canada, the Indian commissioner Hayter Reed wrote in 1908 that it was imperative for schools to prevent parents from taking away their children "as the whim might seize them" and to stop "Indian visitors hanging about the schools, and so unsettling the minds of the children, as well as too often insisting upon carrying them off for visits to their homes, from which they would only be recovered with much difficulty if at all."[4] Did you encounter anything like that while working in the United States?

EC: [Hopi Reservation, Arizona, 1906.] The determination of government officials to enforce education crystallized sentiment, and the party that favored active resistance to restraint packed up their goods and chattels, marched forth from the pueblo, and built the new village of Hotavila about four miles distant. Here they live with only the unavoidable minimum of contact with the white race, whom they unostentatiously but cordially hate…. Their chief, recently released after a prison term of several years, during which no doubt he had abundant time to ponder on the futility of a Hopi insisting that his children be educated in his own ancient fashion when some individual two thousand miles away ordered him to cut their hair and deliver them at the schoolhouse…. Henceforth they will formally obey orders, because they know of the force that lurks behind them, but many years will pass before they enter into the spirit of American education for their children. (Curtis 1907–30, vol. 12:15)

The End Is Near

Fig. E.1.6. Jeff Thomas, *The End Is Near*, 2010.
Left: Edward S. Curtis, *Ndee Sangochonh, Apache*, ca. 1906. Library of Congress, LC-USZ62-106797. *Center:* Jeff Thomas, *Construction Site*, Ottawa, Ontario, 2007. Courtesy of the artist. *Right:* Edward S. Curtis, *Nŏ́va—Walpi [Pursuing a Butterfly, Badger Clan, Hopi, Walpi-Pueblo]*, 1906. Library of Congress, LC-USZ62-124180.

Curtis opens the *NAI* with the image *The Vanishing Race*, which shows a group of Indian people riding single file toward a murky horizon (see fig. E.2.5). The image coveys the sentiment of the time—"the Indian race was dying out." This sentiment was based on the fact that at the dawn of the twentieth century the death rate in Native American communities exceeded the birth rate, and that indigenous peoples were being absorbed into mainstream society through forced assimilation programs such as the residential school system. But by the twenty-first century, a new sense of self and perseverance had surfaced in the indigenous world, and self-determination was increasingly political and being culturally asserted, visualized, and performed.

While admittedly idealized and incomplete, Curtis's photographs can be used, on our own terms, in our efforts to heal. They are a gateway for indigenous people to revisit their own histories and to remember and recall stories that their elders may have passed on to them. I imagine that the metamorphosis Curtis alluded to in the first photograph of the series—*The Vanishing*

Race—was not a statement of fact; it was a question. The question mark had just been left off. Would we be completely absorbed into mainstream society, without a trace of our Indianness left? Or would we do as all previous generations had done—adapt to the new challenges but remain Indian?

1   Throughout this essay, the words attributed to Curtis are direct quotations from *The North American Indian*. All page numbers are taken from the online edition of the *NAI* derived from a copy held by the Charles Deering McCormick Library of Special Collections, Northwestern University Library (http://curtis.library.northwestern. edu/).
2   This description is taken from the caption to plate 213 featured in portfolio 6 of Curtis (1907–30, vol. 6).
3   This description is taken from the caption to plate 117 featured in portfolio 4 of Curtis (1907–30, vol. 4).
4   Dominion of Canada, *Annual Report of the Department of Indian Affairs for the Year Ended 1891* (Ottawa: MacLean Roger & Co., 1891), 201.

Jeff Thomas

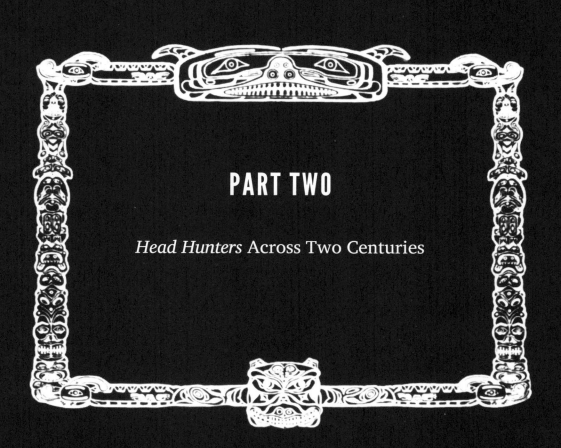

PART TWO

Head Hunters Across Two Centuries

5

CONSUMING THE *HEAD HUNTERS*

A Century of Film Reception

AARON GLASS AND BRAD EVANS

People have a hard time knowing what to make of Edward Curtis, although they always find something to do with him. His huge corpus of romantic, sepia-toned photographs of Native Americans—reproduced on everything from calendars to screen savers—has practically defined the "Indian" in the popular imaginary. He has been alternately valorized and vilified, celebrated for contributing an invaluable record of traditional Native lifeways and castigated for staging scenes and denying the lived reality of Native life. The operational metaphors of photography—"shooting," "capturing," "picturing"—all communicate some of the ambivalence and ambiguity surrounding Curtis and his work.

Since the late 1970s, Curtis has also entered into the discourse of ethnographic cinema, after his 1914 film, *In the Land of the Head Hunters*, was restored, reedited, and released as *In the Land of the War Canoes*. Since then, it has partially displaced *Nanook of the North* (1922) as "the very first narrative documentary film" (Gidley 1998a:3) and the "first full length documentary motion picture of aboriginal North Americans" (Holm and Quimby 1980: preface), although elsewhere in this volume we take issue with its classification as a "documentary" per se, and *Nanook* remains the more famous film by far. Despite the obvious difference in tone between Flaherty's film (sober, humanistic, focused on technology and ecology) and Curtis's (sensationalistic, melodramatic, focused on ceremony and warfare), there are a series of ways in which both films embody a similar set of contradictory tendencies that are characteristic, perhaps, of many ethnographic films as well as of some feature films with ethnographic subjects (Browne, this volume). Both juxtapose desire for authenticity with a reliance on historical reconstruction and imposed narrative devices; both combine specific, localized cultural detail with generalized pictures of regional Natives; both mix artistic and aesthetic sensibilities with claims to ethnographic or scientific authority (to which Curtis also adds a dose of spectacle); and both presented Native people as exotic but humanized and not completely savage.

In fact, the richness of *Head Hunters*—and its lasting effect on critics if not on general audiences—seems to stem in part from this semantic openness, the indeterminacy which, while part of all film practice, is so apparent in Curtis's deeply ambiguous project. This lack of coherence can allow space for new audiences to see it with new eyes, new agendas, new contexts. Here, we track some of the multiple readings of Curtis's film (in both original and restored versions) over time, examining the slippages that occur between his original intentions and various audiences' receptions. Specifically, we attend to immediate responses in 1914, critical interpretation in recent years, and reception of the film in Kwakw<u>aka</u>'wakw communities. In doing so, we explore some of the meanings and messages that Curtis's film has conveyed—some key moments in its recontextualization and resignification.

In Situ, In Tempo

Curtis's original motivation to produce a film was to seek commercial success in order to finance his life work, the twenty-volume *The North American Indian*. The context for his photographic and filmic work was a common notion—reinforced by Curtis's liberal use of the phrase "vanishing race"—that Native people were rapidly disappearing and that records had to be made before it was to late. While anthropologists were out trying to record details of indigenous language, belief, and practice, Hollywood was pounding out Indian-themed melodramas and picturesque travelogues (Evans, this volume). Curtis hoped to cash in on the popular demand for such fare, as well as his growing reputation as a man of adventure, to produce a work that would appeal as art, science, and entertainment (Gidley 1998a:237–45). While critically well received along a variety of these lines, the film was a financial disaster, and Curtis abandoned his hopes of producing a series of such films as fundraising enterprises and dramatic records of Native life. In this section, we discuss the details of the film's distribution and examine four themes that defined critical response at the time of its release: Curtis as an authority on

Indians; the film's supposed authenticity; the film as a blend of science and entertainment; and the film as aesthetic spectacle.

The simultaneous premiers of *Head Hunters* in December 1914 at the Moore Theatre in Seattle (at Second Avenue and Virginia Street) and the Casino Theatre in New York (at 39th Street and Broadway) corresponded directly with the boom of opulent movie palaces around the country, but neither the Moore nor the Casino were known for exhibiting motion pictures. The Casino specialized in musical comedies and operetta; tellingly, it was at the Casino that Theodore Dreiser's *Sister Carrie* used her good looks to get a start on the chorus line, and she delighted after her first night in the fact that it was "still redolent of the perfumes and blazonry of the night, and notable for its rich, oriental appearance … above the common mass, above idleness, above want, above insignificance" (Dreiser 2006:269). While the orientalist decor described by Carrie was like that of many of the movie palaces built at the time to showcase the new silent feature films, vast halls with exotic atmospherics and mighty Wurlitzers, the 875-seat Casino was primarily a musical theater house that occasionally showed a film—not a motion picture house that occasionally staged vaudeville, as was the Strand, its 2,989-seat neighbor at 49th and Broadway that opened in April 1914. Catering to the better classes, with the first theater roof garden in New York, the Casino was run by the Shubert brothers, influential New York show producers who also became major partners in the World Film Corporation when it formed in 1914. At the Casino, the premier of *Head Hunters* was sandwiched between those of two musical comedies, *Suzi*, which perhaps links to the Curtis production by way of the exoticism of its setting in Budapest, and an upscale comedy of manners, *Lady Luxury*. The theater would continue to specialize in musical theater, not cinema, up to the time it was demolished in 1930.[1] Significantly larger than the Casino, seating well in excess of two thousand patrons, the Moore Theatre in Seattle was similar in being not a devoted movie palace but a hall for musical comedy and vaudeville productions.[2] Presentational formats were flexible: vaudeville shows featured short films, while silent films featured live musical prologues and accompaniment.

It has long been thought that *Head Hunters* disappeared shortly after these screenings. We now know that it had a limited, but nationwide, distribution. After opening at the Montauk Theatre in Brooklyn, its run was extended an extra week "owing to the interest aroused" (*Brooklyn Daily Eagle*, December 20, 1914:12). On Tuesday February 9, 1915, a "special rendering" of the film was made at Carnegie Hall in New York City to benefit the Yorkville Social Centre, which serviced the immigrant community on Manhattan's Upper East

Side (see playbill in fig. A.1.16). Later that month, *Head Hunters* was screened alongside other "high class five and six-reel features" at the Orpheum in Eau Claire, Wisconsin, which described itself as a movie house dedicated to "clean and instructive pictures" that could be seen by youth as well as their parents (*Eau Clair Sunday Leader*, February 21, 1915). There was another benefit screening of the film at the end of the month at the Shubert-owned Belasco Theater in Washington, DC, for which the publicity was notably different from most others in that it identified "the Kwakiutl Indians of Puget Sound" by name (if by inaccurate locale) (*Washington Herald*, February 24, 1915). The film showed on September 23, 1915, alongside *The Cotton King*, a drama of business and romance starring George Nash, at the Oakland Municipal Auditorium (now known as the Henry J. Kaiser Convention Center), a building opened in 1914 as a hub for entertainment and sporting events (*Oakland Tribune*, September 23, 1915). In Fairbanks, Alaska, *Head Hunters* was screened in January 1916, and the contextual material from the *Fairbanks Sunday Times* clearly marked it out as a "quality" film (January 23, 1916).[3] In Placerville, a small gold rush town in central California, the film was screened at the Elite, a dedicated movie house that quite frequently showed specialty feature films. The *Placerville Mountain Democrat* described the film as having "sound educational value," but it also suggested that "Mr. Curtis at all times has subordinated the ethnological element to the telling of a thrilling, gripping story" ("Holiday Bill at the Elite," *Placerville Mountain Democrat*, February 26, 1916). In early 1915, the film journal *Motography* (Vol. 13, No. 5:188) classified *Head Hunters* as a "multiple reel educational" and called it "high class," distinguishing it from most films at the time.

A suggestion by Richard Abel (2006) about the way that films were being classified at the time explains why these billings might have accounted for some of the trouble the film had at gaining the wide audience Curtis desired. Abel has argued that critics were busy delineating class distinctions between films for mass audiences and those for discriminating audiences, and that a line had been drawn between action-based Westerns by American companies such as Bison, and art films on Indian and western subjects by foreign companies such as Pathé. Whereas the American Westerns had "snap and go action" and a realist bent, the others were romantic, artistic, and beautifully colored—and this even after James Young Deer, the first major director identified at the time as being Native American, went to work for Pathé after 1910 (Abel 2006:80).[4] Curtis's elaborately artful film would not have played into this narrative about the Americanization of the genre, leading one to wonder what its reception would have been like in Europe and elsewhere around the world. No trace of such a worldwide distribution has yet been found.

The story of *Head Hunters'* distribution by the World Film Corporation also tells us quite a bit about the kind of film it aspired to be, as well as offering some additional clues about its subsequent disappearance.[5] That records of Curtis's film disappeared after its initial screenings in 1914 and 1915 does not necessarily imply that the film itself was unable to hold an audience. Not only were most of the films released during that period lost—and most much more permanently—but the failure of the film may have had as much to do with World Film as with anything in Curtis's control. In 1914, World Film was a brash new company that specialized in importing foreign spectacle films and independent features, and it grabbed much attention in the trade papers. It was founded in a partnership between the Russian-born eccentric Lewis Selznick and two brothers known for their successful New York theaters, Lee and Jacob Shubert. Selznick had gotten his start in the movies only a year earlier, when he became involved briefly with Universal, and then as the importer of Italian spectacle films such as the eight-reel *The Last Days of Pompeii* (1913). For their part, the Shubert brothers had been booking movies for their theaters at least as early as 1908 and, as already mentioned, were the owners of the Casino Theatre, where *Head Hunters* premiered. The company's success was intense but short-lived. In 1914, Selznick managed to lure one of the most famous silent film actresses, Clara Kimball Young, away from Vitagraph, and to hire a number of well-known French directors and filming personnel, including Maurice Tourneur and Capellani. Over the next few years, the company produced or distributed over three hundred films, many of which can be characterized by their technical and artistic aspirations, in line with the foreign films they were importing.

Curtis's own ideas about the art of the motion picture are in line here. Tourneur, for example, was known for his use of natural locations and lighting effects; Albert Capellani for his excellence with actresses. They contributed to World Film's penchant for film adaptations of literary texts, directing such titles as *Trilby* (1915), *The Pit* (1915), *Life's Whirlpool* (based on Frank Norris's *McTeague*, 1916), and *La Vie de Boheme* (1916). World Film also released at least one legitimate documentary alongside *Head Hunters*, called *The Adventures of a Boy Scout* (1915), a five-reel production that featured an appearance by President Woodrow Wilson (Lewis 1987b:167). *Head Hunters* earned $3,269 for World Film in 1915, almost all of it in the first half of the year. By December, its receipts had dwindled to zero. It was not the worst-performing of World Film's special releases, but it was far from the best. The

Boy Scout movie, by way of comparison, brought in $13,726 during the same period, and *America* (1914), a six-reel special feature produced by Shubert, earned $45,105.[6] At any rate, by the spring of 1916, World Film itself was facing considerable troubles, Selznick having bolted from the company with his star, Clara Kimball Young, and investors showing great skepticism about its future. In early 1917, *Head Hunters* was being sold (with its posters) for $60 by the Philadelphia distributor G. W. Bradenburgh (*Moving Picture World*, March 3, 1917:1423), although their relationship with the World Film Corporation is unclear. By the end of 1918, the company had largely shut down, and the number of its films surviving in their entirety is quite low (Lewis 1987a:50).[7] The point for our purposes is that the disappearance of *Head Hunters* is not necessarily a reflection of its success, or its lack thereof. But its association with World Film and the story of its known distribution to the higher class of new movie palaces helps us understand the kind of film it meant to be: artsy, European-influenced, higher-class, dramatic, and spectacular.

As for Curtis, his reputation as a friend of and authority on Native Americans increased steadily after his participation in the famous 1899 Harriman Expedition to Alaska. Theodore Roosevelt wrote the 1907 opening inscription of volume one of *The North American Indians*, assuring readers that Curtis "has lived on intimate terms with many different tribes.... He knows them ... has caught glimpses into the strange spiritual and mental life of theirs" (in Holm and Quimby 1980:13). Curtis often claimed in interviews that he had been initiated into many tribal societies and ceremonial positions across the continent (Gidley 1998a:90). The film's publicity materials as well as press responses constantly presented Curtis as an expert, based on his lengthy time spent with Native people; this is standard fare as a trope of ethnographic authority, shared with the first generation of professional anthropological fieldworkers around the same time (Clifford 1988).[8] Early reviewers highlighted his reputation as a means of authenticating the film. A 1915 article in *The Strand* titled "Filming the Head-Hunters: How 'The Vanishing Race' is Being Preserved in Moving Pictures," began by calling Curtis the "greatest authority on the American Indians to-day," and included an interview in which Curtis himself declared, "Years ago I witnessed some of the performances.... [The film] represents three actual years of work in the field" (in Holm and Quimby 1980:121). Likewise, Bush (1914) subtitled his review in *The Moving Picture World* "Remarkable motion picture produced by Edward S. Curtis, famous authority on North American Indians" and later called him "a profound student of Indian lore." Seattle papers skewed such stories toward the celebration of a hometown hero. The *Seattle Sunday Times*

(December 6, 1914) began a review, "The entry of Edward S. Curtis into the motion picture field has been entirely logical—as logical as he has always been in his life-long devotion to an ideal, the patient, sincere search for the big truths behind the stony face of the American aborigine.... Fidelity to type has always been the moving force of the Curtis pictures and he was determined that his motion pictures must have the same quality to be worthy of him." One industry paper even advertised the distribution of the film with a full-length portrait of Curtis himself (see fig. A.1.23).

Beyond Curtis's own stated credentials, many commentators addressed the accuracy of events portrayed and the authenticity of participants and settings—all heavily promoted on film posters (appendix 1)—even when these facts contradicted the truth. Curtis himself was no doubt responsible for maintaining certain fictions about his production in print. He is said to have hated the artificial nature of most Indian films, and he proposed to the Smithsonian, from whom he sought funding, that his would be "not carelessly caught fragments of superficial, indifferent matter, but rather carefully studied and worked out subjects, in order that every picture be an unquestioned document" (in Holm and Quimby 1980:32). Furthermore, the handbill produced for the 1914 premiere at the Moore Theatre claimed, "Every participant an Indian and every incident true to native life" (15). The extended and somewhat hyperbolic 1915 article in *The Strand* said the film was "the most carefully-worked out and accurate human document ever produced by means of the motion-picture camera. The scenes were taken in exactly the places where they are supposed to have been enacted. The war-canoes are actual war-canoes, while the village destroyed by fire is a real Indian town built by Indians. The totem-poles are actual totem-poles, Indian carved" (122). This is mostly true, except for the fact that some scenes were shot at villages other than the ones named, the canoes were artificially multiplied by repainting, the destroyed village was just a film set, and some of the poles were just flat painted boards. Many reviews suggested the setting was Alaska rather than British Columbia—close enough, perhaps, in continental terms and more familiar to American audiences (Evans, this volume).

The *Strand* article went on to quote Curtis claiming that "appearances did not decide upon the identity of our leading lady.... family history entitled her to play the part" (Holm and Quimby 1980:122), which may be true for one woman, but three different individuals played the part of Naida (introduction, this volume). The authenticity of the actors was one of the most important themes at a time when most movie Indians in leading roles were played by non-Natives. This authenticity was repeatedly suggested by commenting on the participants' inability to "act." Curtis claimed that it was "utterly impossible, for instance, to get any Indian to wear a mask to which by birth and tribal custom he was not entitled," and that it "took months to break down the natives' prejudice against acting" (Holm and Quimby 1980:122). One 1914 article reported problems in getting the superstitious Indians to play dead (in Gidley 1998a:253), another opined that the "Indian does not make a very convincing actor" (*Variety*, December 25, 1914:42), and one claimed outright that the "Indian mind is, I believe, constitutionally incapable of acting" (Bush 1914). The implication was that the dramatic scenes playing out on screen were the direct and authentic expression of Indian culture and not cinematic artifice.[9] However, the lengths to which Curtis himself (in lectures and supplementary publicity material) went to discursively frame the authenticity of his film speaks to the convincing that audiences of the time apparently needed in order to accept the "documentary" reality of a medium known then for imaginative, narrative expression.

The carefully construed veridicality of both filmic image and indigenous performance lent the film its authority as a scientific representation and an educational tool. After its premiere, Alanson Skinner, assistant curator at the American Museum of Natural History, praised the film for "making ethnology alive and of artistic and dramatic interest" (in Graybill and Boesen 1976:87). Curtis drew upon, and likely wanted to surpass, the role of museum displays in picturing and recording ethnographic detail. One film review titled "Ethnology in Action" opened:

> It was thought to be a great educational advance when the American Museum of Natural History and the Smithsonian set up groups of Indians modeled in wax and clothed in their everyday or gala costume. But now a further step of equal importance has been taken by Edward S. Curtis.... The masks and costumes of the eagle and the bear which seemed merely grotesque when we saw them hung up in rows in the showcase at the museum become effective, even awe-inspiring, when seen on giant forms on the prow of a canoe filled with victorious warriors. (*The Independent*, January 11, 1915:72)

It was as if the mannequin-filled war canoe in the American Museum's Northwest Coast hall, assembled just four years earlier, had come alive on screen.[10] Perhaps in 1914, at the dawn of museum institutionalization and academic disciplinary segmenting, people were still more amenable to the rather nineteenth-century notion that scientific advancement and public entertainment could be fruitfully combined. Curtis himself embodied such hopes, and he referred to his life work as "photographic art-science" (in Russell 1999:103). Theodore Roosevelt confirmed this by calling Curtis "both an artist and a trained observer" (Holm and Quimby 1980:13). High praise for the film was won from the sculptor of Mount Rushmore, who wrote to Curtis in 1914, thanking him for "entering the field of educational entertainment and lifting this form of expression into the realm of the fine arts" (Borglum, in Gidley 1998a:254). *The Strand* reported that Curtis approached the film "from a purely educational standpoint" but felt pressure to add "a little romance" to help it sell (in Holm and Quimby 1980:121). Bush (1914) opened his review by stressing the "educational value of the motion picture." He went on to say that although "as a drama it may be a mere curiosity," as a film it is "a gem of the motion picture art," a "study of ethnology as an epic" that could be compared to Wagner. *Variety* (December 25, 1914:42) called the film an "educational exhibition" in one of the only reviews to actually summarize the plot.

Yet Curtis also had clear artistic aspirations for his projects and was very astute as to the love of spectacle and the purely visual forms of aesthetics popular at the time, evidenced by everything from his gold-toned photographic prints to his picture opera (Gidley, this volume). Despite his avowed goal of showing ethnographic details of everyday life, *Head Hunters* is replete with sensational images of warfare, severed heads, skulls, and exotic masked dances. The handbill from Seattle's Moore Theatre mentions the use of "cyclorama stage sets" for its screening (in Holm and Quimby 1980:15), adding a three-dimensional theatrical frame much as Curtis had done for his picture opera (introduction, this volume). Observers in both New York and Seattle commended the extensively colorized film stock (*New York Times*, December 2 and 8, 1914; *Seattle Times,* December 8, 1914). The *Seattle Times* (December 8, 1914) declared it "a vital, virile smashing big dramatic production worthy of ranking with the photomarvels of the decade and more beautiful in coloring, scenic outline and novelty of subject than anything of its kind ever produced heretofore." It was precisely this "spectacular artificiality" which Flaherty decried upon viewing Curtis's film in 1915, perhaps setting a negative example for his own production (in Ruby 2000:73; Browne, this volume).

Most reviewers, likewise, ignored or dismissed the drama and the gore and instead praised the film for its visual aesthetics, repeatedly calling the film a feast for the eyes. Bush (1914) wrote, "You get the impression of having feasted on one of the world's great picture galleries and there follows that most delightful of sensations, a new perception of pleasure in which the

Aaron Glass and Brad Evans

eye and the brain take special share." Bush praised Curtis's "second sight with the camera," which "brought before my eyes a new vista of camera miracles," including the widely revered scenic beauty of the landscape and the majesty of a herd of sea lions (although New York reviewers tended to make more out of the natural scenery than Seattle ones). Many reviewers commented specifically on the play of light, one focusing on the sun, silhouettes, and shadows (*The Independent*, January 11, 1915:72), and another on "some wondrous tableaux" of reflecting waters and glimmering sunshine (*Variety*, December 25, 1914:42). One viewer described the film as a "triumph of art.... The artistic effects were not less pronounced in certain groupings of figures, especially in the dances, than in the marvelous settings of natural scenery."[11] Prominent critic and advocate of film as high art Vachel Lindsay, in an essay titled "Sculpture-in-Motion," described the film as "a supreme art achievement" in its successful presentation of what he called "bronze in action"; relating different styles of films to sculptural materials, he suggested that Curtis's film "abounds in noble bronzes," as stereotypically befits movies about American Indians (Lindsay 1915:86).

While public critics applauded the film's aesthetic vision and some museum anthropologists celebrated its educational value, Franz Boas was consistently critical of Curtis (Jacknis 1984:33), even complaining in 1907 to President Roosevelt about his lack of professional qualification—and this was *before* Curtis's Kwakwa̱ka'wakw work, which Boas would have been in the best position to evaluate (Graybill and Boesen 1976:28; see also introduction, this volume). Likewise, George T. Emmons, an amateur ethnologist and museum collector employed at times by the American Museum of Natural History, wrote to Charles Newcombe, a Victoria-based collector, "I saw some of Curtis's moving pictures and they were very interesting, particularly the canoe ones. The dance ones were in a sense attractive but how true I can not say of course. Curtis is making a living, he is artistic and no ethnologist, and his idea to popularize ethnology is all right for the ignorant public but of little scientific value."[12] For his part, Newcombe had just asked his Kwakwa̱ka'wakw assistant, Charles Nowell, to confirm some of the film's portrayals (of headhunting as well as sea lion and whale hunting), and Nowell responded that while the Kwaguʼł used to hunt heads, they did not hunt those marine mammals.[13]

Curtis sorely lamented his lack of recognition among professional anthropologists. Whether he would have appreciated all the fuss over his natural scenery and lighting effects is not known. It seems that aside from acknowledging the film's "educational" or "ethnographic" import, few reviewers commented much on the details of Native life conveyed. They were more interested in praising Curtis's access to "real Indians" and his fluency in the filmic (if not dramatic) medium. Later critics, scholars, and Kwakw<u>a</u>k<u>a</u>'wakw descendants would read the film very differently, and would mine the footage and narrative for a whole different set of meanings.

In Medias Res

For the six decades between the release of *In the Land of the Head Hunters* and *In the Land of the War Canoes*, Curtis's film seems to have gone largely unnoticed by either scholars or film buffs (the one exception being Hugo Zeiter, who donated The Field Museum's copy in 1947; introduction, this volume). Since 1973, those interested in early cinema or Northwest Coast ethnology have had occasion to revisit the film. Still, there has been markedly scant attention paid to the film, possibly because it was perceived to be wanting as art, science, *and* entertainment by late twentieth-century standards. It is often dismissed by Curtis fans as a bad film (McLuhan, in Evans 1998:222) and by ethnographic filmmakers as bad anthropology (Heider 1976:20, who called it a "scripted epic"). Most historians of ethnographic film ignore it completely, or give it but passing reference, though Emilie De Brigard (1995:19) attempted to redeem it somewhat by calling it "painstakingly reconstructed for precontact authenticity" despite its dramatized narrative. She tried to contextualize it by pointing out that "Indian elements are used to tell the story visually." But the diversity of approaches and density of material present in both the original and 1973 rerelease guarantee that it has something to offer those who wish to insert it piecemeal into their own theoretical or ethnographic paradigms.

To begin with Bill Holm and George Quimby, who discovered and restored the film in the 1960s, is to begin with perspectives on both Native life and the use of ethnographic film much different from those of Curtis's time. Quimby, then a curator in the Department of Anthropology at The Field Museum in Chicago, thought he could use the resuscitated footage in a new exhibition of Northwest Coast material. Bill Holm, a curator, art historian, and Northwest Coast art enthusiast, had extensively studied Native art and was friendly with many Kwakw<u>a</u>ka'wakw. Together they envisioned a newly edited film that would highlight its value as an ethnographic record as well as an artifact of living Kwakw<u>a</u>ka'wakw culture. As such, they restructured the film to play down (some might say, neutralize) the melodramatic narrative (Evans 1998). They also reframed the scenes of violence and increased (by repeating and

Aaron Glass and Brad Evans

drawing out) the scenes of canoe travel.[14] Perhaps most important, Holm and Quimby rearranged and rewrote Curtis's intertitles, pointing out more ethnographic detail and deleting references to "evil magic" and the "gruesome house of skulls" (Evans 1998). In addition to editorial decisions, they showed the film to a number of Kwakwa̱ka'wakw for the first time and subsequently asked them to record dialogue, speeches, and songs in Kwak̓wala for use in the new release (foreword and Harrison, this volume). The resulting *War Canoes* version is both more viewer- and museum-friendly—partly removed from the narrative contrivances of a past era and divested of some of its sensationalism—and provides a document attesting to contemporary Kwakwa̱ka'wakw engagement with widely circulating cultural representations of themselves (introduction and Browne, this volume).

In fact, the Kwakwa̱ka'wakw of Alert Bay used footage from the rereleased Curtis film in their own nascent media production. In 1975, the U'mista Cultural Society produced the film *Potlatch. . . A Strict Law Bids Us Dance,* which combined historical reenactment, contemporary ceremonial footage, and archival photographs and film clips to tell the story of Canada's prohibition against the potlatch and to advocate for the repatriation of confiscated regalia. Although later indigenous productions would eschew this device, *Potlatch* decontextualized and dehistoricized the archival Curtis footage, using it to illustrate purportedly precontact ceremonial culture rather than modern labor in the film industry.[15]

To achieve the same visual pedagogic effect, natural history and ethnology museums had been consistently using Curtis photographs in exhibits of Northwest Coast ceremonial material since the 1950s, and a few immediately integrated portions of the reedited Curtis film into their permanent display. Newly revised exhibits at Victoria's British Columbia Provincial Museum (now the Royal BC Museum) and Ottawa's National Museum of Man (now the Canadian Museum of Civilization) were showing clips by 1976, as was The Field Museum by 1982 (Glass 2006a). Such filmic displays function to authenticate the material culture on exhibit by showing similar items of regalia in what appears to be ceremonial use; when shown silently or in selective clips, Curtis's melodramatic narrative drops away completely and the museum visitor is left with what seems—impossibly!—to be documentary footage of presumably precontact cultural life. Although usually content to let the film footage provide voiceless ethnographic "context" for museum objects, more recently a number of displays have included some discursive contextualization for the film itself. For example, in 1987, the National Museum of Natural History in Washington, DC, in collaboration with the U'mista Cultural Centre, edited a short video for their Northwest Coast exhibit that featured Curtis footage as explicit evidence of cultural persistence during the potlatch prohibition. By the early twenty-first century, the Campbell River Museum in British Columbia was screening *War Canoes* on a daily basis in an exhibition and civic context of contemporary Kwakwaka'wakw vitality.

While Holm and Quimby's aim was to salvage Curtis's ethnographic footage and return it in key ways to the Kwakwaka'wakw as well as the general public, later academic critics would analyze the film through the lens of postmodern, postcolonial, and critical race theory as well as contemporary film practice. Rosalind Morris (1994) places Curtis in the context of filmmaking on the Northwest Coast, focusing on his use of historical reconstruction as evidence of his salvage-minded concern with documenting past authenticity. This effort, she suggests (Morris 1994:39), led to Curtis's selective attention, romantic aesthetic, and ambivalent messages, in which classic barbarity (warfare, headhunting, sorcery) was combined with stereotypical nobility (loyalty, bravery, spirituality). For Morris, the contradictory attempt to fuse ethnographic information with a popular narrative—to stage authenticity—becomes emblematic of the whole project of ethnographic film, in which science is incongruously mingled with imagination and mixed messages abound. Morris also credits Curtis with introducing a "viscerally romantic aesthetic sensibility" into Northwest Coast filmic representation by focusing on the dramatic and the heroic (41). In a somewhat similar vein, Theresa Scandiffio (2001) approaches the film through the lens of the Victorian travelogue and its visual negotiation between an exoticizing and aestheticizing touristic gaze. In addition to promoting foreign locales through picturesque scenery and people, the travelogue genre of film conveyed a desire to accurately record foreign cultures in the name of scientific education. Alison Griffiths (2002) situates Curtis and *Head Hunters* in the context of museum display and popular cinema as contexts for ethnographic representation, noting Curtis's (failed) triangulation between artistic, scientific, and commercial impulses. Griffiths, Scandiffio, and Morris are concerned primarily with Curtis's film as an anthropological—or at least an ethnographic—object, one meant to convey information about another society.

Fatimah Tobing Rony (1996) links ethnographic film to other projects representing racialized bodies. She suggests that ethnographic film is a form of cultural "encapsulation" born of natural history description and thus inextricably mixed up with race, scientific classification, and the determination of identity (inevitably, that of the representer at the expense of the represented) (6–7). Drawing on two modes of visualizing the exotic—taxidermy and the

Aaron Glass and Brad Evans

picturesque—Rony develops the analogy to natural history paradigms. Building on Donna Haraway's (1984/85) classic deconstruction of dioramas, she suggests that taxidermy is a form of "nostalgic reconstruction of a more authentic humanity" that "uses artifice and reconstruction in order to make the dead look alive" (Rony 1996:14). Thus, Curtis's use of sets, costumes, and reconstructed practice is likened to a natural history diorama that kills animals, decontextualizes them in artificially illusionistic settings, and then preserves them in a timeless state for the edification and enjoyment of (specifically Euro-American, metropolitan) others; the comparison to dioramas that a 1915 critic for *The Independent*, cited above, offered as a compliment, Rony posits as critique. This argument has been taken further by Pauline Wakeham (2006, 2008), who situates Curtis's film within a purportedly systematic colonial logic of "taxidermic semiosis," the attempt to use dioramic representations to freeze indigenous people in the past as a means of symbolic as well as actual erasure. Unlike Rony, Wakeham carefully distinguishes between *Head Hunters* and *War Canoes,* additionally taking the latter to task for its attempt to reframe the melodramatic original as a "documentary" in order to recuperate it for an anthropological science that, Wakeham argues, continues to fetishize the lost, authentic, indigenous past (not to mention Curtis's film itself).[16]

Beyond the preservationist mode was an aesthetic sensibility that Rony claims privileged the picturesque—that is, a rough, dramatic irregularity that contrasts with a more sublime, ideal beauty. Rony (1996:90) describes the picturesque as obsessed with nostalgia, loss, death, and memory—a salvage culture which "mythologized" Indians by idealizing and freezing them in the past, erasing history to support the construction of a romantic ideal that was part projected fantasy and part (vanishing) colonial subject. Curtis combined the dramatically picturesque (long scenes of swirling smoke, rocky shores, and gnarled trees) with the stereotypically Indian (vision quests, black magic, and headhunting) (Flint, this volume). Implied here is that the film marks the result of Curtis's quest to hunt Indians through "shooting" them and preserving them photographically. For Rony, the result is a mixed bag of images which both celebrates and savagizes, reflecting the deeply ambivalent Western gaze at the exotic, racialized other.

It is precisely this ambivalence, the "sheer perversity" of *Head Hunters,* that Catherine Russell (1999:114) celebrates. Her goal is to resuscitate the film as an "experimental ethnography" that plays with the line between creativity and certainty, art and science, although not quite in the same way as Curtis may have intended. She associates Curtis's contradictory messages and agendas—his discourse of authenticity and his practice of staging—as a fusion of premodern and postmodern sensibilities resulting in "an authentically inauthentic text" (98). Due to what she calls the "performative doubling" of the film—by which she means the fact that the Kwakw<u>a</u>ka'wakw were "playing themselves" in so many styles (naturalistic, costumed/melodramatic, serious/ceremonial)—the resulting narrative is so indeterminate that it can be read only allegorically and not ethnographically (102, 107). Russell suggests that it took Holm and Quimby's intervention and erasure of the narrative spectacle to reclaim the film's ethnographic validity. Obviously, Russell is reviewing the film through her own very contemporary lens, and we might want to query exactly to whom it is obvious that the film is "so clearly a spectacle of the primitive" (108). To original metropolitan viewers who bought its truth claims? To subsequent anthropologists who saw past the drama? To Native people who recognize their relatives? Or to postmodern critics predisposed to such a revisionist reading?

Russell claims that the staged authenticity of the film "blurs the distinction between native performers and their ancestors," while the very "failure of *Head Hunters* as narrative realism invites that historical difference to be read back into the film" (110). In other words, the fact that Kwakw<u>a</u>ka'wakw in 1913 were "playing" their more traditional ancestors allows contemporary Natives to better relate to *their* ancestors as actors in the movie. This opens the space for their "virtual reappropriation" of the film in many ways. First, it grants a degree of agency to the Kwakw<u>a</u>ka'wakw participants in the original production. Second, it suggests that in reclaiming the narrative space of the movie through an added voiceover that remains untranslated, the contemporary Kwakw<u>a</u>ka'wakw keep a certain amount of cultural knowledge private even as it is displayed on screen.[17] Russell points out that in removing Curtis's dialogue intertitles—which conveyed direct address and character subjectivity—and replacing them with running dialogue in Kwak̓wala, *War Canoes* has Kwakw<u>a</u>ka'wakw speaking to themselves and not to the general audience (101, 111). And third, by transforming the film from a spectacle of primitivism into a record of indigenous custom and language, *War Canoes* becomes a testament to the vitality of the Kwakw<u>a</u>ka'wakw. Joanna Hearne (2006) makes a similar argument for the capacity of Curtis's film to be resignified and repurposed by contemporary Kwakw<u>a</u>ka'wakw, given its inherent contradictions and semantic indeterminacy. Ironically, perhaps, Curtis's staged yet authentic memorial to the Vanishing Races ended up not only picturing their nineteenth-century past but participating in their twenty-first-century present.

Aaron Glass and Brad Evans

It is worth pointing out that all of the above-mentioned critics were analyzing Curtis's film through the editorial decisions made by Holm and Quimby in *War Canoes*, the only version of the film available to them. One of the motivations for the current film reconstruction project was to make available, for the first time, something closer to Curtis's original film for the benefit of future film critics and scholars. We anticipate that the reconstruction will fuel both critics and defenders of the film along lines similar to those outlined above. But academics comprise simply one of the film's lasting audiences, and another goal of the project has been to shift a certain degree of critical attention away from Curtis's artistic intentions and toward the agency of the indigenous people with whom he worked.

In Perpetuum

It is a shame that Holm and Quimby did not film their encounter with the Kwakw<u>a</u>ka'wakw upon first returning Curtis's film to the communities. There is now a well-established, reflexive genre of ethnographic film that records such returns, including *Chronicle of a Summer* (1960), *Jero on Jero* (1980–81), *Nanook Revisited* (1994), and *The Return of Navajo Boy* (2001), to name just a few. All of these films reveal the fascinating, multidimentional relationships that obtain between participants in filmmaking and their later experiences and memories, as well as those of their descendants. Holm and Quimby (1980) share some of this in their text, as they relate that people enjoyed identifying the actors and locating specific sites, offered memories of the filming or told stories that had been passed down, and broke spontaneously into song relating to the on-screen performances. What non-Native audiences never noticed—that there were inconsistencies in location and multiple women playing the lead role—the Kwakw<u>a</u>ka'wakw were keen to pick up on; as Catherine Russell (1999:112) suggests, these Native viewers read the film indexically (for what it captured to nitrate) rather than symbolically (for what it represents narratively).

Around the time of its release in 1973, two films documented Kwakw<u>a</u>ka'wakw attitudes toward the film by recording the memories of a few of its original cast members. Holm and Quimby participated in the production of a short film that told the story of *Head Hunters* and that was ultimately attached to the commercial release of *War Canoes* by Milestone Films. In it, Holm pays a visit to Fort Rupert, where he speaks with two of the surviving cast members of the film, who report that they enjoyed themselves while making it. Helen Wilson Knox identifies both herself as a child and her mother, Emily Hunt Wilson, in photographs taken on the set. Her brother Bob Wilson, who was nineteen years old at the time and paid in silver coins to tow the crew and the dugout canoes with his gas boat, tells the story of filming the scene in which he humorously drops a paddle while running on a rocky shore. In viewing photographs taken on set, Bob Wilson offers an ethnographic interpretation of the *ḥamspek* ("cannibal pole") used by Hamaʦa dancers, although no such scene is included in the film. This suggests that knowledgeable viewers are motivated to read beyond Curtis's scripted narrative to identify culturally meaningful elements latent within it.

In 1974, T. C. McLuhan released her documentary *The Shadow Catcher*, a key contribution to the Curtis revival of the period.[18] She too interviews Bob Wilson and Helen Wilson Knox, along with Johnny Hunt—another crew member—and Gloria Cranmer Webster, a Kwakwa̲ka'wakw anthropologist, curator, and descendant of George Hunt. Webster starts out by clarifying that the "hokey" film reconstructed a past moment in history, fully erasing the modernity in which its cast and crew participated in 1914. For her, as for earlier anthropologists such as Boas, the real pleasure and value of the film lies in its recording of giant war canoes and elaborate ceremonial regalia *in action* rather than resting dormant in museums; even while freezing the Kwakwa̲ka'wakw in what Rony and Wakeham would call a "taxidermic" mode, the film also brought certain aspects of material and performative culture to life in a unique and important way. Knox, speaking in Kwak̓wala, remembers how much fun they had on the set, which earned them a "balling out" from Curtis as he was trying to capture serious episodes on film. Hunt adds that Curtis also got angry with his cameraman Edmund Schwinke whenever technical difficulties arose with the camera. The group also described how they had to shave their whiskers and don black wigs and cedar-bark clothing to recreate the appearance of earlier generations. Hunt recalled being paid fifty cents an hour as an extra, with a bonus of five dollars for scenes in which the canoes capsized. With her own camera focused on a group of family portraits resting on a coffee table in the Fort Rupert home, the interviewer asked the cast members to comment on being stereotyped by Curtis as a "vanishing race." Hunt used the prompt to reflect on the lasting damage wrought by residential schools, which seriously disrupted the transmission of language and culture before and after Curtis's visit, situating the two films—Curtis's and McLuhan's—in terms of colonial history. Bob Wilson countered optimistically that language education for children was beginning in the 1970s in Fort Rupert and that as a people they would not disappear. The segment ends with the three elders singing a song in Kwak̓wala along with their younger translators, a demonstration of the cultural transmission and persistence attested to by Wilson's comments, if not by *Head Hunters* and *War Canoes* themselves.

Two more recent films track the continued return of Curtis's movie (the *War Canoes* version) to Kwakwaka'wakw communities and observe its contemporary reception by one participant and multiple descendants of the cast. Ali Kazimi's *Shooting Indians: A Journey with Jeffrey Thomas* (1997) follows the Iroquois/Onondaga photographer as he researches Edward Curtis for an exhibit he is curating at the National Archives of Canada (see also Thomas, this volume). Upon discovering Curtis's film, Thomas travels with it to British Columbia to interview the last surviving cast member, Margaret Frank—a granddaughter of George Hunt and one of the three women who played the leading lady, Naida—along with her grandson, Andy Everson, a graduate student in anthropology and an accomplished dancer and artist (photo essay 2, this volume).[19] They all watch the film together in Frank's hospital room (she died the following year) as she laughs and reminisces about the production.[20] In 2000, Anne Makepeace released *Coming to Light,* a documentary about Curtis's life told from the multiple perspectives of his family, scholars, and indigenous people. Included in her film are interviews with two children of *Head Hunter* stars, Stan Hunt (son of Stanley Hunt and grandson of George Hunt; see fig. 15.3) and Mary Everson (daughter of Margaret Frank; see fig. 15.14), as well as Gloria Cranmer Webster, all of whom comment while watching the film.

All of the people interviewed by Holm and Quimby recalled fond memories of the project as a pleasurable experience, which is corroborated by a series of photos taken by Edmund Schwinke during the film shoot that show jovial and relaxed cast members lounging around between takes, often playing with the severed-head props (see fig. 1.8 and Holm and Quimby 1980). Margaret Frank, in *Shooting Indians,* recalls that Curtis was very charming and that the cast was well-treated and fairly paid. She admitted that at first they questioned Curtis's motives, since most Euro-Canadians were there to eradicate Native culture. As Webster expressed it in *Coming to Light,* "This white guy is going to *pay them* to do these dances they would otherwise go to jail for? This, in the middle of potlatch prohibition? And from all accounts they just really enjoyed being a part of this." She then joked with Stan Hunt about how Curtis had to rent the dead whale from a commercial fishery up the coast to film the famous hunt scene, even though the Kwakwaka'wakw had never hunted whales. People also laughed about the problems Curtis had with making a dummy body drown properly, his impatience following a series of rather comic canoe mishaps, and the way that actors' newly shaved moustaches and false nose rings tickled their faces (in Holm and Quimby 1980:16; Makepeace 2000).

As for the contemporary descendants, the Curtis film provides a document with which they can trace genealogies and claim status. Stan Hunt said, "If it weren't for the film here we wouldn't have had the opportunity to look back and see some of our older people again. For me to sit here and watch my father and my other relatives, it's very moving for me" (in Makepeace 2000). The film becomes a way of authenticating present identities through hereditary links to the past. Over some footage of him dancing in a potlatch, Hunt explained, "When I'm dancing, I'm reenacting one of our stories. You kind of look within yourself to find yourself, where you fit into the scheme of things here." It is interesting to note that the middle-aged Hunt began dancing only in recent decades as an embodiment of the hereditary status to which he is entitled; being the son of the star of *Head Hunters* gave him an opportunity to display that claim on film. Likewise, Mary Everson pointed out, "That's my mom. She's seventeen. She was picked for this movie because of her high ranking. She was trained to be one of the noble women of her village" (in Makepeace 2000). In this way, reclaiming the film means using it as a document of individual and family status. Current Kwakwaka'wakw communities have the advantage of being able to hear one generation of speakers and singers on the 1973 soundtrack on top of seeing the older generation of actors and performers in the film. Furthermore, Webster articulates both ownership over the film and a historical status claim for the whole Kwakwaka'wakw community (or at least the specific crew members, some of whom were her relatives): "Eventually people discovered that it was the *first* ethnographic film. For years people had thought that Flaherty's *Nanook of the North* was the very first. But Curtis beat him. We were there first" (in Makepeace 2000).[21]

Such sentiments reveal the complex and multilayered valences of Curtis's film. Perhaps the overly ambiguous and contradictory nature of the original project ensured its longevity. Financial success, the one thing Curtis wished for the film, was an elusive goal. Yet the film did end up providing a lasting record of the nineteenth-century Kwakwaka'wakw, or at least of certain reconstituted aspects of their culture at that time. But more important perhaps, it remains an ever-evolving document of the colonial and the (not yet fully realized in Canada) postcolonial encounter, in which indigenous people actively participate in the shifting conditions for their own representation (Glass, this volume). Curtis probably would have been quite surprised to learn that his film took a radical turn in narrative force and underwent a physical return to the very-much-not-vanished Indians he hoped to salvage. What we—as a twenty-first-century audience of anthropologists, film buffs, and Kwakwaka'wakw alike—are left with is a document of boundless possibilities. A *Head Hunters* for all seasons.

1   For pictures of the Casino Theatre, see http://xroads.virginia.edu/~MA02/volpe/theater/theater/theaters.html and http://www.ibdb.com/venue.php?id=1085 (accessed March 17, 2013).

2   For more on the Moore Theatre, see http://www.stgpresents.org/moore/ (accessed March 17, 2013).

3   Including it with several other features, among them an adaptation of the Frank Norris novel *The Pit,* directed by Maurice Tourneur (also released by World Film), the *Fairbanks Sunday Times* (January 23, 1916) assured readers that it "costs more to get the best, but it is worth more for the people who appreciate a good feature, and they have so many of them that they know what they are like."

4   Young Deer self-identified as Winnebago, however his name does not currently appear on the tribal register (Aleiss 2005:176n2). See Aleiss's updated research at http://brightlightsfilm.com/80/80-james-young-deer-silent-movies-pathe-producer-black-native-american-indian-aleiss.php#.UdqyRhZQ0gR (accessed July 8, 2013).

5   This account is largely based on the extensive history of the World Film Corporation given in Lewis (1987a and 1987b).

6   The Shubert Archives, file 2890, correspondence Aug. 1916–Dec. 1918.

7   In 1987, the number of films surviving in their entirety was only ten. Film historian Richard Koszarski (personal correspondence, summer 2010) has noted that many more have since been recovered.

8   Bronislaw Malinowski, an early proponent of participant observation as a method, left to conduct his major Melanesian fieldwork in 1914, the same year *Head Hunters* was released.

9   Ironically, one of the few notices to acknowledge that the stars of the film were "acting" mistakenly identified them as being Eskimo: "The pictures show a real Indian drama, acted by amateur actors chosen from the Alaskan Eskimo tribes" (*Takoma Times,* December 12, 1914:5).

10   This canoe and its inhabitants were later immortalized by J. D. Salinger in *Catcher in the Rye.* Notice the further correspondence between Curtis's attention to whales, giant canoes, totem poles, and mummies, and the competitive scramble to display these same items in metropolitan natural history museums at the time.

11   Kelsey to Curtis, December 8, 1914, MS 7.NAI.1.7, Southwest Museum.

12   Emmons to Newcombe, February 24, 1915, vol. 3, folder 57, Newcombe Family Papers, BC Provincial Archives and Record Service.

13   Newcombe to Nowell, January 12, 1915; Nowell to Newcombe, January 28, 1915, vol. 4, folder 110, Newcombe Family Papers, BC Provincial Archives and Record Service.

14   Holm suggests that this was because canoes were more central to Kwakwaka'wakw life than was headhunting (Holm and Quimby 1980:65), but it also served to reduce the aura of savagery.

15   Bunn-Marcuse (2005:324) notes how U'mista's subsequent film, *Box of Treasures* (1983), features a scene in which masked dancers appear on the prow of a seine boat approaching the shore in Alert Bay, visually quoting the famous scene in *Head Hunters* of the wedding-bound dancers perched on canoe prows.

16   For a critique of this application of semiotics to museum and filmic representations of Native Americans, see Glass (2010).

17   Holm (personal communication) reports that no plans were ever discussed to pro-

vide subtitles for the Kwakwala speech in *War Canoes*. It is our intention to work with the Kwakwaka'wakw to make such a translation available as an optional feature on a DVD release of the newly edited *Head Hunters*, which would also include *War Canoes*.

18 *The Shadow Catcher* was cowritten by McLuhan and Dennis Wheeler, who went on to direct *Potlatch. . . A Strict Law Bids Us Dance* the following year.

19 Andy Everson was also a member of the G̲wa'wina Dancers when they participated in the 2008 Curtis film screening events.

20 This was not the first time that Frank had seen the film. In the late 1970s and 1980s, Jay Stewart (personal communication) used to screen *War Canoes* on the wall of the Campbell River Museum, where Frank would come to watch and point out her relatives.

21 Bunn-Marcuse (2005:322) relates a story told by Webster about the making of *Potlatch*. When the film's director, Dennis Wheeler, hesitated to include clips from *Head Hunters/War Canoes* due to the licensing costs, Webster replied, "Dennis, let's just use it. We don't have to pay for it, it's ours." Howard Morphy (2010) notes a similar proprietary claim by Australian Aborigines on archival film footage of their ceremonies.

6

UNMASKING THE DOCUMENTARY

Notes on the Anxiety of Edward Curtis

COLIN BROWNE

Despite sequences as iconic as any in the history of cinema, Edward S. Curtis's silent six-reel photoplay *In the Land of the Head Hunters* (1914) has never been welcomed into the cinematic canon of either the United States or Canada. Conceived, written, directed, and independently produced by an American off the east coast of Vancouver Island with Kwakw<u>a</u>ka'wakw actors and within a Kwakw<u>a</u>ka'wakw cultural context (although neither the location nor the people who participated are identified), when *Head Hunters* does appear in histories of early cinema it is almost always as a footnote to Robert Flaherty's *Nanook of the North* (1922).[1] This may be due to habit, or laziness, and to the fact that for many years most people were unaware of the film's existence. After much hard work, a version of the film was restored in 1973 and caused a small sensation. Thanks to the 2008 restoration—in a tinted version that may be as close as we'll get to the original—it is now possible to better assess Curtis's achievement. *In the Land of the Head Hunters* is one of the important orphan films of the American cinema, and it should be acknowledged in Canadian cinema histories as well. That it remains an anomaly to this day should be seen as an oversight, but also as a tribute to the courage, imagination, vision, cunning, naiveté, and anxiety of Edward Curtis.

In the Land of the Head Hunters had an inauspicious beginning. On December 8, 1914, the day after it premiered in Seattle and New York, Irving Berlin's first musical, *Watch Your Step*, opened on Broadway, and the Royal Navy scored a decisive victory over the German battle fleet in the Falkland Islands. How could an earnest, complicated, confusing movie about tribal warfare on a faraway, unnamed shore—was it in the South Seas as the fire dancing on the poster might suggest (see fig. A.1.10)?—compete with Vernon and Irene Castle's sophisticated foxtrot or the twelve-inch guns of the battle cruisers *Invincible* and *Inflexible*? In spite of promising reviews and appreciation for the film's technical innovations, *In the Land of the Head Hunters* played for a week, had some spotty distribution, and then seemed to vanish (Glass and Evans, this volume). Curtis had hoped for something better.

Audiences in 1914 might legitimately have been puzzled by the film and its characters. They would not have known that the film was made in British Columbia, or that the unidentified Native actors dressed in cedar bark were modern fishermen, cannery workers, laborers, loggers, and producers of tourist crafts who enthusiastically participated in and were paid for their work on the film. Some were Christian. Who could have guessed that those who danced in their ceremonial masks were simultaneously acting for the camera and preserving a living, if outlawed, tradition? Were the scenes contemporary, or re-creations, or make believe? What was "real": the narrative, the ceremonies, or both—or neither? How might one tell the difference?

Some in the audience might already have been familiar with films in which indigenous actors re-created episodes from the lives of their grandparents and ancestors. Established as a cinematic trope by 1914, the strategy of re-enactment for educational, scenic, or what we might now call documentary purposes would reemerge in films such as Flaherty's *Nanook of the North* and *Moana* (1926), in W. S. Van Dyke's *Eskimo/Mala the Magnificent* (1933), and, more recently, in the thirteen-part *Nunavut* series produced by Zacharias Kunuk and Norman Cohn for IsumaTV in the mid-1990s. The doubled nature of representation is always more complex than it appears to be. In the case of Curtis's film we're offered the rare privilege of watching those who know more about their culture than anyone else in the world—with an art and culture that rival any in the world—interpreting the ways of their ancestors in a time of rapid transition.

A year before shooting *In the Land of the Head Hunters*, Curtis had prepared a scenario titled, rather stiffly, "In the Days of Vancouver," in which he described his film as a "documentary picture of the Kwakiutl tribes, the natives of Vancouver Island" (Holm and Quimby 1980:115). This is one of the earliest uses of the word "documentary" to describe a film. Yet *Head Hunters* was not made as a documentary, or even as a fusion of fiction and documentary. These genres did not exist in 1913. In search of success at the box office, Curtis improvised, borrowing from every dramatic convention that seemed *à propos*, from stagy theatrical tableaux to Belasco-like histrionics to jungle pictures to travelogues to "scenics" to Westerns to matinée reels to melodramas to ethnographic *actualités* to staged Kwakwaka'wakw ceremonial dances; in short, he covered the bases. He and his colleagues—production manager, translator, informant, fixer and, often, codirector George Hunt, and camera operator Edmund August Schwinke—were determined to make a picture that would please the masses. In failing to become a theatrical hit, *In the Land of the Head Hunters* shares the fate of almost every movie ever made. Nevertheless, with the assistance and persistence of George Hunt and his Kwakwaka'wakw collaborators, Edward Curtis helped to create some of the most unforgettable moving-picture images of the twentieth century. And, to give him his due, Curtis was unmasking the documentary even as he helped to invent the genre. Sometimes I feel that he has never been forgiven for this.

* * *

Today, many who have not seen *In the Land of the Head Hunters* are familiar with the images of the dancers on the prows of the great Kwakwaka'wakw canoes and the gathering of masked and costumed dancers that suggests a ceremony associated with the animal kingdom (see figs. 8.3 and 15.6a). These sequences now appear in museum displays or in other people's movies—for example, Chris Marker's *Sans Soleil* (1983) and Daniel Reeves's *Obsessive Becoming* (1995), where, in a nod to surrealism and to psychoanalysis, they represent the energies of the unconscious and, possibly, totemic figures.[2] Until recently, the only available source of these startling sequences has been the reconstruction by art historian Bill Holm and anthropologist George Quimby called *In the Land of the War Canoes*. The story of the film's restoration is well known (Holm and Quimby 1980; introduction, this volume).

Holm had heard rumors of the film's existence prior to its rediscovery at The Field Museum in Chicago. We can only imagine how thrilling it must have been for him and for George Quimby to watch Curtis's footage for the first time, and we should acknowledge Holm's insistence on returning the film to its creators—the Kwakwaka'wakw whose culture is portrayed and who worked side by side with Curtis. We ought to acknowledge too his decision to add a challenging soundtrack created in part by the people whose relatives and ancestors had helped to produce the film. If, as a result, *In the Land of the War Canoes* has come to be misunderstood as a kind of ethnographic documentary of sorts, we should not be so naïve that we fail to see that every frame of the original represents a considered, premeditated performance. In the celebrated ceremonial sequences, the viewer has the privilege of watching performers performing performers performing, an uncanny experience that seems to suggest, on behalf of the Kwakwaka'wakw, a self-conscious commentary on their own ceremonial practices (Glass, this volume).

Viewers of *In the Land of the War Canoes* have been able to rejoice at the breathtaking ceremonial tableaux while forgiving or ignoring the almost incomprehensible melodramatic story. Critics have dismissed the film as an example of salvage ethnology perpetrated by a colonial authority figure saturated in Western aesthetics and ideologies. Reflecting on the film in 2008, artist, singer, dancer, and ritualist William Wasden Jr. of Alert Bay, British Columbia, was of the opinion that the Kwakwa̱ka'wakw actors had purposefully seized the opportunity—and perhaps the means of production—in order to transmit their dances, laws, and practices to future generations via film. He was deeply grateful. The 2008 restoration and its attendant ceremonies inspired the inclusion of one of the film's ceremonial tableaux in the repertoire of a contemporary Kwakwa̱ka'wakw dance troupe. In *Spirit Journey: Encircling Our Ancestors* (2009), the Le-La-La Dancers included "a spectacular scene from the 1914 Edward Curtis film, *In the Land of the Head Hunters*.... Eight masked figures unite together on stage as a tribute to our ancestors," some of whom danced in the original film.[3] Thus are traditions passed on, from the dancer of 1914 to the dancer of today. Thus does the circle remain unbroken.

*   *   *

Quimby and Holm faced technical challenges with their reconstruction. They had to deal with reels of deteriorated nitrate film that had become severely damaged prior to its transfer. As well, the print was missing critical narrative sequences. At the time, archival footage was regarded as a novelty. Silent films, shot at any anywhere from sixteen frames per second to thirty frames per second (with a norm of eighteen frames per second), were regularly shown on television at "sound speed," or twenty-four frames per second, so that the action looked comically speeded up, suggesting that the past was populated by unsophisticated, uncoordinated, simple-minded clowns. The original thirty-five-millimeter release print of *In the Land of the Head Hunters*, originally printed at eighteen frames per second, was transferred to sixteen-millimeter film by means of a process called step printing, which required every third frame to be printed twice. This resulted in a sixteen-millimeter print that could be projected at sound speed with the movement looking more or less natural. Some scenes were brightened up during the optical transfer, and some were made a little darker to improve and even out the contrast. According to Holm, adding extra frames in the reverse sequence helped to prolong some scenes. This occurs, for example, when Motana, the male lead played by Stanley Hunt, returns to his canoe after the witchcraft scene. Holm mentions that if you look closely you will see the waves rolling into the beach suddenly switch to waves rolling out. As well, the tail end of the scene in which Kenada dies was trimmed because the performance looked hyperactive. The shots in which Motana comes to collect his wife were also trimmed so that Motana's entry into the house feels like a natural movement.[4]

Holm and Quimby took a keen interest in the film's ethnographic significance. Holm had heard many anecdotes about the production while visiting Kwakwaka'wakw territory to screen the sixteen-millimeter print. He was familiar with the actors and their families and was able to see the film and its process from their point of view. Whereas Curtis had been careful not to identify the people or communities involved in making the film—after all, he'd taken liberties for dramatic reasons, including the scenes with a rented whale in Haida Gwaii—Holm saw that it was possible during the reconstruction to acknowledge the Kwakwaka'wakw and to return ownership of the traditions and ceremonies represented in the film to the families and the communities involved. He consulted the performers who were still alive and the relatives of those who were not, and took their advice on a number of matters.

Holm and Quimby created two new sequences, one that they used and one that they set aside. The scene they left out showed an actor playing Motana throwing a harpoon (made by Bill Holm) at a site similar to the original location of Pearl Rock. As for the scene they added, Holm says, "At the encouragement of the Kwakwaka'wakw viewers, who kept saying 'Where's the dummy-doll?,' I made a dummy and we shot a scene of the struggle on the cliff, the clubbing of the dummy, and throwing it over the cliff. This was in the original film according to those who witnessed the event in 1914."[5] Interestingly, they excised a scene from the original in which Motana pokes his head out of the mouth of the whale to grin at the camera, a scene that caused some Kwakwaka'wakw viewers to think of Jonah. They felt "it really had no place in the story, and just looked silly," although, as a shot that breaks the fourth wall, Motana's mugging strikes us today as a conspiratorial nod to the audience, perhaps intended to remind us that we're watching a performance.[6] When I first saw it I wondered if it had not been the inspiration behind the opening scene of *Nanook of the North,* in which every member of Nanook's family appears to climb out of a single kayak, or the later scene in which Nanook himself pokes his head from the doorway of his igloo to smile at the camera. Finally, in choosing a new title, *In the Land of the War Canoes,* Holm and Quimby were making it clear that their version was intended to be seen as an interpretation of Curtis's original film.

Brad Evans (1998:222) has shown that Holm and Quimby reduced the number of intertitles from forty-seven to eighteen; composed new, longer, less melodramatic texts; and abandoned the decorative border around the intertitles. With fewer intertitles, the emphasis on dramatic dialogue is reduced and the highly wrought language of 1914 does not have a chance to wrap viewers in its melodramatic spell. The effect is of observing the story from a distance, as a phenomenon, which seems in turn to enhance the sensation that one is watching an ethnographic documentary. The decision to add an occasionally self-reflexive soundtrack by Kwakw<u>a</u>ka'wakw speakers in which they sing, perform an impromptu kind of ADR (automated dialogue replacement, or dubbing), and include a commentary, also enhances the impression of documentary verisimilitude. The voices were recorded in Kwaḵwala by David Gerth, a film student at Rice University, in the Newcombe Auditorium in Victoria, British Columbia. Today that soundtrack is a priceless record for speakers and nonspeakers of Kwaḵwala, particularly for the relatives of those who participated. Holm and Gerth also recorded and added foley, or manufactured sound effects, including the banging of canoe paddles against the hull of a thirty-five-foot cedar canoe, to simulate the thumps one might hear during the arrival of a large marriage party.

In the Land of the War Canoes was released without subtitles—only Kwaḵwala speakers can understand what is being said—and with this rare and intriguing aural gloss it has screened mostly at universities and other institutions. To audiences or students unfamiliar with the film's context, or with the history of motion pictures, the sixteen-millimeter film or video release, with its damaged footage and disjunctive narrative, has often seemed confusing. Are the Indians in the movie dressing up as Indians and acting out an old legend, or is this an accurate depiction of their lives when the film was made? What scenes in the film might be called documentary sequences, if any? The film introduced audiences to a rare treasure—the fierce, enchanting, iconic dances and ceremonies of the Kwakw<u>a</u>ka'wakw— but were these the dances of 1914 or 1790? Or had they been devised for the camera? The distinction is relevant, and I suspect that Curtis's answer would have been that they are "timeless," which is why he so carefully blurred the borders. Regardless, once *In the Land of the War Canoes* became widely available, the iconic sequences of the canoes arriving with dancers on their prows and the gathering of masked dancers entered the world's visual vocabulary almost immediately, becoming, for some, primal representations from an ancestral history that lives on in the collective unconscious—unbidden, magical, destabilizing—and the source of an authentic self.

This interpretation might have appealed to Curtis. He was an accomplished technician; he knew what he was doing. His low angles, dramatic

Colin Browne

lighting, and heroic silhouettes are meant to insist that past and present are indivisible; his portraits of North American Indians are devoted to representing a glimpse of the eternal. Viewers are often troubled by this archetypal iconography, especially in regard to specific subjects and locations, but Curtis was philosophically and aesthetically committed to symbolic portraits, detaching his Native subjects from their everyday, contemporary lives in gestures intended to amplify and dignify the human spirit. It's this commitment to the epic gesture that links Curtis's film to other significant metonymic "documentaries" and "docudramas" of the first part of the twentieth century, including *Nanook of the North* and *Moana*, Dziga Vertov's *Man with a Movie Camera* (1928), John Grierson's *Drifters* (1929), and H. P. Carver's *Silent Enemy* (1930), as well as the great epics of the Soviet cinema by Alexander Dovzhenko, Sergei Eisenstein, and Vsevolod I. Pudovkin. I will examine this relationship later. It may be helpful first, in light of the predominant aesthetic of the epic, to explore the vexing notion of authenticity that haunts films about Native North Americans made by non-Natives. Is the anxiety a sign of a guilty conscience?

*   *   *

Representational authenticity is a rather severe and persistent cinematic convention, easily betrayed (Evans, this volume). At its most insistent it can become a tiresome middlebrow conceit, given that a movie *is* a movie. If we're to speak of authenticity in cinema, we must acknowledge that a movie is a finite representational system devoted to illusion and to concealing more than it reveals. Its sacred compact with an audience is to obey strict dramatic and perspectival rules. This is as true for documentaries as it is for fiction films. The result is a mutually brokered illusion of real life. Ethnographic filmmaker Jean Rouch and philosopher/sociologist Edgar Morin attempted to define this compact for the documentary film when they coined the term *cinéma vérité*, which is often thought to refer to an unmediated portrayal of real life, warts and all. Rouch and Morin, when they devised the term for their film *Chronique d'un été* (1960), had something else in mind. As anthropologists of the everyday, they wanted to experiment with the idea of a "cinema truth," which is to say the very particular kind of truth that would be prompted or stimulated by the intrusion of a camera and a microphone into a subject's life. The final sequences of *Chronique d'un été* show the subjects discussing the completed film. Most were unhappy with the way they were represented and did not find their often revealing portraits to be entirely "true" or fair. The project had in fact been designed as an experiment to test the tolerance of the subjects and the limits of truth and authenticity in documentary cinema.

NOTES ON THE ANXIETY OF EDWARD CURTIS

The audiences who were moved by *Chronique d'un été* were not necessarily fixated on unprompted or "actual" occurrences. The asymptote of authenticity as verisimilitude may in fact be related less to representational transparency than it is to the rules of genre and dramatic structure. Perhaps audiences are not as concerned with certain indicators of authenticity as they are with a film's emotional integrity. They willingly invest their emotions, knowing that scenes are staged and artificially lit, time is elided, the music is manipulative, the picture and the story are snipped up into little pieces, and the sound—even the color—is artificial, as long as the dramatic conventions that preserve emotional integrity are maintained. Indeed, audiences take great pleasure in a mimetic triumph achieved through invisible sleight of hand. All the same, authenticity is often promoted in the marketing, where authenticity's battles are fought, as they were with the Curtis film. Audiences are attracted to films "based on a true story," an oxymoron which they seem to take in their stride. Advertisements for Nicholas Ray's *Rebel Without a Cause* (1955), for example, promised that concerned audiences would discover what was troubling disaffected youth, although what they got was a complex, contemporary meditation on *Romeo and Juliet* and James Dean.[7] Intrigued by Inuit life since his first viewing of *Nanook of the North* at Frank Lloyd Wright's Taliesin in the early 1930s, Ray completed his own "Eskimo" film, *The Savage Innocents*, in 1960. The role of Inuk was played by Anthony Quinn, who made a far greater impression four years later as Zorba the Greek (McGilligan 2011:381).

* * *

Milestone Film and Video, the distributor of *In the Land of the War Canoes*, calls attention to the film's "authentic" audio track. It praises the "appropriate authentic sound effects of the war canoes," adding that "the new soundtrack was meticulously matched to the film and adds an extra dimension of authenticity" (Pierce and Doros 1992:n.p.). While the adverb "meticulously" suggests that the sounds of 1914 are knowable and recoverable, the creation of synchronized sound effects, or foley, is no guarantee of accuracy. Foley is an attempt to duplicate, in a studio or in the field, the illusion of "authentic" sounds and is, in most cases, a matter of mimetic emphasis intended to draw attention to isolated actions or consequences depicted within the frame or off-screen. In the case of *War Canoes*, Holm and Quimby chose to emphasize the canoes by recreating and fulfilling our aural expectations of what they might sound like while being paddled or struck by the paddles. Audio technologies were becoming quite sophisticated by the 1970s. Sound editors had more tracks and better mixing technologies to work with, and it became common practice during the 1970s and 1980s to "improve" silent films by adding "realistic" and/or symbolic sound effects.

Mimetic sound is an emotional signal. Off-screen police sirens and distant dog barks have been used for years in fiction and nonfiction films as shorthand for the urban jungle or a lonely, isolated homestead. Extra tracks of diegetic and nondiegetic sound effects are often added to documentaries to enhance a scene's emotional authenticity. The use of foley in *War Canoes* was in keeping with contemporary practice, and in its claim of authenticity the distributor blurs the distinction between symbolic mimesis and naturalistic location sound. This insistence on authenticity only serves to compound a confusion that seems to have accompanied the film from the time of its original release. For as much as *War Canoes* appears to some audiences to be a faithful document of a contemporary indigenous culture at the dawn of cinema, it is a work of historical fiction and reenactment.

Questions of authenticity have always attended the portrayal of "Indians" in the movies. In Canada, the first filmmaker concerned with the authentic representation of aboriginal people was probably Lumière cameraman Gabriel Veyre, who, in 1898, filmed three Mohawks dancing at Kahnawake, west of Montreal, while crossing Canada on his way to Japan. It is rumoured that Veyre asked the dancers to wear winter clothing, as it looked more authentically savage. His forty-eight-second *Danse indienne* became number 1,000 in the Lumière catalogue (Pelletier 2007:37, 46).

Other brief *actualités* were produced in the early days to document aboriginal life and ceremonies, but for a sustained presence one might consider the early films based on Henry Wadsworth Longfellow's *The Song of Hiawatha* (1855). The first seems to have been produced in 1903 in Desbarats, Ontario, by Joe Rosenthal and cinematographer-photographer-projectionist Charles Leonard Bowden, who filmed a popular, preexisting outdoor pageant titled *Hiawatha, or Nanabozho: The Musical Indian Play*. The actors were members of the Garden River Ojibwe and the libretto was by Canadian Pacific Railway (CPR) colonization agent and showman Louis Olivier Armstrong, who also directed the pageant (Trachtenberg 2004:91). The music was composed by Frederick Russell Burton (Pelletier 2007:37).[8] Rosenthal, a former war correspondent, had been the official cinematographer for the CPR for more than two years and was connected to the Urban Trading Company in London, which released the film in 1903 under the titles *Hiawatha, The Messiah of the Ojibway* and *Hiawatha, The Passion Play of America* (Pelletier 2007:36).[9] The Ojibwe cast would have been of compelling interest to audiences seeking an "authentic" blend of Christian redemption and Native piety.

NOTES ON THE ANXIETY OF EDWARD CURTIS

In 1908, Mohawks from Kahnawake were hired to present Armstrong's durable *Hiawatha* pageant at Quebec City's tercentenary. The CPR had by this time been producing promotional reels for almost a decade, and to record the event Armstrong rounded up cameramen from three companies—British Gaumont, the Charles Urban Company and Vitagraph—and from Quebec theatre owner Léo-Ernest Ouimet. Three years later, in 1911, the Natural Color Kinematograph Company filmed the same Hiawatha pageant—in color—during the intermission at a Montreal lacrosse game. Commissioned, not surprisingly, by the CPR, some of this footage was the following year folded into the Kinemacolor feature *Canada: Nova Scotia to British Columbia* (1912), a promotional film for the railway (Pelletier 2007:37; see also Jacquier and Pranal 1996).

That same year, 1912, Montreal's British American Film Manufacturing Company completed *The Battle of the Long Sault*, a two-reel drama directed by New Yorker Frank Crane (Pelletier 2007:36). In the promotional material, authenticity is a major selling point. The posters promised the true story of Dollard des Ormeaux, although the sets included "buffalo hide tepees ... decorated with gay Indian illustrations." More than 150 Mohawks were hired for the battle scenes and costumed as Plains Indians. Promoting the film in December 1912, the *Moving Picture News* reported with a seemingly straight face that

> the British American Film Co. ... hit upon the idea of posing real Indians, in their native scenery, so that there could be no possibility of the absurd incongruities springing up which so often occurs when ordinary actors pose as redmen. The style of picture will be different from the average picture palace film.... Instead of imaginary conflicts between settlers and Indians, the British American Film Company plan to depict the great battles of Canadian history, and they are taking the greatest care that the picture shall be historically correct. (Pelletier 2007:37)

The claims of accuracy and authenticity may have cleverly served to defuse potential complaints about nakedness or savagery from educators and religious leaders who harped constantly on the sinful nature of the movies—that is, if a film adheres to the historical truth, then savagery is a matter of record, and, moreover, since the film depicts Canadian history, it is one's patriotic duty to buy a ticket. According to an article in the *Montreal Daily Star,* there were, among the actors, "a considerable number of show Indians, some of whom have been round the world with circuses and 'wild west' shows, and who have acquired the rudiments of stage-craft" (Pelletier

Colin Browne

2007:37). It is likely that these "show Indians" were seasoned performers, like the troupe of seventeen Kwakwa̲ka'wakw men and women who, along with George Hunt, had spent the summer of 1893 in the Anthropology Department at the Chicago World's Fair, performing for the public and making and selling objects, all the while being measured and documented by anthropologist Franz Boas (Cole 1999:153–56). Some of these singers and dancers almost certainly later performed in *Head Hunters*.

The best known of the early Hiawatha films appeared in 1913, a four-reel version of a travelling pageant titled *Hiawatha, The Indian Passion Play*. Produced by Frank E. Moore, with cinematography by twenty-year-old Victor Milner, *Hiawatha* was a fairly sophisticated costume drama shot on location in New York State and on the windy shores of Lake Superior. It was Milner's first feature, and he went on to become a veteran Hollywood cameraman, winning an Academy Award for cinematography in Cecil B. DeMille's *Cleopatra* (1935). (Curtis had also worked for DeMille; he was second-unit cameraman and stills photographer on the 1923 epic *The Ten Commandments*.) Years of pageants had taught Moore how to manage large numbers of people, in this case 150 Indians from New York, Canada, and the Dakotas.[10] Choreographed for the camera, *Hiawatha* is often considered to be the first dramatic motion picture to feature an all-Native cast. Victor Milner has left a lovely account of the production; the following excerpts may shed light on the work of all cinematographers at that time:

> My outfit, as before, was composed of a Schneider amateur model, equipped with 200-foot magazines, non-reversible movement, and a crystal view finder.
>
> I had to shoot the visioning of the famine of death visiting the wigwams on a separate negative and double print it. It was my first attempt at a double, and beginner's luck was with me, but my second effort was disastrous. The scene was the last in the picture—Hiawatha, standing in his canoe, slowly drifts toward the setting sun with the visionary face of Minehaha [sic] appearing before him. I effected the vision all right, with the exception of a small detail. I shot Minehaha a little too close to the camera and the vision appeared *behind* Hiawatha.
>
> My job did not end with the completion of shooting—oh, no! I had to develop 10,000 feet of negative on revolving drums, pick out the N.G.'s, make a print, and tone and tint the same. We received a cent a foot extra for tones. In addition, I had to shoot the titles, and wound up by projecting the finished picture. Yes, we were versatile. (Milner 1923:9, 26)

Moore's 1913 production of *Hiawatha* is of particular interest because the music composed for the screenings was by John J. Braham, the man commissioned by Curtis later that year to write the score for *In the Land of the Head Hunters* (Jacknis and Gilbert, this volume).[11] For *Hiawatha*, Braham had sought out and arranged Ojibwe melodies, perhaps in much the same way that he would be asked to adapt and arrange Kwakwaka'wakw melodies for Edward Curtis (Pisani 1997:346).

To return to the idea of "show Indians," it is fair to assume that the repetitive performances demanded by daily tableaux, motion picture production, and long days and nights of exposure to gullible audiences provided the Mohawks, the Ojibwe, the Senecas, the Kwakwaka'wakw, and many other indigenous people with their own profound and telling insights into the nature of "the authentic." It may now be possible to venture a definition of authenticity. Might it be the satisfaction that floods the non-Native mind when Native actors simulate the behaviour of the imaginary Indian? The masquerade of authenticity must have been a source of continuing mirth for those involved. We can smirk at this, but the drive for "authenticity" when representing "primitive" cultures has not changed. The creators of *Avatar* (2009) labored long and hard to make their fictional world of Pandora seem "authentic."

The practice of reassuring audiences of authenticity was probably why an audio prologue was added to *The Silent Enemy: An Epic of the American Indian* (1930), a film produced by W. Douglas Burden and Willam C. Chanler, directed by H. P. Carver, and filmed in the Temagami Forest Reserve in northern Ontario in the winter of 1928–29. The $200,000 silent movie, like *Head Hunters*, was well received by critics but avoided by audiences. In the film, a band of starving Ojibwe search for a migrating herd of caribou while a rivalry plays out between the chief (Chief Yellow Robe), the medicine man (Chief Akawanush), a "mighty hunter" named Baluk (Chief Buffalo Child Long Lance), and the chief's daughter, Neewa, played by the gifted Penobscot actress, dancer, and artist Molly Spotted Elk. The *Saturday Evening Post* declared the film worthy of a Pulitzer Prize and called it "the best American dramatic creation for the year 1930." Premiered at the Criterion Theatre on Broadway, the eighty-four-minute film was praised for its "authenticity," its "superb acting," and Marcel le Picard's "stunning cinematography."[12] Audiences, however, were turning their backs on silent films. *The Silent Enemy* was one of Paramount's last silent releases.

The Silent Enemy took pains to advertise itself as a dramatic portrait of Ojibwe life as it was, or once was, or as it could be imagined. In an attempt

Colin Browne

to weave together what might be thought of as documentary material and a romantic adventure story, *The Silent Enemy* bears a resemblance to *Head Hunters*. It begins with a remarkable recorded speech by Chief Yellow Robe, the Sioux actor who plays Chief Chatoga, who introduces the story and tells the audience, "Now you will know us as we really are." He concludes with a self-reflexive farewell: "We are Indians living once more our old life. Soon we will be gone. Your civilization will destroy us. But by your magic, we will live forever." To untangle these remarks would take some doing, but it's interesting to note the similarity to Curtis's project in the claim that the actors are "living once more our old life" for the camera. It's difficult to imagine that a Native American wrote this speech. It fits too easily into the convention of the Indian as a primitive who'd regard the movies as "magic" in 1930 (Evans, this volume). On the other hand, because of its direct address and its appeal to the audience to witness what is being "destroyed," Chief Yellow Robe's stepping out of character reinforces the claim of the film's authenticity by implicating its viewers and listeners, and perhaps he was saying what he believed to be true.

More than one writer has suggested that *The Silent Enemy* inspired scenes in Kevin Costner's *Dances with Wolves*. If so, it would not be surprising. The "Indian" has been a central figure in North American cinema since the beginning, and has been a vessel into which writers, directors, and actors have poured their hopes, their dreams, their fancies, their ignorance, their prejudices, their admiration, and their consciences. At every turn, Aristotle's dramatic principles, rather than local knowledge or close observation, have ruled the screen. Robert Flaherty was aware that babies and puppies would attract audiences, and in his advertisements for *Nanook of the North*— wrongly called the first documentary film ever made—he stressed the human drama of the family (Flaherty 1922). An early poster promised "a picture with more drama, greater thrills, and stronger action than any picture you ever saw."[13] When Rockwell Kent, the American painter who'd lived in Greenland among the Eskimos, proposed a "dramatized documentary on Greenland life" in 1934, his agent, William Morris, could not sell the idea in Los Angeles. The project lacked "*thrills, sensations* and *Hollywood*" (Traxel 1980:172). The authentic may, by nature, be paradoxical. Audiences eschew the didactic, which they do not trust, and seek out enhanced drama and conflict, the extremes of which they hope will reveal the heart's hidden truths. As silent film pianist Bob Mitchell observed in Los Angeles in 2008, referring to his own music for films, "Once they've heard the imitation, they'll never again settle for the real thing."[14]

Edward Curtis was worried about this paradox in 1914 as he moved toward the release of *In the Land of the Head Hunters*. Naturalism has its limits; good stories require an examination of human behavior under pressure in a time of irreversible transition. This is why the prospectus for *Head Hunters*—perhaps written by Curtis himself—anticipates and attempts to refute a more serious charge: that the Kwakwa̱ka̱'wakw actors and their performances might be too "authentic" to entertain audiences. The anxiety is palpable in this excerpt's use of the passive voice:

> The question might be raised as to whether the documentary material would not lack the thrilling interest of the fake picture. It is the opinion of Mr. Curtis that the real life of the Indian contains the parallel emotions to furnish all necessary plots and give the pictures the heart interest needed. (Holm and Quimby 1980:113)

Curtis was concerned that the "documentary material" would not be an asset, and that "the real life of the Indian" in his film would be found wanting in terms of excitement. The prospectus appears to be a preemptive strike to assure those whose livelihoods depended on "the thrilling interest of the fake picture" that the movie would make money. Curtis feared that audiences seeking "heart interest" and thrills would turn away. When we look at the restored version today, armed with an understanding of Curtis's original intentions and his intense collaboration with George Hunt and the Kwakwa̱ka̱'wakw actors, prop makers, and costumers, we can appreciate and celebrate his achievement. In 1914, he needed to sell tickets. That the above explanation was asked to serve as encouragement suggests, on the filmmaker's part, an act of desperation.

Curtis's anxiety stems partly from his irreconcilable strategies. He wrote *Head Hunters* as a love story with a tangential relationship to *Romeo and Juliet* involving star-crossed lovers and families at war with one another. He wanted to show the "real life of the Indian" and, at the same time, the "real life of the Indian" appeared to lack "heart interest." He introduced sea lions leaping into the ocean, witchcraft, communion with the dead, battles, and a whale to make the story more exciting. The tale is situated in the mists of time, yet in his notes he writes, boldly, "The story, of course, is a minor detail; the real object of the film being to show the customs, amusements, fights, domestic life, and sports of the North American Indians" (Holm and Quimby 1980:125).

Reflecting on his attempts to downplay the contradictions at the core of his movie—trying to have it both ways, to balance the "authentic" portrayal

Colin Browne

180

of "North American Indians" with melodramatic "heart interest"—we can imagine Curtis becoming worried. His 1911 lantern-slide lecture series *The Curtis Indian Picture Opera*, with orchestra and "Indian" music by Henry F. Gilbert, had not been terribly successful (Gidley and Jacknis, this volume). He was a first-time screenwriter who, in watching his film take shape in the editing room, must have been all too aware of its storytelling flaws and short-comings. He was competing against Hollywood Westerns with "real Indians," such as Cecil B. DeMille's first four films, all made the same year (Koszarski 1990:181–83).[15] Curtis would have been acutely aware of the challenges he had set for himself, and he must have known in his showman's bones, like the producer of *The Battle of the Long Sault*, that authenticity without a flair for the inauthentic would translate into box-office disaster.

Mohawks appeared on film seventy-eight years later, near Kahnawake, defending their territory against the governments of Quebec and Canada in the National Film Board's *Kahnesatake: 270 Years of Resistance* (1993). Alanis Obomsawin's documentary of their defence of a sacred burial ground was a watershed in the representation of indigenous people in Canada, the authenticity of which provoked so much anxiety that the Canadian Broadcasting Corporation refused to televise the film for several months until forced to by public pressure. Obomsawin has been the most prolific First Nations filmmaker in Canada, but increased access to the means of production has resulted in a large number of motion pictures produced by indigenous artists, filmmakers, and organizations that speak from within their cultures. Of interest to those familiar with the Curtis film are two documentaries coproduced with the U'mista Cultural Society in Alert Bay, *Potlatch … A Strict Law Bids Us Dance* (Wheeler 1975) and *Box of Treasures* (Olin 1983), both of which make the case for repatriation as a step toward sovereignty. The present-day films of Kwakwaka'wakw filmmaker Barb Cranmer are particularly significant inasmuch as they stress renewal and contemporary social and commercial success within an unbroken continuum (Cranmer, this volume). *Shooting Indians: A Journey with Jeffrey Thomas* (1997), a documentary by Indian filmmaker Ali Kazimi, includes a visit to hundred-year-old Maggie Frank, who performed in Curtis's film as the "princess." She tells Kazimi that, as she recalls it, *In the Land of the Head Hunters* was like a "home movie" (Glass and Evans, this volume).

* * *

As mentioned earlier, Curtis's original treatment was for "a documentary picture of the Kwakiutl tribes, the natives of Vancouver Island" (Holm and Quimby 1980:115). He was among the first to use the word "documentary" in this way, although film historians credit documentary theorist and producer John Grierson with inventing the term in a 1926 review of Robert Flaherty's *Moana* (Grierson 1926). An earlier example occurs in the Charles Urban Company's 1907 promotional pamphlet "The Cinematograph in Science, Education, and Matters of State." Urban reproduces excerpts from a 1903 lecture by a Dr. Doyen, who had been using motion pictures to teach surgery since 1898 and who was proposing to establish a surgical motion picture archive for "the preservation in documentary form of the operations of the older surgeons." The expression took some years to insinuate itself as a genre. When Robert Sherwood praised *Nanook of the North* in 1923, there was no "documentary" category; it was classed with "travel pictures" and "scenics" (Koszarski 1990:241).

Perhaps what we call the "documentary" was just waiting to be born. It was not only a matter of advancing technology. Sometimes it seems, paradoxically, that each new and revolutionary technology is charged with returning us, through representation, to a longed for (and reified) vision of a simple, innocent, if perilous time. The new makes old new again. Audiences by 1914 were enjoying exotic travelogues; Curtis took the next step. He began with a concept—a romantic, enthusiastic response to the modern era—developed a melodrama as a framing device with central characters and families, and employed nonactors to reenact their ancestors' lives. If we look structurally at *In the Land of the Head Hunters*, *Nanook of the North*, or, for example, *Silent Enemy*, it's clear that the documentary film as an art form—distinct from journalism—was from the outset related to the epic; it was Tolstoyan rather than Zolaesque. The characters tend to be archetypal, and their evil or heroic actions follow suit. They exist in a world in which the elements are unconcerned with human fate. Following on the heels of a brutal, dispiriting war, Flaherty's Nanook represents, for example, the human spirit triumphing over a cruel or indifferent universe. In the fiery cauldron of the modern era, Curtis and Flaherty turned to contemporary moving image technology to ally themselves with a conservative, sometimes reactionary strand of romantic modernity. Resisting the ideological battles of the revolutionary Left and Right, the lure of psychoanalysis, and the nihilistic urban aesthetics of futurists, dadaists, and others, their chiefly Anglo-American strand of modernity sought out what seemed to be timeless in human experience.

In Curtis's case, he was well aware that his actor/collaborators were not dwelling in a state of primitive innocence; he knew them as twentieth-century Canadians. His idea of a mythic, "timeless world" speaks to both the past and the present. By setting in motion epic characters who play out the

Colin Browne

ancient and often terrible drama of succession, his narrative is intentionally ahistoric—not prehistoric.

Sadly, in chasing after the timeless, Curtis missed a remarkable opportunity. I have always been sorry that he did not locate his film in his own time—a transitional period critical for the cultures of the Northwest Coast. It would not have been easy, given the cameras of the time and the film stocks, which required high levels of light. Location sound recording as we know it today would have been out of the question. Filmmakers in Curtis's time made the films they did because they made the films they could. If elements of mythology, dance, melodrama, and epic pictorialism appear to coexist somewhat uneasily in *Head Hunters*, part of the reason has to do with the limitations of technology. At the same time, Curtis made a choice, and he missed the story that was right under his nose.

* * *

There's a fascinating link between *Head Hunters* and *Nanook of the North*. After seeing *In the Land of the Head Hunters* in New York, Robert Flaherty, at the time a mining engineer, asked to meet Curtis. He'd been filming on the Belcher Islands in Hudson Bay and wanted Curtis's opinion on his footage. Curtis offered him advice about narrative and dramatic structure as well as shooting for continuity, reverse angles, framing, editing, mise-en-scène, and so on. The result, after two more trips into the Arctic, was *Nanook*. Flaherty's film focuses on the survival of an Inuit family and, like *Head Hunters*, constructs fictional scenes to advance the narrative. Flaherty collaborated with the man he called Nanook (his name was Allakariallak) in order to recreate traditional hunting, fishing, and family life for the camera. He included elements of comedy, concentrating on an intimate portrait of the family and its daily struggle. Thanks to these more intimate strategies, *Nanook* is a more accomplished film than *Head Hunters*.

Curtis and Flaherty have both been criticized for their recreations and for their simplistic portrayals of complex people and societies. Critic Arthur Calder-Marshall accused Flaherty of making a "costume picture," and he was correct in the sense that costume pictures are a way of addressing the present (Koszarski 1990:243). Anxious about the economic and social upheavals of their own time, Curtis and Flaherty dramatized the precontact lives of North American hunter-gatherers as screens upon which to project their own cherished values: self-reliance, independence, and the instinct to protect or to sacrifice oneself for the family or tribal group. Both men have been criticized for practising cinematic salvage ethnography and for concentrating on the vanishing traditions of their subjects, but the truth of the matter is that the way of life that was vanishing was their own.

The romantic poet William Wordsworth believed that the task of poetry was to identify, in the lives and landscapes of ordinary people, "the primary laws of our nature" (Wordsworth 1970:411). In the documentary, it's often an article of faith that the camera and the microphone are able to identify and reveal these primary laws, and, further, that these laws govern the human condition and its innate virtues of courage, loyalty, and dignity. This is the unwritten article of faith to which Frances Flaherty was referring when she wrote in 1927 that "pictures of life, of the dramatic inherent in life, are documentary and philosophic" (Koszarski 1990:241). Artist Paul Klee was thinking of something similar when he wrote, "Art does not render the visible, but renders visible."

Nanook of the North seems to have made a deep impression on the Soviet directors of the 1920s. Writing in the magazine of the National Board of Review in 1943, Soviet director Sergei Eisenstein claimed, "We Russians learned more from *Nanook of the North* than from any other foreign film. We wore it out studying it. That was, in a way, our beginning" (Taylor 1949:28).[16] Thus *Nanook*—begotten by *In the Land of the Head Hunters*—begat *The Battleship Potemkin* (1925) and *October* (1927). In Britain, John Grierson, the Scottish-born founder of the British documentary movement, and later the creator of the National Film Board of Canada, was profoundly influenced by Eisenstein's epic cinema. He had the job of subtitling the films into English when they were screened at the Film Society in London during the 1920s, and took the opportunity to study them frame by frame. Borrowing Eisenstein's epic narrative sense, in 1929 he directed his first documentary film, *Drifters*, a portrait of British herring fishermen who battled the elements to feed the nation. The film's subtext is that Britons have the courage, the stamina, the discipline, the good cheer, the independence, and the faith in one another to triumph over doubt and social upheaval. The primal laws of nature are revealed to be intact in the dignity and work ethic of the herring fishermen. Is this the documentary film as an act of social engineering? Yes, and in Grierson's hand, as a reiteration of traditional British values against the lures of fascism and communism.

Eisenstein's epic treatment of actuality, translated by Grierson, became an organizing principle of the British documentary movement of the 1930s. A film about daily life, for instance, would locate the symbolic elements of epic conflict in daily experience and reveal them dramatically. Grierson, an unabashed propagandist and educator, understood that through exaggeration, repetition, rhythm, defamiliarization, and extreme camera angles, the documentary would reveal what he called the "dramatic nature of the actual," thereby engaging deep impulses and emotions in order to advance democratic principles (Aitken 1990:68–69). He brought these convictions with him to Canada when he founded the National Film Board during World War II. An unbroken line can be traced from Curtis, assisted on his epic by George Hunt and his Kwakwa̲ka'wakw collaborators, to Flaherty, to Eisenstein, to Grierson, and on to the traditions of the National Film Board, where Grierson's definition of documentary, "the creative treatment of actuality" (Grierson 1966:13), guides the hands of filmmakers to this day.

* * *

In devising his complex scenario for *Head Hunters*, Edward Curtis must have felt that he had no choice but to cover as many bases as possible. He was right to be concerned about how his film would be received by audiences enchanted by "fake" pictures, and it must have been a terrible blow for him to watch the film's title being pulled off the marquee after only a few days. Those who wish to gain an understanding of his radical, iconic, melodramatic—and, until recently, confusing—movie, will be intrigued by the 2008 restoration project described in this volume, which replicates, as closely as possible, the movie that premiered in Seattle and New York in 1914. With the replacement of lost footage, the original intertitles, and a reconstruction of the musical score by John Braham, the film as Curtis intended—while still not complete—now stands better revealed, providing an enhanced dramatic context for the extraordinary footage of the Kwakwa̲ka'wakw ceremonial practises.

To stand in for still-missing scenes, single frames of the original film, recovered from Curtis's Library of Congress copyright deposit, were inserted into the current reconstruction. These still images tend, inadvertently, to enhance the film's pictorialist nature. With their inclusion, however, and with the new footage, we can better understand how certain scenes were intended to fit into the narrative. One of the newly discovered sequences— the slave boy summoning help for his mistress—is probably as complete now as it will ever be, and in its extended form is complex and moving. The final scene of the sequence, showing the abject boy on the beach, wounded and abandoned after his sacrifice—he's a slave after all—reveals that Curtis and his assistant George Hunt had an impressive, convincing grasp of cinematic storytelling and its emotional potential (chapter 12, this volume).

As well as confirming his talents as a photographer, a writer, and a visual storyteller, the new restoration reminds us that Edward Curtis was a complex, conflicted, perhaps unknowable character. He is regularly accused—a charge that's partly true—of "antiquing" his twentieth-century Native subjects, yet the persona he fashioned for himself is equally "antiqued," although he spent over 60 percent of his life in the twentieth century (in Seattle, New York, and Los Angeles). He embarked on his projects with the same kind of Adamic intensity as his nineteenth-century analogue, John James Audubon, or perhaps as Melville's driven, single-minded Ahab, yet he was a twentieth-century self-promoter and entrepreneur and gladly embraced new technologies. Perhaps it wouldn't be out of place to suggest that within Curtis himself a battle raged between the old century and the new—between the communal traditions, spiritual beliefs, and nomadic freedom of aboriginal cultures, and the conservatism, fundamentalism, and entrepreneurial individualism of American culture—at a time when the combined forces of both reactionary and revolutionary fury were about to incinerate civilization.

*   *   *

What would happen if we examined Edward Curtis in the intellectual context of his time? He wasn't the only one to be made anxious by the modern condition of alienation, of having discovered that belonging consists in recognizing that one does not belong. What would Freud have made of Curtis? He'd have been intrigued by this capable technician's obsessive quest to stage dramatic, photographic tableaux of the precontact lives of the societies he believed his own culture was aggressively erasing. Is there an aspect of Curtis's work that can be seen as an act of atonement? What was it that led him to devote his life to making images that would symbolically stop time, aging, and death and keep oblivion at bay? Herman Melville would have recognized the anxiety of Edward Curtis, simultaneously paralyzed by and fatally dependent upon his nation's efforts to cleanse its New Jerusalem of its original inhabitants.

Franz Kafka's "Wunsch, Indianer zu werden" or "The Wish to Be a Red Indian" was published in 1913, the year Curtis wrote the scenario for *Head Hunters*. Its single fragmenting sentence, a fantasy of wish fulfilment and escape imbued with longing and melancholy, would not be out of place as a caption for one of Curtis's photographs.

> If one were only an Indian, instantly alert, and on a racing horse, leaning against the wind, kept on quivering jerkily over the quivering ground, until one shed one's spurs, for there needed no spurs, threw away the reins, for there needed no reins, and hardly saw that the land before one was smoothly shorn heath when horse's neck and head would be already gone. (Kafka 1971:390)[17]

Colin Browne

In Kafka's exploding "portrait" the elements of oppression and control drop away, the horse vanishes, and something like the soul alone remains, disembodied, free, leaving no trace, not even a photograph. Michal Ben Naftali suggests that one of the conditions of modernity is living without the presence of one's ancestors. She notes that both Kafka and Walter Benjamin—Curtis's contemporaries—were absorbed by the search for their "primitive" or ancestral history and its present-day manifestations, and tormented by their sense of alienation. In his 1934 essay on Kafka's longing, Benjamin uses an unexpected simile:

> To Kafka, the world of his ancestors was as unfathomable as the world of realities was important to him, and we may be sure that, like the totem poles of primitive peoples, the world of ancestors took him down to the animals. (Benjamin 1999:809–10)

The moment when the animal manifests itself, in Benjamin's mind, is the moment in which one must confront one's suppressed self and its forbidden desires. One is reminded that one is, at once, animal *and* human. What emerges is the sadly tolerable truth that one's fortunes feed on the misery and erasure of others. Here, one might say, lies the universal source of anxiety and guilt, and a lifetime of self-control and sadness.

Curtis had witnessed the dramatic struggles represented by Kwakwaka'wakw ceremonies in which man and animal intercede with one another on the border between life and death, and in which destructive instincts are tamed. Perhaps he sublimated these instincts into his image making. Ben Naftali suggests that Kafka—who wished to be what he thought of as "a Red Indian," and who sublimated what he could into his writing—experienced throughout his life a "sense of organic dread, as well as ... a fear of the immemorial, the fear of an unknown culpability" (Ben Naftali 2007:83). Does this make one think of Edward S. Curtis, who perhaps turned guilt and anxiety into a very North American, that is, redemptive, if paradoxical, process of acquisition and atonement?

What we admire today about *Head Hunters* are the grand ceremonial tableaux. There is nothing like them, or more thrilling, in all of cinema. I hope that one day more people will become aware that the art of cinema found some of its initial inspiration on the rainy beaches of Beaver Harbour and Fort Rupert and in the mythic transformations of the Kwakwaka'wakw. With the newly completed restoration of *In the Land of the Head Hunters*, it may be time to consider rewriting the film histories of North America. And it is time to assign credit to all of those who made props, costumes, and wigs; who assisted in other ways; and who coached and performed for Curtis's camera. He could not have made the film without them, and they ought to share the credit. The Kwakw<u>aka</u>'wakw, cannot, this time, be overlooked.

1   In the Western cinematic canon, *Nanook of the North* is known as the world's first documentary film. In fact, both Flaherty's and Curtis's films must bear considerable responsibility for devising what are now conventional dramatic and narrative strategies for working on location with nonactors—strategies still used in observational documentaries today, although portable cameras and sound equipment have made the machinery almost invisible. Now that we have a newly restored version of *In the Land of the Head Hunters*, with added scenes and stills, perhaps we should begin to think of Flaherty's film as a footnote to Curtis's … but more on this later.

2   It's interesting to consider that Curtis's contemporaries included Marcel Duchamp, Albert Einstein, D. W. Griffith, Marcel Proust, Bertrand Russell, Alfred Stieglitz, Igor Stravinsky, Leon Trotsky, Pancho Villa, and Sigmund Freud, who in 1913 published *Totem and Taboo*. During the time that Curtis was in production on his film, Freud's colleagues presented him with a small Egyptian figure as a totem animal at a "totem feast" in Vienna to celebrate the book's publication. See http://www.freud-museum. at/freud/chronolg/1913-e.htm (accessed August 17, 2012).

3   This description is taken from the Le-La-La Dancers promotional material. See http:// ca.groups.yahoo.com/group/AboriginalArtsAdministrators/message/1207 (accessed March 18, 2013).

4   Bill Holm, email correspondence with author, January 31, 2010. Holm uses the name Modana. He writes, "The Awikenoxw name is Mudana, pronounced Moodahnah (accent on the first syllable), and means something like 'Four Man Eater.' So I habitually spell it with a D. However … Curtis spelled it with a T. Still, it isn't *moe*-TAN-a, as I hear it pronounced! I don't know why Curtis used the Awikenoxw Hama͡tsa name for his hero." I'm grateful to Bill Holm for sharing this information and for permitting it to be published. (On Motana/Mudana, see also introduction, this volume, note 18.)

5   Bill Holm, email correspondence with author, January 31, 2010.

6   Bill Holm, email correspondence with author, January 31, 2010.

7   One poster claimed, "Warner Bros. put all the force of the screen into a challenging drama of today's juvenile violence!" Another announced, "This is how a teen-war starts!" The movie is promoted almost as if it's a public service announcement; audiences are encouraged to go to the movie as an act of concerned citizenship.

8   See Nancy Watrous, Judith Miller, and Andy Uhrich, "A Pictorial History of Hiawatha (1904)," online at http://sites.google.com/site/orphans7/home/notes-on-a-pictorial-story-of-hiawatha (accessed March 22, 2013).

9   See the IMDB entry at http://www.imdb.com/title/tt0000443/releaseinfo#akas (accessed March 22, 2013).

10 See the Library of Congress listing for *Hiawatha* in their invaluable research aid for "American Indians in Silent Film" at http://www.loc.gov/rr/mopic/findaid/indian1. html (accessed March 18, 2013).

11 Both John Braham's original 1914 manuscript score for *Head Hunters* and David Gilbert's 2008 transcription are available in complete form through the Getty Research Institute's online library at http://www.getty.edu/research/library/ (accessed July 14, 2013).

12 See the research collection at the Abbe Museum, Bar Harbor, Maine. Online at http://abbemuseum.org/research/collections/curator-features/molly-spotted-elk. html (accessed March 22, 2013).

Colin Browne

13 Poster online at http://en.wikipedia.org/wiki/Nanook_of_the_North (accessed March 22, 2013).

14 Bob Mitchell was a legendary silent film pianist who began his career as a teenager. He died on July 4, 2009, in Los Angeles, at the age of ninety-six. He made this remark while adressing a research gathering at the Getty in support of the Curtis film project.

15 DeMille's 1914 Westerns were *The Squaw Man, The Virginian, The Rose of the Rancho,* and *The Girl of the Golden West*, based on David Belasco's play of the same name (1905), which also inspired Puccini's *La fanciulla del west* which premiered at the Metropolitan Opera in New York in 1910.

16 Taylor (1949:28) adds that Flaherty was "inclined to consider [Eisenstein's] compliment with mixed feelings. A few years ago, at a social function in London, he was assailed bitterly by several Soviet officials who accused him of suppressing facts. 'Nanook was a dog,' one of them said. 'He was a victim of capitalism. It was your duty to make all clear about living conditions.' Flaherty nodded politely and replied, 'You're right, of course. I'm very anxious to make a clear documentary of life in Russia. Perhaps you can arrange it for me.' He gave the officials the name of his hotel and asked them to get in touch with him when they had hashed things out with Stalin. He waited around town several weeks, checking with his hotel every hour or so, but the word never came."

17 Kafka's sentence was composed earlier, but was first published in a collection of short texts entitled *Betrachtung* [Meditations] in 1913.

7

INDIAN MOVIES AND THE
VERNACULAR OF MODERNISM

BRAD EVANS

In the Land of the Head Hunters epitomizes and complicates the classic modernist juxtaposition between "primitive art" and "mass culture." This familiar pattern of contrasts between the assumed integrity of traditional cultures and the kaleidoscopic fragmentation of mass-produced cultural commodities can be found in almost all genres of early twentieth-century cultural production: from the dialect of the minstrel shows popular on the vaudeville stage to the orientalism characteristic of the grand movie palaces; from collections of folk songs attentive to the orthographic details of ethnic dialect to classical renditions of such songs in symphony halls; and from the portrayal of the "Indian" in dime novels to their appearance in high modernist poetry and cubist paintings.[1] *In the Land of the Head Hunters* offers a particularly rich encapsulation of this dynamic. I hope to expand our understanding of what Curtis's film represents by suggesting a path for reading its historical documentation of the Kwakw<u>a</u>kwa'wakw neither in opposition to cultural forces of modernity nor fully embraced by the aesthetics of high modernism but rather as part of a middle ground being forged within the entertainment industry. For most white audiences and philanthropic supporters, then and now, *Head Hunters* was both part of the culture industry felt by many to exemplify modernity's fragmentation of traditional cultures, and also part of the attempt to "shore up its ruins" by aesthetic means.[2] The film falls squarely into the gap between crass, mass-market commercialism and the aesthetic recuperation of "primitive art," which makes it even more difficult to recover a sense of how to situate the scores of indigenous people who were involved

190

in its production and the thousands of spectators who would have seen it in movie houses across North America.

The initial line of questioning about the film in our own time properly concerns its intentions, and our own understanding of them. These concerns are not entirely distinct from the juxtaposition between the primitive and the mass cultural to the extent that they turn on the issue of authenticity—on the dynamic between what is real and what artificial, what is true and what fiction (Browne, this volume). The primary question has been whether *Head Hunters* is a documentary or a feature film. Is it more properly grouped with Robert Flaherty's *Nanook of the North* (1922) or with D. W. Griffith's Indian movies, such as *The Mended Lute* (1909) or *The Battle at Elderbush Gulch* (1913)? Is it more fact or fiction, more cultural history or modern art, more authentically ethnographic or crassly commercial? Does it portray the Kwakwaka'wakw enacting authentic scenes from their own, and to some extent their neighbors', cultural past—doing, basically, the same things they have always done and still do? Or does it reveal a different kind of history, that, say, of paid Kwakwaka'wakw actors performing a bowdlerized version of their own past in a melodrama for the most modern of early twentieth-century mass-cultural entertainments, the motion pictures? Is it the kind of thing that was correctly archived in the American Museum of Natural History and The Field Museum, or should it be at MoMA instead?

Since at least 1947, when an eccentric collector from Indiana named Hugo Zeiter donated his orphaned copy of the film to The Field Museum, the overwhelming emphasis of its reception has been in the direction of under-standing the film in documentary terms (Glass and Evans, and Browne, this volume). Indeed, the preoccupation with authenticity has been so prevalent with *Head Hunters*, and for so long, that one is tempted to offer a diagnosis: that in viewing it, we seem to be suffering from something of a documentary fixation. The interest of The Field Museum in 1947 in obtaining "portions of the film hav[ing] great merit as a scientific record," as its deputy director John Miller put it at the time, mirrored exactly the assessment of Boas and others at the American Museum of Natural History twenty years earlier when, "solely for Museum purposes" and "for the record," they negotiated with Curtis for the negative and copyright.[3] While one of Zeiter's letters to the Field expressed his interest in the film's color tinting and toning, his main pitch to the museum was that aspects of the film reminded him of *Nanook of the North* and of articles he had seen in *National Geographic*.[4]

Bill Holm and George Quimby's rediscovery of the film decades later contributed to the continuation of its reception as a documentary. As I have argued before, the production values of their restoration effort, *In the Land of the War Canoes*, encouraged a reemphasis of the film's ethnographic content by altering the melodramatic style of the title and intertitles and adding a soundtrack very much out of keeping with a 1914 silent movie (Evans 1998). And even with the current reconstruction, which has restored the melodramatic intertitles, the colorization, and the original 1914 musical score, it has proven difficult to focus any sustained attention on *Head Hunters* as a piece of motion picture history. The questions at public screenings and lectures inevitably turn to the Kwakwa̱ka̱'wakw themselves, and whether this or that aspect of the film was an accurate representation, whether they still did things in just the same way. It is as if the very idea of Kwakwa̱ka̱'wakw individuals "acting" in an outrageously melodramatic love story with cannibalism as its backdrop were somehow inimical to any conceivable notion of what it would have meant "to be Kwakwa̱ka̱'wakw" in 1914, and also as if a suggestion that they had so "acted" would be offensive to or threatening of the claims of cultural self-identification made by Kwakwa̱ka̱'wakw community members today.

The documentary fixation not only oversimplifies the historical record of cross-cultural encounter, but also diminishes the kind of understanding that can take shape even in deeply flawed works of art. It is a reflection of the deep suspicion with which, as anthropologists, activists, cultural historians, and literary critics, we now approach works of art about "other" cultures— a reflection of a postmodern suspicion of representation, of the ability of a work of art to reflect anything but its own cultural perspective (Evans 2007:436–37). In what follows, I nonetheless would like to consider what can be learned by treating *In the Land of the Head Hunters* as a piece of fiction, a commercial entertainment recognizable in the historical context of the movies. This essay examines this forgotten side of *In the Land of the Head Hunters*—its history as part of the emerging motion picture industry—in order to recover some of the complexity of the historical moment of the film's release in 1914, making three points about the relationship of *Head Hunters* to other feature films.

First, the lingering tendency to think of *Head Hunters* exclusively in documentary terms, even once we know that it was not a documentary in any simple sense, perpetuates the naïve idea that Kwakwa̱ka̱'wakw cultural identity (and by implication cultural identification more generally) is situated strictly in opposition to the cultural market and, one might say, against the idea of modernity itself. If that were the case, any participation by Native Americans in something like a Curtis film deeply inflected by primitivist imaginings, as *Head Hunters* obviously was, would only weaken or cheapen their own identity. But, as I have suggested elsewhere, the consumption of such images at the time, made newly available not only in motion pictures but also in illustrated magazines, was integral to the emergence of the very idea of "cultures" in the modern, relative, pluralized, ethnographic sense: historically speaking, one does not even have a notion of "cultural identity" before mass media's objectification of the "culture concept" in the anthropological sense in the early twentieth century (Evans 2005:24–50). Before then, "culture" was used only in the singular in English, and you either had it or you didn't. So in the first section of the essay, I explore the implications of this argument about the emergence of new ideas about cultural pluralism and cultural identity in particular relation to Native American viewers of early film. What happens, I ask, if we work to imagine the indigenous community in 1914 not merely as participants in the production of film (as others in this volume have done regarding both the film and Curtis's photography), but also as consumers and spectators of it, and as such as authors of the culture concept in its modern sense?

The second point has to do with what has always been cast as the failure of *In the Land of the Head Hunters* to find a popular audience. In what follows, I place the reception of *Head Hunters* in three contexts: as one of hundreds of other Indian movies being produced at the time, including not only the ubiquitous "Westerns" but also "Northerns"; as an attempt to be identified as one of what were then coming to be known as "spectacle films," extravaganza pieces that were experiencing a vogue at the time; and, more broadly still, as a prime example of the modern art movement's well-known thirst for and exploitation of "primitive" materials. What I suggest is that *Head Hunters* offers an opportunity to reconfigure the relationship of Native American materials to modernity more generally when we understand the very particularized kind of traction they were able to gain in the modern art market.

Finally, the essay revisits the legacy of *Head Hunters* as a feature film, attempting to understand the complexity of the encounter it documents between the Kwakw<u>a</u>ka'wakw, Curtis, and the cultural marketplace of the early twentieth century in artistic terms. The effort here is to consider the film not on the grounds of history but in terms of the fictional story it attempted to portray, and especially to account for the cultural resonance of its exceedingly dark portrayal of love and war on the Northwest Coast.

Indian Spectators and
the Vernacular of Modernism

The first thing to keep in mind when imagining *In the Land of the Head Hunters* in the historical context of early film is that, by the time it premiered, the film industry was well established and moving quickly toward a new era. The period of the nickelodeon storefront viewing rooms had already faded, being replaced by that of the vast movie palaces of the silent-film era, and the nickelodeon's fare of a balanced program of four or five shorts was giving way to multireel features of increasingly ambitious scale and technical proficiency. The idea of *Head Hunters* being in any way a groundbreaking film on its technical merits is one that runs into immediate problems. It was not the first to eschew non-Native actors in Indian roles, film in an exotic location, commission a musical score, or take an ethnographic interest in cultural ceremonies and costumes.[5] In promotional materials, claims had been made about its technical innovation in the development of something called the "Hochstetter process" of color film developing, but, as it turns out, the film's tinting and toning were simply an elaborate version of already well-known techniques (Guldin, this volume).[6] Similarly, the advertising claim that its score featured "native music symphonized"—as if following in the footsteps of Dvořák, who had cited the significance of Native American music and African-American spirituals in the composition of his *New World Symphony*—turns out to have been in large measure an exaggeration as well (Gilbert and Harrison, this volume).

Just as filmmaking had evolved by 1914, so had film viewing. It is clear from the evidence that at least some of those involved in making *In the Land of the Head Hunters* would also have been audience members of it and other motion pictures that were being shown with regularity in the area around Victoria and Vancouver at this time. Here, in particular, the documentary fixation can take us astray. It is no longer surprising, when thinking of a film like *Head Hunters,* that critical attention would turn to the relationship of its actors to the broader field of representation, to the participation of Native Americans as actors in and directors of this and other movies. While the attention to more complex histories of the production of these films is welcome, it is nonetheless notable that far less attention has been paid to the subject of their historical reception among Native communities. It is almost as if, even while acknowledging an Indian presence in the motion picture studio, we still manage to internalize the conceit that the subjects of these films did not, themselves, go to the movies.[7]

Brad Evans

Not only do we know this to be false, but it also tends to cloud our understanding of how the production of cultural identity depends on the manner of its consumption—on the way, for example, that a viable market for cultural commodities might even secure the viability of a cultural heritage in moments of extreme political or economic duress (for a recent theoretical overview of this subject, see Comaroff and Comaroff 2009:22–29). What we now know of the active participation of hundreds of Native Americans in the production of motion pictures in the early 1900s should encourage us to begin speculating about the phenomenon of film's historical reception by indigenous spectators. In this case, we are looking at the process by which the reception of cultural identity, mediated by a popular market for cultural commodities, inevitably shaped the production of that identity, even then. Historically speaking, this reception not only informed its content, but given that we are at the dawn of the modern idea of culture in the anthropological sense of the term, it also would have contributed to elaborating the notional contours of what cultural identity might even be. As Paul Chaat Smith has put it recently, making a similar point, and perhaps stating the case more forcefully than I would care to do, "Everything about being Indian has been shaped by the camera" (Smith 2009:4). And that includes the very idea that "being Indian" meant being part of "a culture" in the modern, anthropological sense of the term.

With one significant exception, we are largely in the realm of speculation when contemplating the possibility that any of the Kwakwaka'wakw involved in the production of *Head Hunters* might have been to the movies. The exception, however, speaks volumes. In a letter to Franz Boas that George Hunt sent while visiting New York in March of 1903, Hunt describes having been to a moving picture show twice, once in Victoria and again in New York the night before writing. If he had been to the movies twice already in 1903, one would assume that by 1914 he would have been many more times.[8] And given this evidence, it seems more than reasonable to suspect that at least some of the other participants in Curtis's film had been to the pictures as well. After all, many coastal Natives were highly itinerant through the late nineteenth and early twentieth centuries, as the colonial economy offered labor prospects throughout the region in canneries, fisheries, logging camps, and hop fields, not to mention urban markets for crafts and occasionally prostitution (Lutz 2008). The film was made in Fort Rupert, which was relatively "cosmopolitan" for the time, as was nearby Alert Bay, although some individuals in the film were from surrounding villages, including Blunden Harbour, which were more remote. The Kwakwaka'wakw involved with the film likely had quite different histories of urban experience, and yet the specific individuals whom we know to have been involved in projects like *Head Hunters* would also have been those who traveled to the world fairs, participated in Boasian ethnographic projects, and catered to the tourist trade, and thus would have been the ones most likely to have seen films (introduction, this volume). And they would not have had to go so far afield as the fairs in Chicago or Saint Louis to have done so, the history of showmanship in British Columbia being quite well documented.

Opportunities for the Kwakw<u>a</u>ka'wakw to see motion pictures in Vancouver, Victoria, or elsewhere in the province would have been ample starting as early as 1898. The first permanent theater in Canada devoted exclusively to showing motion pictures, the Electric Theater, was established in 1902 at 38 Cordova Street in Vancouver, and there were soon at least three more theaters advertising regularly in the daily newspapers (Macdonald 1992; Matthews 1937; Moore 2004; Morris 1978). The British Columbia and Vancouver directories, which would not have included most of the small nickelodeons—and do not for that matter, include even the Electric or the Savoy—list four theaters in 1907 and forty-four in 1914; as was the case in other cities, many of these likely included film in their programs even if they were devoted to musical theater and vaudeville. We know this to be the case at the 675-seat Pantages, for example, which opened in 1907 and was the first of an extensive chain of Pantages theaters that stretched across Canada. By 1921, Vancouver had at least one of the lavish movie palaces that so defined the silent film era, the Capital Theatre at 820 Granville; and by the later 1920s and by the 1930s, it had many more (Lazecki 1997:714).

But well before then, traveling showmen were projecting films up and down the Northwest Coast, bringing the movies to new audiences. One documented report is of particular interest. John Schuberg, who opened the Electric Theater, started out as an itinerant showman, with his first Vancouver film, *The Spanish American War*, being projected there in 1898. That same year, there is a record of someone as far north as Hazelton, 760 miles to the north and 186 miles east of Prince Rupert, at the head of the Skeena River, showing a film to a mixed audience of white frontiersmen and Indians, presumably Gitxsan from the area. Ingenious and determined, Schuberg had excavated the side of a hill overlooking the side of town, where he rigged a screen and lantern to show his motion pictures (Morris 1978:14; Talbot 1912:132–33). The point for us is that the movies made it to very remote locales years before Curtis even got the idea of doing a movie at Fort Rupert. So would it have been possible for the Kwakw<u>a</u>ka'wakw performers in *Head*

196

Edward S. Curtis or Edmund A. Schwinke, ca. 1914. Hand colored lantern slide depicting a scene from *Head Hunters*, similar to those used by Curtis in his 1911–13 musicale. Burke Museum of Natural History and Culture. See fig. 1.6, p. 53.

Top: Emily Carr (Canadian, 1871–1945), *Indian Village, Alert Bay,* ca. 1912. Oil on canvas, 25 x 32 in. Gift of Lord Beaverbrook. Beaverbrook Art Gallery, 59.30. See fig. I.7, p. 20.

Bottom: Emily Carr (Canadian, 1871–1945), *War Canoe, Alert Bay,* 1908. Watercolor on board, 10 5/8 x 15 in. This is an image of one of the dugout canoes used for the filming of *Head Hunters.* Private Collection. Photo by Brian Goble, Heffel Fine Art Auction House. See fig. I.8, p. 20.

Jeff Thomas, *Returning the Gaze: Black Eagle and Kevin Haywahe*, 2005.
Left: Edward S. Curtis, *Black Eagle [Wa"bŭdi-sápa—Assiniboin]*, ca. 1908. Library of Congress,
LC-USZ62-105371. *Right:* Jeff Thomas, *Kevin Haywahe in Powwow Dance Attire, Assiniboine
tribe*, Carry-the-Kettle Reserve, Saskatchewan, 1991. Courtesy of the artist.
See fig. E.1.3, p. 136.

Jeff Thomas, *Medicine Crow*, 2010.

Left: Edward S. Curtis, *Medicine Crow—Apsaroke*, ca. 1908. Library of Congress, LC-USZ62-106886. *Center:* Jeff Thomas, red-tailed hawk photographed at the Alberta Birds of Prey Foundation, Coaldale, Alberta, 2006. Courtesy of the artist. *Right:* Edward S. Curtis, *Medicine Crow*, ca. 1908. Library of Congress, LC-USZ62-98537.

See fig. E.1.4 p.138.

Jeff Thomas, *Indian Families*, 2010.

Left: Photographer unknown, Jim Abikoki and family in front of the fence surrounding the Anglican Mission on the Blackfoot (Siksika) Reserve, Alberta, ca. 1900. Glenbow Museum Archives, NC-5-8. *Center:* Edward S. Curtis, *Yellow Bone Woman [Arikara tribe]*, ca. 1908, North Dakota. Library of Congress, LC-USZ62-10183. *Right:* Jeff Thomas, *Good Eagle Family*, Bismarck, North Dakota, 1996. Courtesy of the artist. See fig. E.1.5. p. 141.

fig. E.1.6. Jeff Thomas, *The End Is Near*, 2010.

Left: Edward S. Curtis, *Ndee Sangochonh, Apache*, ca. 1906. Library of Congress, LC-USZ62-106797. *Center*: Jeff Thomas, *Construction Site*, Ottawa, Ontario, 2007. Courtesy of the artist. *Right*: Edward S. Curtis, *Nó·va—Walpi [Pursuing a Butterfly, Badger Clan, Hopi, Walpi-Pueblo]*, 1906. Library of Congress, LC-USZ62-124180. See fig. E.1.6, p. 143.

Top: Interior of the Big House in Alert Bay, British Columbia, 2011. Photo by Christina Cook. U'mista Cultural Centre. See fig. 14.1, p. 311.

Bottom: Canvas drops (here projected digitally) designed and painted by William Wasden Jr. for use by the Ǥwa'wina Dancers in 2008. Photo by Sharon Grainger. U'mista Cultural Centre. See fig. 14.2, p. 311.

Top: Kwan̓wala (Thunderbird) Dance as presented by the G̲wa'wina Dancers in the 2008 restoration project. Photo by Sharon Grainger. U'mista Cultural Centre. See fig. 15.5b, p. 330.

Bottom: Tuxw'id (Warrior) Dance as presented by the G̲wa'wina Dancers in the 2008 restoration project. Photo by Sharon Grainger. U'mista Cultural Centre. See fig. 15.4b, p. 329.

Top: Galsgamliła Dance as presented by the G̲wa'wina Dancers in the 2008 restoration project. Photo by Sharon Grainger. U'mista Cultural Centre. See fig. 15.6b, p. 329.

Bottom: Hamat'sa Dance as presented by the G̲wa'wina Dancers in the 2008 restoration project. Photo by Sharon Grainger. U'mista Cultural Centre. See fig. 15.7b, p. 333.

Hamat'sa masks and *dantsikw* ("power boards"), original Curtis film props now on display at the Burke Museum, Seattle, 2008. Photo by Aaron Glass. Burke Museum of Natural History and Culture. See fig. 15.11, p. 340.

William Wasden Jr. (Canadian, b. 1967), *Samdzuyawes: The Mouth of Heaven*, 2008–9.
Acrylic paint, graphite black paint, and mica flakes, 54 x 74 in. This painting is based
in part on Edward Curtis's photograph of Hamat'sa masks used in the film.
Courtesy of the artist. See fig. 15.12, p. 340.

In the Land of the Head Hunters billboard, 1914. 24 pieces; 8 x 20 ft. (assembled). Printed by the H. C. Miner Litho Company, New York (#17676). Private collection.

See fig. A.1.1, p. 364.

Original advertising card depicting "The Bridal Party" from *In the Land of the Head Hunters*, ca. 1914. The Seattle Public Library, Photographers Scrapbooks: Asahel & Edward Curtis #180.

See fig. A.1.2, p. 364.

Original Curtis film props, ca. 1913, now in the Burke Museum.
Top: Neck Ring (7719). Cedar bark, diam 15.75 in. See fig. A3.1, pg. 381.
Bottom: Head Ring (7720). Cedar bark, H: 4 in, W: 7.5 in, L: 9 in. See fig. A3.2, pg. 381.

Original Curtis film props, ca. 1913, now in the Burke Museum.
Top: Basketry Hat (7739). Spruce root and paint, no dimensions given. See fig. A3.3, pg. 383.
Bottom: Drum (7740). Hide and wood, no dimensions given. See fig. A3.4, pg. 383.

Edward S. Curtis, *A Tsawatenok House-Front*, 1914 (*NAI,* vol. 10).
Charles Deering McCormick Library of Special Collections,
Northwestern University Library. See fig. A.1.7, p. 366.

Hunters to have been to the movies, just like George Hunt? Or, even, is it at all likely that they would not have?[9]

Again, one can only speculate. A drive today from Fort Rupert to either Vancouver or Victoria still takes well over eight hours and may involve a long ferry ride. It obviously took much longer than that in 1914. It was isolated. And yet, it seems to me a mistake to assume that people at Fort Rupert were naïve to the pleasures and problems of film spectatorship. It is, of course, true that posing for still cameras and performing dances for tourists were more common experiences than seeing movies in movie theatres. However, it seems important not to rule out the possibility, and it is highly useful to assume, at the very least, a kind of cognizance of the kind of thing likely to be produced with the moving picture camera. The government had outlawed the potlatch but not the movie palaces. With this in mind, it is interesting to reconsider the relationship of the Kwakw<u>a</u>ka'wakw to *Head Hunters*—as both actors in and spectators of it—without the rather insulting assumption that the motion pictures were foreign to them either technologically or culturally. The Indian movies generally, and *Head Hunters* in particular, are useful in modeling the vernacular of cultural reception in the early twentieth century, and there is little reason not to include indigenous populations in the period's emerging mass public engaging the new phenomenon of the motion pictures.

Once arrived at this point, we may still find it quite easy to dismiss what would seem to be the reverse movement of culture—from the mass market back to indigenous communities—as a cheapening or weakening of the original's value, especially when so many Indian films were notoriously stereotypical. The sentiment is certainly not a new one. As early as 1909, film critics were complaining in trade journals about the inaccuracy of Indian movies, about what one article titled the "'make-believe' Indians," which upset both purists wanting "real Indians" and also the "real Indians" who saw the movies and "most justly resented the untrue, unreal and unfair representations of themselves and their habits."[10] As a critic in the *Nickelodeon* wrote in 1911, the Westerns did not portray "real Western conditions" but only looked west to find a novel "stomping ground for melodrama" (quoted in Abel 2006:63). American Indian studies specialist Ted Jojola has recently argued that the Indian Westerns produced by the major studios "reduced native people to ignoble stereotypes" (Jojola 2003:12), and, already in 1911, the *Motion Picture World* covered the trip of a delegation sent to Washington from the Shoshone, Cheyenne, and Arapaho reservations to protest against misrepresentation in the Indian pictures.

By the same token, pushing too far in this direction quickly becomes patronizing. In an Associated Press report describing a protest about the movies lodged by California Indians from 1911, also republished in *Moving Picture World* (vol. 10, October 7, 1911:32), W. H. Stanley, superintendent of the Southern California Indian Agency, is quoted saying that the "Indian of today will spend his last cent on a moving picture show when he visits the city.... We are trying to teach the Indian that he should be a good farmer and forget about being a warrior, and when he visits the city and sees nothing but the Indian depicted with gun or arrow in his hands, instead of a hoe or rake, he becomes confused, and the better educated among them are deeply grieved." It is hard, today, to take these words from the good white father seriously.

Here, however, is the crucial point: Indian movies were about more than just Indians. They were fundamentally about modernity and the changes it wrought on the economic, moral, and cultural structures of society, about narrating the future as well as the past.[11] It may well have been for this reason that Indian Westerns were the most popular American export from the very beginning of the film trade in the first years of the century, and hundreds of them were even filmed outside of the United States—in places as far afield as Italy, France, Japan, India, and Finland (Salmi 2003:40). These were well-known "genre films," and much of the fun would have come from suspending disbelief, even if as an audience member you knew exactly what was coming next. Surely not everyone took them as the literal truth.

In this regard, film historian Miriam Hansen's notion of "vernacular modernism" is particularly useful. She uses the term to describe a way of thinking about the conjunction of early cinema and modern art, which she frames as "cultural practices that both articulated and mediated the experience of modernity," as opposed to thinking of them in terms of their formal, artistic characteristics. These practices could range from fashion, design, and advertising to photography, radio, and cinema; and although Hansen does not address them particularly, the widespread representations of Indians in photography and film would serve as particularly apt examples because of the way they evoked the destructive capabilities of commercialization, industrialization, expansion, and colonization. Hansen's argument is that vernacular modernism was not merely a symptom of such destruction but also a modality for reflecting upon it. Making a particular case for cinema, she argues that it was "not only part and symptom of modernity's experience and perception of crisis and upheaval; it was also, most importantly, the single most inclusive cultural horizon in which the traumatic effects of modernity were reflected, rejected or disavowed, transmuted or negotiated" (Hansen

1999:68). The packaging of the "primitive" together with "modernity"—the "real" Indian with the feature film—thus makes perfect sense as an example of what Hansen describes as the juxtaposition both exemplifying and mediating these traumatic effects.

Hansen's version of this story is, of course, quite different from many of those with which it might be compared. It does not, for example, exhibit or account for the anger that anthropologist Renato Rosaldo writes of feeling at recent films that portray "imperialism with nostalgia"— "mourning … what one has destroyed"—a criticism frequently leveled, with good reason, at Curtis (Rosaldo 1989:107; for application of the critique to *Head Hunters*, see Rony 1996:95). Taking it even further, Jojola has written that the "Hollywood Indian is a mythological being who exists nowhere but within the fertile imaginations of its movie actors, producers, and directors.… The only remedy from such images was a laughter, for these portrayals were too surreal and too removed from the reservation or urban Indian experience to be taken seriously" (Jojola 2003:12–13). Hansen certainly acknowledges the destruction and loss of the period, but her intent is to explain the "new modes of organizing vision and sensory perception"—new modes that could, of course, include imperialist nostalgia, but that also permitted the development of "different forms of mimetic experience and expression, of affectivity, temporality, and reflexivity, a changing fabric of everyday life, sociability, and leisure" (Hansen 1999:59).

The distinction between these approaches is one that reveals, once again, the essential documentary problem and the vagaries of imagining reception. In a discursive landscape so dense with representations, and a commercial landscape in which the reception of films varied so widely from one location to another, it is quite difficult to specify who was watching the movies. Production can be critiqued, but it is never quite clear how the movies were taken up and to what effect; whether, for instance, the laughter and sense of surrealism described by Jojola was not, in fact, built into the response. There are many ways to see a film, and being appalled is certainly one option. We can, however, expand our attention to imagine the local contexts of reception that might help to bridge the apparent boundary keeping the "traditional" Kwakw<u>aka</u>'wakw customs in one place and their history with the movies elsewhere—keeping the primitive and modern in Kwakw<u>aka</u>'wakw life figuratively apart. If one simply follows the conventional argument that Curtis erased all signs of modernity from his images, figuratively freezing the Indian in the past, then one is stuck in a rather static version of reception history. It assumes that "being modern" would mean Indians consuming images of themselves looking like themselves—modern, integrated, impoverished, harassed—and not, say, of themselves dressing up for old-time photographs. And it certainly leaves little room for "surreal" experiences, in both Jojola's sense and in the sense more broadly conceived, as, for example, by James Clifford (1988) to describe the likes of André Breton's engagement with anthropology.

Hansen describes the movies as a "new sensorium" to which modern spectators—the "mass public"—adjusted and shaped their lives. To include Native American spectators in this mass public adds a new layer to the history both of Curtis's work and that of the Native Americans who played in the movies. These new layers become particularly visible if we make the assumption that at least some Kwakwa̱ka'wakw at the time of *Head Hunters* would likely have been familiar with the notion of going to see motion pictures, and thus would have seen screen representations of Indians. If that were the case, then it follows that to be traditional was also to be modern, and, although historical research would be needed to confirm the point, we might assume that the traditions were inflected by the movies, just as the movies were inflected by the traditions.

"A Mighty Spectacle Drama of Exotic Thrills"

As we move in to consider *In the Land of the Head Hunters* itself as part of Hansen's modernist vernacular, it might be useful simply to situate the discussion in the context of the quintessential modernity of Curtis's project when taken as a whole, and by implication the ways in which his indigenous collaborators were also integrated into modern life. The issue is not merely Curtis's potential involvement with Alfred Stieglitz, the 291 Gallery, and the journal *Camera Work* (Egan 2006); nor is it the seriousness of his social scientific ambitions and his resentment at not being taken seriously by established anthropologists and museum curators (Gidley 1998a). Rather, it is the extent to which the entire body of his work finds its match in the aesthetic proclivities of the period's primitivist turn in both high and popular culture. This is evident in the realm of fine art in everything from Joseph Henry Sharp's contemporaneous oil portraits of Plains Indians (1900–10; Watkins 1998) to the decorative screens by Robert Chanler featuring Native American subjects that greeted visitors to the famous Armory show of 1913, which initiated American audiences to European cubism and modernist abstraction (Staples 2001), and Marsden Hartley's *Indian Fantasy* (1914), which combined Chippewa canoes, Pueblo pottery, and a Northwest Coast carved eagle, all of which he studied at Berlin's Museum für Völkerkunde (Rushing 1995:57).

Brad Evans

And it is equally apparent in works of popular culture, from dime novels and Wild West shows to the scores of Indian Westerns—many of which featured Native American actors—coming out of Hollywood studios in the early 1910s, culminating in D. W. Griffith's seminal, long-format Indian movie *The Battle of Elderbush Gulch* (1913). One of the defining characteristics of high modernism of this period was its reaction against what was understood to be the standardizing effects of routinized, industrial capitalism. The turn to the "primitive," like analogous interests in the "handmade" and "arts and crafts," registered in contradistinction to what were perceived to be the flattening and sterilizing tendencies of the new economy of consumption (Lears 1981; Torgovnick 1990; North 1994; Bramen 2000; Sollors 2008). Taken in this light, it would seem uncontroversial to suggest that the relentless antimodernism of Curtis's oeuvre epitomizes at least some of the aesthetic and market dynamics of modernism itself.

Within this context, *In the Land of the Head Hunters* makes sense not merely as the cinematic legatee of the Buffalo Bill Wild West shows of the late nineteenth century, nor merely of the first decade of Indian movies produced by the nascent film industry. These were, of course, both influences. So, too, was the emerging genre of what we might call "the Northern": scientific, fictional, and exploratory efforts that looked to the North as the new and perhaps last frontier.[12] Following a long history of imaging and imagining the North—especially as a passage to the East—the late nineteenth century celebrated numerous heroic expeditions, the most famous being the Alaska Gold Rush and Robert Peary's search for the North Pole, which ignited the popular imagination and unleashed a flood of iconic images of the Arctic and its indigenous peoples (Condon 1989; Potter 2007). At the time of Curtis's work in British Columbia, there was also extensive activity in the lands and with the people of the Arctic, including the production of motion pictures in both fictional and nonfictional modes (King and Lidchi 1998; Huhndorf 2001; Fienup-Riordan 2003; Harber and Potter 2010).[13] Curtis likely intended *Head Hunters* to be firmly embedded in this emerging genre of the Northern, with advertising posters touting the film not as a "Western" but as an "Indian Epic Drama of the Northern Sea." At least one newspaper followed Curtis's lead in their advertising for the film, incorrectly describing it as being "acted by amateur actors chosen from the Alaskan Eskimo tribes" (*Tacoma Times*, December 12, 1914).

However, I would suggest that in terms of its aesthetic aspirations, as a work of cinematic art, *In the Land of the Head Hunters* was even more in line with a very different kind of filmic context. At its most ambitious, Curtis's film situated itself alongside the large-scale art movies being produced by the early 1910s, and especially with works like those produced in Italy at precisely this time, which became known as "spectacle" productions. I am thinking in particular of films such as the famed Gabriele D'Annunzio photo-play *Cabiria* (Pastrone 1914), a massive three-hour (fourteen-reel) Italian art drama that had come out in the United States six months before *Head Hunters*. *Cabiria* had quickly become a touchstone for early film critics looking for art in the motion pictures because of its expansive sets and the innovative camera movement that brought audiences deep into them. *Head Hunters* was explicitly compared to *Cabiria* at the time, a *Seattle Times* (December 8, 1914) review of the screening at the Moore Theatre calling Curtis's film "a companion offering to … *Cabiria*, as enthralling and as beautiful." The *New York Clipper* (December 5, 1942:12) called it "a thriller."

Such an association may have been prepared in the audience's mind by the growing reputation of Curtis's ambitious book project, *The North American Indian*, and the elaborate musicale he had undertaken in the preceding years (Gidley, this volume). But there was also a very clear attempt to promote Curtis's film in terms of "spectacle," which had become associated with works like *Cabiria* and other Italian films such as *Dante's Inferno* (1911) and *Quo Vadis?* (1913) (Bowser 1990:251, 257–58). Both the advertising and the posters for Curtis's film hailed it as an "epic" and a "mighty spectacle drama of exotic thrills" (appendix 1). This last phrase bore a close similarity to advertisements for other big American films produced at the same time, most famously Griffith's *The Birth of a Nation* (1915), which was also advertised as a "mighty spectacle"—indeed, the "mightiest spectacle ever produced" (figs. 7.1a and 7.1b).[14] It is perhaps not a mere coincidence that posters for the two films were produced by the same printer, the H. C. Miner Litho Company (introduction, this volume, note 24). The *New York Times* announcement for the *Head Hunters* premier at the Casino, moreover, referred to *Head Hunters* as a "spectacle play," and it did the same in announcing *Birth* three months later, calling it a "spectacular film production." The next year, Griffith's *Intolerance* was also billed as a "stupendous spectacle."[15] By identifying *Head Hunters* with spectacle films, promoters encouraged audiences to expect the sense of awe inspired by such things as impressive landscapes, enormous archaeological specimens, innovative camera sequences, and acting crews numbering well into the hundreds—to expect, in short, an expansive, epic sensorial experience.[16] The grandiosity of these large-scale spectacle productions also distinguished themselves qualitatively from the mass of industrially produced short films, and especially the popular genre of the Indian Western.

Brad Evans

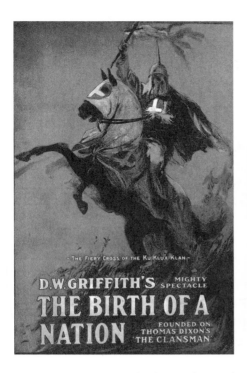

Figs. 7.1a and 7.1b. Two theatrical posters for *The Birth of a Nation*, 1915.
Printed by H. C. Miner Litho Company, New York, which also printed the posters for
Head Hunters.

Modernist spectacle neatly explains the critical reception *Head Hunters* received, with critics repeatedly emphasizing the "scenic beauty of the film," as Stephen Bush put it in the most famous review (Glass and Evans, this volume). Bush went on at length about the "low flight of the birds over the waters tinted and burnished by the setting sun," which he called "a veritable revelation of motion picture art" (Bush 1914:1685). Given this context, it is perhaps not surprising that advertising and press releases almost never mentioned the Kwakiutl (as the Kwakwa̱ka'wakw were known at the time) but instead referred to the film as a "real Indian drama enacted by natives" and, again, as an "Indian epic drama of the northern seas." That the Kwakwa̱ka'wakw were not simply unspecified but framed in such a way as to evoke a wide variety of exotic subjects—perhaps Chinese Orientals or Mongolians, or even epic heroes in the Homeric sense—would only have been to the motion picture's advantage in attracting a broader audience and drawing to the film the cultural cache of a more universally "spectacular" subject. We also know that some viewers (such as those at the *Lima Daily News*) mistook the actors for Eskimos, and it is remarkable the extent to which advertising referred to a relatively minor scene in the film, the "fire dance" (see fig. A.1.10), which sounds almost oriental in its exoticism.[17] The *Brooklyn Daily Eagle* (December 15, 1914:10) reported that the film's accompanying music was "weird, yet enchanting," while the *New York Dramatic Mirror* (December 16, 1914:51) called it "barbaric, stirring, and yet with an unforgettable lilt," suggesting that period audiences may have found Braham's score more genuinely exotic, and less stereotypical, than we do now. With raven masks and grizzly bear costumes instead of the eagle-feather headdress and tipis familiar from many hundreds of other Indian movies, the point of reference for audiences would have been welcomingly strange, evoking a range of cinematic associations that would have taken the subject well beyond that of merely the natural history museum or world's fair. As Bush wrote in his review, the "Indians" in the film are "natural in every move; the grace, the weirdness and the humor of their dances have never been brought home to us like this before" (Bush 1914:1685). In aligning itself in this way, Curtis's film used the associative fantasies of primitivism and the expanded sensorial experiences of the motion pictures to settle *In the Land of the Head Hunters* neatly into the rift between modernity and tradition, crass entertainment and high-art spectacle.

Suspending Disbelief

The attention of audiences today, judging from the screening series we produced in 2008, skews sharply in the other direction, away from cinematic "spectacle" and toward an understanding of what the film might actually "document" about the Kwakwaka'wakw. We are subject to a documentary fixation that turns our attention away from a register for understanding either the epic beauty of the figure cut by Motana, a figure that may have inspired Vachel Lindsay to write in 1916 that the film abounded in "noble bronzes" (Lindsay 1915:86). Instead, we drift toward an equally interesting but very different history of the young Kwakwaka'wakw man who played Motana's role, Stanley Hunt, son of the famous culture broker George Hunt, who had worked extensively with the anthropologist Franz Boas as well as with Curtis in the making of *Head Hunters*. It is this impulse that turns us toward the study of what Alison Griffiths has called the "semantic architecture of Indian representations" that played such a central role in the emergence of American mass culture from the time of the dime novels and Wild West shows to that of early film (Griffiths 2001:100). It drives the desire to disentangle fact from fiction in the film, to disregard spectacle in order to recover cultural continuity from the mechanical artifice of the melodramatic story.

I wonder, nonetheless, about this strapping young character, Motana. Bare-chested throughout most of the film, in an era when the nakedness of male actors playing Indians is said to have been a major draw for audiences (Bowser 1990:173), Hunt delivers his role with playful bravado, entirely believable as dancer, whale hunter, warrior, and general heartthrob (see figs. 1.9 and E.2.10). What might happen were we to take this performance seriously as such? What might happen were we to go back to the question of Stanley Hunt's acting and, more generally, to that of what we actually see when we watch *Head Hunters* both as a "spectacle" in the early twentieth-century sense, but also, more in line with our own time, as a fictional melodrama of love and war?

Before considering the question, a quick aside would seem to be in order. If Holm and Quimby's *In the Land of the War Canoes* (1973) looks today like one of the opening salvos in the reform of anthropological practice that has come to be known as postmodern ethnography, then the project to reconstruct a 1914 version of *In the Land of the Head Hunters*—as we have tried to do—may at first appear to be a retrograde move in terms of contemporary cultural politics. As sociologist Paul Apodaca suggested during a question-and-answer period at a symposium at the Getty in 2008, it is as if the desire were to leapfrog backward, taking the voices of the Kwakwaka'wakw that registered so clearly on the *War Canoes* soundtrack back away from them. As I hope to have made clear so far, understanding the historical context more fully helps us hear the Kwakwaka'wakw role in the film differently, such that we might begin to imagine a history of indigenous voices sounding in ways that were not always autoethnographic—to break the documentary hegemony on ways of being in modernity. Because these questions continue to resonate, it seems worth thinking about how we see the spectacle and the drama of *Head Hunters* today. It may have been significant for its aesthetic innovation in historical terms, but now that it has been reconstructed, are we able to say whether it is any good as a feature film?

D. W. Griffith's *The Mended Lute*, a one-reel film from 1909, offers a storyline in many ways similar to *Head Hunters*, and thus can help point out the differences that Curtis may have hoped to build upon with his all-indigenous cast. As in *Head Hunters*, two young lovers are held apart by the girl's father promising her to an unsavory suitor. Despite the promise, the lovers in both films run off together, and this initiates (among other things the movies have in common) a canoe chase scene that ends with the hero and heroine navigating through treacherous waters. Like Curtis's film, *The Mended Lute* takes place entirely within the Indian community. The Indians are presumably Sioux in this case, but the only clue comes from the stereotypical tipis and eagle-feather headdresses. *The Mended Lute* was filmed in New Jersey, and although the Native American actor and director James Young Deer does have a minor role, the film's major players were all white idols of the silent era—Florence Lawrence, Owen Moore, and James Kirkwood.[18] There are no Sioux cultural elements to speak of beyond those essential to the plot, namely, again, tipis and canoes. The film made no nod to either ethnography or spectacle, and was clearly not meant to educate. It addressed itself to a vernacular, not elite, modernism.

Our hope is that the restored film makes *Head Hunters* recognizable as a feature film sharing, at least to some extent, a genealogy with *The Mended Lute*. The recovery of missing scenes and the use of still photographs to fill in known gaps in the narrative has made it clear that well over three-quarters of the film is devoted to developing the storyline, and that its ethnographic content was directed at developing not only science but also spectacle. Like *The Mended Lute*, *Head Hunters* is very effective in defining its hero and heroine. In the film, Motana and Naida's love for each other is framed melodramatically not by one but two scenes in which they canoe off into the sunset. Curtis's picture, however, takes place on an entirely different scale than Griffith's. It is an ambitious spectacle piece, so that the love story's melodrama is juxtaposed with panoramic shots of hundreds of sea lions diving into the water from the cliff as Motana rounds the corner in his boat, as well as more familiar technical effects, such as having the ghosted image of Naida appear in the smoke of Motana's prayer fire (on vision scenes like this one, see Bowser 1990:62–65). There is purple prose in the intertitles—"Oh! that I might go with you walking hand in hand along that misty path of copper!"—but also impressive camerawork from the rear of a war canoe, as its rampaging oarsmen begin an attack on some fishermen, that is taken from a camera mounted out over the water.

This is not to say that there are not problems with the fictional narrative. In fact, one feels that Stanley Hunt's "failure" as an actor, such as it was, had quite a bit to do with Curtis's failure as a storyteller. While the first half of the film is quite successful at defining the scope of the love story between Motana and Naida, as well as the threat posed to it by the evil Sorcerer, there is a problem in the second half of the film, where it is increasingly difficult to keep track of the characters and their allegiances. Confusion comes from all corners. To start with, three different women play the heroine, Naida, and it is not easy to distinguish this character from the Sorcerer's daughter, who is

Brad Evans

206

also interested in Motana. In the course of events, however, this is the least of the film's problems. Instead of Motana leading the attack against the Sorcerer to win Naida's hand, it is his father, Kenada, who does the deed. And when Kenada subsequently returns to Naida's village to claim the princess for his son, he stands in the front of his canoe gruesomely swinging around his enemy's severed head. It's not exactly the best way to garner sympathy for his son. To further muddy the issue, props and scenes get interchanged. That same scene is repeated later in the film, only with Kenada's own head swinging: after the Sorcerer is revenged by his brother, Yaklus, who leads a massacre of Kenada and his village, the young warrior chief returns home in what may well be the very same canoe that Kenada had taken earlier in the film, and does the same grizzly dance—most likely swinging the same (fake) heads. Props, indeed, were frequently reused: the canoes were repainted for the different parties; the totem poles were reused and only slightly altered in Yaklus and Kenada's house interiors; and the same Thunderbird, Bear, and Wasp regalia are used in both Yaklus's and Kenada's ceremonies (introduction, this volume). Even more disorienting for the storyline is that the most culturally significant and aesthetically interesting dances of the entire film take place at the home of the evil Yaklus. They are staged in celebration of his massacre of Kenada and Motana's village. Although it may be the case that any suspenseful drama needs an engaging villain, the narrative here unfolds as if some kind of mistake has been made. Rather than being told from the sympathetic perspective of the hero, the most dramatically striking and ethnographically complex scenes are given over to the evil Yaklus.

Even without the confusion, I would suggest that, from a fictional perspective, Curtis has given us an incredibly dark film. Not only are the "good Indians" perpetually under siege, but they are also at the mercy of remarkably violent and vengeful enemies. Nowhere is this better illustrated than in two scenes that are entirely new to the current restoration, which, as Jere Guldin describes (this volume), were salvaged using recently discovered nitrate fragments of the original picture. The first is that of the destruction of Kenada's village, Watsulis. Some of the power of the scene as it now appears is the luck of the archive; in his reconstruction, Guldin played through some of the decomposed film and used stills from the Library of Congress that are among the most grizzly and dramatic that Curtis ever took. Especially with the blue tinting and the smoke from the burnt village hugging close to the detritus, the dramatic effect is quite profound, as one imagines the movement of the medicine man awaiting the heroic resuscitation of Motana. The other example is a stirring scene toward the end of the film where Naida is forced to dance for her life. With a red tint and the haze of smoke drifting across it, the scene is heavily saturated by the threat of sexual violence, as Naida and her slave dance before Yaklus and a group of machete-wielding warriors. Because the scene was restored from an original thirty-five-millimeter nitrate print, we know the coloring to be accurate, and the sharpness and clarity of the picture in this section are unsurpassed. Naida's dance is exceptionally beautiful, and it is entirely possible to read fear and vulnerability in her facial expression. Good and evil clearly make their return in this section of the film, as well as in the next scene, also new in the restored version, in which Naida's slave escapes to alert Motana of her plight.

The good, however, is always just on the verge of destruction. From the start, when the evil Sorcerer peers out at the pair of lovers, to the final scene in which Yaklus is defeated by the treacherous waters of the "gorge of Hyal"—and not directly by the superior strength of Motana—the film swims deeply, and seemingly not without a certain pleasure, in the waters of evil. Curtis does not even seem willing to indulge in the "right" ending for the melodrama of his love story. As everyone knows—even everyone in 1914, having already seen it in scores of other movies—the ending of a melodrama is the nuclear family, with the hero and heroine joined safely back together and a child on the way. We never get there with *Head Hunters*, which instead ends fixated on the dead body of the evil Yaklus, which floats covered with seaweed in the turgid surf. Perhaps this is Curtis at his most Homeric, the good outcome nonetheless clouded by the tragic, leaving viewers with a fictional nod to Curtis's "vanishing Indians," dying off and setting with the sun. The seagulls mentioned by Stephen Bush presumably flew in right after that. The footage for that scene is part of what is missing from the restoration, and we have only the Library of Congress still image to go on, but the effect that one can imagine is that the childless couple survive only to fade into the natural environment, part of the land's natural history.

There have always been moments in the film that reveal its actors "acting"—being aware of themselves as actors. These include the scene in which the evil sorcerer's daughter steals a locket of the sleeping Motana's hair and wags her finger over him for spurning her love; the wildly exaggerated death throes of Motana's father, Kenada, after he has been pierced by one of twenty or so arrows shot weakly in his direction; and the scene toward the end in which the heroine's escaped servant, who has been pierced by an arrow but nonetheless journeys on to find someone to rescue his princess, has the arrow yanked from his back as he lies facedown on a rocky beach. What is interesting is that when enhanced by the musical cues of the score,

Brad Evans

208

scenes such as these can be recast with varying emotions (chapter 12, this volume). This last scene with the escaped slave was particularly striking at the UCLA Philharmonia's performance of the score at the Getty in 2008. For most audiences of *War Canoes*, this scene has invariably held a laugh line straight out of vaudeville. Motana forces Naida's faithful slave down onto the rocks, puts his foot on the slave's shoulder, and rips out the arrow. The action often registers as slapstick, and in every other performance, Motana's exaggerated gesture got a big laugh. But at the Getty, the orchestra played up the drama of the slave's escape in the scenes leading up to this one, and then recycled a more somber theme from earlier in the film instead of using the music indicated in the Braham score. The effect was entirely unlike that at any of the other screenings in that Motana's pulling out of the arrow elicited not a laugh but a collective squirm from a suddenly captive audience.

The scene as it was played at the Getty speaks against our documentary desires. Given the historical record and the current reconstruction of the film, I would find it worth resisting the notion that, if there had to be a film, what we really would have preferred would have been a genuine documentary, one set not in a historically unidentifiable past but in the historical present of cultural transformation. Even today, when the film is there before our eyes as a fiction, we have a hard time seeing anything but the history of that transformation. But we would understand the transformation more fully, more critically, less nostalgically, less naïvely, were we to see for one moment the full implication of *Head Hunters* as both fiction and spectacle, and the Kwakwaka'wakw as party to both its production and reception as such. *In the Land of the Head Hunters* is not just a useful anthropological record for cosmopolitan museums, nor merely a record of the survival and recovery of indigenous cultural traditions, but it also provides a record of the historical complexity of an era. Curtis's work with the Kwakwaka'wakw can be carried beyond documentary realism into the equally compelling aesthetic register of modernist spectacle, and the Kwakwaka'wakw can be seen as having been both party to and audience of the new cultural sensorium.

I would like to thank Andrew Martin at the Vancouver Public Library for archival assistance with this project. Also, my thanks to Paul Apodaca, Aaron Glass, and Russell Potter for their suggestion of "the Northern" as an emergent film category during the period, as well as for documentation of the craze for northern subjects.

1   For representative studies of this juxtaposition of "primitive culture" and "modern mass culture" in the early twentieth century, which generally tracks with the related melange of "art" and "anthropology," see Clifford (1988); Torgovnick (1990); North

(1994); Hegeman (1999); Bramen (2000); Griffiths (2002); Manganaro (2002); Evans (2005); Sollors (2008); Braddock (2009); and Hutchinson (2009).

2   The last lines of T. S. Eliot's *The Waste Land* (1922) epitomize the modernist juxtaposition I am describing by ending with a nod to the *Upanishads*, similar in many ways to Curtis's nod to the Kwakwa̱ka̱'wakw (as I argue in what follows).

3   John R. Miller, Deputy Director, to Clifford C. Gregg, Director, March 18, 1947, Field Museum Archives; Pliny E. Goddard, Curator of Ethnology, to Edward S. Curtis, January 25, 1923, and January 17, 1924, Division of Anthropology Archives, American Museum of Natural History.

4   Hugo Zeiter to Field Museum of Natural History, February 7, 1947; Hugo Zeiter to Clifford C. Gregg, March 5, 1947, Field Museum Archives.

5   Early nonfiction films of Native Americans date from the earliest actualities, and there were also early "documentaries" being made by the major film companies at the time that Curtis was thinking of his own project, such as Vitagraph's *Indian Basket Making* (1909) and Edison's *Camping with the Blackfeet* (1910) (Griffiths 2001:109; Abel 2006:171–82; and Browne, this volume). Exotic locales were also familiar by 1914; for example, the Kalem Company had filmed in Florida and Ireland; the Selig Company sent groups to shoot in New Orleans and Mexico; and Vitagraph sent a company to Jamaica and Maine (Bowser 1990:153–60).

6   The Hochstetter process claim was made, among other places, in the *New York Times* announcement for the Casino Theatre premiere ("Notes Written on the Screen," *New York Times*, December 6, 1914:25), and on the playbill for the Casino Theatre screening of the film. The process was supposed to provide natural color photography without postproduction manipulation (Hochstetter 1913:12–13).

7   For recent work on the representation and participation of Native Americans in early film, see Buscombe (2006); Buscombe and Pearson (1998); Kilpatrick (1999); Jay (2000); Griffiths (2002); Simmon (2003); Rollins (2003); Deloria (2004); Aleiss (2005); Marubbio (2009); and Smith (2009). For an invaluable guide to Native Americans in early films, see the Library of Congress's comprehensive guide "American Indians in Silent Film," at http://www.loc.gov/rr/mopic/findaid/indian1.html (accessed June 28, 2010). My sense of the need to consider Native American spectatorship has been inspired, in particular, by Jacqueline Stewart's work on black film audiences of this time in *Migrating to the Movies: Cinema and Black Urban Modernity* (2005). The best work on Indian spectatorship to date comes in Griffiths 2001 and 2002.

8   The American Council of Learned Societies Committee on Native American Languages, Franz Boas Collection of Materials for American Linguistics, American Philosophical Society, 497.3 B63c [Series 28: Boas, Franz—Kwakiutl ethnographic materials]. My thanks to Isaiah Wilner for this discovery, and to Judith Berman for confirmation.

9   These numbers are comparable to those from various cities in the United States. For example, in 1908, Grand Rapids, Michigan, population approximately 112,000, had fifteen nickelodeons (Etten 1926). The population of the greater Vancouver area in 1911 was estimated at 162,000, so one might expect something in the same range (for the historical population of Vancouver, see http://www.altiusdirectory.com/Travel/vancouver-history.html, accessed July 4, 2010). Rochester, New York, had seventeen houses for a population of 200,000. By 1919, even a fair-sized town like Toledo, Ohio, was boasting forty-five movie theaters, and the six downtown theaters were drawing 75,000 patrons each week (Koszarski 1990:12).

10 "The 'Make-Believe' Indian," *Moving Picture World* 8 (March 4, 1911, 473). Similar articles from *Moving Picture World* include "Accuracy in Indian Subjects (vol. 5, July 10, 1909, 48); "Chief Blackfoot's Vindication" (vol. 6, May 21, 1910); "Indians War on Films" (vol. 8, March 18, 1911, 581); "Indians Protest Against Indian Pictures" (vol. 8, March 18, 1911, 587); "The Vogue of Western and Military Drama" (vol. 9, August

Brad Evans

5, 1911); W. Stephen Bush, "Moving Picture Absurdities" (vol. 9, September 16, 1911); and "Indians Grieve Over Picture Shows" (vol. 10, October 7, 1911).

11 My thinking about Westerns has been informed by a number of insightful recent works on the genre, and especially by Abel (2006); Verhoeff (2006); Simmon (2003); and Smith (2003).

12 Aaron Glass and I began thinking of Curtis's film as a "Northern" after we discovered the *Head Hunters* advertising posters (appendix 1). As this book went to press, we learned that Russell Potter is using the same phrase (independently invented) in his current work on Arctic films and Eskimo attractions. We'd also like to acknowledge Paul Apodaca's research into this topic, some of which he presented at a 2008 Getty Research Institute symposium in support of the Curtis film project.

13 It would not be an exaggeration to claim that between 1890 and 1920 there was an "Eskimo craze" (c.f. Hutchinson 2009) as newspapers, universities, cinemas, world's fairs, carnivals, and other forms of American and European popular culture sought to cash in on the interest in Peary's adventures in the North. One of the most remarkable aspects of this trend in popular entertainment was the consistency of image and theme as well as Inuit performers. For example, the same group of increasingly professionalized Inuit lived and performed in Eskimo village concessions at the 1893, 1901, and 1904 World's Fairs as well as at Coney Island (which for years featured variations on a "Journey to the North Pole" theme park attraction), and they starred in some of the films set in the North but shot in California around the same time (Russell Potter, personal communication; Harber and Potter 2010). A very small sample of films with northern subjects released as Curtis was making his own includes *Into the North* (1913), *Breed of the North* (1913), *Pierre of the North* (1913), *An Odyssey of the North* (1914), *The Call of the North* (Cecil B. DeMille, 1914), *Star of the North* (1914), *Aurora of the North* (1914), and *Sonny Jim at the North Pole* (1914).

14 For a very different take on the relation of *Birth* to Native American issues, see Jay (2000).

15 For *Head Hunters*, "Notes Written on the Screen," *New York Times*, December 6, 1914:25; for *Birth*, "Notes Written on the Screen," *New York Times*, February 28, 1915; for *Intolerance*, "Intolerance Stupendous Spectacle," *New York Times,* September 6, 1916.

16 I am using "spectacle" here in a much more technical sense than Fatimah Tobing Rony (1996) does in her treatment of "race, cinema, and ethnographic spectacle." Hopefully, our project to reconstruct and recontextualize *Head Hunters* will strongly qualify Rony's assessment that the Curtis film "is really an excuse to string together footage purporting to offer a view of the Kwakwaka'wakw way of life before the nineteenth century" (94). This assumption simply does not hold when the reconstructed film and its historical contexts are taken into account.

17 "Our 'Reformed' Alaskan Head Hunters." *Lima Daily News* (Ohio), January 16, 1915.

18 Young Deer's tribal affiliation is complex. See Glass and Evans, note 4, this volume.

8

MUSICAL INTERTEXTUALITY IN INDIGENOUS FILM

Making and Remaking
In the Land of the Head Hunters

KLISALA HARRISON

Many silent films about indigenous Canadians, including a number about Northwest Coast First Nations,[1] have staged or been accompanied by indigenous music, but *In the Land of the Head Hunters* is unique for having done so differently on numerous occasions over the course of its history. Music for *Head Hunters* has been revived, rewritten, and reframed each time the film has come back into public attention. Made in 1914 by the renowned photographer and ethnographer Edward Curtis, and the first feature film to depict Northwest Coast First Nations, *Head Hunters* contains at least eighteen scenes showing Kwakwa̱ka̱'wakw music and dance performance.[2] The film's plot focuses on a love triangle between the hero Motana, Naida (the "maid of his dreams"), and a jealous sorcerer from a rival village to whom Naida has been promised; the scenes of ceremony mostly accompany ritual practices associated with Motana's youthful initiation, with wedding rites, and with celebrations surrounding warfare.

In 1914, silent film footage was paired with an orchestral score by John J. Braham, a New York composer long associated with Gilbert and Sullivan productions (Jacknis and Gilbert, this volume). A reedited 1973 version, *In the Land of the War Canoes,* included for the first time a Kwakwa̱ka̱'wakw musical soundtrack featuring recordings of Kwakwa̱ka̱'wakw songs that may have accompanied the actual filming of *Head Hunters* in 1913–14 but were not recorded then. *War Canoes*, edited by Bill Holm and George Quimby, with sound direction by David Gerth, aimed to accompany Curtis's silent footage with historically appropriate music by contemporary Kwakwaka'wakw singers as well as with Kwakwala language dialogue. Then, in 2008, *Head Hunters'* original musical score for orchestra, based in the "Hollywood Indian" music tradition (Pisani 2005; Deloria 2004), was revived when a newly edited version of the film was accompanied by performances of the score in a tour titled "Edward Curtis Meets the Kwakwaka'wakw" (discussed throughout this book). Following these *Head Hunters* screenings, a Kwakwaka'wakw dance and singing group, the Gwa'wina Dancers, performed some of the dance songs and dances shown in the film, interpreting them through speeches for audiences in a new century.

This article focuses on intertextuality as a means of analyzing struggles for cultural authority by the Kwakwaka'wakw singers who recorded the soundtrack for *In the Land of the War Canoes* and by the Gwa'wina Dancers more recently. Drawing on my ethnographic and ethnomusicological research on Kwakwaka'wakw music, dance, and culture, I describe Curtis's silent footage of Kwakwaka'wakw music and dance in *Head Hunters*, and consider how the Kwakwaka'wakw singers who recorded the *War Canoes* soundtrack in the summer of 1972 responded to it. The singers watched Curtis's footage before recording the soundtrack and when making the recording, and they had agency to choose which music genres to perform (Holm and Quimby 1980:16–17). In 1972, how did contemporaneous indigenous Canadian political and cultural contexts filter into interpretations of the *War Canoes'* soundtrack for the 1914 feature film? And, conversely, how did the varied contexts of the 1914 film filter forward to affect indigenous musical recording six decades later? Central to my analysis is the Kwakwaka'wakw political and cultural concept of *u'mista*, which refers to the process of returning something valuable. A final section, which draws on ethnographic fieldwork that I conducted in 2008 screening situations, considers the current relevance of the historical presentation of indigenous music, and suggests that the Gwa'wina Dancers' performances in some ways extended the efforts of those involved in *War Canoes*.

Intertextuality and Kwakwaka'wakw Music

Developed by Julia Kristeva in the 1960s, the concept of intertextuality has origins in the work of Ferdinand de Saussure and M. M. Bakhtin, and has influenced literary and cultural studies ever since (Kristeva 1980; Allen 2011).

In film studies, "intertextuality" usually refers to any specific film (or text) referring to other films/texts. In film music studies, the term most often means film music referencing music that has occurred previously in another film, or alternatively in a recording, score, or live performance (Siôn 2007). The term has also been used to refer to instances when another genre of expression—for instance, speech—comes together with music, in order to facilitate separate, intertextual analyses within the different genres (the music referring to previous music and the speech referring to previous speech). Bonnie Wade's study of how the Japanese Noh play *Ataka* was adapted for Kabuki theatre and film, for example, deals separately with how orally told story and musical works each undertake what she calls "the intertextual effort," by which she means "the complex and variegated play of borrowing, citation, implicit or explicit references and substitutions, which substantiate the relationships between the texts of a given culture (and even between texts of different cultures)" (Wade 2006). Wade demonstrates that when the play was taken from Noh to Kabuki to film, the music moved farther away from Noh in content and musical style. I will extend the current literature on musical intertextuality to consider how the circulation of indigenous ritual music presents new angles for considering the concept.

Northwest Coast First Nations presentations of music and dance, especially in the ceremonial context, are executed according to strict conventions, and thus provide a useful starting point for a textual reading. In fact, it would be fair to say that these conventions have been developed precisely in order to limit the influence of "intertexts" deemed external to Kwakwa̱ka'wakw traditions and history. In the Kwakwa̱ka'wakw winter ceremonial, each dance is accompanied by a particular song type and in a set order. Mistakes of type or sequence during the ceremonial performance are punishable—today by considerable fines, and historically, some Kwakwa̱ka'wakw artists say, by death. In general, performance practices for each genre are highly specific and predetermined in terms of timbre, rhythm, vocables, melodic contour, structure, and tempo (Halpern 1967). Kwakwa̱ka'wakw regulate other creative practices, including who can perform dances and songs, or who can use regalia associated with them. In addition to hereditary individual ownership, there are at least four types of hereditary collective ownership of Kwakwa̱ka'wakw ceremonial song and dance (Harrison 2002).[3] These proprietary guidelines, when combined with the rules around genre and protocols governing what Kwakwa̱ka'wakw consider an error in song and dance performance, go some way toward ensuring that musical expressions are replicable over time. In such ways, and indeed others, customary or "traditional" Kwakwa̱ka'wakw song and dance performance involves set conventions, is predetermined, and is in certain ways replicable.

Songs and dances that Kwakwa̱ka'wakw perform in ritual contexts at the same time are considered to constitute *one expressive genre* by Kwakwa̱ka'wakw. For instance, a Hama̱t̕sa ceremonial dance and a Hama̱t̕sa song are both called "Hama̱t̕sa." A Ṉan refers both to a Grizzly Bear dance and a Grizzly Bear song. Dance and music together constitute one ritual event that is imbued with a set of ritual meanings shared also with visual art, myth, and oral history. In the Kwak̕wala language, the word k̕ik̕esu describes song and dance privileges that go together with rights to own and present regalia and masks in ceremonials. (Some versions of the music, dance, visual art, or myth may be presented separately—outside of ritual contexts, particularly in contemporary renditions—and for Kwakwa̱ka'wakw ceremonial music this can be contentious). An intertextual analysis of indigenous ritual performance must consider music, dance, and other human expressions presented together in ritual to make up unified "texts."

From another perspective, though, Kwakwa̱ka'wakw music and dance in the ritual setting—similar to how filmic texts are often understood—may *also* be understood to constitute what Bakhtin called a "secondary" or complex genre, which links to more than one set of generic features (Bakhtin 1986). For example, the Kwak̕wala word k̕amda̱m describes song as distinct from dance or any other art-making category; likewise, ya̱xwa̱mł designates the generic category of mask. So while ritual units need to be identified in Kwakwa̱ka'wakw parlance, they are built up from analytically separable components.

It is through putting music recorded for the *War Canoes* soundtrack in direct relation to conventions for presenting live Kwakwa̱ka'wakw song together with dance, regalia, and myth that the 1973 soundtrack involved the politics of u'mista. The literal return of voice necessarily engages with the politics of silencing, in film as in history. In order to parse my discussion of silent-film footage from the quite distinct notion of silencing (Spivak 1988), I will look briefly at the role of silence in the silent film, with attention to its implications for musical sound.

The Silence of the Silents

There is a problematic adage about silent films attributed to early film producer Irving Thalberg that goes, "There never was a *silent* film" (in Altman 1996:648), implying that film audiences would have always heard music to accompany them.[4] This sentiment is constantly reiterated in histories of musical practice for the silent film (Stilwell 2002), which was called "silent drama" before 1926 (Altman 1996:669). It is true that in the era of the silents (1894–1927 and later), live music performance often accompanied public film showings. The live music consisted of improvised scores, composed scores, and compiled scores (Sauer 1998). As Martin Miller Marks notes, renditions varied greatly in terms of performance skill, instrumentation, and musical sound:

> The tens of thousands of theatres across Europe and America varied enormously... in the number and types of musicians employed. There were amateurs and professionals, pianists, organists, small ensembles, and orchestras. Rather like musicians of the Baroque period, these silent film players enjoyed a great deal of freedom to realize their music according to talent and circumstance; ... it was fundamentally as new an art as playing from a figured bass had been three centuries earlier. (Marks 1997:9)

However, as Rick Altman explains, *silence* also was regular practice at early silent film exhibitions in America. Often, films had no "countersounds," in other words, no musical accompaniment or sound effects. A lack of musical accompaniment to silent projections was not systematically criticized by knowledgeable observers until 1911, after which the absence of music slowly declined as popular support for music increased.[5] Newspaper comments, cartoons, and theater reports show that from 1911 through the early 1920s—the years surrounding *In the Land of the Head Hunters*'s release—the American public contested and debated the use of music *and* silence during film exhibitions (Altman 1996).

What was also relatively silent about silent film was its projection. Early on, film projectors were often relegated to projection booths. If they weren't, there is little evidence that audiences were disturbed by projector noise. It is the noise of audiences, in fact, that claimed the attention of early critics (Altman 1996:670). On physical pieces of projected film media, dialogue or music was neither recorded photographically or electromagnetically on a band beside the image (as in sound film from 1894 to 1933 and later) nor digitally together with a digitized image. This meant that music—if it was performed during a silent-film exhibition, as was the intention for John J. Braham's composed score for *In the Land of the Head Hunters*—did not correspond specifically to sounds that one might reasonably expect to be produced during the dramatic action on screen.

Silent films were silent in a third respect, in terms of diegetic music.

Diegetic and nondiegetic music are the two types of film music generally identified. Diegetic music exists within the film narrative or diegesis. It is heard by the film's audience and presumably by the film's characters. The source of the music is apparent onscreen. "Nondiegetic" music refers to music that is not part of the diegesis, but occurs outside of it. Nondiegetic music therefore may be more precisely called "extradiegetic music" (Wierzbicki 2008:23). This type of music is heard by a film's audience but not by the film's characters, and the source of the music is not apparent onscreen. Silent films, when accompanied by improvised scores, composed scores, and compiled scores performed live, feature nondiegetic or extradiegetic music.

What specifically happens with the reception of film footage of music and dance performance that is silent? The visual image is disarticulated from the musical sound through being presented without music when projected. This is a particular type of decoupling that means that, for the film viewer, information is missing about sounded aspects of musical expression such as melody, lyrics, volume, phrasing, timbre, and instrumentation, as well as related social and cultural meanings. Braham's score for *Head Hunters* was separated from the film after 1915. In the 1970s, the silent film footage was all that was available. This left the dance and musical performances pictured in the film not only audibly silent but also culturally decontextualized.

Curtis's Silent Footage of Kwakwa̱ka'wakw Dance

Bill Holm and George Quimby described the process of a group of Kwakwa̱ka'wakw recording the dialogue and songs for *War Canoes* in the Newcombe Auditorium of the British Columbia Provincial Museum in Victoria in 1972 as follows:

> [The silent film footage from *Head Hunters*] was shown ... so that everyone could fix the story in mind and catch the mood. Then the first scene was projected several times, until those viewing had a chance to think through and discuss the appropriate dialogue or song. Finally the scene was projected.... The recording was spontaneous; there was no script or any rigid plan. (Holm and Quimby 1980:16–17)

The Kwakwa̱ka'wakw singers watched *Head Hunters* from 1914 in order to get inspiration about which songs to sing. The singers were Henry Bell, Dusty Cadwallader, Agnes Cranmer, Jonathan Hunt, Tom Hunt, Emma Hunt, James King, Helen Knox, Katie Scow, Peter Smith, and Bob Wilson, a few of whom had worked on the film in 1913–14 (see appendix 2). To give a sense of what is missing from the film musically—and what is missing from Braham's score too—I'll provide a single extended example from early in the film.

In the first dance scenes in *Head Hunters*, Motana appears on a towering rock, wearing a red cedar-bark neck ring and headband, and dances around a small fire before smudging himself (wafting the smoke over his head) and laying down to sleep. As Motana dances, his fingers relax toward his palms, his legs are bent, and his soles drop flat each time he steps. In the second scene, after finding a human skull in the forest, Motana makes stylized dancelike movements in which he turns his head quickly from side to side. Then, wearing the cedar-bark neck ring with an added hemlock headdress, Motana enters what the film implies to be a Kwakwa̱ka'wakw grave house, but which appears to be a Nuu-chah-nulth whaling shrine hung with human skulls (Glass 2009b; Jonaitis 1999). To the dance movements of the first scene, Motana—now wearing four skulls on his neck ring—adds quivering hands and newly holds his elbows at right angles (fig. 15.7a). The third scene shows Motana resuming his quest for power on "the heights," a bluff outdoors (fig. 8.1). Motana again layers new dance movements into his performance of those just described, adding very rhythmic footsteps, counterclockwise and clockwise turns of the body, and the alternate raising of each quivering hand.[6]

In these opening scenes, Motana's movements, as well as the cedar regalia and skull paraphernalia, indicate the Kwakwa̱ka'wakw Hama̱tsa ceremonial, although the dramatic context brings various incongruities between how the dance movements appear in the film and how they would appear in Kwakwa̱ka'wakw ritual (for example, outdoors instead of in a ceremonial Big House). In the Hama̱tsa, an individual is initiated into the Hama̱tsa secret society and in so doing acquires the right to display, for reasons of public and community witnessing, Hama̱tsa masks and hereditary dance privileges. Before and during a Kwakwa̱ka'wakw winter ceremonial, the initiation typically occurs through the following dance sequence. After a ritual seclusion, a Hama̱tsa dancer and initiate is said to be possessed by the spirit of Baxw-bakwalanuxwsiwe', the mythic "Cannibal at the North End of the World" (for versions of Baxwbakwalanuxwsiwe' myths that relate to origins of Hama̱tsa dances, see Boas 1897:394–408). Song gradually "tames" the initiate, who at first dances frenziedly (Curtis 1907–30, vol. 10:182). A successful initiation moves progressively through at least four dance types to unique song genres: a first dance in which an initiate traditionally emerges from the forest wearing hemlock branches, and runs wildly around a ceremonial fire, a movement

Fig. 8.1. The character Motana uses movements excerpted from the Kwakwa̱ka'wakw
Hama̱tsa dance in opening scenes of *In the Land of the Head Hunters* (1914).
UCLA Film & Television Archive, The Field Museum, and Milestone Films.

called *xwasa̱lil*; a second dance in which the initiate dances more calmly; the
Ha̱msa̱mala, which features other (noninitiate) dancers wearing dramatic
bird masks; and the Hilik'ala or tamed Hama̱tsa in which a female dancer
called a *hiligaxste'* dances in front of the initiate in an effort to entice him
into a ceremonial house in order to complete the taming process (see Powell
et al., n.d.:18–23).[7] In *Head Hunters*, one sees Motana using movements and
regalia that are present in all four of the dances, but most intensely in the
Hilik'ala. Each of Motana's three performances thus blends dance movements
from the four stages of the Hama̱tsa dance sequence.

The Hama̱tsa songs implied by Motana's ritualistic dance movements in
Head Hunters are, similar to other Kwakwa̱ka'wakw song types, highly specific in terms of instrumentation, vocables, singing techniques, and microto-
nality. Kwakwa̱ka'wakw ceremonial songs are frequently sung in unison by
men and are accompanied by percussion, including the log drum, wood plank,
and frame drum (Boas 1966:192) played with beaters that historically could
have alternative uses as torches (Boas 1966:437). Other Kwakwa̱ka'wakw
instruments are box drums (made of cedar wood), clappers, rattles of wood
and shell, bullroarers, multitoned whistles called *ma̱dzis,* and, in twentieth-

and twenty-first-century contexts, bass drums derived from brass bands. In the Hamaṫsa dance cycle, log drums and rattles are used throughout, whereas *maḏzis* are heard before the appearance of the Hamaṫsa bird masks. Hamaṫsa songs and other historical Kwakwa̱ka'wakw song genres use Kwak̓wala lyrics together with syllables that have lexical derivations and meanings, and both are employed in highly sophisticated ways in song composition (Halpern 1981:4). These vocables unfold in microtonal song compositions in which a vocal line—always sung in unison and in the Big House context by a lead singer directing other vocalists, all of whom may be hired (Spradley 1969)—undulates according to a rhythmic cadence that can be entirely different from that of a concurrent percussion part. Each song genre has a specific contour, and most songs have "recitative" and melody sections (Halpern 1967).[8] Deep knowledge of such singing traditions informed the sorts of musical and intertextual decisions made by the singers during the recording of the soundtrack to *War Canoes*. They helped restore to Curtis's silent footage a sense of the rich aural and cultural environment of Kwakwa̱ka'wakw ceremonial practice.

Kwakwa̱ka'wakw Song and the Politics of *U'mista* in *In the Land of the War Canoes*

If the Kwakwa̱ka'wakw singers performing and recording a traditional song soundtrack to *War Canoes* are understood as reconstituting what most Kwakwa̱ka'wakw consider to be a unified ceremonial performance text and event experience—consisting of music and dance together with regalia, masks, and mythical relevance—it is also tied to what Kwakwa̱ka'wakw call *u'mista*. Gloria Cranmer Webster offers the following definition of *u'mista*. In the film *Box of Treasures* (Olin 1983), she suggests that before colonial contact, people who were captured during raids but later returned home were "said to have u'mista"—that is, to have the quality of being returned.[9] At the time *War Canoes* was produced, the term was also used figuratively to refer to a desire for "the complete u'mista or repatriation of everything [Kwakwa̱ka'wakw] lost when [their] world was turned upside down" (Webster 1992:37). It referred to the return of cultural property through what are now called decolonizing processes (Smith 2000), for instance repatriations of material culture confiscated by Canadian authorities during the colonial period and returned to Kwakwa̱ka'wakw-run museums such as the U'mista Cultural Centre, operated by the U'mista Cultural Society (founded in 1974; the Centre opened in Alert Bay in 1980), as well as the Kwagiulth Museum (opened in Cape Mudge in 1979). *U'mista* also referred to revitalizations of

Kwakwaka'wakw ritual practices primarily after 1951 (Webster 1992:37). From 1884 to 1951, Section 3 of Canada's Indian Act legislation prohibited the practice of certain indigenous ceremonials, music, and dance. Kwakwaka'wakw who participated in potlatch ceremonials were legally persecuted and jailed, although even during the ban, some Kwakwaka'wakw persistently practiced ceremonial customs in remote and private places, or resisted and defied the ban in other ways (introduction, this volume). Webster (1992:37) notes, "The renewed interest of younger people in learning about their cultural history is a kind of *u'mista*. The creation of new ceremonial gear to replace that held by museums is yet another *u'mista*."

The possibility and interest of Kwakwaka'wakw in making a traditional music soundtrack was undeniably shaped by the legalization and revitalization of ceremonialism after 1951. The soundtrack to *In the Land of the War Canoes* was *u'mista* in that it brought into greater vitality and aural vividness the music by recoupling sounded and voiced Kwakwaka'wakw song with Curtis's silent footage of dancing and ritual performance. When applied to music, Webster's metaphorical notion of *u'mista*—involving the revival and return of music and other cultural practices after their prohibition—literally means making what was often silent (in public spaces at least) newly sounded.

In fact, by recording new musical accompaniments to the film, the Kwakwaka'wakw also helped to subtly reshape and recontextualize its thematic and cultural focus. The songs that the singers recorded for *War Canoes* underscored some narrative themes in Curtis's film, but not others. During the opening "spirit quest" scenes, for example, the singers chose to sing Hamaťsa songs to go together with Motana's Hamaťsa dance movements. This emphasized the film's narrative theme of human death, linked to motifs of cannibalism and war, in the following way. Hamaťsa songs use the syllables *ha, ma,* and *mai,* derived from the Kwak'wala words for "eating" (*hama-hamap*) and "food" (*hama*) (Halpern 1967:255). *Hap,* derived from "eat," is called out in a ritual Hamaťsa sequence by dancers who are said to be possessed by the man-eating spirit Baxwbakwalanuxwsiwe'. These syllables are references to the myth and mock-cannibalistic acts by dancers who undergo initiation into the Hamaťsa secret society. Beyond the connection to eating human flesh, Hamaťsa songs are also associated with war. Franz Boas concluded that Kwakwaka'wakw secret societies originated with war custom, and most detailed discussions of Kwakwaka'wakw war practices show a relationship between secret societies and war (Boas 1897:664; Holm and Quimby 1980:96).

Song choice further emphasized the theme of war musically during a "capturing the bride" ritual.[10] The plot unfolds as follows: At the bridegroom's village, three canoes are loaded with paddlers, bentwood boxes ostensibly filled with animal furs, cedar-bark mats, large ladles, a ceremonial copper, and a feast dish. The bridegroom's party paddles to sea. A scouting party on the shore of the bride's village spots the canoes. As the film shows, the beginning of the ritual involves the groom's family paddling their canoe toward the bride's village, in front of which the ritual will occur. The ritual builds up to a display of dance privileges of the groom's family, which today is still a part of traditional Kwakw̲ak̲a'wakw marriage ceremonies (Holm and Quimby 1980:77).

During such bride-capture rituals, the Kwakw̲ak̲a'wakw sing war songs. The Kwakw̲ak̲a'wakw singers in 1972 chose to record war songs for when the groom's family paddles toward the bride's village. The symbolic implication is that the family is going to capture the bride by force (in reality, they lure her and her family through the display of property that will form the bride price). If specific ritual scenes in *War Canoes* are understood as secondary or complex genres, à la Bakhtin, consisting of more than one set of generic features, the Kwakw̲ak̲a'wakw singers' musical choices resulted in the inclusion of a greater number of genres—not only dance and mask display but also song—that addressed war. The intertextual musical choices for *War Canoes* thus amplified culturally specific themes of human death and war in the film by reattaching the relevant Kwakw̲ak̲a'wakw musical and lyrical traditions.

Of course, Curtis and his audiences had generic (rather than culturally specific) themes in mind too. As Claudia Gorbman notes in her seminal article "Scoring the Indian: Music of the Liberal Western," North American indigenous people have been manifested in film either as "bloodthirsty marauders" or "romanticized noble savages" (Gorbman 2000:235). The connection to war has also been expressed in so-called Indianist music—Western art and orchestral music, including music for early film and eventually Hollywood Westerns—that signified the "Indian" through specific musical gestures. Some such musical tropes derived from concert works in the war dance genre of 1830s Europe and America, which included driving rhythmic accompaniments, fast tempos, and intense chromaticism, as well as angular melodies and diminished-seventh chords. For example, in John J. Braham's score for *Head Hunters,* a forty-four-bar movement called "No. 11" (fig. 8.2) features a steady quarter-note rhythm in the "Indian Drum" (bars 1–33, 35, 37, and 39); pulsating chords (bars 33–40); the quick, lively tempo of allegro ("No. 11" in its entirety); and chromatic runs in the violins (bars 11–12, 17–18, and 23–24) and cellos (bars 11–12, 17–18, and 23–24) that are echoed later by chromatic notes in runs in the clarinets (bars 29–32), violins (bars 29–32 and 41–42), and

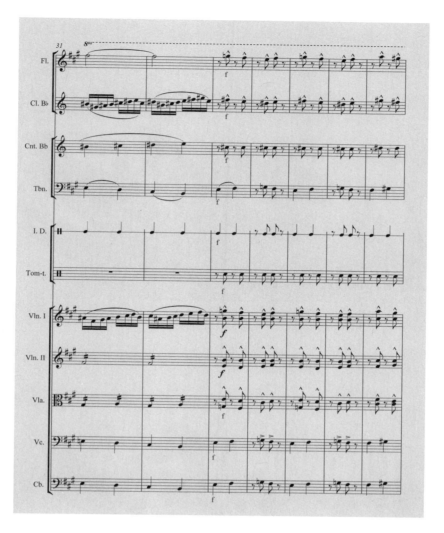

Fig. 8.2. John J. Braham, *In the Land of the Head Hunters* (1914),
"No. 11," Allegro, bars 31–37, from the 2008 performance score by David Gilbert.
J. Paul Getty Trust. Getty Research Institute, Los Angeles, 2008.M.58.

cellos (bar 43).[11] Another set of musical tropes that came to connect Indianness with war in orchestral music was derived from British marches that had
"Indian" in their titles and that used open fourths and fifths, pulsating per-
cussive chords (identified above), and minor modes (Pisani 2005). Braham's
"No. 11" is in F-sharp minor. There are recurring and arpeggiated open fifths
in the cellos (bars 1–4, 7–10, 13–16, and 19–22) as well as double-stopped perfect fourths and fifths in the violins (bars 33–40). Although a comprehensive
analysis of Braham's score is beyond the scope of this chapter, it is worth

MUSICAL INTERTEXTUALITY IN INDIGENOUS FILM

Top: Fig. 8.3. Dancers of the N̲an (Grizzly Bear) dance, Kwan'wala (Thunderbird) dance, and H̲amasalał (Wasp) dance appear in a Kwakwa̲ka'wakw "capturing the bride" ceremony, ca. 1914. Photo by Edmund Schwinke. Burke Museum of Natural History and Culture, 1988–78/144.

Bottom: Fig. 8.4. The Kwakwa̲ka'wakw N̲an (Grizzly Bear) dance, ca. 1914. Photo by Edmund Schwinke. Burke Museum of Natural History and Culture, 1988-78/142.

noting that musical tropes of the war dance persist in the score, including in "No. 11," which was matched in the 2008 performances to Motana's spirit quest scenes. Braham's music for *Head Hunters* scored the Indian as generic warrior, while the examples of music for *War Canoes* that I just discussed connected culturally specific Kwakwa̱ka'wakw practices—from the Hama̱t́sa dance to wedding rituals—to warfare and war symbolism.

In other cases, though, Curtis's footage of musical and dance performance strongly suggests certain themes underscoring human death and war, whereas the Kwakwa̱ka'wakw singers made other decisions in 1972. Selected examples are the N̠an or Grizzly Bear dance, Kwa̱n'wala or Thunderbird dance, and H̠amasa̱laɫ or Wasp dance. Later in the bride-capture ritual, the three masked and fully costumed dancers each perform on one of the canoe prows (fig. 8.3). The grizzly claws the air while the bird and insect dancers outstretch their arms, the thunderbird fluttering its wings. With paddles upturned, a singing bridegroom's party drums on the gunwales. In this part of the ritual, three separate song genres would typically be heard, each one correspondent to the different dance and regalia type.

For *War Canoes*, the Kwakwa̱ka'wakw soundtrack singers recorded one dance song that bears none of the obvious or specific genre markers of a Grizzly Bear song, Thunderbird song, or Wasp song. The featured song includes the spondaic drumbeats (which are absent in some declamatory sections) and singing in seconds that distinguish songs shown in the peace dance ceremonies (*Tła'sa̱la*) of the winter ceremonial. In a ceremonial, such a song would signal that a mask is about to be shown. A mask is one type of *długwe'* or "supernatural treasure" of a family unit ('*numaya̱m*)—a special category of owned aesthetic expression that may also include other visual arts, songs, and dances (Harrison 2000:125–26). This song's vocables include *ha, hi, ho, hey, ya, yo,* and *yay* (and, less frequently, *la, lo,* and *ley*)—all of which particularly identify dance songs as opposed to other types. While a single song in *War Canoes* seems a practical choice (because the dances are shown concurrently, for instance), it would have been possible to layer excerpts of song genres that are specific to the masks, especially during close-ups of individual dancers. The bear dancer is the main visual focus for twenty-five seconds (fig. 8.4), and there is close-up footage of the thunderbird.

When making the soundtrack for *In the Land of the War Canoes*, the Kwakwa̱ka'wakw performers also circumvented themes of human death and war in Curtis's film footage. The most appropriate choice for the Grizzly Bear dance, for instance, would have been a Grizzly Bear (mask) song. Grizzly Bear songs use the typical song syllables *na-na*, which means "grizzly" in Kwaḵwala, and *hi-ho-hu,* the sound that a grizzly bear makes according to Kwakwaka'wakw. Kwakwa̲ka'wakw recognize the grizzly bear as an impressive peacemaker that salves conflict, but also a great warrior. Grizzly Bear songs can also connote diverse types of fighting (Halpern 1967:11). The Thunderbird dance and Wasp dance are typically performed to Thunderbird and Wasp songs, respectively, which are associated with war in different ways. Thunderbird songs often accompany the Hilik'ala or tamed Hamaťsa genre associated with cannibalism. As secret societies have a relationship with war, Thunderbird songs that are also Hamaťsa songs indirectly imply war. In Kwakwa̲ka'wakw culture, the wasp is respected for its intimidating and warrior-like qualities. Young warriors have been known to seek it as a guardian spirit through vision quests.

The song choice that I just discussed avoided referring to war and, by extension, to modal stereotypes of North American indigenous people in film and music as bloodthirsty and warlike; to cannibalism, the historical existence of which on the Northwest Coast is contested but the symbolism of which is clear in the Hamaťsa and other dances; and to stereotypes that have prevailed in Canada (intensively before the 1950s) about the mistakenly "savage," "wild," "uncivilized," and "primitive" nature of indigenous cultural expressions, and that were articulated by Canadian authorities involved in the antipotlatch legislation and provided as justification for enforcing it. The results of either amplifying or tempering Curtis's narrative themes of war and death through the selection of culturally appropriate music would have been primarily available to Kwakwa̲ka'wakw audiences for *War Canoes,* as well as to have culturally knowledgeable non-Natives such as Bill Holm, and we can see such decisions as a specific act of filmic reclamation or *u'mista* on the part of the soundtrack recorders.

Intertextual Gaps in
Performed Indigenous Responses to *Head Hunters*

The intertextuality literature offers an additional perspective for examining musical sound and musical image in film. Charles Briggs and Richard Bauman draw attention to an intertextual *gap,* by which they mean the spaces that are produced by the process of linking utterances to generic models. Briggs and Bauman write,

> Although the creation of this hiatus is unavoidable, its relative suppression or foregrounding has important effects. On the one hand, texts framed in

some genres attempt to achieve generic transparency by *minimizing* the distance between texts and genres, thus rendering the discourse maximally interpretable through the use of generic precedents. This approach sustains highly conservative, traditionalizing modes of creating textual authority. On the other hand, *maximizing* and highlighting these intertextual gaps underlies strategies for building authority through claims of individual creativity and innovation (such as are common in 20th century Western literature), resistance to the hegemonic structures associated with established genres, and other motives for distancing oneself from textual precedents. (Briggs and Bauman 1992:149)

From this perspective, the literal and musical utterances of Kwakwa̱ka'wakw singers recorded for *War Canoes* can be understood to have minimized the intertextual distance between the filmic text and the "texts" of Kwakwa̱ka'wakw ritual genres in some scenes more than in others, especially when contrasted with the maximal gap existing between those Native genres and the orchestral score that Braham wrote for *Head Hunters*. I suggest that these minimizing and maximizing moves reacted to the big-P Politics of the antipotlatch legislation in Canada, but the intertextual decisions also are small-p political in that they assert the cultural authority of an ethnic and indigenous group.

In 2008, the G̱wa'wina Dancers' performances following the screenings of the reconstructed *In the Land of the Head Hunters* presented another opportunity in which Kwakwa̱ka'wakw engaged with Curtis's silent footage of ritualistic performance, even once it was reunited with Braham's orchestral music. The dance group had its own stage space and time block—a parallel presentation space to the *Head Hunters* film and score. The audience for most of these performances was largely nonindigenous, although many Kwakwa̱ka'wakw and other Northwest Coast First Nations attended a Vancouver screening.

The G̱wa'wina Dancers—many of whom are descendents of the crew of *Head Hunters* and the singers for *War Canoes*—claimed an opportunity to define the Kwakwa̱ka'wakw music and dance genres that Curtis had filmed through speeches as well as song-and-dance presentations (see also Wasden and Glass, this volume). The dance group presented a program selected from dances explicitly featured in the film (including the Hamaṫsa, Kwan'wala [Thunderbird Dance], Na̱n [Grizzly Bear Dance], Tuxw'id [Warrior Dance], and G̱alsgamliła ["First to Appear in the House" Ceremony]); those present in the film but incorporated into larger group scenes in a manner at odds with indigenous ceremonial practice (such as the Tła̱lkwała [Ladies Dance] and the Długwala [Wolf Dance]); and those that are not featured in the film at all but that are part of the Gwa'wina Dancers' standard presentation format (the 'Yawitłalał [Welcome Dance], Me'dzawesu' [Salmon Dance], Am'lala [Play Song and Dance], and Halakas'lakala [Farewell Song and Dance]).

Following the current practice of other Northwest Coast First Nations dance troupes that perform publicly (Harrison 2000, 2002), the Gwa'wina Dancers explained the song and dance genres presented. This mirrors Kwakwaka'wakw ceremonies and rituals, which are interspersed with speeches by chiefs and speakers for chiefs. The sequencing of the songs and dances presented also replicates ritual order. Yet the song-and-dance explanations, which could have emphasized the narrative themes of human death and war in the film, instead minimized or negated them. The group leader Hiłamas's (William Wasden Jr.) speech about the Hamaťsa, which is approximated on the Curtis project's website, is one such example:

> The Hamaťsa is the highest-ranking and most sacred T'seka "Winter Ceremony" of the Kwakwaka'wakw. The Hamaťsa is the reenactment through song and dance of a young man's possession by the dreaded man-eating spirit Baxwbakwalanuxwsiwe', who lived at the north end of the world. Through rituals, song and dance the initiate is purified and tamed, thus bringing him back to his human state. The Hamaťsa dancers that will perform are initiated members of the sacred Hamaťsa secret society.[12]

Other examples of speeches that maximized the gap between the narrative themes of human death and war—and thus Curtis's *Head Hunters* film/text—addressed Gwa'wina Dancers' performances of the Tuxw'id, the Nan, and the Kwan'wala, genres associated with war or warrior spirits but that were not presented in that light to audiences.

Compared to *War Canoes*, the Gwa'wina Dancers' performances in 2008 similarly involved an *u'mista* of musical sound and voice, but *after*, not during, Curtis's film itself. Through live performance of speech—which had not existed in 1914 exhibitions of Curtis's film—Kwakwaka'wakw explained on their own terms the Kwakwaka'wakw music and dance genres that Curtis had filmed. In fact, the Gwa'wina Dancers performances left the impression of maximizing the textual distance between their performances and those in the Curtis film by not even mentioning the film in some shows. At the same time, the dancers also minimized an intertextual gap between their performances and those in Kwakwaka'wakw rituals through replicating ritual protocols for performance format and order, as well as through sharing performances of Kwakwaka'wakw ritual genres themselves (Glass, this volume).

When it came to presenting the Curtis film and music, the Kwakwaka'wakw were not alone on stage in their strategic manipulation of intertextual gaps. For instance, the Coast Orchestra, an all-indigenous group, notably departed from the efforts to replicate a period performance by the UCLA Philharmonia (which performed Braham's score at a Los Angeles screening) and by the Turning Point Ensemble (performing in Vancouver). Instead of the instruments used by these two ensembles, drawn from those that Braham wrote for (see fig. 8.2), the Coast Orchestra featured violin and cello together with drum kit, voice, saxophone, and Native American flute. This represented not only different instrumentation but a smaller ensemble than Braham's score requested. The ensemble used Braham's score as a starting point, but then individuals in the group improvised based on their own (non-Kwakwaka'wakw) musical and Native cultural backgrounds.[13] Several of the musicians told the organizers that they felt that they were "reclaim[ing] the images" in the film in a personal way—through improvisation based on their individual artistic impulses, which sometimes involved using generic "Indian-sounding" music or, in the case of the Native American flute, instrumentation (personal communication with Aaron Glass, June 1, 2012; see chapter 12, this volume). The intertextual gaps that were often minimized in the Kwakwaka'wakw soundtrack for *War Canoes*, and maximized in the 1914 score and (at least some) 2008 performances accompanying the restored *Head Hunters*, constitute different kinds of assertion of cultural authority through intervention via Curtis's film and Braham's score.

Conclusion

Indigenous struggles for cultural authority are ongoing through aesthetic texts, media, and performances that are presented to the general public and, over the mid-to-late-twentieth and early twenty-first centuries, that often reflect an intensifying push toward indigenous self-empowerment and toward decolonization efforts. I have described textual strategies for asserting cultural authority that the Kwakwaka'wakw voiced over a period of over three-and-a-half decades. The earliest one, in *In the Land of the War Canoes,* involved pairing Kwakwaka'wakw traditional music with silent film footage of ritual dance. The Kwakwaka'wakw understand the music and dance together with regalia and mythological significance to constitute single ritual performance genres. I suggested that this act could be interpreted as a musical *u'mista* — the return/revival (having political connotations) of Kwakwaka'wakw music to Kwakwa̱ka'wakw dance that minimized the intertextual gap between the soundtrack, musical scenes in the film, and live ceremonial performance. This was a traditionalizing mode of creating textual authority. A similar intertextual strategy occurred, via a greater number of expressive modes (such as speech making and dancing as well as singing) in the G̱wa'wina Dancers' performances after the screenings of *Head Hunters* in 2008.

A complementary strategy of maximizing the distance of meaning between narrative themes in Curtis's 1914 film—specifically of human death and war—and meanings of ritual performance also intensified between the Kwakwa̱ka'wakw song recorded in 1972 to the 2008 G̱wa'wina Dancers' presentations. This strategy resisted the characterization of Kwakwa̱ka'wakw in terms of colonial modalities such as the blood-thirsty marauder that defined Hollywood Indian-style films and their music and promoted the prohibition of ceremony in Canada in the late nineteenth century. In such ways, the assertion of cultural authority via strategies that both minimize and maximize intertextual gaps has characterized certain politicized aesthetics of music for indigenous film, including the various versions of Edward Curtis's *In the Land of the Head Hunters.*

1   Other silent films about Northwest Coast First Nations include Harlan Smith's four short ethnographic films on the Bella Coola (1924), Tsimshian (1927), Coast Salish (1928), and Nuu-chah-nulth (1928–29), all of which include music or dance performance; *Saving the Sagas* (1928), a documentary film about Marius Barbeau and Ernest MacMillan's work on recording Nisga'a music and dance; and Franz Boas's raw footage (1930), edited by Bill Holm and released as *The Kwakiutl of British Columbia* in 1973, which features drumming and eighteen Kwakwa̱ka'wakw dances (see Morris 1994 and Bunn-Marcuse 2005).

2   This number is taken from the 2008 reconstructed version of *In the Land of the Head Hunters*, although additional footage of music or dance is likely still missing. *In the Land of the War Canoes* (1973) contains twelve music or dance scenes.

3   The four levels of collective ownership: groups of Kwakwa̱ka'wakw tribes or nations; Kwakwa̱ka'wakw nations; groups within these nations, such as *numayms* or extended family units; and subgroups within Kwakwa̱ka'wakw numayms (Harrison 2002:144).

4   This section title is taken from Altman (1996).

5   As late as 1912–13, silence was the dominant accompaniment to film showings in some American cities; intermittent and no musical accompaniment for films continued in certain cases through the early 1920s and beyond (Altman 1996:649, 680–87).

6   The scenes discussed follow these intertitles in *In the Land of the War Canoes* (1973): Intertitle 1: "Through fasting and hardships, Motana, the son of a great chief, Kenada, seeks supernatural power. In his vision-sleep the face of a maiden appears to him. It is Naida, the daughter of Chief Waket." Intertitle 3: "He resumes his spirit quest at the Island of the Dead. Then testing his courage and skills he harpoons the sea lion and whale." Intertitle 5: "Motana has again built his fire on the heights where he fasts and dances, still seeking spirit power. The sorcerer's daughter resolves to spare him [from sorcery practiced by her father] and win his love, but he spurns her and she returns to her father with Motana's hair and neckring." The 2008 reconstructed version of *In the Land of the Head Hunters* split the five scenes into seventeen, added

additional footage and still photographs, and used Curtis's original intertitles from 1914 (appendix 4). The 2008 intertitles that substituted for those above and that introduced the same dance footage are: Intertitle 17: "Motana lands on an island to build his first prayer fire. In a dream appears a maid." Intertitle 22: "Motana continues his vigil by journeying to the Island of the Dead." Intertitle 29: "For his final invocation to the gods, Motana again builds the sacred fire on the heights."

7   My description of the dance sequence is based on my ethnographic work on the Hamaťsa among the Kwaguʼł of Fort Rupert on Vancouver Island, British Columbia, and elaborates on Boas (1966:443), who identified only dancing done before the taming (such as the first dance) and after the taming (by some interpretations, part of the tamed Hamaťsa dance) without detailing all dances of initiation.

8   Kwakw<u>a</u>kaʼwakw singing generally exhibits a highly complex assortment of musical traits. Ethnomusicologist Ida Halpern listed these features of special voice production: manipulation and repetition with emphasis on single tones; glissandi; sharp contrast between long and short tones; forceful accents on sustained tones produced by guttural pressure on long notes; long sustained tones separated by pulsations; nasal quality, no falsetto; ornamentation; unusual simultaneous sounds as though the singer were producing two tones at once; prolongation of tones at the end of verse; beginning of polyphony; octave leaps common, also leaps to the fifth and sixth; melody pattern based to a great extent on seconds; extensive use of clusters of seconds; extensive use of vowels sung to important melodic material; extensive use of microtones; clearly defined melodic lines; descending melody; microtonal rises undertaken within techniques of melodic variation; intentional breath-taking as part of a melody and a stretto in breathtaking; slight variation of single tones in beating (rhythm) or melody, when the original subject is repeated; dramatic drum beat changes from many small beats to slower beats with some tremolo effects; and changes in dramatic sense and intensity built up also by drumming without singing and by singing without drumming (adapted from Halpern 1967:7).

9   Kathryn Bunn-Marcuse observes that films produced by the U'mista Cultural Society, such as *Box of Treasures* (1983) and *Potlatch ... A Strict Law Bids Us Dance* (1975)— both of which also define *u'mista*—are "part of a larger Native-directed effort to document their own history" (Bunn-Marcuse 2005:305).

10   In *War Canoes*, the bride ritual follows this intertitle: "Waket accepts the [marriage] proposal and Kenada and his tribe come for the bride in their great canoes. The Thunderbird, the Wasp, and the Grizzly Bear dance in the prows."

11   Both John Braham's original 1914 manuscript score for *Head Hunters* and David Gilbert's 2008 transcription are available in complete form through the Getty Research Institute's online library at http://www.getty.edu/research/library/ (accessed July 1, 2013).

12   Wasden's description of the dance is online at http://www.curtisfilm.rutgers.edu/index.php?option = com_content&task = view&id = 28&Itemid = 49 (accessed March 18, 2013).

13   For a profile of the Coast Orchestra, see http://www.myspace.com/thecoastorchestra (accessed March 18, 2013).

9

REFLECTIONS ON WORKING WITH EDWARD CURTIS

BARBARA CRANMER (ṪLAḴWAGILA̱'OG̱WA)

I have sat many times at my computer to write about my thoughts on the work of Edward Curtis and could come up with no definitive outcomes. In his early work he called us the "vanishing race," and today that is far from the truth. We live today as Kwakwa̱ka̱'wakw; we show great pride in the culture into which we were born.

For many years I have had great interest in the work of Edward Curtis as it relates to my own documentary filmmaking experience. I started sharing the stories of our people some twenty years ago, and the ultimate goal was and still is the telling of our own stories, our own perspectives, and the giving of voice to our communities. In my career, I have achieved what I set out to do in the ten documentaries that I have directed. I have given voice to our communities, one that has been absent for way too long.

Today in 2013, we celebrate who we are. We have been given a beautiful and distinct culture, one where we celebrate every facet of our lives. In my opinion, it is the threads of our cultural history that we shared with people like Edward Curtis. I have often thought that if he had not taken all of those photographs and made the film *In the Land of the Head Hunters,* we may have not been given the exposure as a people. He has added his work to the many others that travelled and worked among our people at the turn of the twentieth century, at a time when our people were being looked at with a magnifying glass and condemned for practicing our customs.

I have appreciated the work of Curtis from the version of the film *In the Land of the War Canoes*, and in particular the scene where two men are hold-

Fig. 9.1. Scene from *Head Hunters* (1914) with a grease feast.
UCLA Film & Television Archive, The Field Museum, and Milestone Films.

ing huge feast spoons and throwing *t̓łi'na* (eulachon oil) at each other as a way to compete against one another (fig. 9.1). I incorporated this scene in *T̓łi'na: The Rendering of Wealth,* my 1999 documentary about the tradition of catching the eulachon fish, rendering the oil, and giving the t̓łi'na out in a potlatch ceremony we call *T̓łi'nagila*. This ceremony is the highest honor a chief can bestow on his guests—the giving of t̓łi'na. I dedicated this film to my grandpa Arthur Brown Dick, and his voice can be heard throughout the documentary. The *T̓łi'nagila* ceremony, where we shared t̓łi'na with people who attended the memorial potlatch for him, was filmed to honor his memory. Of all of the documentaries that I've done, this is one of my favorites because I was able to incorporate historical and present-day perspectives, showing that this is still part of our living culture.

I actually never gave Curtis much thought in choosing that particular scene, but I'm glad I had access to footage that may have never otherwise been photographed or filmed at that time. I had seen *In the Land of the War Canoes* and was fascinated by the scene with bear and thunderbird dancing on the bows of the great canoes (see fig. 8.3). That was amazing to me. Curtis managed to catch a small glimpse of how our people were living at that time

REFLECTIONS ON WORKING WITH EDWARD CURTIS

Fig. 9.2. Edward S. Curtis, *A Chief's Daughter—Nakoaktok* [Francine Hunt], 1914. (*NAI,* portfolio 10.) Charles Deering McCormick Library of Special Collections, Northwestern University Library.

while incorporating much of the ceremony and tradition that was lived by our people way before 1914, when the film was made. That scene is world famous, and I acknowledge Curtis for filming it.

Yet there are many aspects to this period in time about which I have questions. I have wondered about what our people were thinking. Did our people even know what a camera was, or what making a movie meant? From all accounts they seemed to get right involved and enjoy this once-in-a-lifetime experience.

What was going through Edward Curtis's mind as he developed his film? He worked with a full Native cast of actors with no acting experience. Though the film is ethnographic in nature, many elements were created out of his own romanticized view of our people.

At that time in the history of our people, there seemed to be so much turmoil. Our people were being looked at under the microscope for our heathen ways, for cannibalism, and with total misunderstanding of who we were. People were living in fear because of the government ban on the potlatch. And here was Curtis working among our people, having developed a trust and relation to gather the great regalia, dances, and culture of our people.

I was a part of an Edward Curtis photo exhibit, developed for the film restoration project, where we were asked to chose a photo and write about it (photo essay 2, this volume). I chose the photo of George Hunt's wife Francine (fig. 9.2; see also fig. 1.2). To me she is a woman of great nobility. She sits showing her wealth and status among our Kwakwaka'wakw people. The abalone shell on her hat signifies her status in the social structure of our people. The photo struck me because of the continuation of our culture and my own personal experience in my early teen years. My grandfather Arthur Dick Sr. gave a potlatch where I was in the Coming of Age Ceremony passed down from my great-grandmother, Agnes Alfred (Axu). I wore a hat like the ancestor in the photo, covered in abalone shell. I stood and danced on a wooden box with two family attendants on either side wearing Peace Dance headdresses. I had a dance screen behind me painted with two slaves holding up a copper. The design comes from the Starface House of the Mamalilikala (at Village Island). The story tells of my grandfather's great-grandfather, Maxwayalis, the first man that ever brought our people together after years of war among each other. People arrived with guns because they thought he was just trying to trick them. He brought people together in peace and got them to know each other. This ceremony was of great significance in my early life. It shows my family lineage and recognizes my mother's side of the family through my grandfather Arthur Dick Sr. from the Mamalilikala.

REFLECTIONS ON WORKING WITH EDWARD CURTIS

Over time I have come to acknowledge and respect the work of Edward Curtis. I watched Anne Makepeace's 2000 documentary *Coming to Light*, about his life and work, and I came to understand a bit more of what Curtis was attempting to achieve. We should be grateful for the contribution he made to all of us.

I also wish to acknowledge having being present in 2008 at the Chan Centre for the Performing Arts in Vancouver, while watching our dancers share our culture, listening to a full score of the music, and seeing the film again. It will be with me for a time to come. In this current time, we witnessed something from history with a contemporary First Nation feel to it. It was great.

Barbara Cranmer (Ṫłakwagilạ'ogwa)

PHOTO ESSAY 2

"Old Images / New Views: Indigenous Perspectives on Edward Curtis"

DR. E. RICHARD ATLEO

PAM BROWN

MARIE CLEMENTS

KARRMEN CREY

MIQUE'L ICESIS DANGELI

ANDY EVERSON

LINC KESLER,

DAVID NEEL

EVELYN VANDERHOOP

AND WILLIAM WASDEN JR.

This photo essay features the reflections of ten First Nations artists, scholars, and community leaders on the north Pacific coast, each responding to an Edward Curtis photograph that they selected. In the diversity of perspectives, we find nuance regarding Curtis's images and their complex relationship to indigenous peoples today.

This essay was adapted from an original exhibit developed by the Museum of Anthropology and the First Nations Studies Program at the University of British Columbia for the 2008 public presentation of Curtis's 1914 film *In the Land of the Head Hunters*. For the complete exhibit, which included twenty contributors, see www.curtisfilm.rutgers.edu. Unless otherwise indicated, all images are from Edward Curtis's *The North American Indian* (*NAI*).

Fig. E.2.1. Edward S. Curtis, *Naida, the Proud Princess* [Margaret Frank, née Hunt],
from Curtis's 1915 book *In the Land of the Head-Hunters*.
UBC Library, Rare Books and Special Collections.

Andy Everson (Nagedzi)
K'omoks First Nation

Underneath the fur robes and the clip-on nose ring in this picture, Edward S. Curtis managed to capture something he probably didn't expect. When I gaze at this photograph, I don't see Princess Naida from his film and book *In the Land of the Head Hunters*. Instead, I see youth and beauty and a long life still to be fulfilled. I look into this profile of my grandmother and see that the wrinkles that I knew for most of my life are absent. At the same time, I see the waves in her hair that she always carried with pride. I gaze into the photograph and see a seventeen-year-old daughter of a chief whose cultural taboos restricted what she could and couldn't do on film—so much so that Curtis was forced to hire two additional women to also portray the princess in his film. I recognize that although she is wearing a costume, she carries a sense of poise and grace that belies her age. I see in her the eyes of a woman who would live to ninety-nine years of age and who, as a true *princess* amongst our people, would live up to her ancestral name U'magalis, or "Noblest Over All." I thank Curtis, not for capturing his vision of our people before European contact, but for capturing a moment in time in my grandmother's life.

Fig. E.2.2. Edward S. Curtis, *Bowman*, 1915. (*NAI,* portfolio 11.)
UBC Library, Rare Books and Special Collections.

Umeek of Ahousht (Dr. E. Richard Atleo)
Associate Adjunct Professor,
University of Victoria

The Bowman represents, for me, a photograph of intense irony. Since a major cultural theme of the Nuu-chah-nulth is the hidden world made manifest in origin stories—such as the story of Son of Raven that unveils the astonishing intimacy between the physical and the metaphysical—it is natural for me to view this Curtis photograph through that cultural theme. On the surface, it is evident that the photograph is meant to illustrate the kind of natural pristine moment that had excited the imagination of Enlightenment authors such as Sir Thomas More, John Locke, and Jean Jacques Rousseau. Rousseau imagined that the Bowman wandered in the forest, here without clothes, without laws, morals, intelligence, society, or family, and perchance would meet a female, then copulate and continue to wander instinctively, never to know his offspring. The Indian Act of 1884 that declared aboriginals to be nonpersons is one outcome of Enlightenment thinking and *The Bowman* photograph is another.

Consequently, as I gaze at this photograph, I am filled with the familiar sense of fear, oppression, helplessness, and powerlessness that I felt as a small child of seven when I entered residential school. Like the Bowman, frozen in time, captured and imprisoned in Western technology, speechless and dumb, the photographer distorts reality so that Renée Dupuis, who served on the Royal Commission on Aboriginal Peoples in the 1990s, could say, "We should not be surprised to find ourselves, at the beginning of the twenty-first century, confronted with a wall of mutual misunderstanding when it comes to Aboriginal questions."

Fig. E.2.3. Edward S. Curtis, *A Fair Breeze*, 1914. (*NAI*, vol. 10.)
UBC Library, Rare Books and Special Collections.

Karrmen Crey
Sto:lo, Cheam Band

As a student, I spent the better part of a decade studying the ideology around images of aboriginal people in the visual arts. Edward Curtis's portraits figured largely in this experience. In classes, we would discuss these portraits in relation to salvage ethnography in art and visual anthropology, a way of thinking about aboriginal people as a "vanishing race" that need to be documented before they become extinct due to the influence of colonial newcomers. This way of thinking couldn't imagine aboriginal people capable of survival, adaptation, and creative interaction with different social and cultural influences. Abstracted from a lived reality, these images document an "idea" of who First Nations people are. However, if I've learned anything from my education, it's that a uniform characterization is probably a very flawed one. Here, I thought, is an opportunity to look at more of Curtis's photographs, and maybe to change the way that I've come to see and imagine his work within a particular colonial framework.

I can't say that I've seen all of Curtis's portraits, but that was my introduction to his work, and so I chose to look at his other photographs. I went through droves of photos before coming across one called *A Fair Breeze*. This photograph shows three Kwakwa̲ka'wakw canoes at full sail moving across the water. Not only was it not a portrait, and so not something I would have conventionally associated with Curtis, but the image of sails on dugout canoes is something I've not frequently seen, and probably an image that most people don't immediately associate with aboriginal peoples of this area. More than that, though, the photograph immediately called to mind conversations I've had with my father, when he'd talk about how aboriginal people traveled along the water—in this photograph it looks like the ocean, but my father spoke about it in relation to both the ocean and the Fraser River. He'd describe the river as a kind of highway for the First Nations people, and talk about the traffic on the water—social, economic, or otherwise. One image he described that I couldn't get out of my head was how people would travel upriver using sails in the canoes to take advantage of the winds, the same winds that would be used to dry salmon up by Yale in the Fraser Canyon. What I was looking for, and part of what I see in this photo, is a practical reality of travel for First Nations people—how things "work" in an everyday sense. I think it strikes me because it points to the reality of a way of life based on water systems, and how people work with local conditions to live here.

Images like these are interesting to me not just because they connect to something personal but also because they show something almost colloquial that tells me more about how people lived, and not just how they have been pictured. It reminds me that it is possible to see more of the people Curtis documented than the examples I have been shown that were intended to illustrate a mode of Western thought. For me, this photograph connects to an impulse to continually rethink, or think more about, what we think we know about First Nations people from images, which here also involves considering Curtis's body of work in a way that allows for this possibility.

INDIGENOUS PERSPECTIVES ON EDWARD CURTIS

Fig. E.2.4. Edward S. Curtis, *A Haida of Massett*, 1915. (*NAI,* portfolio 11.)
UBC Library, Rare Books and Special Collections.

Evelyn Vanderhoop

Massett Eagle Gitan Clan

Haida Naaxiin Weaver

While attending university, my mother gave me a copy of the Edward Curtis photograph *A Haida of Massett,* a portrait of her father, Alfred Adams. Alfred was a leader in Massett, as a teacher, entrepreneurial store owner, music teacher and band organizer, art agent for carvers and weavers, and Anglican lay minister. He was a moving force for the establishment of the Native Brotherhood of British Columbia. In his role as the first grand president of that organization, he asserted Native rights for fishing and land title with the Canadian government. My mother, Delores Adams Churchill, had told me stories when I was young about her father. I could hear her affection and pride for him in her voice. He sounded like a stern yet kind man. Alfred Adams passed away when my mother was just fourteen, so I never met my grandfather. I know that my mother gave me that Curtis photograph to motivate me to do my best in my university studies. He had been such a great inspiration and mentor for so many.

One of the stories my mother told me was about the Curtis portrait. She said that I would never find it in any publication of Edward Curtis photographs. Alfred requested from Curtis that his image not be reproduced beyond the original portfolio. Curtis had talked him into donning a wig and chief's robe to produce a conspicuous image of bygone days. As Curtis continued to photograph people in his work at Massett, Alfred could see that the "costume" was being used over and over by Curtis's Haida subjects. Cultural authenticity was a concern for Alfred, and Curtis's attempt to portray precontact Haida with a trunk of costumes was counter to his principles.

Fig. E.2.5. Edward S. Curtis, *The Vanishing Race—Navaho*, 1904.
(*NAI,* portfolio 1.) UBC Library, Rare Books and Special Collections.

David Neel
Kwakiutl Nation
Photographer

In his lifetime, Curtis stated that this photograph, *The Vanishing Race*, epitomized his photographic vision and was the motivation for his lifelong work. Fortunately, history proved him wrong: Native Americans did not fade away, and the people and much of their culture survived.

Curtis's commitment to his photography is unmatched, and his photo essay, the *NAI*, was a formidable undertaking that consumed his life. Unfortunately, he chose to recreate images of his subjects according to his vision of a precontact era, rather than of the time period they were living in. This helped to create the "noble savage" myth surrounding Native Americans, which survives to this day. Curtis's approach, to create photographs of Native people as vestiges of an idealized past, oversteps the boundaries of documentary photography and taints what is otherwise an impressive body of work.

His methods included supplying authentic-looking props and wigs, and cropping out contemporary items from photographs to achieve his vision of an "authentic" past. This was a tragic misjudgment, as it undermines the value of the images in a social/historical context, and it becomes difficult to separate the fact from fiction in his images. Had he chosen to document the conditions of Native American people as they were in his lifetime—during a time of conflict and rapid social change—the photographs would contribute much more to our understanding of both the people and the time, as do the stirring images by photographers such as Jacob Riis, W. Eugene Smith, and Sabastiao Salgado. It is unfortunate that an extremely talented and committed photographer created a superb body of work that is based on a false premise: the (non)vanishing race.

Although the images are impressive from an artistic perspective, the ideas they represent, and the misconceptions they perpetuate, will remain a problem for contemporary viewers and for the descendants of Curtis's subjects. On a personal note, Curits's images taught me a lot about photography, including how not to photograph Native American people.

Fig. E.2.6. Edward S. Curtis, *A Klamath*, 1923. (*NAI*, portfolio 13.)
UBC Library, Rare Books and Special Collections.

Linc Kesler
First Nations Studies Program,
University of British Columbia

When I first became aware of Edward Curtis's work, I spent hours looking through his Plains photos, especially the Oglala ones, looking for people who resembled my relatives. Many years later, in a bin of unpublished Curtis prints in a Seattle art gallery, I came across a photograph of another person I felt that I recognized, a man I knew from a tribe in southern Oregon. I asked him about it later and he said that that was his great-grandfather, who had been photographed by Curtis and later hung by the army at the end of the Modoc War. Around that time, I also began work with a friend from that same community on an oral history project, for which I had trained myself in digital video. The first man eventually decided to join this project, and sometime later I was setting up my camera in his living room when one of his family members came in. "A hundred years ago we had Edward Curtis and his camera, and now we have you," she observed. We talked for a while about our families and their histories and the project, and the desires of its participants and their control of the results, but I knew that at some level she was right, and would be right in some ways whether the person using the camera was Indian or not, or from that community or another. A record is a record, and although the circumstances surrounding its generation most certainly matter and can become part of its later interpretation, as a record it always captures, reveals, and obscures, preserves and falsifies all at once, in spite of the intent of all of those involved in its making. Curtis, for instance, is often charged with recreating history in the arrangement of his work (a kind of practice more recently and deliberately undertaken by Inuit filmmaker Zacharias Kunuk and others), and in the recollections of its participants, perhaps our oral history project has done that too. In addition to the records Curtis has left and the controversy surrounding their interpretation, he has given us the challenge of thinking about the past, about our own actions in recording and remembering, and about the ambiguities surrounding any account with which we become engaged.

INDIGENOUS PERSPECTIVES ON EDWARD CURTIS

Fig. E.2.7. Edward S. Curtis, *Hop Pickers—Puget Sound,* 1898.
(*NAI,* vol. 9.) Charles Deering McCormick Library of Special
Collections, Northwestern University Library.

Mique'l Icesis Dangeli

Tsimshian Nation of Metlakatla, Alaska

Doctoral Student, University of British Columbia

While I loathed the thought of mulling over the assortment of romantic images taken by Curtis during his stint on the Northwest Coast, I was surprised to find myself filled with emotion when viewing this photograph of a hop picker in Washington State. It provoked simultaneous feelings of sadness and pride, which is far from my typical reaction to Curtis's pseudodocumentary photographs. While he was frantically trying to capture the "disappearing Indian" by shooting us with his colonial weapon of choice—the camera—our people's lives were in dramatic upheaval. The Euro-American/Canadian intrusion on our land and waterways caused our way of life to be challenged, demeaned, and eventually outlawed. In an effort to reconstruct "authentic" images of First Nations people, Curtis used wigs, costumes, and props to mask evidence of our adaptation to our colonial oppressors.

Unlike Curtis's highly constructed images, this photograph is different. It reflects the challenges and hardships that First Nations people faced during their transition from a trade-based economy to a cash economy. This shift forced us to accept that our survival no longer depended on our ability to utilize the bounty of our land and waterways or our adeptness to negotiate in trade, but instead survival meant working for others in exchange for an alien currency. Starting around the turn of the nineteenth century, hundreds of First Nations people from British Columbia and Alaska began a seasonal migration to Washington State to take advantage of the opportunity that hop picking presented to supplement their income. Most left their families and communities in the hopes of earning enough to return home with money to spare. I've seen images of my own people, Tsimshians from Metlakatla, Alaska, working in these hop fields, and heard stories of hop picking that are maintained in the oral histories of First Nations people all along the Northwest Coast. Although this image appears serene, it speaks volumes to the sacrifices and resilience of generations of our people.

Fig. E.2.8. Edward S. Curtis, *Lahkeudup—Skokomish*, 1912. (*NAI,* vol. 9.)
UBC Library, Rare Books and Special Collections.

Marie Clements
Dene/Métis
Playwright

I have selected this photograph because it represents many of Curtis's deep portraits—"deep" meaning that there are layers of textures, both artistically and culturally, and that behind the pure beauty of his "subject's" architecture, there seems to be more of a story: a hint of humor in the eye, a slight reflection of anger, a tilt of the head that reveals impatience, or a stance that is long bored. Perhaps this is where Curtis's eye is most dynamic—here we can still bear witness to the meeting between humanity and art because it is still breathing, still asking more questions than it is answering.

Having said this, I feel that Curtis's portraits are infantilized by his descriptions of them. Many times he only describes his "subject" in the most generic manner, as if labeling only for his consumption. Content: man. Where he took it: place. What his subject is wearing rather than their name. What "type" they are often seems more significant than who they are. Many would say that this was a product of the time, but if time can stand still when looking at great art ... it can also stand still when it betrays its own good intention.

All that being said, it is reassuring to understand that romanticism is more complex than a simple meeting of eyes.

Fig. E.2.9. Edward S. Curtis, *Gathering Abalones—Nakoaktok*, 1914.
(*NAI,* portfolio 10.) UBC Library, Rare Books and Special Collections.

Pam Brown
Heiltsuk Nation
Curator, Pacific Northwest
University of British Columbia Museum of Anthropology

This picture arouses bittersweet feelings because it evokes a time before aboriginal culture and the resources vital to our existence were affected by colonization. Abalone in particular were so depleted by overfishing in the 1970s that none can now be taken, even for a wedding or feast. I say "bittersweet" because this is how a Tsimshian hereditary chief described seeing cultural objects in the exhibition *Treasures of the Tsimshian from the Dundas Collection* that had been "collected" by the Reverend Robert J. Dundas in 1863: bitter because they were taken, sweet to have a chance to see them.

This picture was taken in 1914, the first year of the Great War in which many First Nations men fought and died. Veterans Affairs Canada estimates that one in three able-bodied First Nations men volunteered. This woman, pictured gathering abalones, may have been the mother, grandmother, wife, or sister of a man who died far from home. She may have been related to one of those pictured on the walls of the British Columbia legislature in 1930. She may have been a schoolteacher, or many other things. Like many First Nations women of the time, she is anonymous, and listed simply as "Nakoaktok" [Ed. note: although see Holm, this volume]. One thing is certain: her normal life was not lived in a traditional blanket and hat. Not only was traditional clothing discouraged by missionaries (and regalia associated with the potlatch banned from 1884–1951), but by 1914, Native women were just as interested in modern fashion as anyone. So it is sweet to think about the fun this woman and her friends may have had when they took part in Curtis's staged photo shoots—the laughter they probably shared at the idea of dressing up in cedar-bark regalia to gather abalone.

Fig. E.2.10. Edward S. Curtis, *Motana* [Stanley Hunt],
from Curtis's 1915 book *In the Land of the Head-Hunters*.
UBC Library, Rare Books and Special Collections.

William Wasden Jr. (Wax̱awidi)

'Namgis Tribe

Artist, Singer, Composer, Educator

My favorite photograph taken by Edward Curtis during the filming of *In the Land of the Head Hunters* is of Stanley Hunt (the character Motana) standing by one of the Kwa̱nu'sila (Thunderbird)-over-the-Grizzly Bear-Grasping-a-Man house posts. The posts for the film were inspired by original totem poles that stood outside of head 'Na̱mgis Chief Tła̱wudła̱s's (Ned Harris) house. These poles were intended to be built into a Big House by the grandfather of Ned, who was Chief Tła̱wudła̱s before him. The house was never finished, and the poles were then given to Paul Rufus as part of a dowry when he married Ned's oldest daughter 'Wadzidalaga (Martha Harris). Stanley's father George Hunt had him arranged in marriage to Ned's second oldest daughter G̱wa̱nti'lakw (Mary Harris). Stanley received from his 'Na̱mgis wife the name Ła̱lgamlilas, as well as a traditional dowry from his father-in-law.

To me, this photograph shows a connection between my great-grandmother Mary and my great-grandfather Stanley, and the two families that make up who I am today. The picture captures the cultural strength and identity that both the Harris and Hunt families hold and maintain with the guidance and teachings of our ancestors.

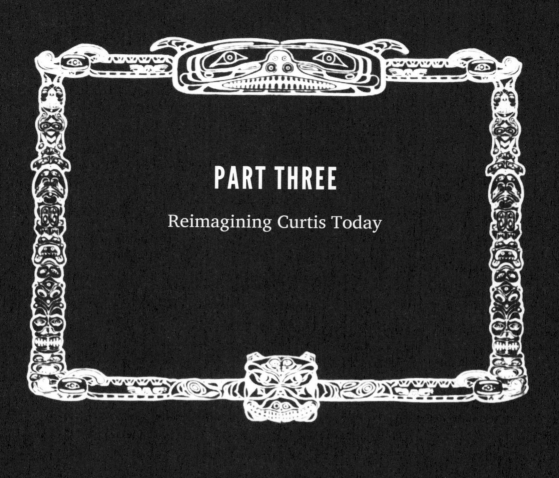

PART THREE

Reimagining Curtis Today

10

IN THE LAND OF THE HEAD HUNTERS

Reconstruction, not Restoration

JERE GULDIN

There are many reasons why archives restore films, the chief one of course being for the intrinsic value of those films. But restorations happen also for programming purposes, prestige value, financial consideration, political and sociological concerns, and sometimes as personal crusades on the part of the archivists involved. *In the Land of the Head Hunters* may be unique, however, in being the only restoration undertaken initially not to rescue the film itself but to bring back to prominence the musical score that accompanied the film upon its original release (Gilbert, this volume).

Yet labeling what has been done with *In the Land of the Head Hunters* as a "restoration" is being kind. Even with the addition of titles, frame enlargements, and stills to fill in for some of what has been lost, so much remains missing that the finished product must be regarded instead as a "reconstruction." Many organizations and individuals, only a very few of which are mentioned below, contributed to returning *Head Hunters* to a semblance of what it once was in 1914. Here is how that reconstruction came to be.

When Aaron Glass began casting his net among archives for one that might undertake a restoration of *Head Hunters*, the task seemed daunting. Searches had been made at many institutions, and the only footage known to survive resided at The Field Museum in Chicago. Unfortunately, that footage was not in the theatrical thirty-five-millimeter film gauge but in the smaller, nontheatrical sixteen-millimeter format.[1] In the late 1940s, a nitrate thirty-five-millimeter print of *Head Hunters* had been preserved at The Field Museum by reducing it optically to a sixteen-millimeter duplicate negative.

Following that, the nitrate was discarded. Due to the expense of copying films in thirty-five-millimeter, preserving silents in sixteen-millimeter rather than thirty-five-millimeter was often standard practice even through the 1960s. This ensured that more silent films survive today than might have otherwise, but, sadly, in lesser-quality copies, as was the case with *Head Hunters*.

Even if the *Head Hunters* nitrate hadn't been discarded, it never would have lasted to the present day. There are numerous places in the Field's sixteen-millimeter footage where blemishing and mottling of the image caused by nitrate decomposition are evident. Once nitrate film begins decomposing—an inevitable process—its life expectancy is quite short. At best, the Field nitrate might have lingered only for another few years, perhaps longer if someone had removed the affected sections from the rest to retard the decomposition. But there was never a hope of its hanging on for another six decades until it could have been copied under today's improved techniques.

One can only mourn the loss of pictorial quality, definition in image, and subtleties in shading and tone that might have been captured if the nitrate had been copied to thirty-five-millimeter. The sixteen-millimeter footage is disappointing: soft and murky, sometimes out of frame, frequently unsteady. This is not entirely the fault of the preservation work done years ago. Curtis, an immaculate still photographer, was not much of a hand with a motion-picture camera. It was determined during the reconstruction that some of the visible unsteadiness was due to problems Curtis had with a camera during the shoot. Still, much of the remaining unsteadiness, and all of the out-of-frame footage, undoubtedly would have been eliminated if a more knowledgeable technician had been at the helm while making the optical reduction negative in the 1940s.

Besides being in a lesser gauge of regrettable quality, the Field's *Head Hunters* was severely incomplete to boot. The total footage timed out to half of its probable original six-reel length, and far less if the original ran to as much as ten reels, as claimed by some sources.[2]

The UCLA Film & Television Archive indicated interest in *Head Hunters* to Aaron Glass, but made no commitment. So much seemed to be expected of the project, yet with so little footage surviving, the best that might be done would be to give it a cosmetic improvement through judicious editing and by fixing the many fragmentary intertitles. Also, any kind of a restoration was going to cost a great deal of money. All of that, plus the potential impediment of many different institutions and individuals being involved in making decisions about the restoration, made the prospect of getting involved not all that appealing.

RECONSTRUCTION, NOT RESTORATION

Then the first break in the project came along. Soon after Glass's visit to UCLA, we checked in a preservation department nitrate holding vault containing deteriorating items inventoried and uninventoried, identified and unidentified, for a barely remembered can that might have been labeled as "head hunters." Not just one, but two such cans were found. One held a fairly full reel in which only a slight amount of decomposition was present; the other contained several small rolls with heavier decomposition. Both were identified tentatively as being from *In the Land of the Head Hunters*. This was confirmed by Glass after a transcription was made of the intertitles. Many of these titles were not present in the Field sixteen-millimeter, so it was hoped that missing scenes also would surface in the UCLA nitrate.

That indeed proved to be the case. The large roll was identified eventually as reel six, the final reel of the film, while the small rolls came from reel five. The latter reel was probably complete, or nearly so, when we acquired it, but these fragments were all that had been salvaged from it once decomposition had begun.[3] Since the Field footage was missing much of reel six, this was welcome news indeed. Even better, the pictorial quality of the nitrate in overlapping footage, though still far from pristine, would improve those sections as well. The nitrate contained scenes in numerous different tints and tones, providing a good idea of how the Field sixteen-millimeter (which was copied in black-and-white, with no tinting record—again, standard practice for its time) should be colored.

Now that there was more to work with, we became excited about the project. UCLA Film & Television Archive curator Eddie Richmond and then–associate curator Rob Stone approved *In the Land of the Head Hunters* as a project. Richmond secured funding from the National Film Preservation Foundation, which paid for the work performed at institutions such as YCM Laboratories and Title House Digital. The match component of the NFPF grant was met by the Packard Humanities Institute, which funded the work done at the Stanford Theatre Film Laboratory, our in-house lab.

The nitrate was copied first, then the Field sixteen-millimeter, which was made available in the form of a fine-grain master positive rather than the dupe negative. The fine-grain had been made from the Field negative only a few years previously, also with funding from the NFPF, as the sixty-year-old negative was exhibiting symptoms of the "vinegar syndrome," a popular expression for acetate film decomposition.[4] Everything was copied optically at the Stanford lab. This included making an enlargement to thirty-five-millimeter dupe negative at 1.37 Academy aspect ratio from the Field sixteen-millimeter fine-grain; a reduction of the full aperture UCLA nitrate

Jere Guldin

to thirty-five-millimeter dupe negative, also at Academy aspect ratio; and matching cuts within individual shots between sixteen-millimeter and thirty-five-millimeter for size and contrast when those shots were incomplete in both gauges.

Other problems with the Field footage included frequent shifted frame-lines and several shots printed out of frame. Only rarely had the shifted frameline been corrected by the optical printer operator when copying the nitrate. Adjustments were usually made on the fly, sometimes during the middle, or even at the tail end, of a shot. Because the shifted frameline is built into the dupe negative, it cannot be fixed optically today, only disguised slightly. With deadlines looming and much optical work remaining to be done, only the worst of the shifted frameline shots were "corrected." Those shots rendered out of frame due to improper splices left in the nitrate, causing the top part of the frame to be on the bottom and vice versa, were copied to rectify the problem. However, this created a horizontal frameline bisecting the image that could not be eliminated.

Judicious editing also was employed to improve the look of the picture. A large number of individual frames in the Field footage jumped drastically up or down due to unrepaired damage in the nitrate. Many of these were excised to provide a smoother viewing experience; only a trained eye would be aware of their removal.[5] Some shots were out of order in both the Field and the UCLA footage. Evidence from the one allowed us to reorder the other, but there were still a few shots for which the proper sequencing remained in doubt.

Like the live-action footage, titles in the Field sixteen-millimeter were soft-focus, unsteady, scratched, splicey, and fragmentary. Titles in the UCLA nitrate were of much better quality, but those coming from heavily decom-posed sections were practically illegible. Fixing the titles was thus impera-tive. But rather than employing methods such as lengthening the titles by copying them multiple times or making freezes of individual frames, it was decided instead to re-create them. Numerous frames were provided to Title House Digital in order for them to re-create an alphabet of the font. Bor-der artwork also was re-created from the original design by Dugald Walker (introduction, this volume; fig. I.10). Words were arranged and spaced to match the originals exactly. Besides enhancing the overall look of the film, this allowed us to make facsimile versions of how the missing main and end titles might have appeared originally. Credits were devised similarly to those of other World Film Corporation releases from the same time period as *In the Land of the Head Hunters*. Documents made available from the Getty Research

Institute also provided possibilities as to how the main titles might have read.

There remained the dilemma of what to do about all of the lost footage. Photographs exist (in Curtis's publications from 1915 and in the collection of Edmund Schwinke photographs taken on set) that were presumed to represent some of the missing shots, while files at the Getty indicated scenes that might have been included in the finished picture.[6] A combination of titles and photos bridging the missing footage could fill in the gaps but still would leave us with little more than half a movie.

Then the second big break in the project came along. A symposium on *Head Hunters* was organized at the Getty Research Institute to which representatives from participating organizations and other interested individuals were invited. During one of the discussions at the symposium, Bill Holm surprised us all when he unrolled photostats in his possession of frame enlargements taken from dozens of shots in *Head Hunters*. Holm had come upon these "copyright frames" during his research at the Library of Congress in the 1960s.[7] The frames were eye-openers; many came from shots that no longer existed. In lieu of finding the rest of the missing film footage, this was the best we could have hoped for to aid in the reconstruction.

But because many shots that did exist were not represented on the photostats, the copyright frames could not be relied upon as a precise guide to the exact number of shots in the film. Also, the content of the individual frames often proved disappointing. These were not chosen carefully as being the best representatives of their respective shots, but were instead clipped haphazardly from wherever the scissors happened to fall.[8] However, the copyright frames were mounted and labeled in consecutive order, allowing us to determine precisely where the rest of the mixed-up shots in the Field sixteen-millimeter and the UCLA nitrate belonged. The labeling system for the frames confirmed the length of the film as being six reels. And although there are a few too many frames showing nothing more than the prow of a canoe or a nondescript view of foliage, just as many provide glorious depictions of the content of missing shots.

So the copyright frames would indeed prove indispensable to the reconstruction, but first they needed to be secured. Presumably they had not been accessed in four decades and, being nitrate, quite possibly no longer survived. At first they could not be located at the Library of Congress, but eventually they were tracked down. The Library made digital scans of them, which were cleaned up and output to thirty-five-millimeter negative by Title House Digital. No attempt was made by us at dramatic enhancement through zooming and cutting, as we've sometimes done in the past when employing stills in the reconstruction of incomplete Hollywood films from the 1920s. To have used those methods in a film as leisurely paced and static as *Head Hunters* would have been dramatically incorrect. Only one still image was employed to fill in for a known missing shot not represented in the copyright frames.[9] We had hoped to locate good still images that might supplement or replace some of the frames, but with deadlines to be met, we elected to go all the way with frame enlargements except in this one instance.

Not only live-action footage was lost; intertitle cards were missing, too. Here, the files at the Getty proved invaluable. There were outlines, story ideas, and concepts, all containing descriptions of proposed scenes, many of which were deleted or never filmed, but some of which were filmed intact or modified only slightly (see note 6). Suggestions for titles also were included in the files, and several appeared verbatim in the completed picture. For those spots in the reconstruction that cried out for a now-lost intertitle, if a match was found in one of the outlines, it was lifted intact (see appendix 4).

There remained concern over the reconstruction of *Head Hunters* servicing the original musical score. Since so little actual film survived, the decision was made to maximize reconstructed footage whenever possible so that large portions of the score would not have to be cut. So the heavily decomposed nitrate fragments from reel five (during the scene depicting the burning of Watsulis), in which practically nothing but decomposition is visible, were included intact, bracketed with copyright frames from those shots. All copyright frames were held onscreen for a uniform ten seconds; the actual complete shots of course would have run longer. Intertitles were made at lengths greater than usual for silent films; in *Head Hunters*, however, intact titles originally ran nearly half again as long as was normal, so no liberties were taken in making this decision.[10]

The final task was to reproduce the tints of the nitrate in the answer print. The UCLA nitrate indicated that at least twelve different tints and tones, and multiple shots with combined tinting and toning, had been utilized in *Head Hunters*. A tinting scheme for the black-and-white Field footage was extrapolated from the tints found in the nitrate. The Stanford Theatre Film Laboratory tints film the old-fashioned way, albeit with modern equipment, by immersing black-and-white prints in dye baths of the appropriate color. Most of *Head Hunters* was tinted in this manner.[11]

No film ever gets a perfect restoration, so there were bound to be compromises and disappointments. There simply was not enough time to have a fully tinted print ready for the scheduled 2008 premiere screening at the Getty Center, and so one print was projected with the frame enlargements

RECONSTRUCTION, NOT RESTORATION

and titles left in black-and-white. A second print in which the tints did not match the desired intensity could not be corrected to meet several later confirmed bookings.

In regard to the actual preservation of the film, there were more vexing problems. Some of the copyright frames wound up not being centered as well as they might have been, or were cropped excessively. The matching between sixteen-millimeter and thirty-five-millimeter footage in the same shots, usually flawless, went awry in one shot. The shifted frameline problem was mentioned previously. Due to time and financial constraints, these were not and will not be corrected.

The biggest disappointment, however, was an inability to reproduce the many different combinations of tinting and toning found in the nitrate. Tinting colors an image in its entirety; toning colors only the darker portions of the image, leaving the highlights clear. Combined tinting and toning provided a pleasing two-color effect in an era when films in color were rarities. A common combination was "blue-tone pink," used for scenes at sunset, the sky being pink and the shadows blue. Such a combination was undoubtedly used in *Head Hunters* in the image in which Naida appears to Motana in the smoke from his fire.

Today, this effect is achieved not through the dyes and chemical processes of old but by flashing the black-and-white negative with two different colored lights onto color film stock in two separate passes. Unfortunately, due to the lack of definition in the Field sixteen-millimeter footage, this effect could not be achieved photochemically. YCM Laboratories is a master at this work, and they tried but were unsuccessful at achieving the effect. For these scenes, we opted instead to use the flashing technique to reproduce one of the two colors onto color film print stock, knowing that the look would be different enough from the surrounding dye-tinted black-and-white footage to set them apart. But that was an unsatisfactory alternative. Six different tinting-and-toning combinations were employed in *Head Hunters*—probably more than in any other existing silent film—and the inability to reproduce those effects is regrettable.

Would *Head Hunters* have benefited from a digital rather than a photochemical restoration? If done well, certainly.[12] Digital should be able to improve some things we didn't fix, or couldn't fix, such as image unsteadiness. However, it could not improve the lack of contrast and detail in the Field footage (although the benefit of no generational loss provided by digital would have helped somewhat). Except in one recent restoration, tinting films digitally has also left much to be desired. But the biggest reason for not

Jere Guldin

going digital was the expense. Even though prices have come down, digital restoration still costs a great deal more than photochemical restoration. Only by doubling the *Head Hunters* budget could digital restoration have taken place.[13]

As of this writing, full preservation of *In the Land of the Head Hunters* remains uncompleted. For various reasons, work on it was halted in the years following the first rush of screenings. A thirty-five-millimeter fine-grain protection master positive was eventually made from the dupe negative, but no new thirty-five-millimeter print with correct tinting was produced. The need for a projection print may be immaterial, as future public screenings will likely come from the digital transfer made by Milestone Films in 2012.[14]

Although not the most complex preservation project undertaken by the UCLA Film & Television Archive, *In the Land of the Head Hunters* proved to be more time-consuming and complicated than most restoration projects. From its genesis as a way of resurrecting the original accompanying musical score, it became a restoration in which prestige, programming, politics, and financing all played a part. Given those influencing factors, the challenge was to reconstruct the film to a satisfactory degree with the constraints of time, technology, and quality of available film elements. In meeting that challenge, we were relatively successful.

1   The sixteen-millimeter film frame is about a quarter of the size of a thirty-five-millimeter frame. The quality of its image is lessened proportionally.
2   In 1914, a single reel of thirty-five-millimeter film would have run close to fifteen minutes. The total running time of the Field footage at the proper speed is a little less than forty-five minutes.
3   The nitrate print was not inventoried at the time of acquisition, probably because some of it was deteriorating even then. It came to UCLA, contained in a box labeled *In the Land of the Head Hunters*, as part of a larger collection of nitrate deposited by David Shepard in 1988. The number of reels originally within that box is not known.
4   Like nitrate, manufacture of which was halted in 1951 due to its hazardous properties, acetate film also decomposes. It decomposes in a manner different from nitrate, but the end result is the same.
5   Only the UCLA dupe negative was edited; the Field sixteen-millimeter remains intact.
6   Archival scenarios used to help reconstruct the film are held by the Getty Research Institute Research Library, Special Collections and Visual Resources division, "Edward Curtis Papers" (accession #850111, box 1, folder 33, series II). Selections are available at www.curtisfilm.rutgers.edu. See also Holm and Quimby (1980:appendices 2 and 3).
7   In the early days of the motion picture, copyright could be secured only if copies of films printed onto rolls of photographic paper were deposited with the Library of Congress. This odd requirement proved fortuitous because it inadvertently ensured the survival in "paper prints" of many pre-1915 subjects that otherwise would not exist. Copyright rules were soon relaxed to allow excerpts from a film, rather than the entire subject, to be supplied on paper. In the case of *Head Hunters*, a collection of single frames clipped from a nitrate print must have been deemed permissible.

8   Obviously it was an onerous task, to be dispensed with quickly. If the person making the cuts had suspected that these frames would someday have to be employed in a reconstruction of the film, possibly more care might have been taken.

9   The missing shot (or possibly shots) referred to comes at the conclusion of the sequence depicting the fight atop the cliff. The Schwinke photograph employed here is of Yaklus after having vanquished his adversary by hurling him over the edge.

10   As it turned out, there was more footage than music for some sequences in the reconstruction, necessitating many repeat phrases during the musical accompaniment (Gilbert and chapter 12, this volume). This was nothing that composers and arrangers of silent film music hadn't coped with previously. Due to varying projection speeds, most scores for films of the silent era were imprecise, requiring repeats in the music until individual sequences were concluded.

11   When the silent-film era ended, tinting processes were all but abandoned. Since then, new prints of silents that originally contained multiple tints of different colors were usually manufactured only in black-and-white. But that situation has changed in recent years, and there are several methods today by which tinted prints can be made.

12   Digital restoration is not always a guarantee of improved quality. Bad digital work can be seen in many proclaimed restorations, particularly of silents. The term "digital restoration" currently encompasses a wide range of endeavors, from mere commercial ballyhoo, through varying degrees of image cleanup strictly for DVD-release purposes, to extremely costly scans of the film elements with extensive cleanup, corrections, and enhancement, and output back to film. Since no distinction is ever made for consumers regarding levels of digital restoration in the product, confusion runs rampant.

13   To date, the reconstruction of *Head Hunters* has cost more than sixty thousand dollars. Nearly half that amount was subsidized at The Stanford Theatre Film Laboratory, which is strictly photochemical. Digital restoration would have pushed that figure well over a hundred thousand.

14   The digital work performed by Milestone from UCLA's thirty-five-millimeter print for its DVD release has resulted in a satisfactory final product in which, as in the photochemical work, compromises had to be made. The shifted framelines in many shots were disguised by enlarging the image slightly and framing it upward or downward as required, resulting in some image loss but eliminating the annoyance of the visible frameline. Digital cleanup removed some of the blemishes built into the film elements for a more pleasing effect. Tints were reproduced to match the originals as closely as possible, but because the digital process tends to shift tints toward tones, these could be accurate only to the degree the medium would allow. The distinction between dye-tinted shots and tints reproduced on color stock in the thirty-five-millimeter print could not be achieved here.

Jere Guldin

11

IN THE LAND OF THE HEAD HUNTERS AND THE HISTORY OF SILENT FILM MUSIC

DAVID GILBERT

Edward Curtis's *In the Land of the Head Hunters* premiered at the Casino Theatre in New York City, December 7–14, 1914, accompanied by an orchestra
performing a musical score written especially for the film by John J. Braham.[1]
Audiences in Seattle, Curtis's hometown, enjoyed a premier simultaneous
to the one in Manhattan. From December 15 to 26, the film played at the
Montauk Theatre in Brooklyn, also with Braham's music accompanying the
drama (Holm and Quimby 1980:15; *New York Clipper*, December 26, 1914:20;
Brooklyn Daily Eagle, December 15, 1914). These constitute the only known
performances of Curtis's film with its special music; as far as we know it was
not heard again for the rest of the twentieth century. The discovery of a draft
orchestral score and the performance parts used at the Casino (and probably
the Montauk) provided the occasion for a reconstruction of Curtis's film from
available sources, reuniting *In the Land of the Head Hunters* with its original
music for the first time in ninety years. While the instrumental parts preserve
almost all of the music, the film exists only as a fragment (Guldin, this volume), preserving a little more than half of an original two-hour production
(if one includes the musical prelude and interlude). This chapter considers
Curtis's film as a *Gesamtkunstwerk,* a film with music essential to the drama;
discusses its place in the formative years of film music, a period for which
there is a dearth of primary sources; and presents some of the problems in
matching the complete score to the fragmentary film.

Film Music around 1914

Original film scores such as the one Braham composed for *In the Land of the Head Hunters* were termed "special music" because they were written or compiled especially for a specific film and also because at the time they were not common but reserved for special or "art" films. One of the earliest and best-known is Camille Saint-Saëns's music for *L'Assassinat du Duc de Guise* (1908). In 1914, the moving picture as a form of entertainment was, like the twentieth century itself, still in its adolescence, and like an adolescent was poised to grow into maturity over the next several years. The business of presenting moving pictures in family-owned store-front "nickelodeons" moved to larger theaters built for live entertainment and subsequently to specially built movie palaces owned by large corporations. (The process mirrors very well the evolution of the rental of videotapes, which began in the 1980s in thousands of small mom-and-pop stores and ended with consolidation into Blockbuster and a few other large businesses, now of course migrating to Internet streaming through companies such as Netflix.) Programs of short one- or two-reel films alternating with traditional vaudeville acts gave way to an evening-long, six-reel, feature-length film. Many actors began to specialize in performing in films and left the vaudeville and theater stages altogether, following the burgeoning film industry to Los Angeles, where the sunlight and mild climate allowed filming year-round, and where stars and the so-called Golden Age of silent film were born.

Standardized musical accompaniment became part of this maturation process. Although we now know that the silents were, early on, sometimes silent, accompanied only by comments from the audience or noise from the street, distributors and theaters beginning later in the first decade of the century looked to musical accompaniment to increase their profits and control audience behavior (Altman 2004:231). Early on, the accompanist in a silent film venue simply played music alongside the film, relevant or not. Later, distributors provided cue sheets, lists of songs or musical themes matching the scenes in the film to be played in order as the film progressed. Getting from one theme to the next depended on the accompanist's talent for improvisation. One company in the early teens, Kalem, experimented with distributing films to theaters along with special scores to accompany them. Much of the music during this period, however, consisted of familiar folk or popular songs with a little newly composed music mixed in, assembled together in a sequence to match the film. Instrumentation was generally limited to piano, organ, or at most a small ensemble of instruments. Although theater opera-

David Gilbert

tors complained of the expense, several factors came together in the middle teens that helped convince picture producers and theater owners to invest in live musical accompaniment. Beginning around 1914—the year *Head Hunters* was released—continuous musical accompaniment relevant to the scenes in the film became part of the experience that audiences expected. Composers and theater musicians explored techniques for performing live music timed to action as it moved inexorably across the screen. These practices slowly became standardized and persisted through the late 1920s until a successful method of synching recorded sound on film developed.[2]

A milestone in the development of narrative film, D. W. Griffith's *The Birth of a Nation* (1915) is also key in the history of film music. Similar to promotional notices for Curtis's film, advertising for Griffith's picture touted the special music: "an orchestral score of 40 [instruments] synchronized to several thousand thrilling scenes" (see similar notation in fig. 7.1b).[3] The composer of this music, Carl Jacob Breil, had several years of experience composing special music for films. After his enormous success with Griffith he began billing himself as the "Father of Film Music" and lectured to audiences on how it was done.[4] Breil's score for *The Birth of a Nation* is analyzed in detail in Martin Marks's bedrock census and study of silent film music (Marks 1997:198) and demonstrates that Breil knew what he was talking about. He fashioned his score from short repeatable slices of music for each scene and provided detailed cues to the action in the film, giving the musicians both flexibility to account for changes in tempo and firm instructions for following the film's action. He probably had access to the film or a final scenario to accomplish his task. Cutting a large number of familiar and pre-existing melodies into his original score not only made Breil's job quicker and more efficient—he "composed with scissors"—it also improved the audience's experience, streamlined characterization, and added local color and depth to the plot and depicted scenes. Although composed for orchestra, as were other contemporary film scores, Breil's *Birth of a Nation* music is known today only from the existing piano score or new orchestrations of it that are often used in contemporary releases of the film.

The Composer

John Joseph Braham came to the United States from England in 1855 aboard the steamship *Ocean Queen* bound for New York. He was about nine years old and accompanied his mother Margaret and younger sister Elizabeth.[5] His father, Joseph, had probably emigrated earlier to find work, since the whole family appears in the 1860 United States census of New York City. Joseph was thirty-three and a musician. John himself was fourteen years old and also employed as a musician, possibly at Tony Pastor's Opera House in the Bowery, where his father served as musical director. John's two younger brothers, William and Henry, also grew up to be musicians. Indeed, the (male) members of the very large Braham family infiltrated the musical theater and vaudeville scenes of New York and Boston to an exceptional (and highly confusing) degree. The fame of the most notable member of this family, Dave Braham, Joseph's brother and John J. Braham's uncle, rests on his association with the "Irish" comedy duo Harrigan and Hart,[6] and their long string of hit sketches and shows as the Mulligan Guard for which Dave Braham wrote songs and music.[7]

Over the next several decades John J. Braham appears in the historical record as a musical theater director and conductor in Boston and surrounding towns and vacation spots. In the 1870s he began publishing songs on the usual popular and contemporary themes: sentimental ("I'm Weary, So Weary," 1871); the coon song ("Oh Dat Watermelon," 1874); parodies of recent immigrants ("The Dutch Policeman," 1874); and the celebration of New York ("Coney Island Down the Bay," 1880).[8] Probably Braham's sole claim to significant historical importance is his association with Gilbert and Sullivan. On November 25, 1878, at the Boston Museum theater he conducted the first performance in the United States of *HMS Pinafore* that in many ways introduced Gilbert and Sullivan to America. Over the next decades Braham conducted many American premiers and productions authorized by the D'Oly Carte Opera Company, even possibly traveling to London to rehearse and bring musicians back for American productions (*New York Times*, February 18, 1894:7). The notice of his death in the *Brooklyn Daily Eagle* (October 28, 1919:3) lauded him as the "Father of Gilbert and Sullivan in the United States."

By the 1880s most of Braham's engagements were in New York, where he conducted and directed the music at several theaters over the years, including Koster and Bial's Music Hall, Daly's Music Hall, and at various times the Casino and the Casino's rooftop garden. Musical directors during this period not only hired and conducted the orchestra but often provided orchestrations and contributed musical material to the "show." Braham's songs were certainly inserted into the musical comedies on which he worked, and he contributed to several over the years including, for example, *An Arabian Girl and 40 Thieves* (1899). Two musical comedies bear Braham's name along with that of Edward E. Rice, one of the most important figures in American

David Gilbert

272

musical theater of the later nineteenth century. The most successful, *Conrad the Corsair,* ran for 180 performances at the Bijou Opera House in New York during the 1887–88 season.

After touring as far as Louisiana, Colorado, and Oregon with a highly successful production of *San Toy, or the Emperor's Own* in the opening years of the twentieth century and serving as musical director for *The Regatta Girl* (1900), *Matilda* (1906), and other musical comedies, notices of Braham's activities begin to decrease remarkably. Unfortunately for scholars of silent film music, the record of his musical activities all but disappear until his obituary appears in the *New York Times, Variety,* the *Boston Daily Globe,* and several other musical theater and entertainment journals and magazines. Braham died on October 28, 1919, survived by his wife and three children. The composer/conductor may have been ill or weakened with old age for quite some time, for his son, John J. Braham, Jr., reports on his 1917 draft card that he is the sole support for his invalid father.[9]

Sparse in Braham's known biography is any association with the new form of entertainment that would have eventually cut off the source of his very bread and butter, the movies. Also sparse is music by him related to Native Americans at a time when composers both popular and classical were incorporating into their compositions Native American music collected, notated, or recorded by anthropologists and ethnomusicologists to create a new American sound (Pisani 2005:182). Braham's sheet music publishing seems to come to an end in the 1880s, before the rage for Indian melodies really began, and none of his popular songs in the Library of Congress or other sheet music collections share the "Indianist" genre. Relevant work preceding his score for Curtis and *Head Hunters* is limited to a score for F. E. Moore's *Hiawatha, The Indian Passion Play,* another film claiming a Native cast as well as "specially arranged Ojibway music" (*Motion Picture World,* March 8, 1913:908; Griffiths 2002:276–78; see also Browne, this volume). The Library of Congress preserves the printed and manuscript instrumental parts for *Hiawatha,* and their relation to the *Head Hunters* music is worth noting.

First of all, Braham's music for *Hiawatha* does indeed incorporate Ojibwe songs arranged for orchestra, the tunes derived from Frederick R. Burton's (1908) *American Primitive Music, with Special Attention to the Songs of the Ojibways.* Second, the orchestration for Hiawatha is the same as that eventually used for *Head Hunters*: flute, clarinet, cornet, trombone, piano, percussion, and strings—common orchestration for live theater of the period. Third, the surviving sources for Moore's *Hiawatha* parallel that for Curtis's *Head Hunters*: the two films are fragmentary, but their music, as far as is known, is whole. Music accompanied only certain scenes in *Hiawatha*, particularly those with diegetic music such as for dancing, but for long sections of even the surviving film no music appears to have been composed. The music consists of the Burton tunes, elaborated upon and varied, and with some original material composed by Braham. Writing the music for this production would not have aided the composer or provided relevant experience for his work on the more extended production that *Head Hunters* came to be, where continuous musical accompaniment seems to have been the goal.

Songs for an 1878 musical parody on Longfellow's poem that Braham composed for a production at the Boston Museum theater can be dismissed in a few sentences. The cast for this comedy featured Siamese twins, a character named Mr. Tel O'phone, and a book laden with uproariously funny double entendres and puns such as "*He a wath a charming follow.*"[10] The music does not survive, but it is difficult to believe that this Hiawatha music would find its way thirty-five years later into works of a more serious character.

Although how Curtis came to ask Braham to write the music for his film is unclear, Braham's score for Moore's *Hiawatha* may be a clue. Curtis would certainly have been aware of the passion play, which had been touring for several years, and also of another Indian-themed film of an artful character released very near the time he was making his own.[11] Braham's former relationships with the Casino Theatre, the site of *Head Hunters'* New York premier, may also have been a factor, and indeed the Casino may have commissioned the music from their former music director.[12]

Premiere Performances

The Casino served as the flagship theater of the Shubert Company. In the process of building their theatrical empire, the Shubert brothers leased the Casino from the Bixby estate whose ancestors had purchased the land when it was still being farmed. New York newspapers covered the blow-by-blow action between the Shubert brothers and the syndicate that controlled most New York theaters of the time as they tried to take possession and open for business.[13] Built in 1882 as a European-type entertainment center in a luxurious Moorish style with a rooftop garden and café (but no gambling), the theater featured high-class entertainment: musical comedy, opera, and operetta (see also Evans, this volume). Opposite the Casino at 39th and Broadway stood the original Metropolitan Opera house. Over the years, many notable events in American musical theater occurred on the Casino's stages. In 1898 the rooftop garden hosted the first presentation of an African American musical comedy to a white audience, Will Marion Cook and Laurence Dunbar's *Clorindy, or The Origins of the Cakewalk* (1898). The theater's inaugural production had been Johann Strauss's operetta *The Queen's Lace Handkerchief,* while Charles Gounod's opera *Faust* in 1929 marked the end of the Casino's long history. Other important productions during the heyday of American operetta included Rudolf Friml's *The Vagabond King* (1925) and Sigmund Romberg's *Desert Song* (1926).[14] Obviously the opulence and high reputation of the venue matched Curtis's aim to present his film as an artistic and cultural event.

In the Land of the Head Hunters was only the second film to be shown at the Casino. *The Seats of the Mighty* starring Lionel Barrymore opened a week earlier, on November 29, and also featured a special musical score by professor Harper Garcia and Ludwig Marum (Marks 1997:194). A *New York Times* article published the following day explains one reason why a palace such as the Casino would turn to showing films: live theater productions had exceeded demand, particularly as audiences turned to the movies for a less expensive evening's entertainment. "In each instance" that a theater turned to film, "the announcement has been made that when business in a theatrical way picks up the theater will go back to playing 'legitimate' attractions."[15] For most theaters, of course, that time never came. A suffrage motion picture play, *Your Girl and Mine,* opened at the end of December, but live musical comedy returned to the Casino for the holiday weeks (194).

The audience that attended the presentation of *In the Land of the Head Hunters* during the second week of December was treated to a film colored with the "Hochstetter Process" and "Native Music Symphonized," as the display ads boasted (appendix 1). (By odd coincidence, up the street at Carnegie Hall on the same opening night, the New York Philharmonic Society also performed "Native Music Symphonized" in the form of Edward MacDowell's "Indian" Suite).[16] Here is what is known about the performances of Braham's score at the Casino Theatre as it accompanied *In the Land of the Head Hunters.* The surviving instrumental parts at the Getty were produced by the Arthur Tams Agency and consist of one copy each for the following instruments: flute (doubling piccolo), clarinet, cornet, trombone, tympani (including other percussion: "Indian Drum," bass drum, triangle, and cymbals), and strings.[17] As only one copy of each part exists—and if these are all of the parts that ever existed—the orchestra must have been small, one instrument on a part at most, except for the strings and the two percussionists. (The draft score includes some music for additional instruments—oboe, bassoon, and horns— that were not used, perhaps indicating that the musical aspirations narrowed

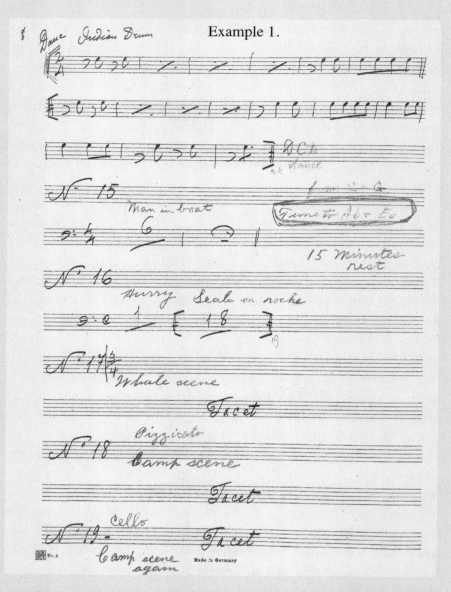

Fig. 11.1. John J. Braham, *In the Land of the Head Hunters* (1914), timpani/percussion part, page 8, nos. 14–19. Since the percussionists do not play in every number, they wrote in what was happening on the screen to keep track of the action and where they had to be ready to play next. They also wrote in performance instructions—when and how to tune the timpani, repetitions, etc. This sequence covers Motana's second vigil. The Indian drum accompanies his dance around the fire, followed by the seal hunt, the whale hunt, the scene with the sorcerer, and finally the girl putting in the nose ring ("camp scene").

The Getty Research Institute, Los Angeles, 850111.

as the project proceeded.) We know the names of four of the musicians who took part in the performance. The program preserved in the Brooklyn Museum Archives lists two: Ludwig Marum, the conductor, and Walter Pick, the pianist.[18] Although the only piano parts found in the Getty collection are for numbers that were cut during rehearsals (and at some time renumbered) and evidently not performed, a pianist did participate in the performances, because the musicians make numerous references to the piano in their parts. Ludwig Marum made his living in New York as a violinist with the Metropolitan Opera and conducting in various theaters. His string quartet, the Marum Quartet, performed works from the standard classical repertoire at Cooper Union and in salons and society events. As mentioned above, music for *The Seats of the Mighty* is also attributed to Marum.[19] Unfortunately neither the music Marum used to conduct *Head Hunters* nor the piano parts Pick played survive in the Getty collection.

The two percussionists wrote their names into the timpani part: "W Braham, 1st timpani. G Maurer, 1st tom tom." W. Braham is almost certainly John J. Braham's younger brother, William, a percussionist who later played with the Boston Symphony Orchestra.[20] One other clue to the musicians who performed appears in the trombone part, which has an annotation: "Casino. New York. Dezbr. 7–13, 1914." This clue provides both the dates of the performances as well as the probable national origin of the trombonist, a German speaker, not uncommon in orchestras during this time since German émigrés made up a substantial portion of musicians in New York theaters of the time.

We do not know whether either or both Braham or Curtis were present in the theater during the rehearsals, or whether the conductor, Ludwig Marum, shouldered the responsibility for making the music fit the film. Several musicians wrote instructions to themselves into their parts so that they could follow the progress of the music with the film, notations such as "repeat last strain till signal, stop, then Dance," and "short piano solo until buzzer then 41," and "very long number, play several times." These annotations seem to indicate that only the percussionists could actually see the film during performances, since references to the actual drama occur only in the tympani part (fig. 11.1).

How was the Casino, a theater that for four decades had featured only live entertainment, physically adapted to show movies? Unfortunately archival material from the Casino Theatre is rather sparse in the Shubert Company archive, and no material related to the Curtis film is to be found there. One assumes that the screen for the film was hung in front of the fire curtain and the orchestra played either from the pit or on stage.[21] Since the percussionists do not play in all of the movements and both performers had long periods of rest, we are fortunate that they found it necessary (and entertaining?) to write cues to the action into their part, leaving us essential clues to how the music fit the film.

Still, there is much that we do not know about how early silent film performances took place. Is it possible that Marum, a violinist, conducted the orchestra in the eighteenth-century manner from the position of concertmaster and first violinist—a practice not unknown in the theater at this period—explaining the lack of a conducting or short score? The first violin part lacks evidence for this possibility. Were the piano parts, also missing from the Getty archive, used in later performances in place of the full orchestra? For instance, a Knabe piano was mentioned as having been used at a special screening of the Curtis film at Carnegie Hall on February 9, 1915, although no other orchestral music was indicated and the identity of the piano music not stated.[22] Although the film traveled widely during 1915 and even into 1916 (Glass and Evans, this volume), most advertisements and announcements from the theaters do not mention musical accompaniment. But that does not mean that Braham's score in piano form or other music did not accompany it in the smaller theaters around the country where it played.

The Music

Whatever Braham's experience with music for moving pictures or with Native American subjects, his score for *In the Land of the Head Hunters* has the style and form that he knew from musical theater. In form, the draft manuscript consists of sixty-two short musical numbers preceded by an overture or prelude that—just as in operetta and musical theater to this day—reveals many of the musical themes the audience will hear over the course of the evening's entertainment. The manuscript is in ink but with some instrumentation and sketching in pencil. The writing becomes much more sketchy and hasty during the last several numbers. Although the manuscript is surely a draft of the complete work, the performance parts match this score except for several corrections and changes in harmony and voice leading. The differences are substantial enough, however, making it unlikely that this was the basis for the performance parts copied by Arthur Tams. It seems likely that at least one source score is missing or has not yet been located. Is the present manuscript in Braham's handwriting? There are many documents (although no music notation) written and signed by Braham in Harvard's Houghton Library, Bijou Theatre Collection: letters of application for the position of music director and receipts for payment, for example, but all date from the 1870s. The signatures appear to be similar to the one at top of the *Head Hunters* manuscript. The music notation in the *Head Hunters* score is also similar to that in the *Hiawatha* manuscript at the Library of Congress Music Division, and it seems unlikely that Braham himself used a copyist or amanuensis.

Braham incorporated the usual tropes of "Indian" and theater music current at the time and that would continue to reappear in future decades. These characteristics are visible from the beginning in the prelude (fig. 11.2) and include short phrases repeated sequentially, pentatonic and modal writing, tom-tom drum beats, and the melodic use of fifths and augmented fourths (Browner 1995). If there is any influence from Curtis's recordings of Kwakwaka'wakw music as advertisements for the film and Curtis himself claimed (appendix 1; Holm and Quimby 1980:15), it is very subtle, most likely engulfed by Braham's Anglo-American and mainstream theatrical background. Unlike in his score from the Hiawatha film, Braham used no identifiable quotations of music from the Native people portrayed in the film. Frederic R. Burton, whose *Hiawatha* cantata was well known and who published the Ojibwe themes that helped to establish many of the signs for "Indian music," felt that the melodies of the Ojibwe were "more beautiful, more conducive to 'translation' than other North American Indian styles" (Pisani 2005:247). Given Braham's background, it seems likely that he heard very little melody on Curtis's cylinders of the Kwakwaka'wakw—if he heard the cylinders at all—given the character of their music.

The *Head Hunters* prelude opens and closes in sections of 5/4 time in D minor, the opening majestic and the ending fast and exciting and incorporating the vaudevillian signs, or what would become the signs, for generic "other": Indians, Gypsies, Eastern Europeans, and so on. The theme in the opening section provides a motivic framework for several themes Braham uses throughout the score, an economical way of working used in the theater but also a method for providing unity in an extended work made up of fragmentary sections. The framework consists of repeated notes followed by a descending scale in a minor key. The musical examples reproduced here (e.g., fig. 11.2) illustrate Braham's derivation of several different themes of varying character from this framework.

A long, placid *Andante* section interrupts the war-march-like music that pervades the prelude and is also (perhaps symbolically) unrelated to the other themes. It is characterized by pedal points and harmonies based on open fifths accompanying a highly ornamented melody (often given to the clarinet). Due to the fragmentary nature of the film, it is difficult to match

Fig. 11.2. Musical themes used in the film. The prelude begins with a musical theme from which Braham generates several others used in the film. The example shows all of them and the movements in which they occur. These examples also illustrate the musical signs and tropes for "Indianness" as discussed in the text. Musical example by David Gilbert.

music to the film for any extended period of time, but it seems clear that this theme is associated with Naida, the girl Motana falls for, who plays the role of Helen of Troy to the two rival Kwakw<u>a</u>ka'wakw nations. The *Andante* undergoes several changes and recurs throughout the film, always (as far as we can tell today) in association with Naida. The theme makes its first appearance during the film when Motana falls asleep by his sacred fire and Naida appears in his dreams and in the smoke above the flames. She later appears in her canoe ("boat with girl arrives" as the percussion players described it), and Motana paddles after her. After the battle, when she has been captured by Yaklus's people, the intertitle "Bring in Naida" also brings forth her music in the orchestra. (In the 2008 performance at the Getty's premiere of the recent restoration, this music also accompanied the dance that saves Naida's life at the end of the film. Whether this is how Braham and Curtis timed the music for this scene is unclear, but the contrast between Naida's frenetic dancing and the slow emotional music provided an effective commentary on the scene; see chapter 12, this volume.) Braham employs the *Andante* also when Naida is present in spirit but not on the screen. After Motana returns to his vigil and dances and then sleeps in the house of the dead, the orchestra intones Naida's theme; they are in love, and she is never very far away from his heart whether he is awake or asleep. While other music repeated during the course of the film may also serve as signs and motives for characters or actions (leitmotifs in the Wagnerian sense), this is the most obvious example and the one that can be firmly established based on the archival materials. It is perhaps this aspect of the score that gave one reviewer of the 1914 performances reason to hail the epic nature of *In the Land of the Head Hunters* as "reminiscent of the musical epics of Richard Wagner" (*Moving Picture World*, December 1914:1685).

The Music and the Reconstructed Film

So far we have attempted to resurrect on paper the performances of 1914 and describe what occurred based on the remaining historical evidence. Perfectly recreating the historical performances in the theater today is hardly possible given the deteriorated state of the film. For the 2008 restoration, Jere Guldin from the UCLA Film & Television Archive linked together available footage using the scenarios Curtis left behind (see Guldin, this volume; the plural is necessary here, since more than one scenario exists and there are inconsistencies among them). It is clear, however, that some complete scenes no longer survive and that individual frames (a few here and there) and longer sequences are missing from the footage that does, leaving a film that is substantially shorter than the original. The original flow of the story, timing of shots, and dramatic continuity are severely damaged. Thanks to the photographic prints filed for copyright with the Library of Congress (which also served as evidence for reassembling the film), some missing images could be inserted in the proper places to restore a sense of the scene if not the action. But they are still images, not moving ones, and therefore do not reflect the pace of the story. How much time from the film is lost will probably never be known, and music—being an art that takes place in time—cannot easily wait or mark time for a still image. An analogous situation occurs in the music where several numbers lack tempo indications. We do not know how long the music lasted as the film moved forward, especially if the particular scene has cuts or breaks. Is it possible to match music Braham and Curtis intended for scenes in the film with the scenes that remain?

The answer is "partly," but of course there are problems. The draft score contains only eight references to the action in the film: "No. 16. Sea Lions"; "No. 17. Whale"; "Nos. 18 and 21. Sorcerer"; "No. 26 (at end). Till warriors land"; "No. 31 (at end). Repeat till end of battle"; "No. 48. Wind Dance"; "No. 49. Thunderbird Dancer"; and "No. 53. Bear Dance" ["Bear" is crossed out, "Fire" written in]. To the list we can add the tempo or character indication "Barcarolle" for numbers 6 and 24, the music that accompanies scenes following two surviving intertitles, "Go my son, the time has come to prove your manhood …" and "Motana returns to his father" (see appendix 4 for a complete set of intertitles). Number 6 accompanies Motana leaving for his vision quest in his canoe, and number 24 his return, having completed it. So far so good. Numbers 48 through 53 are associated with the sequence of dances of "mythic animals and monsters" and "Bear, Wolf, Mountain Goat, Wasp, and Dog" that culminates Yaklus's victory celebration. Number 53, titled "Bear Dance," lacks a tempo indication, but the lumbering dotted rhythm tune of a somewhat comical nature played slowly by the basses and trombones is perhaps appropriate for a dancing bear. It is not appropriate for the Fire Dance, although as noted the original title "Bear Dance" is crossed out and "Fire Dance" is written in pencil. At some time the "Bear Dance" had to become the "Fire Dance" because the tempo given in the parts is *allegro vivace*, although this has been added by the players, not the copyist, and is not in the draft score. At the slow tempo the music is a Bear Dance, at the fast tempo it seems out of place for the more serious Fire Dance. Therefore, even in the orchestra pit before the premier, movements were being changed and rearranged to comply with the action in the film. This situation also implies that Braham did not have a final scenario or access to the film when he composed his music. Tragically, the film for this important sequence illustrating key Kwakwaka'wakw lifeways is quite damaged and fragmented. Although the music for the Wind Dancer exists and is identified in the score, the frames are entirely missing, replaced in the 2008 reconstruction with only a still image of the dancer in costume from the Library of Congress copyright deposit.

Although the parts contain many more clues to the synchronization of

David Gilbert

the music and the film, the character of the comments leaves much room for interpretation. The lack of tempo indications on some movements has been mentioned. Metronome marks of course would have provided the conductor with the exact tempo to match the musical number to the scene in the film, but none exist in the draft score or parts. During this period, several methods were used to show the musicians how to accompany the film, including providing the number of feet of film a scene took on the reel.[23] Breil's method of short sections with adequate cues to the film was the most successful. The biggest mystery related to timing in *Head Hunters,* however, is what the pianist was playing given the numerous references to the piano that appears in the parts. Did Walter Pick play from missing piano parts, or did he improvise between the orchestral numbers? Did he improvise from his head or did he use Braham's tunes or even popular songs or music from the classical repertoire, as was common? And how long did he play? So, while it is possible to match some of the music to the existing film, the problems lie in continuity and in getting from one scene to another. The experience of synchronizing the music to the film for the 2008 reconstruction probably mirrored what took place in the orchestra pit in December 1914 (see chapter 12, this volume). The more recent experience also demonstrated that there can be more than one "final" musical accompaniment to the version of *In the Land of the Head Hunters* that remains.

My work as the music editor in preparing for the 2008 restoration performances with live music consisted of adapting the available musical materials to the available film. I had the same complaint that composers of original film scores have had from the time of Braham and Breil up to the present: inadequate time with the completed film to fit the music to it. Film composers have the advantage, however, of knowing the complete film for which they are composing music; I had a complete score to fit to an incomplete film from which sections known and unknown were missing. Given these constraints, my job became to provide a score cut and adapted to the film as it exists today while preserving as much as possible the music Braham actually wrote for scenes and action remaining in the film. Unfortunately, several of the numbers Braham composed and audiences heard in 1914 could not be included in 2008. I also needed to provide as much information as possible so that conductors and performers could perform the music with the film in front of an audience. This included not just numerous cues to the film in the score (such as Breil had learned to do) but also a diagram (fig. 11.3) showing all of the scenes in the film, with their length, the musical number in the edited score intended to accompany them, and performance notes explaining tempos, repetitions,

Action, Title, etc.	Timing	Number	Instructions	Tempo
——	——	No.1	Overture "Before Picture"	
1 Main Titles	0:31:08	No.2	End bar at 15	Q=120
Title: Vigil of Motana	0:52:12			
2 Shot of the Sea	0:58:19	No.3	Play 5 bars to end only	Q–7
Title: Principle Characters	1:10:18	No.4	Repeat 3 or 4 times	Q=100
3 Intros (Kenada, Motana, Waket)	1:28:19			
Title: Naida. Daughter of Waket	2:22:25			
4 Intros (Yaklus, Soorcerer, Naida, 3 dancers)	2:40:21		at 3 dancers fade or end	
Title: "go my son...isle of dead...."	4:26:00	No. 5	no repeats	DQ–58
5 Motana with Kenada; Motana departs	4:47:02			
view of some sea lions	5:16:29			
Title: Motana lands on island...fired...dreams	5:23:13			
Dance around fire...Naida in smoke	5:35:15	No. 6	tom-toms can play also	Q=88
Title: It is Naida, the maid...	6:08:13	No. 7	no repeats	Q=66
Motana on rocks...Naida in canoe	6:18:29			
Naida paddles into sunset	——			
Motana paddles after Naida	——	No. 8		DQ=66
Title: Motana overtakes Naida	7:28:25			
Motana and Naida walking	7:45:24		at Adantino	
Sorcerer in bushes	——	No. 9	Sorcerer in bushes, bars 1–5 or so	Q=80
Title: O that I might go...copper	8:15:09	No. 10		Q=108
Motana and Naida on beach	8:28:29			
Title: It is a tribal law...isle of dead	8:36:06			
Motana shoves Naida off in her canoe	8:54:18			
Naida paddles off into sunset	——			
6 Motana journeys to Isle of Dead	9:26:24	No. 11		Q=108
Motana climbs down to skulls	9:45:13	No. 12	Adantino, no repeat	Q=76
Dance among skulls	——		Dance	Q=96
Title: through the night he sleeps...	10:41:29	No. 13	No repeat	Q=94
Motana sleeping	10:51:00			
Title: with his slaves...quest of sea lions	11:04:27	No. 14	repeat 3x, fade to Title	Q=126
Motana in boat...	11:13:08			
Motana crawls on rocks	——			
7 Continuation of Sea Lion hunt	12:22:12			
Title: After weeks of prep...leads a whale...	12:42:09	No. 15	play 3x, fade when man crawls out of whale	DQ–56
8 Whale hunt	12:53:12			
Title: Awarding the portions	13:53:03			
more whale	13:58:10			

Fig. 11.3. First page of the guide matching the music to the existing film supplied to the musicians in the 2008 Curtis film event series, the first performances of the score since 1914. There is no doubt more than one way to accomplish the task using the existing materials. Diagram by David Gilbert.

and pauses. I also calculated metronome markings. In the end, I counted it a success that for the performances I heard each of the conductors used the information I provided to adapt the score in their own way.

Conclusion

Given the difficulty the musicians had in matching the music to the film and the disappearance of the music from later showings as well as the historical record, it is probably likely that, from a musical point of view, the performances at the Casino, Moore, and Montauk Theatres were not the hoped-for successes. However, Braham's musical score for the film, although vague in certain aspects, remains one of the most complete artifacts of Curtis's concept as realized in the New York, Seattle, and Brooklyn performances. Although

David Gilbert

the film will almost certainly (and sadly) remain a fragment of Curtis's original intent, Braham's music is complete and can serve in the future as a source for further reconstruction of the film should new material come to light. Furthermore, the music has survived in the form of an orchestral score and parts rather than in just a piano score, as is the case with many other films of the era. It is also, as far as we can determine, not based on preexisting music or well-known popular songs but is completely original. Whatever fame John J. Braham attained rests on his association with Gilbert and Sullivan rather than his musical compositions, but we may revise his footnote status in the history of music and cinema due to his relationship with Curtis and *In the Land of the Head Hunters*. The accumulation of these characteristics leads us to a final conclusion: the passage of time and the subsequent loss and decay of sources for silent film music from this nascent period has endowed John J. Braham the honor of having composed what is so far the earliest existing orchestral score for a feature-length silent film. Or, from another perspective, Curtis's *In the Land of the Head Hunters* is now the earliest surviving feature film with a complete original orchestral score.

1   Both John Braham's original 1914 manuscript score for *Head Hunters* and David Gilbert's 2008 transcription are available in complete form through the Getty Research Institute's online library at http://www.getty.edu/research/library/.
2   This necessarily short background summary of the development of film music is based on several recent histories, particularly Altman (2004); Cook (2008); Marks (1997); and Wierzbicki (2008).
3   Display ad, *New York Evening Telegraph*, Sunday, July 25, 1915:12.
4   "Composing with Scissors," unpublished typescript, Carl Jacob Breil Collection. UCLA Library, Performing Arts Special Collections.
5   Braham biographical information found at Ancestry.Com, Library Edition, US Immigration Collection (accessed November 14, 2011).
6   Edward Harrigan and Tony Hart; see E. J. Kahn (1955).
7   See Franceschina (2003). No evidence links this Braham family to the notable English baritone and song composer John Braham (1774–1856).
8   All of these Braham songs are included in the Library of Congress, American Memory Project, Historic American Sheet Music, 1850–1920, and Music for the American Nation, 1870–1885, both at http://memory.loc.gov/ammem/index.html (accessed March 28, 2013).
9   Ancestry.com, Library Edition, Military Records (accessed November 14, 2011).
10   Review clipped from an unknown newspaper, Harvard Theatre Collection, Boston Museum Scrapbook.
11   Moore's *Hiawatha* screened in New York City in April 1913 at the American Museum of Natural History, which had loaned Moore objects from its collection to use as costumes and props (Griffiths 2002:276–78). Curtis was most likely in New York at that time (Holm and Quimby 1980:29).
12   Ira Jacknis (this volume) discusses Curtis's ca. 1913 falling-out with Henry Gilbert, who otherwise would have seemed a logical choice to compose the *Head Hunters* score, having arranged Curtis's field recordings for his 1911–12 musicale (see also Gidley 1998a:208–15). In fact, Braham's manuscript score was misfiled among Gilbert's

musical papers in the Curtis collection at the Getty Research Institute until volume coeditor Aaron Glass discovered the mistake (see preface, this volume).

13 Shubert Theater Archive, Casino Theatre File.

14 "Forty Years at the Casino," *New York Times,* January 7, 1923; and "Casino Theatre, Built in 1882, Reported Doomed by March of Business Buildings on Broadway," *New York Times,* January 4, 1930.

15 "3 More Theatres Join Movie Fold," *New York Times,* November 30, 1914:9.

16 The complete programs of the New York Philharmonic are provided in a database at http://nyphil.org/.

17 Getty Research Institute, Curtis Collection.

18 Brooklyn Museum Archives, Culin Archival Collection, object 4.2.004.

19 Marum died in 1952 at the age of eighty-eight (Obituary, *New York Times*, July 31, 1952:23).

20 Obituary, *New York Herald,* May 3, 1941, Music Division, New York Public Library for the Performing Arts clipping file. He is misidentified as brother-in-law to Dave Braham.

21 Moreover, an advertisement for the premiere screenings in Seattle mentions "cyclorama stage sets" designed by Frank Cambria, a New York–based theater designer, although we don't know what these would have looked like or how they would have functioned (see introduction, this volume, note 25).

22 From a program in the Carnegie Hall archives. See also the playbill for this event (fig. A.1.16).

23 For example, in "Let Katie Do It" (1916), with musical accompaniment by William Furst (Furst 1916).

David Gilbert

12

PERFORMING BRAHAM, INTERPRETING CURTIS

A Conversation on Conducting

NEAL STULBERG, OWEN UNDERHILL,
TIMOTHY LONG, AND LAURA ORTMAN

As part of the Head Hunters *screening series in 2008, four different orchestras performed John J. Braham's original score for the film, each of them finding very different solutions to the cultural, historical, and aesthetic challenges it presents (see preface, this volume, for a list of the screening and performance events). The following conversation, held by phone on June 9, 2010, was organized as a way of documenting and discussing those variations, as well as the experience of the musicians before and after the performances. Brad Evans and Aaron Glass circulated a number of questions in advance. In addition to Evans and Glass, the following were present on the call: Neal Stulberg (UCLA Philharmonia), Owen Underhill (Turning Point Ensemble), Timothy Long and Laura Ortman (the Coast Orchestra, an all-Native American classical ensemble). The transcript has been edited for clarity and sequencing.*

BRAD EVANS (BE)/AARON GLASS (AG): What were your initial impressions on seeing the score? Did the music have any resonance for you with other period music? And having worked now with the score quite extensively, did your impressions change? How would you now assess the score as a piece of music?

NEAL STULBERG (NS):   My initial impression about the music was that it was fairly conventional movie music from that period, but that it had some unusual rhythmic twists (like compound meters) that I didn't quite understand at first, some interesting things happening harmonically, and some unusual orchestrational indications. But the score itself seemed incomplete and somewhat skeletal in its orchestration. The organization of it wasn't really clear to me either, in terms of how it went with the film; that was a later part of the process. My sense was that the film was probably better than the music, but the fact that it was a commissioned score—something quite rare at the time—elevated it in terms of its musical interest. I did have a chance to look at copies of Braham's original score because David Gilbert was working on it at the time. We puzzled over the interpretation of some details in the score, because it's not clear at all how much of a rush job this was on Braham's part, what the circumstances were of the music's composition, or the conditions of its rehearsal and performance. It was a bit of a detective process, like it always is when you work with a restoration. And it was fun to work with David, who did such a great job restoring the score.

I liked the score more as I got to know it. I guess you start to own it and become affectionate toward it. And the ways it appeared to sync up on film were sometimes very effective, very powerful. I think that what you have is a score that has to be interpreted in a pretty broad way, and maybe completed too, to make it a finished product. And of course that's controversial. For example, the orchestration is so skeletal. Certain instruments appear once or twice and then don't really come in much at all after that. There are musical numbers that trail off in a musically incomplete way. It all had to be reconciled with trying to make a performance that was satisfying to an audience. So, is the score an undiscovered masterpiece? I don't think so. Does it deserve to be presented and heard and polished up and put in its best possible light? Sure.

OWEN UNDERHILL (OU):   I don't think it could exist without the film.

NS: No. Typically, a concert suite of music from the film might be extracted. But I agree; I don't think it would stand up to that. The overture is strong, though—it could stand on its own.

OU: I agree with Neal about the score itself. It is what it is, in a sense. It was back in 1913–14, this guy—with experience in vaudeville, bringing things like Gilbert and Sullivan to New York—was commissioned to write a piece for Edward Curtis. Having said that, I think that there are, as Neal pointed out, some interesting aspects to it in terms of the use of 5/4 and various other things. You get the sense that Braham was trying to do something different, a cut above just standard silent movie music of the period.

The issues about how to synchronize the score and the film are really complicated. I did have some of the handwritten score, but for the most part we worked off of what David had scored and the detailed instruction handout he produced. I also had the opportunity to talk to Neal over the phone and to view his performance on video. Ultimately, I understood our performance task to be a kind of historical reenactment of the original score with the film. But there are so many different ways to synchronize the two. And we don't know whether some of the pieces were missing. Some things were quite clear, other things weren't. The tempos that you used would affect it dramatically. Each of us had to develop our own roadmaps, if you like. But I think I did use some of the ideas Neal had developed, where he added orchestrations, ran repeats, changed up the orchestration.

LAURA ORTMAN (LO):   Some years ago, I went to the Museum of Modern Art here in New York, one of the great art film institutions, and there was this guy performing the original score from Victor Schertzinger's *Redskin* from 1929, a film for which I had also composed and performed an original score for audiences in Italy, Santa Fe, and New York. I approached him afterward and asked him how he did it, and he said he had music. But he said, "I finished all the music before the film was over, so I just started back again at the very beginning, started playing the score over again." I was really mad about that! I was pretty enraged, because I didn't know if it was just laziness.

So when I saw the music to *Head Hunters*, I saw that some of the cues were pretty weird, and I could tell that the music was quite simple. In approaching Tim Long, I said, "Well, this is what we have to work with. It seems like there's a lot we could pull out of this and make our own." I'm a violinist and a composer, and I am super-heavy into improv and just trying to make something out of a moment where there might not be so much energy. We had such a great group and an opportunity for this Native orchestra to be together. It seemed really important to make use of our thoughts about the music, to bring more issues and ideas to light.

TIMOTHY LONG (TL): I think everybody is right on about this. It was really complicated. There are markings on the score about what it should sync up with, but it didn't always work out. And we didn't have that much time. The first time we rehearsed we were doing the score as is, and on top of that it was the first time a lot of us were meeting, so I had no idea what kind of players we had, if they were strong classical players or improv players. We basically had to approach this like a classical chamber group. When we finally got to work with a video of the film, and we had the group there in Washington, DC, the score and the film were not synching up at all. We only had time to run through it twice, and I remember the second time it was better because I had changed tempos around, and we repeated some things. But we figured out at the end of that three-hour rehearsal that the film had been running at the wrong speed, which meant that we had to forget that entire rehearsal because the timing was off.

So I was given a DVD, and I think we had only one other rehearsal opportunity with the film after that. I took the DVD to my hotel room to work out the timings; I don't remember whose recording I was listening to either (it may have been Neal's). Like the others, I noticed that since there wasn't a lot of music for certain scenes, some pieces would be repeated many times, altering the orchestration, which, of course, is very helpful. And we did some of that as well. And sometimes the recording would take pieces that were previously done and put them in the middle, so it was reordered a bit. But by that point, we didn't have enough time to sit everyone down and say, "We're going back here, and then we're going to the regular order and then we repeat this seven times."

I figured out where we could just keep the order going as is, and by then I also knew that we had some great improv players in the group. We had a Native flute in the group as well, which of course wouldn't be in a regular orchestra. We had Laura, and Dawn Avery, who is an improv and a classically trained cellist, and we had a percussionist who does a lot of Native music. So we added our own improv elements to fill in holes in the piece.

We started out the entire live performance with Steve Alvarez on the drums, and Don Harry, who is a tuba player from Eastman, giving out a big war whoop. We then began with Native music to lead into the overture. When we had run the piece in that last rehearsal, I would just point at a person to improv—and at a certain point we had duet improvs going on as well. I would just motion for them to fade or keep going or to get more energetic or whatever until we got to the time for the next piece.

Somewhat miraculously, it worked out very well in the performance, and we lined up really well—I thought it was pretty extraordinary. Of course, it became a new composition, because we were adding so much new music. In a way, we acted as composers of this new score. But I thought it added a really interesting element to it.

I had problems with Edward Curtis before becoming a part of this project, though I don't think I really knew that much about him. My sister had also had problems with him, and I think some of the others in our group had as well. And this might seem silly, but in a way it felt like we could reclaim the film's images in a strange way. Because the film music was very basic and for the most part very light-hearted, we could juxtapose it with, say, a Native flute player suddenly going solo out of C-major music. Doing so brought something a little more personal to the images we were seeing. I found it very moving in the end.

BE/AG: On a technical note, could you briefly tell us how you adapted the orchestration to your particular set of players, so we can understand how the instruments changed with each orchestra?

NS: I didn't tinker too much with the existing orchestration, although I made some changes here and there. David Gilbert himself wrote some cues into the score for what appeared to be missing instruments, and we generally played those. The main changes had to do with altering the orchestration on repeats so as not to fatigue the ear of the listener too much. And also there was the interesting question about an instrument listed as the "Indian drum." We tried out a bunch of different drums, including what appeared to be a Native instrument. But the Native drum didn't cut through the orchestral texture too well—it was very hard to actually hear it distinctly in the hall. So we ended up using a more conventional drum that spoke a little bit better, a little more clearly. We had about thirty-three players, and used a string section as opposed to just a quintet, which of course created some balance issues that we had to work out.

TL: Wow, that's a different experience entirely. We were more like one of those concentration camp orchestras, you know, as in Viktor Ullmann. I did an opera by him once [*Der Kaiser von Atlantis*]. He would write for whatever players were there. That's what we did. We didn't have any complete sections, we didn't have complete strings. I mean, we had individual players, but we didn't have all the groups covered. We had a Native flute. We originally had an oboist who became a singer, and then decided not to continue. We had a pianist. It was a ragtag group, and we had to double certain things. I think everything was covered, but it was certainly a different beast entirely from a group with complete sections.

LO: We had a saxophone cover the clarinet part. Yeah, we had to make do with what we had, because gathering a Native orchestra is tricky. I had about a million submissions from guitarists, all the way from classical to blues guitarists. And a lot of Native flute players, but I thought one would suffice.

OU: We had fourteen players, so it was a string quintet instead of a string section. Probably, that's closer to what Braham would have had at the time. It would have been scored for something like fifteen players, I would guess. In terms of alterations to the sections, the kind of things we did on repeats—we'd do some with the strings, add the winds and timpani with the others, go back to the strings, and put everybody together. I did some things to build up the music. For example, for Motana's "prayer fire" dance in the first part, we started with drums only and then added some string players, bit by bit, building it up, constructing the music additively.

BE: One of our challenges has been trying to place the score in the historical period and to understand its musical aims and ambitions. In the advertising for the film, Curtis made very big claims for this music—as was his regular mode of operation—calling it "Native music symphonized." This seemed to place it alongside Bartok or Dvořák, as if it were making one of those moves, familiar during that period, of taking folk inspirations and trying to make them into classical music. When you listen to the score, is there anything like that in it, or is this more like vaudeville?

NS: I think when he used the word "symphonized," it might have also implied not only the size and nature of the ensemble but an attempt to create a "high-toned" atmosphere for the audience he was trying to attract. It's certainly not music by a journeyman. It's a big score, and there is substantial musical interest in it. A lot of it is repetitive, but I think it was a serious attempt. Where it fits into the genre of silent film scores is a little hard to say because it's so fragmentary, particularly in its orchestration. If that was better fleshed out you could judge it more fully. But there are just pages and pages that look as if they weren't finished.

AG: With it seeming like there is not a lot of actual Kwakwa̲ka'wakw melody in the music, I'm interested in the ways that you hear Braham signaling "the Indian" in musical tropes, in ways that were perhaps stereotyped. What is in the score that Braham may have put in there to make it sound Indian, whether that was borrowing from other silent film tropes or from ones we have come to know from later periods?

NS: When I had a chance to listen to some of the Native music that Braham was supposedly exposed to when he wrote the music, it seemed like he had made a real effort, at least in some places, to incorporate some of the musical gestures from those tapes. And I found that really interesting.

OU: I feel that there is no kind of transcription going on in the Braham score, but I do get the sense that he listened to the recordings, because quite a few of the Kwakwa̲ka'wakw pieces are in a 5/4. By the way, this project led me to do another project with Turning Point Ensemble involving William Wasden Jr. and Chief Robert Joseph in the UBC Museum of Anthropology. I did interviews with Chief Joseph in the Kwak̓wala language. My sense, from having now spent some time with Kwakwa̲ka'wakw music, is that the use of the 5/4 was based upon Braham listening to the recordings that Edward Curtis had made (Jacknis, this volume). When we listen to it now, in a contemporary light, it sounds very stereotypical and quite possibly offensive in terms of its attempt to take on some of the characteristics of that Native music. But we should remember that this was a historical project. And one of the things I would note from my conversations with William Wasden and others is that the G̲wa'wina Dancers seemed very proud of the appearance of their ancestors in the film and some of the footage in there. Especially the Thunderbird Dance and the group dance scene. The quality of the dancing, and the scenes with the canoes coming in, are remarkable footage. Clearly, putting this music by a New York, English-born composer with that footage has nothing to do with the real music. In a sense, what made that whole performance work was that you had this other half with the actual cultural performances [by the G̲wa'wina Dancers]. Ultimately, that made the Braham score seem like a kind of pale imitation. But it was what it was—it was the music written for the film.

TL: On Indian music and hearing Indian music in the score—it's such a difficult thing, transcribing the Indian melodies that I know, and every tribe is different. It's very easy to get offended, and I'm sure we can always find reasons to be offended. And we can always rationalize either side. Stereotypes are there for a reason; you have the drumbeats in the music, but you go to a powwow and it's all about drums, it's all about dancing. What I think he probably did was combine several types of Indian music that may not have originally been played at the same time, such as the drumbeats along with a melody that came from their tribe.

I'm in a project right now where I've been asked by the Cherokee Nation to tape some of their old, old lullabies and transcribe them for contemporary voice and some instruments. And it's shocking, because they gave me some sound bytes of these ancient Cherokees, and these pieces are not written down and these people are not musicians either— they just sang into a recorder. I have those, and, I tell you, it's next to impossible to find a meter. It's really difficult unless you know the language well to figure out where the stress falls. I grew up around Creek singing, and it's a little easier for me because I've been around the tribe a lot, but with a lot of these people, the singing *is* like improvisation. They'll shift keys, they'll shift modes, they'll shift meters. And once you set it in a strict meter, it naturally becomes more Westernized, which is fine for something like this. We just hear the melody in a different way then. But it makes me understand why he would choose 5/4: it feels a little bit less stressed, and the stress can shift around a little more. I think that makes a bit more sense for some of these Native melodies.

BE: I wonder if I could jump in and get Neal and Owen to respond to what Tim has just said. There was a scene that Aaron and I had wanted you to talk about in particular, which I think poses a lot of problems. We've always referred to it as "the curtain-drop scene." It's the scene where there's a curtain across the front, and when it drops down you have twenty or so masked figures dancing in the back [the Kwakw̲a̲ka̲'wakw call it the G̲alsg̲amlil̲a; see Wasden, this volume]. It's a scene that presents all sorts of issues in terms of how to sync a pre-Hollywood film score with one of the more ceremonial and ritualistic parts of the film.

Stulberg, Underhill, Long, and Ortman

Do you remember what you did with that scene in particular or with some of the issues that Tim was raising?

OU: One thing I would say about the Los Angeles, Seattle, and Vancouver performances is that it was great to have the G̲wa'wina Dancers doing the second half of that performance. In a sense, that's why I felt that when we were doing the first part we were doing a historical reenactment, and that you actually got the real thing in the second part with descendents of the actors in the film presenting. And to me that was the fascinating juxtaposition of those performances. Tim, what you were able to do [on the East Coast] sounds exciting and I wish I could hear that. As you say, it was a different project.

NS: From what Tim was saying, it strikes me that the way he approached this may well have been the way it had to have been approached when it was originally shown in 1914. These kinds of productions probably had very little or maybe no rehearsal. And there was of course no videotape to consult, so there was no opportunity to view the film, stop the action, and practice pacing and timing the way we can now. My assumption is that they were flying more blindly than we generally do nowadays. If you have a large ensemble of musicians who need to do things at the same time, there is a limit to how much they can turn on a dime in terms of the actual written music in front of them. So the idea is that in a given passage, you would play the printed music until it stopped, and then maybe proceed to having the conductor improvise at the piano or organ for a while, or, as in Tim's case, have the players improvise. In terms of performance practice, this may well be more in line with what happened at the time. The question of what is a more "successful" or "affecting" performance is very subjective, and my guess is that an audience could enjoy both [more historicist renderings and improvisational interventions] a lot, even though they would be very different.

AG: There were two scenes especially in which your different musical decisions seemed to affect the experience of the film—the "curtain drop" being one of them, and the other being when Naida's slave has the arrow pulled out of him at the end (Evans, this volume). These were moments where the different takes on the music cued very different kinds of emotional responses among the audience members. So I'd be curious to hear your thoughts about that, from either working on these particular scenes or others in which you made a conscious choice to make one particular kind of reading that may not have been indicated in the score one way or another.

TL: I would say it was very difficult to take some of that music and do a vastly different kind of reading. What was possible was to end a certain piece and move on to another piece, if you could line it up. But probably the way it originally happened was with a little bit of luck harmonically, as it did in our case. When we were doing improvs, we had to decide how many repetitions we were doing, because we were changing the orchestrations that Neal and Owen did. Sometimes we got lucky, and the music would be incredibly moving. And sometimes the music would shift in the middle of a scene. For instance, we would be in the middle of a scene and we would get to the end of a musical part and go into an improvisation, and it was like looking into a prism—you would get a completely different vision of that scene. But our project was, from the start, quite different from just doing the score as it was written.

NS: In my case, I had a few goals in mind. First of all, to do no harm. That is, if I saw spots that really demanded precision, emotionally speaking, I highlighted those and tried to figure out how I could get them to work. Then I moved out from there. So being a "good" classical musician, I planned this all out. I had extensive cue sheets for all the players that had them moving backward and forward in the score and repeating pieces a precise number of times, when necessary. I know that's not probably how they did it back in 1914, but given the larger orchestra I was using, it seemed sensible. I tried to avoid inappropriate juxtapositions of sounds to images. I also tried to approach the score with the idea that I wanted to put it in the best light possible. For example, Braham didn't write in metronome markings. He wrote expressive indications, which are very subjective, of course, but I often tried to find tempi that seemed, first and foremost, musically logical. And then we'd repeat the music if necessary, or fade it out if necessary rather than choosing a "shoe-horned" tempo based solely on the length of a scene. That's one reason I moved things around in the score the way I did. If there was a spot that struck me as particularly serious and emotional, I tried to find a way to highlight that in the accompaniment.

OU: I did a similar thing, and I think you had to do that. I had four pages of instructions. Seattle had less rehearsal time than the Vancouver performance. The Vancouver one came afterward, and I actually made it a little more complicated because I had more rehearsal time and it was with my own ensemble. Particularly in the second half, there was more film than music, so we did repetitions and we developed certain synchronization points all the way through that I worked toward. Some of the "action" sequences developed with repetitions. I did have to choose when to stop in order to coordinate things; on the last repetition, I would put my fist in the air. I developed some ways of doing things on the fly. But I did find that with the arrow coming out or the burning of Watsulis, some of those scenes were kind of moving with certain pieces of music. So there was some choice there to try and choose which piece of music for what part of the film, and to make it as effective as possible. Mostly there wasn't much improvisation, but in the Vancouver performance the percussionists were able to improvise in certain pieces rather than following the score directly.

AG: In terms of the idea that the Coast Orchestra made a kind of musical intervention that was different from the historicist project, the scenes that struck me most strongly were the ceremonial scenes where Braham's score makes the least sense historically or culturally. I don't think he knew what to do with the scenes of ceremony, which were very different from chase scenes or love scenes that would demand more standard cinematic emotions. The burning of the village isn't a ceremonial scene exactly, but what the chanting and the solo improv did for me was to turn it into a scene about mourning rather than just a scene about the devastation of this village. This had a very different kind of emotional, maybe even cultural, character than the kind of melancholy music that is in the musical score for that scene.

LO: When we were practicing the score, we left the synchronization of the music and film up to Tim, with his wonderful opera experience. I remember practicing with the group and simply trying to get the music down as best we could. But when Tim approached all of us and said, "Alright, who does improv?" it was a moment in which I thought, "Oh cool, something's about to happen." The times when Tim started instructing us and said, "Okay, Laura you go," or "Dawn goes," or "Elaine sings," it just ended up being that much more special because of our own voices. I didn't want us to come across as selfish, but it was important for us to become even more a part of whatever scene was going on in the film; our goal was to make it a little more personalized.

AG: Yes, definitely. And among New York audience members who were also familiar with the film—who, of course, had never heard the score either—we got a lot of positive feedback about that. It gave them a really strong and interesting experience of the film that they wouldn't have expected otherwise.

BE/AG: We feel really fortunate to have worked with all of you on the project at various stages. It has taken directions that we would never have conceived of on our own when we first started thinking about making the film available. It has been really exciting for us. Looking back on the project, what kind of feedback did you all receive? What did you take away from it, in terms of things that worked well or things that didn't?

NS: I loved being involved in the project. And the feedback was extremely enthusiastic. We had a full house in Los Angeles; there is something about a unique event like this—and a premiere—that carries its own excitement. I think people loved seeing the movie. I didn't get the sense that people were put off in any way by the score. And maybe pleasantly surprised in certain instances, too. Of course, the project had its particular challenges, in terms of preparing the music. But in other ways it wasn't so different from some of the other orchestral silent film projects I've been involved with, where you just have to make an arrangement and a performance that you think somehow works. In our particular case, because it was a student orchestra, I had to decide how much time was appropriate for them to spend on a project that, musically speaking, was a little thin, but educationally speaking was very, very rich. And I think I got the balance right. Certainly for the students in the orchestra, I think it was a great experience, although it was a little bit tough on them in terms of trying to deal with the complicated "roadmap" I had created for them in their parts. I think they were quite fascinated with the subject matter, though. In the rehearsal process, I tried to make sure that they weren't just a backup band and that they really understood something about the context of the film and score. And we invited David Gilbert to talk to everybody about why this was an important project.

OU: I thought it was a really unique project. And actually both the Seattle and Vancouver performances had special features. In Seattle, it was really a treat to be in the Moore Theatre, where the film was shown in its original run, and which is the oldest vaudeville theater in Seattle. I liked the way the projector was sort of hanging from the balcony. They built a special platform there and you could hear the sound of the thirty-five-millimeter projector right in the theater. It had a real kind of authenticity as a historical reenactment in there. It was also part of the Seattle Film Festival, and the theater was packed. I could remember afterward that Bill Holm was not very happy about the use of the Braham music because he created the *War Canoes* film with authentic examples of Kwakwa̱ka'wakw music. But overall I thought the Seattle performance worked extremely well, and what really made the whole evening work was the fact that there was the performance of the G̱wa'wina Dancers as part of it. I thought that was a fantastic pairing.

In Vancouver, what was incredible was that the project really caught fire. There was a full house at the Chan Centre and it sold out days in advance. There was something like twelve or thirteen hundred people there. You probably could have sold out three shows of it! But what was very special about that evening was that there were so many Kwakwa̱ka'wakw in attendance, and the events that happened afterward, spontaneously in the hall, were quite remarkable (Glass, this volume). You got the sense that it was a one-of-a-kind event. And ultimately, when you sat down and accepted what was going on there, and the kind of music it was, it was quite exciting. To have this film that was reconstructed with the original music, there was lots of positive feedback about that, as well as the spontaneity and excitement of hearing live music synchronized with the film.

LO: This project was a dream come true for me, especially the performance in New York. I was running around before the show trying to get food and get people situated. Walking down that great hall [at the American Museum of Natural History] and seeing people I knew—colleagues, friends, family. Just seeing it all come together for the Coast Orchestra and the film and the opening night of the Margaret Mead Film Festival. And then to get up there on stage and play with this all-Native orchestra, doing things in our own unique way. I never knew something like that would ever be possible.

TL: I got great feedback. And despite my reservations about the score I had a fantastic time. I thank you all; it has been a very worthwhile project. And none of this would have happened without Laura's hard,

hard work. It was a big personal victory for all of us to be able to come together and to take on a difficult project like this and to enjoy it and play with emotion and succeed. And to have such a great audience like we did in that New York performance.

It's interesting having done it a couple of times now. It would be fun to do it again knowing what I know now, and having a chance to look further at the score. To see other ways we could work it. I would certainly keep the improv aspects in it and probably elaborate even more. Basically, music is subjective, but for me the written music doesn't have anything to offer. It's very simplistic, very basic, but it gave us a starting point, it gave us a point to jump off from. I think if we were to do it again, we could use the score and take more melodies, maybe some of the original melodies that are in there, and use those as improvisational starting points. I also think it would be interesting to take a Native composer such as Raven Chacon and ask him to come up with something, give it a real contemporary spin, using a Native composer. I think it would be fascinating to see that.

LO: I remember seeing Gerald McMaster, a Native curator up at the Art Gallery of Ontario, put together this whole program called "The Double Entendre of Re-Enactment." That was a huge influence for me to get the Coast Orchestra to do the music for the Curtis film. Just re-presenting it and making it our own, it couldn't have been better timing to have this come about for the kinds of projects I'm interested in. Now that I've done this, it just inspires me that much more to have the Coast Orchestra work on other film projects. Hopefully our next project could be a Native film by a Native filmmaker telling the white man's story (laughs)—just something that keeps the ball rolling and brings a bunch of ideas within Native culture that are not talked about nearly enough.

TL: I'd love to see that. Also just to present contemporary Natives in front of people. Because so many people still see us as part of mythology, part of history—they see us like a Curtis photo. And they don't always realize we are alive and kicking.

13

"WHAT THE CREATOR GAVE TO US"

An Interview with
William Wasden Jr. (Waxawidi)

William Wasden Jr./Waxawidi ('Namgis Kwakwaka'wakw) is the founder and creative director of the Gwa'wina Dancers, a professional adult dance group whose members represent many of the sixteen tribes of the Kwakwaka'wakw people. Members of the dance group live and work in the region of northern Vancouver Island, British Columbia, and come together to perform by invitation or by special arrangement for private events. Since its inception in 1999 the group has performed in Canada, the United States, Europe, and New Zealand.

Under the auspices of the U'mista Cultural Centre, a major institutional sponsor of the Curtis film project, the group was contracted to share a cultural presentation and answer audience questions following the screenings of the restored film in 2008 at the Getty Center in Los Angeles, the Moore Theatre in Seattle, and the Chan Centre for the Performing Arts at the University of British Columbia in Vancouver. Funding the project was an ongoing challenge, and only a smaller group of five interpreters were able to accompany the film at screenings on the East Coast. Many of the individuals involved in the presentations, including Wasden, are direct descendants of the cast and crew of the original film.

The following transcript was compiled and edited from email exchanges between Wasden, Glass, and Evans over the course of 2010 and 2011.

Q: Do you remember the first time that you saw the Curtis film? What was the occasion? Did you talk to elders or to others about it?

WW: It was in the Alert Bay high school when I was a young boy. Everyone told us our great-grandfather Stanley Hunt was the main actor [see figs. 1.9, 8.1, and E.2.10]. We didn't talk so much about it, but I heard comments about who the people in the film were, and then we found out when we got home what kind of great-grandfather we had. I did not know him. He passed before my time.

Q: What do you most value about the Curtis film? And what do you like least about it?

WW: I most like the dancing and the drama of our people. It is a great resource today. I didn't like the scene with the whale hunt, because we didn't hunt whales. Also, the Grouse dancer in the Galsgamli̱la scene [see below]—those don't go together in our ceremonies. And the wigs.

Q: How accurate or inaccurate is the film in terms of Kwakwa̱ka'wakw culture, aside from the story?

WW: From what I grew up with and what I was taught, the dancing was classic Kwakwa̱ka'wakw ceremonial drama at its best.

Q: Do you hear any traces of Kwakwa̱ka'wakw music in the 1914 score by John Braham?

WW: No.

Q: Are there any parts of the movie that you think should not have been filmed at all, or should have been filmed differently?

WW: I would have gone bigger on the budget and wouldn't have recycled the totems and canoes and artwork to represent different groups and villages.

Q: What is your sense of the new restoration, with the original score?

WW: It was done to the best of its potential. I enjoyed it, and the film seemed more complete. The story was more understandable.

Q: When and why did the G̱wa'wina Dancers form, and what does the name refer to?

WW: We formed in the late 1980s. The goal was to represent Alert Bay and our Kwakwa̱ka'wakw Nation during tourist season in The Bay, and to preserve and maintain our traditional Kwakwa̱ka'wakw culture. G̱wa'wina means "Raven" and refers to the Kwak̓wala Raven's Arts and

Wax̱awidi

Crafts Society, which was a huge local movement back in the seventies that promoted traditional dancing and singing as well as tourism and the selling of arts and crafts.

Q: When Andrea Sanborn, director of the U'mista Cultural Centre, first approached you about putting together a presentation to accompany the restored film, what interested you most about participating in this project?

WW: I thought my great-grandfather was the star, so I as much as anyone else had a right to be a part of the story. Also, I know our dance group's caliber is second to none, and if anyone were to represent our tribes and really lift all our people up, it would be our group. I understood that many people wanted to do the gig but didn't have the talent or the professionalism. Why allow the poor representation of our culture to continue when we could do a great job? We knew that what we were able to offer was legitimate and traditional.

Q: How did you go about preparing for the events? How did you decide what dances, songs, and masks to show, and which dancers and singers to include in the group?

WW: We rehearse our programs months in advance and tune our singing and refine our regalia so nothing is undone, literally. I choose dances we are entitled to, or we get permission from the chiefs and families that own them. I have four young ladies that are unquestionably the best female dancers among our tribes. For singers, I take the best among the young traditional singers today that can represent and can work together. It is hard today, because we face so many obstacles when it comes to respect and self-pride among our people.

Q: To open the performance on the West Coast, the G̲wa'wina Dancers restaged a scene from the movie, where a curtain was dropped and all of the dancers appeared behind it. Could you describe that particular dance?

WW: It is called G̲alsgamlila [see figs. 15.6a and 15.6b]. It is a sacred ceremony that the Kwagu'ł of Fort Rupert used to perform. My ancestor John 'Nulis had a box that was part of commencing this dramatic winter ritual. I am a descendant of his and knew that we needed to bring this ceremony back to life in our lifetime or it would never have come back. I researched the ceremony and eventually helped bring it to life in Edwin Newman's potlatch in the winter of 2010 in Alert Bay (Edwin is the present Chief 'Nulis). An old treasure box, which was inherited from Chief Hamdzid from Bella Bella as dowry through marriage around 1800, was brought by the current owner, our aunt Doreen Fitch, to validate and add spiritual power to the family's treasures.

Q: How did you decide how long to make each song/dance? How important was it to you to perform after the film rather than before it?

ww: We were told by our elders to sing everything and perform everything to its fullest, the way it is done for our own people. It is not a "performance" to us; we are generously sharing our culture and spirituality. Out of respect for our ancestors in the film, they should always go first.

Q: How did the presentations for the Curtis events differ from other public Gwa'wina events? Do such presentations feel different than when you do these dances in the Big House, at potlatches?

ww: This dance program was geared to coincide with dances used in the film. The lack of the central fire, and the energy of family and witnesses, lessens the energy flow coming inwards. So dancers must generate more from themselves to project back to the audience as well as to the singers. It is a one-way channel.

Q: At the beginning of the public events, you often explained that the songs and dances the group would be performing are the property of certain families and that you had to have permission to use them. Can you say a few words about this?

ww: Kwakwaka'wakw ceremonial songs and dances are personal property belonging to specific families and are used to relay a history of a family. The only way a dance can be transferred is through dowry in marriage from one family to another. A song cannot be used without permission, and the same is true of dances. Potlatches are a traditional way of sharing a family's history through song and dance and ceremonies. It is considered stealing when someone without the right or proper permission uses another family's songs or dances or names.

Q: What were your experiences in the different venues of the tour?

ww: I felt all the venues were really helpful and did their best to help us make it happen. I was grateful. We always adapt but do our best to persuade our venue owners to work with us to make it more real or authentic, concerning space and presentation. I really enjoyed the crowds everywhere. They were all very receptive and I think it had a lot to do with the promotion. They knew exactly what they were getting and that it was real Kwakwaka'wakw people performing.

Q: In Los Angeles and Seattle, you faced a challenge because your elaborate ceremonial regalia—exceptionally valuable traditional masks, drums, and other instruments—were held up by customs. What did you have to do when your regalia did not show up?

WW: We had to make do and adjust our dance program according to the regalia that did make it and traveled with us. We are a versatile group that can work with what we have.

Q: At the Getty, you had to make do with a drum improvised from two-by-fours and dance blankets adapted from black restaurant linens, but in Seattle you borrowed regalia from Bill Holm. How did you feel about using Holm's pieces?

WW: I was very grateful to our relative Ho'miskanis for his kindness and generosity. He really came through for us, and that is what being Kwakwaka'wakw is about—helping each other out, especially when the chips are down.

Q: When the regalia finally arrived in Vancouver, a number of the pieces had been broken in transit. Can you tell us a little about the cleansing ceremony you did for the broken pieces?

WW: It was sad and hard for me personally, because my family masks were damaged. I felt total disrespect from the shipping company. We did something we call "brushing off," which was the extent of a cleansing that we could do at that time [see fig. 15.13]. We did more later when we got home. The tour ended on a very sad note for myself and for some of our people.

Q: If you were to present alongside the film again, would you do anything differently?

WW: I'd like to see more involvement by our own people making decisions on the level of organization and coordination. No matter how qualified in the white world some people are, what can they offer a culture that is ancient, authentic, and more in-depth than anything they have ever known? How can people understand or appreciate it, especially when pan-Indianism and modern dancing is the norm now? We are just fortunate that we have our traditions intact, and we need to work with people that will value that and treat it as sacred.

Q: What do you hope audiences went away from the evenings with?

ww: We want people to know that the Kwakwaka'wakw and their culture are alive and thriving, and that any stereotypes that they may have should be clarified. Also, that we own our culture and that we are the custodians of it, no one else. We are a proud and strong people with teachings that could help all people. We are not reviving or reinventing our culture. Our elders hung on, and we are strengthening it and are in control of what the creator gave to us.

14

CULTURAL INTERPRETATION

DAVE HUNSAKER

I came late to the *Head Hunters*/Gwa'wina Dancers project, and essentially acted as a "friend of the production," or a kind of artistic advisor. I heard of the project because I had recently been hired to write a feature screenplay about Edward Curtis, and, in studying the man's life, I had come to the conclusion that a terrific subject for a movie would be his shooting of *In the Land of the Head Hunters*. So I was thrilled to learn that a restored copy of the film was being prepared, along with a newly discovered score, and—most exciting of all—that a dance troupe made up of some of the descendants of Curtis's actors (among others) would be incorporated into the production and would be doing some of the very dances that Curtis had attempted to capture in his film.

My basis for offering my services to the production was ten years' experience as the Artistic Director of the Naa Kahidi Theater, a touring troupe based in my hometown of Juneau, Alaska. Naa Kahidi was made up of Alaska Native performers (storytellers, musicians, and dancers) who were Tlingit, Haida, Athabascan, Yup'ik, Aleut, and Inupiat. I cofounded the company in 1985 at the invitation of a Board of Elders of the Sealaska Heritage Institute, a regional organization founded for the preservation of Tlingit, Haida, and Tsimshian cultures and languages. The Elders wanted the new theater to have two primary audiences and functions: one hope was that it would help people from outside the culture have a better understanding of and appreciation for Native people through their stories, masks, and performance artistry; the Elders were also worried that they were losing the interest of their own children to movies and television, and hoped that the company, in presenting dramatic interpretations of ancient stories, would help regain the interest of the children and youth who saw our performances. Competition for *Star Wars*, in other words … a fairly daunting prospect.

For these reasons, I felt that my role was as something of an interpreter, not of language but of culture. How does one stay true to complex performance traditions of one culture and make them meaningful and moving to people who know little or nothing about it? The Tlingit Elders felt that while the visual art of the Northwest Coast nations was very well represented in the world, it was often seen out of context and was overly exploited by artists who had no right to do so. So one mandate from the Elders was to use masks and clan regalia in a culturally appropriate way. The Elders also felt that although there was a fair amount of dance taking place within the culture, the songs weren't being passed down as much as they would like, especially songs owned by particular clans. Dance groups were very often made up of people from different clans and moieties, so songs owned by specific clans were inappropriate for a mixed group. As a result, people were dancing only to a very limited number of songs—those few that were seen as being more or less in the public domain. So the Naa Kahidi Theater was encouraged to work not only with the clans but also with actors who were actually members of those clans, to select songs as well as stories that were appropriate to what we were doing. Some clans were enthusiastically cooperative, others less so, and we were not able to use all of the material I would have liked because of some individuals' reluctance to have sensitive clan property publicly displayed in what seemed, to some, an inappropriate forum. (From many reports, including his own, Curtis had a similar experience.)

The problem remained: how to present what we were given rights to? After a year or so of trial and error, we finally hit on a style of performance that worked artistically, didn't trivialize the culture, and was still accessible to highly diverse audiences. We invented a style in which we had a storyteller tell a story from onstage, while dancers in masks essentially illustrated it, not literally but in highly stylized ways, using traditional dance moves. The telling of the story gave the audience context in which to view the masks and dances. We experimented with telling certain stories in Tlingit (or, in one case, Yup'ik), and we attempted one or two story dances for which we provided only a short synopsis. I found it was a thin tightrope to walk, this respect for privacy protocols and allegiance to our original charter—assisting in the preservation of cultural performance. But by and large we felt satisfied that we had reached our goal of creating works that could be appreciated by people outside the culture, without compromising traditional material.

Dave Hunsaker

Still, it was far from a pure form of representing Alaska Native perfor-mance traditions. Added to a rather liberal departure from storytelling tradi-tions, I also actively promoted the use of modern theatrical effects. I tended to use dramatic colored lighting, smoke and fog machines, artificial fire, and trap doors in the stage floor. My justification for this approach was that the traditional setting for Tlingit dances was a capacious Ceremonial House, with a fantastically painted screen, carved house posts, and a central fire, which would have dramatically illuminated the performance. Certainly trap doors, transformation masks, and stage trickery were used to enhance the mystery of the ceremonies and dances being performed. We used as many modern devices as we could acquire to give the audience a similar, contemporary theatrical context.

There were other cultural compromises, no doubt. It would not bother a Tlingit spectator to see a dancer wearing a Raven button blanket, dancing in blue jeans and Nikes; he would be more interested in the regalia the dancer was wearing and would simply not see or care about other clothing. We learned that things such as this were often viewed as anachronistic by out-sider audiences, and tended to take them out of the spirit of the performance. (There were a few times we used such devices deliberately—putting Raven in a black leather motorcycle jacket, for instance—as a reminder that these old stories endure and that the performers are modern-day people, actively living their culture in the present century.) We went to great lengths in a story to clarify a cultural reference that would have been easily understood by a Native audience member. We also made concessions to audiences' atten-tion spans, trimming dances that, done in their entirety, may have seemed overlong and/or repetitive. Again, to a person from within the culture, to whom the dance had personal meaning or significance, or who was able to recognize fine and subtle nuances in a dance, the repetitions and slight varia-tions would have been important and riveting to watch. But to unschooled people from outside it, there was a danger it would simply become boring.

So while we certainly made concessions, our intentions were good. We tried to carry out our Elders' wishes in making the cultures we represented accessible to as many people as possible, including people in foreign coun-tries, including our own children. For ten years, this worked very well. Perhaps not surprisingly, the end of Naa Kahidi came when the company management decided we were missing a good opportunity to make money by performing for the million-odd tourists who visit Juneau every summer on cruise ships. For reasons I still don't completely understand, this ended up feeling like self-exploitation to all of us, perhaps because it seemed to the performers that few of our audience members were interested in anything more than a photo op: they liked Indians in their colorful "costumes" and outlandish masks … but they didn't seem to be interested in hearing the stories or learning much about the values and traditions of the people.

We all decided we had done it long enough and it was time to stop.

* * *

So this was the experience that I brought to the G̲wa'wina Dancers in 2007. I had visited Alert Bay (along with other Kwakwa̲ka̲'wakw places of significance to *Head Hunters)* prior to hearing about the project, as part of my research for my feature screenplay. Having met Aaron Glass and Andrea Sanborn, I was very happy to return at their invitation to meet with some of the G̲wa'wina singers and dancers and discuss what their—and my—part of the production might entail.

I was extremely impressed with the G̲wa'wina Dancers and their leader, William Wasden Jr. They are extraordinarily polished dancers and singers, seasoned performers. Wasden had a very clear idea of what he wanted in the performances to accompany showings of *In the Land of the Head Hunters*. I was able to see some of the dances and hear the songs, and was pretty sure they would go down very well with audiences in Los Angeles, Seattle, and Vancouver. I had some of the same thoughts I'd had about Naa Kahidi performances, and offered suggestions as to how to appeal to non-Kwakwa̲ka̲'wakw audiences.

We all agreed it would be important to try to create a performance space that suggested, as much as possible, a Kwakwa̲ka̲'wakw Big House. Andrea showed me the enormous and magnificent Big House in Alert Bay, which set us a very high standard (fig. 14.1). Wasden offered to paint canvas drops that could be rolled up for transport and suspended (or projected digitally) onstage to show at least two dimensionally the design and shape of Big House posts and lintels (fig. 14.2). This was very effective, and very much like the sort of thing we used to tour with in Naa Kahidi. Instead of a painted dance screen, we agreed we would attempt to project slide images of either the screen or photographs pertaining to each dance onto the motion-picture screen with which we would be sharing the stage. The post-and-lintel drops would frame the screen, with dancers in front of it. Although I felt that this was not an entirely satisfactory solution because of the difficulty of rear projection in venues (front projections throw dancers' shadows onto the screen), it would suffice for a touring show. Wasden accepted many of my suggestions for dramatic lighting designs (see figs. 15.4–7). (In the event, the design ended up being highly limited in two of the venues. Only Seattle's

Top: Fig. 14.1. Interior of the Big House in Alert Bay, British Columbia, 2011. Photo by Christina Cook. U'mista Cultural Centre.

Bottom: Fig. 14.2. Canvas drops (here projected digitally) designed and painted by William Wasden Jr. for use by the G̲wa'wina Dancers in 2008. Photo by Sharon Grainger. U'mista Cultural Centre.

Moore Theatre was really rigged for the kind of theatrical lighting I had worked out in a design plot.)

One area where Wasden and I disagreed was on the order of the evening's events. He felt that the orchestrated motion picture should be the first act, as it were, with the G̲wa'wina Dancers following after an intermission, during which time we would clear orchestra chairs and rig the drops. My other hometown is Los Angeles, and I know audiences there to be more interested in cinema than in traditional dance. LA audiences can also be fairly rude. I was afraid that many would come to the Getty to see the restored Curtis film and then simply leave at intermission. In other words, it was a question of which would be the main event—the film or the live dance presentation. Both Wasden and I understood that it would be the second one. Wasden was adamant that the main event was absolutely the dance performance, and if anybody cared enough to be interested in Curtis's fictitious representation of Kwakwa̲ka'wakw culture, they should stick around and learn something about the real thing. It was a strong argument, and even though I feared there would be walkouts, I admired his attitude and pride; I dropped the issue.

I also believed that most of the songs exceeded my idea of what the average non-Native audience attention span could handle. Each song was repeated (it seemed to me) four times, with little or no variation. The first time through was very effective—the masks and regalia themselves were absolutely dazzling, and the dances always engaging. The second time through was even more so, due to a certain degree of familiarity. My admittedly ignorant assessment was that any further repetition beyond that became less interesting to the culturally uninformed observer. Wasden agreed that some of the dances could be shortened; others could not. He wanted them to be presented in their correct form or not at all, even if we risked losing audience attention. Here I realized that the goals of the G̲wa'wina Dancers and what I had done with the Naa Kahidi Theater were very different. Naa Kahidi was a working theater company making a living based on audience acceptance and attendance. With them, I had been in a position much more similar to Curtis's—an outsider trying to package and present a culture for a wider audience. Wasden and his troupe were presenting a true vision of their culture, in many ways as an answer to and correction of Curtis's film. These were very different ends. In the event, Wasden dropped a few of the songs, kept most, and performed them, with the dancers, in their entirety.

The three venues presented unique challenges, none more than the place we premiered, the Getty Center in Los Angeles. In keeping with the museum campus's overall architectural design, the theatrical space (which was actually more of a lecture hall) was entirely white—the worst possible color to present any sort of stage magic with lights. In the showing of the film, some nuances were lost, too, due to all of the light bounce. There was no rigging system in the Getty, so we had to jury-rig anything we wanted to hang. Consequently we had little time to rehearse with the dancers, between having to share the space and precious rehearsal time with musicians, film technicians, and stage crew. Worst of all, we were confronted with an impossible situation in that somehow most of the priceless and magnificent regalia and masks that were being shipped down from Alert Bay had gone missing and could not be accounted for. This was frustrating and anxiety-provoking for me; I cannot even imagine how the people from Alert Bay must have felt.

The show went on as scheduled, without most of the masks. The film and orchestra were very well received. We had a few walkouts at intermission, but most people stayed to watch the G̲wa'wina Dancers, whom we lit dramatically the best we could. They performed their dances fearlessly, and though there was, at times, a certain amount of restlessness in the audience, and thirty or forty walkouts (the evening was long), it was not nearly as bad as I had feared. Most people who saw the dancers perform felt that they had been afforded a real treat, and had learned a good deal about the true Kwakwa̲ka'wakw culture, as opposed to the cartoonish story in Curtis's film. I had also had misgivings about Wasden's introduction to each dance, fearing that they would make the evening even longer and would reduce the effect of the performance, but in the event, he kept his words short and informative, and his considerable charm and ease on stage more than outweighed my ungrounded fears.

The historic Moore Theatre in Seattle proved to be a much better venue: a real theater with lights and curtains and rigging, and an amazing history with Curtis's film. Despite this, we continued to be hounded by production problems. As had been the case in Los Angeles, we had very limited access to the stage on the day of set-up and performance. We shared it with the crew who were organizing the projector and cinema screen; then with the orchestra (a different set of musicians from those who had performed at the Getty), who had to rehearse the music with the film; then the lighting/rigging crew. I worked with them to devise different looks for each dance and to determine how much of the stage we needed to light for each piece. Wasden and his troupe seem to have had little experience with the tedium of a theatrical tech rehearsal (always a trying experience), and they became understandably frustrated by the process. We ran out of time and couldn't run through the lighting cues for the whole show. We winged it for the performance, and, as usually happens, it all came together. The dance performance looked especially good on that venerable old stage, with the group using masks and regalia generously loaned by Seattle scholar Bill Holm to replace the still-missing shipment from Canada (it was wonderful to see the dancers try on this gear as if they were being reunited with long-lost relatives; see fig. 15.10, and Wasden and Glass, this volume). The Seattle audience no doubt knew a lot more about Northwest Coast cultures than the LA audience. It seemed to me that people were very absorbed throughout the dances; we didn't have nearly as many walkouts.

Although the Vancouver venue—the Chan Centre for the Performing Arts at the University of British Columbia—also had its own set of challenges, the lights and rigging worked pretty well there, and the audience responded very favorably to the film, the score, and the G̲wa'wina Dancers. The missing masks had finally resurfaced (although, sad to say, somewhat the worse for their travels), and looked very striking on the dancers. There were many more Kwakw̲a̲ka'wakw people in the audience than there had been at either other venue, which gave the performance a hometown feel. I am sure that the more knowledge and appreciation one had for Kwakw̲a̲ka'wakw culture, the more interesting and moving the evening was.

Assisting with this unique project was extremely rewarding and interesting—I learned a lot, and, I believe, took a lot more than I gave. I suppose that during my years with the Naa Kahidi Theater, I had identified a good deal with Edward Curtis. Although it was not the self-image I would have preferred, the fact was that I had been a kind of impresario, "packaging" and presenting Native culture to audiences who otherwise might not have had much exposure to it. I cannot presume to understand Curtis's motives—I think he was a very complex individual—but he does seem to have been genuinely respectful of the cultures he documented, if not always correct or entirely truthful. It was fascinating to see Kwakw̲a̲ka'wakw culture as Curtis presented it a hundred years ago, then see it again as contemporary Kwakw̲a̲ka'wakw people present it now. And it was particularly interesting to note that the biggest compromise in the film is what its creator tacked onto it: a sensational Hollywood plot. The place where Curtis's heart was (it seems to me), and the part that mattered then and matters still, is presenting a rich and vibrant culture with its masks, ceremonies, and dances to a world that I am sure will always find it fascinating and worthy of artistic appreciation and serious consideration.

Dave Hunsaker

15

THE KWAKWAKA'WAKW BUSINESS OF SHOWING

Tradition Meets Modernity on the Silver Screen and the World Stage

AARON GLASS

Almost a century after Edward Curtis debuted *In the Land of the Head Hunters* at Manhattan's Casino Theatre, the newly restored film returned to New York. It opened the 2008 Margaret Mead Film Festival, an annual showcase of recent as well as classic documentary and ethnographic cinema, at the American Museum of Natural History, to which Curtis had sold his motion picture in 1924. The all-Native American Coast Orchestra performed a live rendition of the film's original musical score, and five Kwakwaka'wakw members of the Gwa'wina Dancers followed with a song presentation and discussion about their ancestors' participation in the film's making (fig. 15.1).[1] The visitors from British Columbia joined me the following day to present two more recent films—the now-classic *Box of Treasures* (1983), produced by the U'mista Cultural Society to tell the story of the repatriation of masks once confiscated by police under the Canadian potlatch prohibition, and my own *In Search of the Hamaʼsa: A Tale of Headhunting* (2004), which explores the history of the Kwakwaka'wakw's ethnographic representation with explicit reference to Curtis's film. Taken together, the three films encapsulate a crucial aspect of Kwakwaka'wakw experience over the past hundred years: the frequent and sometimes conflicted engagement with anthropologists, museum collectors, filmmakers, and government officials in various media and

Fig. 15.1. Members of the Gwa'wina Dancers (*left to right:* Maxine Matilpi, William Wasden Jr, and William Cranmer) looking at *dantsikw* ("power boards") in storage at the American Museum of Natural History, New York, 2008. Photo by Aaron Glass.

Fig. 15.2. Bob Harris performing a Hamaťsa at the Louisiana Purchase Exposition, St. Louis, 1904. Royal BC Museum, BC Archives, PN 2618.

venues of intercultural exchange. As a means of tying together many of the themes of this volume, this essay brings *Head Hunters* into direct dialogue with the Gwa'wina Dancers' presentations to explore this complicated legacy of collaborative cultural production and ethnographic display. Both the original film and its recent re-presentation highlight indigenous strategies of harnessing traditional culture under the unsettled conditions of colonial modernity.

Watching the two newer films at the museum, my copresenters chatted volubly—recognizing themselves as children, laughing at their outmoded clothes and haircuts, pointing out relatives who have since passed away—and then took the stage to answer questions from the audience. All are seasoned public performers and interpreters, and they proved unflappable in the face of well-intentioned but often naïve and even primitivist lines of inquiry from the New York festival crowd. In response to a query about their presumed protectionist stance toward nature, the speakers avoided invoking a spiritualized custodianship and instead educated the audience—in rather gruesome biological detail—on the horrors of farmed fish and their ongoing political struggle over resource management. Just as the film *Box of Treasures* does, their reply built on public interest in stereotypical markers of Indianness (ritual masks and environmental spirituality, respectively) but reframed the conversation toward colonial and neocolonial political conflict. When asked directly about their feelings toward the legacy of anthropological objectification and touristic performance—topics covered in all three films from different vantage points—and whether they feel differently when dancing in ceremonies at home versus for tourists abroad, they passed up a chance to simply contrast the ritual with the commercial. Rather, the group described how hereditary restrictions govern both contexts, allowing for a degree of integration between ceremonial and nonceremonial dance and speech. This presentation nicely illustrated what I think of as a specific Kwakwaka'wakw culture of display: a characteristic mixture of ritual protocol and cultural (even ethnographic) self-awareness, a tendency to transform awkward exchanges into moments of declarative claim—claim on/to identities, properties, status, sovereignty.

As the speakers and the trio of films made clear, the Kwakwaka'wakw have a robust history of anthropological exposure in ethnographic texts, photographs, films, museums, and world's fairs. The heritage of such experience not only provides prototypes and models (both positive and negative) for current intercultural productions but also furnishes today's presenters with a font of narrative resources to draw on. At the Mead screening, Kevin Cranmer volunteered a long story—frequently recounted in Kwakwaka'wakw communities today—about how a couple of ancestors, Bob Harris and Charles Nowell, frightened crowds at the 1904 Louisiana Purchase Exposition in St. Louis. During a public dance presentation like the one pictured in figure 15.2, the duo convincingly staged the theatrical decapitation and miraculous recovery of a bystander (who just happened to be an African "pygmy" living in the neighboring house at the fair's ethnographic village) at the hands of a Hamaťsa or "Cannibal Dancer," just as they might have done back home in the potlatch had it not been outlawed at the time.[2] Nowell himself recorded this tale in his autobiography (Ford 1941:188), where he also told of his journey with Harris to The Field Museum in Chicago to help curators there document and install their large Kwakwaka'wakw collection, much of it acquired in the run up to the 1893 World's Columbian Exposition, where a larger troupe of Kwakwaka'wakw had lived and performed. While at the museum, the two men not only posed for photographs wearing the museum's Hamaťsa masks, but they were themselves installed inside the glass walls of a Hamaťsa diorama, startling and then educating visitors as if they were mannequins come to life (191; Glass 2009a:107).

Such narratives describe and declare a long tradition of intercultural display, one anchored both in ceremonial culture and in economic and political adaptation to conditions of colonial surveillance, scientific scrutiny, and touristic interest. Much of my own work has focused on this legacy of knowledge production, and on the specific role that Kwakwaka'wakw have played as coproducers as well as consumers of ethnographic depictions of themselves (Glass 2004a, 2004b, 2006a, 2006b, 2009b). I have come to see their cooperation with ethnographers as a kind of extension of the culture of the potlatch, in which conspicuous visual display, oratory, performance, and material exchange govern the ratification of personal and lineage identities and status, cultural reproduction through hereditary transmission, and the refiguring of social and political relations both near and far, between various types of insiders and outsiders. The current indigenous reception of anthropology is a byproduct of this shared history, as the Kwakwaka'wakw tend to read Franz Boas texts and Edward Curtis photographs through the lens of kinship relations to the previous culture brokers that made those books and images possible in the first place, evaluating the veracity and thus utility of the depictions accordingly. Today's visual artists, professional dancers, and semi-professionalized cultural interpreters often debate the decisions their ancestors made to transform and recontextualize ceremonial practices in spaces of intercultural exchange. In part, they see their work as the continuation of earlier attempts to use cultural production as a mode of economic labor as well as a means of asserting political agency and aboriginal sovereignty (see Mahon 2008; Bourdieu 1993). The embodied preservation and strategic mobilization of "traditional" dance in the face of colonial assimilation efforts also define the contours of a uniquely indigenous experience of modernity, even though modernization is typically thought to accompany and encourage the abandonment of Native traditions. The very modern—and in some cases modernist—history of intercultural art display and ethnographic knowledge production is also a history of indigenous cultural practice, and my interest in recuperating archival material as evidence of this imbricated history is shared by many Kwakwaka'wakw themselves, who see in such practices the efforts of their ancestors to keep culture itself alive.[3] The current collaborative film restoration project is the result of just such a conjuncture (preface, this volume).

In this essay, I offer an ethnography of the restoration project itself, focusing on the ways in which both the project producers and sponsors, as well as the Gwa'wina Dancers, negotiated the fraught conceptual binary that pits modernity against traditional indigeneity. This collective effort entailed three related tactics: arguing for the quintessential modernity of the Curtis film participants' cinematic (re)enactment of earlier cultural practices; promoting audience recognition for the Kwakwaka'wakw adherence to certain traditional potlatch protocols even in intercultural presentations; and ensuring that the current public events were kept in direct dialogue with the film as a historical precedent. By keeping Curtis's original film production and the conditions of our own project in view at the same time, I suggest how understanding the cultural and intercultural dynamics of each might help us to complicate our understanding of both, as well as of the conceptual binary ("tradition vs. modernity") under which both types of project are often evaluated. Obviously, as one of the coproducers of the restoration project and coeditors of this volume, I intend to further the pedagogical goals of the project itself while also attempting to evaluate its realization. My complicity with the Kwakwaka'wakw in the production of cultural representations in this context instantiates the more general predicament in which anthropological research partners and advocates find themselves in sites of contemporary global cultural production (2004 Glass film; Marcus 1997; Myers 2006).

Regardless of the Curtis project's academic and historicist intentions, the Kwakwaka'wakw put it to work for themselves in multiple ways. I address the specific material, discursive, and performative strategies they used to articulate genealogical connections to their ancestors in the film and to voice current political concerns. Both onstage and backstage, objects, speeches, and dances passed through various cultural registers and regimes of value, demonstrating an ontological flexibility—an ability to move between standard categories as context demands—that is characteristic of a people who have long adapted ritual forms to commercial, popular, and academic venues.[4] Through dynamic combinations of masked dancing and public demonstrations, along with ceremonial oratory and film interpretation, the Kwakwaka'wakw draw on traditions of both potlatching and ethnographic display to fashion their present—and future—in terms of their various pasts.

Presents: Performing the Past and the Business of Display

Presenting cultural heritage to non-Native audiences is a serious affair. Like other indigenous people on the north Pacific coast today, the Kwakwaka'wakw possess a complex culture of visual art, hereditary status, and ceremonialism that has to a significant degree withstood the trials of colonial intervention over the past two centuries, albeit with requisite adjustments and adaptations. At the center of these social dynamics is a particular approach to display in which individual and lineal status is made conspicuously public through an elaborate system of material adornment—in the application of hereditary crest designs on everything from masks and totem poles to T-shirts—and ritual presentation, most famously at potlatches. Individual, social, and cultural identities as well as properties (material and ephemeral) are claimed and maintained through public display and validation by witnesses, who in the potlatch context are paid with "gifts" in order to seal the twin obligations of remembrance and reciprocity in the future.

Ritualized displays and exchanges—what Marcel Mauss (1990) called "prestations" in his classic account of the potlatch and its gifting procedures—are spoken of in coastal Native parlance as "business," regardless of the specific context in which this is done. This quasieconomic discourse reflects the seriousness of their role in mediating social relations and qualifies any sense that dances are simply done for entertainment, or that gifts are just given for holidays. The act of validating births, namings, initiations, weddings, and commemorations at potlatches constitutes the business of the events, but such business can also occur in less ritually marked settings (such as museums and other intercultural venues) as long as proper restrictions and protocols—frequently including the distribution of gifts—are observed (Ostrowitz 1999). While highly conventionalized styles of visual art and cer-

Aaron Glass

emonial oratory encourage a certain degree of public legibility, hereditary restrictions on ownership of material or immaterial prerogatives entail a proprietary relationship to certain forms as well as the private knowledge necessary for their full interpretation. Thus the culture of display and accessibility is tempered by equally active protocols of strategic withholding and restricted access (Townsend-Gault 2004), regardless of where and in front of whom important business is to be conducted.

By the late nineteenth century, the intercultural dynamics of colonialism offered new, quintessentially modern venues (such as museums and world's fairs) and technologies (such as photography and film) for strategic display as a means not only of advertizing hereditary identities and claims to property but also of helping to ensure their survival in the face of increasingly interventionist assimilation policies such as the potlatch prohibition, rampant missionization, and forced attendance at residential schools (introduction, this volume). With this advent of colonial modernity came a reevaluation of the status of something newly objectified as "traditional culture," which the colonial authorities were trying to eradicate at the same time as anthropologists and tourists were promoting (and financially rewarding) its retention and public availability (see below and Glass 2011). In the wake of devastating mortality rates due to introduced diseases, and in the context of restricted land bases and outlawed ceremonialism at home, opportunities to perform and preserve indigenous traditions may have appealed to salvage-oriented scholars, nostalgic settlers and travelers, and indigenous people alike, albeit for different reasons. Around the turn of the twentieth century, the Kwakwaka'wakw who attended the world's fairs or who posed for Curtis's cameras may have deceremonialized (and to some degree commercialized) aspects of their material and performance culture as a strategic measure to forestall its total eradication (Glass 2004a).

At one level, the legacy of such ethnographic display and intercultural collaboration has resulted in enormous colonial, scholarly, and popular archives of material representations now frequently deemed "traditional" (and thus authentic) due to their nineteenth-century pedigree. This archive is now being mined by scholars and the Kwakwaka'wakw alike for insights into this past world and as a resource for current indigenous self-fashioning, although the veracity of any specific representation may be locally contested (see Glass 2004b, 2006a). At another level, however, participation in ethnographic demonstrations, touristic displays, and photographic or filmic reconstructions provided individual Kwakwaka'wakw with an experiential method of rehearsing and thus maintaining a degree of cultural knowledge as embodied practice rather than as "representation," even under conditions of reframing and recontextualization.

Performance studies scholar Diana Taylor (2003) emphasizes the importance of such embodied practices, which she calls "repertoires" in contrast to archival repositories, to the maintenance and transmission of cultural identity and collective memory under—and against—colonial histories of violent disruption and repudiation (see also Nyong'o 2010). Rather than relying on static models of ritual or mimetic reproduction, Taylor suggests that embodied repertoires are adapted and performed under recurrent "scenarios," which are not rigidly scripted texts that recur in identical fashion but rather typical narrative sketches or outlines with familiar characters and scenes, generic plots, formulaic choreographies, and predictable contours (Taylor 2003:28–32). For example, we might identify different typical Kwakwaka'wakw performance scenarios, some linked to ceremonial contexts and others emergent in intercultural settings, each with their own choreographic repertoires of movement, discourse, gesture, and object use. Like some kinds of archival (especially academic) knowledge, scenarios are "citational" in their reuse and reiteration of previous forms, however they are distinguished from the archive by the embodied nature of the transmitted knowledge and experience, for both performers and witnesses to the repertoire's enactment. Such scenarios structure but do not fully determine any given iteration of the repertoire; indeed, they can be recast over time through regular variations in embodied practice given current circumstances. I am suggesting that the degree to which social, economic, artistic, and political structures were integrated into the embodied, expressive aspects of Kwakwaka'wakw life—what Mauss (1990:3) called the "total social phenomena" of masked dramas, musical performances, and oral literatures displayed at potlatches—may have contributed to the survival of such structures, if in altered form, through the early decades of the twentieth century. In other words, because expressive culture was deeply political in the context of the potlatch, it provided a means of maintaining a real and deeply politicized repertoire of Kwakwaka'wakw self-fashioning even when presented outside of a ceremonial context under reiterative scenarios of intercultural exchange.

Intercultural display is not only dramatic and often aestheticized, it is specifically "performative" in a way analogous to potlatch prestations, although with somewhat different goals and parameters.[5] The public demonstration of individual hereditary prerogatives or collective cultural identity in the potlatch not only claims a particular affiliation but also *enacts* it; such presentations are *constitutive* of a new state of being, not only reflective of an

Aaron Glass

existing state. Through strategically displaying certain ceremonial privileges in intercultural settings, the Kwakwaka'wakw today continue a century-old scenario of performing—and thus articulating—their lasting alterity as indigenous people in a modern multicultural democracy, building on the model of displaying and enacting hereditary personal and clan affiliations in intertribal ritual contexts. In presenting themselves to non-Native audiences, they are not merely passively reproducing past forms but are engaged in an active and agentive form of "culture making" in the present (Myers 1994, 2002).

Moreover, both potlatch prerogatives and intercultural displays are discursively and materially framed with explicit references to history, although with discrepant temporalities in each case. In the former context, the demonstration of ceremonial privileges such as masks, songs, and dances is typically accompanied by oral testimony as to the mythological or ancestral origins of these forms as well as the paths of inheritance or marriage transfer that resulted in their current owner's proprietary claims. If particular regalia such as masks, headdresses, or blankets are based on earlier prototypes, then these material pedigrees are also explained, not so much to authenticate the specific object but rather to validate the family's claim to the prerogative that it makes manifest. In fact, the Kwakwaka'wakw tend to view most such objects as the temporary—and potentially alienable—embodiment of the hereditary rights themselves, which are the true and inalienable form of ephemeral wealth that they index and objectify (Weiner 1992).[6] There is thus an ontological and mutually corroborating relationship between material forms (masks and regalia), performance types (song, dance, and oratory), proprietary ephemerals (hereditary prerogatives), social identities (clan titles, genealogies, and dance society positions), and historical trajectories (ancient and recent paths of circulation and exchange).

While such perspectives and ontologies are also clearly explained to intercultural audiences, an additional historical frame is introduced in the latter case that places current cultural production in the context of the potlatch prohibition and colonial efforts at assimilation. By using cultural presentations to educate the public about First Nations culture as well as past and current political struggles, dramatic masked dances are made to enact both individual and collective claims to identity, property, and continuity. As Chief William Cranmer declared to project participants at a Getty-sponsored symposium, he sees the Curtis film restoration as one component of a much larger "repatriation" process that includes the physical reclamation of objects removed under the potlatch prohibition, the reassembly of ethnographic records and recordings, the preservation of indigenous language, and the reestablishment of control over resource management and cultural practice more broadly through contemporary treaties and land claims (Peabody 2012).[7] He added that intercultural presentations and exhibitions are intended in part to enlist widespread public knowledge of and support for their efforts. Such discourse refigures the audience members as "witnesses" being offered the privilege of learning about authentic indigenous culture along with the contingent responsibility to recognize indigenous claims to survival and sovereignty. As in other kinds of ritualized contexts, live performance enters the audience into an "emotional economy" marked by protocols and expectations of obligation, exchange, and ongoing relation (Schieffelin 1998:203, 206).[8]

In an important sense, Kwakwaka'wakw ceremonial dances and regalia forms are always already historical "reenactments" at multiple orders of temporal remove from their origin, thus providing a flexible model for other kinds of citational, performative displays. Most Kwakwaka'wakw potlatch dances stage the legendary moment of acquisition at which rights to the dance itself as well as accompanying regalia were obtained from supernatural or human beings in the ancient or historical past. These origin claims are discursively validated and explained by song lyrics, narrative traditions, and family histories of exchange and diffusion. When certain initiates to masked or unmasked privileges are performing their dance in the ceremonial Big House (*gukwdzi*), they are also symbolically reenacting their own recent, private encounter with the presiding spirits of their prerogative, which itself reiterates the ancestral encounters that brought the prerogative into the lineage to begin with. For example, a Hamaťsa initiate dances in a potlatch in order to validate—and constitute performatively—his claim to the new hereditary position; his dance reenacts for public witnesses his own private encounter with and subsequent possession by the initiating spirit Baxwbakwalanuxwsiwe', while at the same time re-reenacting the legendary encounter from which his family obtained their first Hamaťsa.

In addition to looking backward, potlatch prestations also look forward, as witnesses are expected to validate and recall the claims to personal and familial identity and property in the future—an obligation sealed with a gift. Every (re)performance thus validates its prototypes while setting the conditions for future iterations, and this is true in both ceremonial and nonceremonial contexts. For Curtis's actors, the decision to perform for the camera was all the more significant in the context of the potlatch prohibition, which disrupted the ceremonial channels for the embodied reproduction of identity at the time. Their cinematic prestations were not mere "representations" of Kwakwaka'wakw culture; they were direct and performative means of per-

Aaron Glass

petuating it both by recording it on celluloid and by anticipating a future for performance. Recurrent moments of intercultural display may have resulted in ethnographic objectifications (such as the film itself) but they also helped perpetuate embodied knowledge and memory. As Diana Taylor (2003:57–58) suggests, the "scenario functions as the frame that enables the transfer from the repertoire to the archive," bridging the past and future, the here and there of cultural transmission. After the premiere Curtis film screening and performance in Los Angeles, G̱wa'wina leader William Wasden Jr.—a song leader, visual artist, hereditary chief of the 'Na̱mgis, and great-grandson of Stanley Hunt, the star of the film—explained the hereditary basis of their presentations: "It all goes back to the legends of the families. We're dancing our history through these songs and dances. That's what we're sharing with you today." In offering traditional culture as a kind of gift to their audiences, the G̱wa'wina Dancers were also making the past present for themselves.

"Sharing Culture" While Looking Both Ways

In both principle and practice, the G̱wa'wina Dancers based their participation in the Curtis film restoration project on the precedents set by their ancestors who acted in the film (appendix 2), as well as those who visited world's fairs—as Kevin Cranmer described at the Mead Festival—and those who developed educational dance presentations for fundraisers and steamship tourists in the mid-twentieth century (Wasden, this volume).[9] In thinking about ceremonial precedent and protocol, the history of intercultural performance, and the Western stage tradition, the group carefully positioned itself along distinct but overlapping continua between the film and the stage, between ritual and theater, between modernity and tradition.

Early in the course of the project, we screened the *War Canoes* version of the film for members of the Kwakwa̱ka'wakw community at the U'mista Cultural Centre in Alert Bay in order to open discussion about what the G̱wa'wina presentation to accompany the film might look like (fig. 15.3). We initially turned the volume off in order to better simulate the experience of it as a silent film and to record the commentaries of those gathered, but the Native audience missed hearing the voices of their old people from the 1960s, with which they had become accustomed, and they asked that the volume be restored.[10] Along the way, Andrea Sanborn, Colin Browne, Dave Hunsaker, and I asked questions and paused the film to discuss specific scenes of quotidian activity, object handling, and ceremonial dancing.

Stan Hunt immediately identified his father Stanley as the "handsome

Fig. 15.3. Members of the G̲wa'wina Dancers and Kwakwa̲ka̲'wakw community viewing the Curtis film at the U'mista Cultural Centre, Alert Bay, BC, 2007. *Left to right:* Beau Dick, Stan Hunt (the son of Stanley Hunt, who played Motana in the film), William Wasden Jr., and K̓odi Nelson with his young son. Photo by Sharon Grainger. U'mista Cultural Centre.

guy" who portrayed the hero Motana when he was around eighteen years old. As a young boy, Stan heard stories from his father about the rented whale used in the film, and was shown a photo of Stanley standing next to the dead beast, possible evidence that Curtis left at least a few field prints with his models and actors. He joked about his father adjusting his long wig during a dance sequence, and about the staging of the scene in which Motana builds the prayer fire, rapidly collecting tinder from just offscreen despite the apparent paucity of wood on the rocky beach nearby. Wasden confirmed the use of small harvesting canoes like the one paddled by Naida in an early scene, but he observed that a later scene with clam diggers was implausible, as they were filmed working at half tide, when there would have been no clams. People laughed as Paddy 'Ma̲lid, the actor playing Kenada, gestured dramatically when shot with an arrow during the raid on his village, and when the actor playing Naida's slave struggled against the removal of an arrow lodged in his back. My sense is that they appreciated the melodramatic acting effort as an extension of the familiar local culture of showmanship; at one point, carver Beau Dick called the film participants "natural actors." He also suggested that 1914 audiences in New York were convinced by the acting and the veracity of the film—"they thought it was like a newsreel," he said—when their ancestors at the time of filming were really quite modern,

Aaron Glass

with short hair, pin-striped suits, and motorized skiffs. Fellow carver Wayne Alfred later told me that his grandfather Jonathan Hunt, who was an extra in the film, frequently told Wayne's mother about being in it, boasting that he was a genuine "movie star."

Despite their recognition of the film's clear artifice, the viewers confirmed that the majority of ceremonial scenes contain accurate renditions of Kwakwaka'wakw ritual, although they were clearly shaped to support Curtis's melodramatic narrative (Holm and Quimby 1980:36–43, 65–105).[11] Dances that were typically performed indoors were presented outside, likely to ensure proper lighting. In a couple of instances—most notably in the round dances of numerous masked figures—individual dancers demonstrated proper choreography but the ensemble as filmed represents a departure from known ritual prerogatives.[12] Motana repeatedly dances with the movements of a Hamatsa, although it is not contextualized as such in the film but rather performed to enact his prayer vigils (see below; Harrison, this volume; Glass 2009b).

Viewers thought it plausible that George Hunt and the cast of performers improvised such scenes in order to give Curtis the spectacle that he desired while remaining true to established cultural practice and respecting certain ritual prohibitions. Based on their skillful execution of the dances, the performers in the film were speculated to have been among the most talented dancers in or near Fort Rupert at the time. According to Curtis's own publicity claims (cited in Holm and Quimby 1980:122), as well as oral history suggested by the audience at U'mista and other Kwakwaka'wakw film viewers, most of the actors likely had hereditary rights to the main dances they presented to the camera, a criteria for public presentation dating back to the world's fair troupes and active to this day in dances for tourists or in other nonceremonial settings. The masks and regalia in the film demonstrate equal fidelity to their ritual prototypes, and most were thought by project consultants to have been either borrowed or purchased from families, or commissioned by Curtis as film props (see appendix 3 for a list of extant props).[13] In the later category is the idiosyncratic set of *hamsaml* or "Cannibal Bird" masks used in and likely made for the film (see fig. 15.11). The shared and distinctive crescent emerging from the beak tops are not found on other known Hamatsa masks of the period, and their slight deviation from the norm might be seen as a material analogue to the dances that may have been strategically altered to make them appropriate for presentation in the film (introduction, this volume).

In some realms of both regalia and ritual performance, the restoration project mirrored the contexts of production of the original film, as singers and dancers were chosen based on skill, kinship ties to the film stars (mostly the Kwagu'ł as opposed to the 'Naḵwaxda'x̱w actors), and personal potlatch prerogatives that authorize them to dance both ceremonially and in intercultural venues.[14] Acting as emcee at the screening events, Wasden repeatedly emphasized the presence of both kinds of genealogical links—familial descent from film actors, and histories of initiation and hereditary rights to the masks, songs and dances—in addition to offering more general interpretive comments and descriptions about the sources and significance of the selections. Prior to the beginning of the public film screenings, we predisposed audiences to keep the past in dialogue with the present by playing Kwakwaka'wakw music in the auditoriums (alternating archival and contemporary recordings) while still photographs dissolved into one another on the film screen (juxtaposing published Curtis photographs with contemporary portraits by Sharon Grainger that were inspired by the earlier images).[15]

Specific dances were chosen by Wasden to illustrate those pictured in the film. For some of these, like the Grizzly Bear (Nan) and women's Warrior (Tuxw'id) Dances (fig. 15.4), the group decided not to imitate the particular choreography used in the film itself but rather to present specific variations that group members inherited or secured the rights to perform. For instance, the Thunderbird (Kwan'wala) dance presented in Vancouver by Kevin Cranmer showcased Wasden's personal transformation mask and regalia (an inherited 'Namgis privilege), which is quite different from the one pictured in the Curtis film although the dance's characteristic gestures were apparent (fig. 15.5).[16] For other presentations, the dancers corrected inaccuracies in the film. In Curtis's famous version of the Galsgamliła, in which a curtain drops to reveal a tableau of masked dancers (fig. 15.6), the assembly is guided by a Grouse dancer, even though in Kwakwaka'wakw potlatches the Grouse introduces a different masked dance series, the Atlakima. The Galsgamliła is a rare ceremonial prerogative owned by only a few families, including one connected to Wasden. In the potlatch, it is offered as a kind of preview of the prerogatives to be displayed by the host family (Boas 1966:174, 292–94; Curtis 1907–30, vol. 10:171; Holm and Quimby 1980:96); in the film project, it followed directly after the film screening in order to serve a similar function, although it featured masks and regalia not otherwise presented at the public events.

In at least one case, current cultural protocols demanded the exclusion of dances as pictured by Curtis. As mentioned above, typical Hamatsa gestures and choreography are present in the film, during Motana's solitary vigils and in the *hamsaml* masks present in the curtain-drop and round-dance

Aaron Glass

Top: Fig. 15.4a.
Tuxw'id (Warrior) Dance in the
Curtis film (1914). UCLA Film &
Television Archive, The Field
Museum, and Milestone Films.

Bottom: Fig. 15.4b.
Tuxw'id (Warrior) Dance as
presented by the G̱wa'wina
Dancers in the 2008 restora-
tion project. Photo by Sharon
Grainger. U'mista Cultural
Centre.

Top: Fig. 15.5a. Kwan̲'wala (Thunderbird) Dance in the Curtis film (1914). UCLA Film & Television Archive, The Field Museum, and Milestone Films.

Bottom: Fig. 15.5b. Kwan̲'wala (Thunderbird) Dance as presented by the G̲wa'wina Dancers in the 2008 restoration project. Photo by Sharon Grainger. U'mista Cultural Centre.

Top: Fig. 15.6a. G̲alsg̲amliła Dance in the Curtis film (1914). UCLA Film & Television Archive, The Field Museum, and Milestone Films.

Bottom: Fig. 15.6b. G̲alsg̲amliła Dance as presented by the G̲wa'wina Dancers in the 2008 restoration project. Photo by Sharon Grainger. U'mista Cultural Centre.

sequences. Onstage, the G̲wa'wina Dancers presented the final, "taming" stage of the Hamaťsa cycle to acknowledge its presence in the film and its cultural importance (fig. 15.7), although they avoided including the stages pictured in the film itself, as those are held by some Kwakw̲a̲ka'wakw to be too important to include in intercultural events and are instead restricted to potlatches (see Glass 2006a; Glass film, 2004). As Wasden told the audience at the Getty symposium, the younger generation is now "putting things away" that are the most sacred but that have been overexposed in the past. He also politicized his introduction to the Hamaťsa by explaining its centrality to the Canadian prohibition of the potlatch, pointing out the historical contingencies of cultural displays promoted by ethnographers while prohibited by colonial administrators.

Other dances, not directly pictured in the film, were chosen to satisfy different criteria. The Welcome Dance ('Y̲awiťlalał) and Farewell song (H̲alakas'lak̲ala) are frequent components of intercultural presentations by the G̲wa'wina Dancers and other Kwakw̲a̲ka'wakw groups, and hearken back to the standardized repertoires that were developed by groups such as the Kwaḵwala Arts and Crafts Society for tourist presentations half a century ago. A Wolf Dance (Długwala) and a Ladies Dance (Tłalk̲wala) showcased new regalia (see next section) and the skill of the group's women even though these were minor features in the film. While the Salmon Dance (Me'dz̲awesu') is a staple of public cultural presentations, at these events Wasden interpreted the dance according to both ancestral legends of the salmon (which often relate the fish to twins) and the current political crisis surrounding fish farms, aquaculture, and resource management in British Columbia.

Drawing a balance between the extended duration of potlatches and the compressed framework of intercultural displays is a challenge for many dance groups. The G̲wa'wina Dancers decided to present most songs and dance segments in something approaching their entirety, much like they would be displayed at potlatches (see Wasden and Hunsaker, this volume). This is a key factor in the frequently heard pronouncement among the Kwakw̲a̲ka'wakw today that one shouldn't "play with the culture" by disfiguring songs and dances too much in their recontextualization for outside audiences. In telling audiences that the group is not allowed "to touch" the old ways of doing things, or that they always have to answer to their families back home, Wasden is conveying a sense that the critical judgment of elders and fellow community members applies even to intercultural events. While certainly encouraging the dramatic staging of dances—an essential

Top: Fig. 15.7a.
Hamaťsa Dance in the
Curtis film (1914). UCLA
Film & Television Archive,
The Field Museum, and
Milestone Films.

Bottom: Fig. 15.7b.
Hamaťsa Dance as
presented by the G̲wa'wina
Dancers in the 2008
restoration project. Photo
by Sharon Grainger.
U'mista Cultural Centre.

component of Kwakwa̱ka'wakw potlatch displays—Wasden warned against allowing the lighting design to get "too extreme" or "too Hollywood." During the repeated and extended standing ovations that the group received at the Curtis events, they never offered stage bows or other nods to the Western theatrical tradition. As occurs at feasts and potlatches, the final presentation was an Am'lala or "Play Song" (Hana'ɬdax̱w'la) in which witnesses are invited to join the performers onstage or in the theater aisles to celebrate the successful completion of the event. This intermingling makes active participants out of the otherwise observant audience, a component of drawing them into a social relation with the presenters.

In general, there is a careful negotiation to maintain the sanctity of ceremony in the space of museums, theaters, and performing arts centers. While dancing on the customary dirt floor of the Big House provides a more direct sense of "connection" to the Earth and to the ancestors, according to Wasden, similar protocol is observed in other venues. To help convey the architectural environment of a traditional Big House, Wasden designed screens that were printed and suspended around and over the singers to represent carved house posts and cross beams; where these could not be hung above the stage, life-size digital images were projected onto the film screen (see fig. 14.2). The group also shipped large log and box drums to better approximate the acoustic effect of a community event, although they decided not to place a simulated fire at center stage. One common choreographic tactic is to transfer, from the Big House to the theater, the practice of entering and exiting the dance floor/stage by circling once in place—always counterclockwise, the same direction one travels along the dirt floor or the stage while dancing. Wasden explained to audiences that this motion mimics a baby being born and signifies the transition from a human to spirit realm and back again as people enter and depart the performance space. The group also chose to have their honorary speaker, Chief William Cranmer, stand to the left of the singers (on "stage right") when he introduced the events, just as he would while performing his customary role as the main orator at potlatches.[17]

As at other intercultural presentations, some of the ceremonial framing was handled discursively. Audiences that may feel uncomfortable in not knowing the cultural or spiritual status of what they are witnessing are guided through the experience. When Chief Cranmer opened the academic symposium at the Getty with a traditional blessing in Kwak̓wala, he assured the audience that they did not need to stand. Wasden, like similar group leaders today, frequently tells people that they are free to clap after dances or to take photos for their own use, as restrictions operative in the context of

Aaron Glass

334

a potlatch are suspended in such venues. At the same time, he does not promote the use of the term "performance" to describe what it is the group does, preferring to say that they offer "cultural presentations." The term "costume" is rigorously eschewed in favor of the more ritually marked term "regalia," all the more apt when intercultural groups wear the particular items that they also use in potlatches. Announcing hereditary claims to the prerogatives and individual histories of initiation does more than just create an aura of authenticity around presentations that are obviously and incontrovertibly recontextualized (see Kirshenblatt-Gimblett 1998:65, 74); it also validates the right of the presenters to be there in the first place according to the restrictive and proprietary protocols active at home. One of the most conspicuous analogies between such events and the potlatch comes in the use of phrases such as the "sharing of culture" to describe intercultural presentations as a kind of gift, as suggested above. In return the presenters expect a degree of reciprocity from their audiences/witnesses, not only financial compensation but also attention, respect, and recognition for their displays of identity and their cultural sovereignty over the terms of their public representation.

The events also provided public spaces in which to manage intertribal relationships, much as potlatches do. In almost all of the venues, we began the program by inviting delegates from local First Nations or Native American tribes to welcome the presenters and audience members to their territories, which helped ensure that the events unfolded with the atmosphere and temporality of Native cultural protocols. For example, in Los Angeles, Chief Anthony Morales from the Gabrielino-Tonva (San Gabriel Mission Indians) opened the two-day events at the Getty Center with a ceremonial welcome in the museum's auditorium. Leonard Forsman, chairman of the local Suquamish Tribe, offered the first words at the Moore Theatre in Seattle. In Vancouver, the Kwakwaka'wakw reinforced statements of friendship with the Coast Salish, on whose territory stands the Chan Centre for the Performing Arts, and with whom they used to wage war in past centuries. Musqueam Chief Larry Grant welcomed audiences to his community's "traditional, unceded territory," as has become custom at official events held on the campus of the University of British Columbia and other sites around Vancouver.[18]

In addition to the blurring of ritual and theatrical boundaries onstage, the Gwa'wina Dancers conducted transactional "business" both onstage and behind the scenes. While hereditary restrictions on public display characterize one key facet of the potlatch, perhaps its most famous aspect is the gift distribution with which it is generally concluded. Throughout the entire project, the Kwakwaka'wakw presenters exchanged gifts with key players.

For example, in Seattle scholar Bill Holm privately distributed prints of one of his Kwakwa̱ka'wakw-themed paintings to the group, who in turn recognized him publicly at the event itself—calling him by the Kwak̓wala name that he had been given decades before at a potlatch—for his years of friendship and assistance, and more specifically for his loan of the regalia that they danced that evening (see Wasden, this volume). Wasden promised Holm, "I'll square it with you in the Indian way when we get back home," pledging future returns of some kind. Likewise, public recognition was also offered to the project's coproducers before sold-out audiences in New York and Vancouver. At the American Museum of Natural History, the dancers gave clothing appliquéd with Kwakwa̱ka'wakw designs by Maxine Matilpi to Brad Evans and to my wife Helen Polson and me, which we wore onstage and during the reception afterward.[19]

Finally, on behalf of the U'mista Cultural Centre, Andrea Sanborn offered new Hudson's Bay Company point blankets to her coproducers, to key project participants that had volunteered their labor, and to the descendants of the original Curtis actors who were in the Vancouver audience (Richard Hunt, grandson of Stanley Hunt; and Mary Everson, daughter of Margaret Frank). This was done with an explicit reference to the past as well as to current ceremonial protocol, as HBC blankets were the standard medium of both the fur trade and of potlatch exchange on the mid-nineteenth-century coast, as well as being the original substrate for the ritual button blankets that are now ubiquitous at indigenous gatherings. As project gifts, they indexed multiple orders of social, cultural, and historical relations. Ensuring the proper conduct of such business is itself a historical feature of the scenario of intercultural display, as players adhere to a repertoire of reciprocal exchange modeled on that of the potlatch.

Performing Objects and Ontologies: Materiality and Native "Art"

The G̱wa'wina Dancers' discursive and performative framing of their presentations was mirrored by their use of objects designed with reference to both the original film props and contemporary ritual. Following the selection of dances and group members, the group attended to the need for the appropriate regalia. In some cases—such as Wasden's Thunderbird mask and full-body covering, and all of the button blankets worn by dancers and singers—troupe members provided their hereditary potlatch gear, the same items they wear in the Big House. Carvers and weavers studied the film in

Fig. 15.8. William Wasden Jr. painting the face of K̓odi Nelson at the Chan Centre for the Performing Arts, Vancouver, 2008. Photo by Sharon Grainger. U'mista Cultural Centre.

order to produce some reproductions based on the original film props.[20] To stage the G̱alsg̱amlila, the group assembled a large set of masks and regalia forms that were basic equivalents to, but not exact copies of, similar items pictured in the film, so that the general effect of the tableau would be the same. In addition to the dance regalia, the line of male singers wore distinct face-painting patterns that Wasden and others have been actively reviving in recent years based on multiple kinds of records, including elders' memories, old photographs, and ethnographic repositories (fig. 15.8).[21]

This pattern of material iteration has both art world and potlatch precedents, as carvers have long reproduced forms for ceremonial transmission or sale, whether based on the physical presence of the prototype, on personal recall, or on published or archival images (Blackman 1982, 1990; Ostrowitz 1999). In order to be validated as proper (or "authentic") reproductions, the subsequent versions do not need to be exact visual or material replicas, although they certainly could be. Rather, they may provide alternative interpretations of the same characters or constellations of forms, or they may introduce individual or idiosyncratic design elements unique to each generation's maker, as long as the maker or commissioner has valid hereditary rights to the prerogative. Since the late nineteenth century, it has been common for a chief or artist to sell a certain mask to a museum collector and then simply reproduce it, with variable degrees of visual fidelity, for ceremonial use (for example, Holm 1983b:92). While providing the cultural logic behind protocols of material replication, the Kwakwaka'wakw also invoke this local regime of value—as they did onstage during the Curtis events—to explain their current policy of very selective repatriation claims. They do not require all of their old objects back from museums, they publicly claim, because these can be replaced legitimately as long as artists exist and families can prove appropriate genealogical ties to the rights they represent (Webster 1992).

Unfortunately, the logistics of international circulation forced the hand of material flexibility on multiple occasions. En route to the Getty Center in Los Angeles, the project's first venue, the shipping containers with the new and borrowed regalia were temporarily misplaced. The night before the world premiere screening, the Gwa'wina Dancers stayed up late in the courtyard of their Sunset Boulevard hotel retooling their performance (bemusing the other guests) so as to require only the small headpieces that had traveled in their checked or carry-on luggage. Skilled adaptability being a key feature of intercultural repertoires, at the last minute they fashioned a plank drum from a piece of lumber lashed to wooden crates, and they borrowed black tablecloths from the Getty's restaurant to sling over their shoulders in lieu of customary blankets (fig. 15.9). A few days later, the group arrived in Seattle only to find that their regalia had still not cleared customs. The morning of the event at the Moore Theatre—where Curtis had premiered his film in 1914—the troupe put a call in to Bill Holm, who generously opened up his personal storehouse and loaned the group over twenty masks, blankets, and headpieces, some made by Holm himself and some by renowned artists of past generations, such as Willie Seaweed (fig. 15.10). That night, Holm sat in the front row as the Gwa'wina Dancers performed his art collection onstage.

Meanwhile, across town, similar objects were moving in the opposite intercultural trajectory along the hazy continuum between art and nonart. The Burke Museum of Natural History and Culture had just put on exhibit a number of the original film props used in *Head Hunters,* which had been purchased recently on the private auction circuit. These *hamsaml* (Hamatsa masks) joined *danisikw* ("power boards") and other items from the collection that were commissioned for the Curtis film and now stand as museum displays alongside the ceremonial regalia of that and earlier eras in adjacent cases (fig. 15.11; see also appendix 3). Here they are appreciated not only for their aesthetic style and ritual significance but also for their contribution to this historic motion picture; they are multivalent artifacts of various overlapping Kwakwaka'wakw visual and material cultures.

Aaron Glass

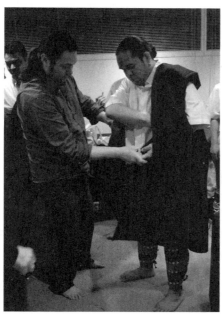

Left: Fig. 15.9. William Wasden Jr. helping Ian Reid don a black tablecloth in lieu of customary regalia at the Getty Center, Los Angeles, 2008. Photo by Sharon Grainger. U'mista Cultural Centre.

Top: Fig. 15.10. The G̱wa'wina Dancers adjusting a Hamat̓sa mask by Willie Seaweed (in the collection of Bill Holm) backstage at the Moore Theatre, Seattle, 2008. Photo by Sharon Grainger. U'mista Cultural Centre.

The *ḥamsaml̕* masks in particular have had a fascinating and mobile social life. Curtis published a now-famous photograph of two of these masks in the tenth volume of the *North American Indian*. Based on this image, carvers have been known to copy the masks for the commercial market or for use in the communities, although the black-and-white photograph is silent as to the masks' color scheme.[22] After seeing the original masks for the first time at the Burke Museum, Wasden produced a large painting, titled *Samdzuyaẉes: The Mouth of Heaven* (2008–9), based on the Curtis photograph (fig. 15.12). The

Top: Fig. 15.11. Hamaťsa masks and *danťsikw* ("power boards"), original Curtis film props now on display at the Burke Museum, Seattle, 2008. Photo by Aaron Glass. Burke Museum of Natural History and Culture.

Bottom: Fig. 15.12. William Wasden Jr. (Canadian, b. 1967), *Samdzuyawes: The Mouth of Heaven*, 2008–9. Acrylic paint, graphite black paint, and mica flakes, 54 x 74 in. This painting is based in part on Edward Curtis's photograph of Hamaťsa masks used in the film. Courtesy of the artist.

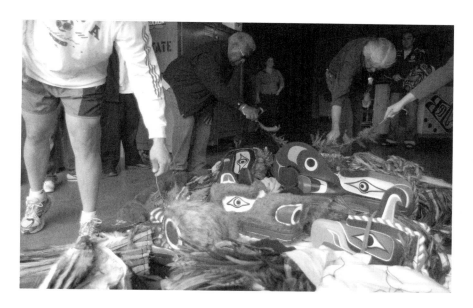

Fig. 15.13. The G̱wa'wina Dancers conducting a "brushing off" ceremony over their regalia at the Chan Centre for the Performing Arts, Vancouver, 2008. Photo by Sharon Grainger. U'mista Cultural Centre.

work returns the green color to the birds' eye sockets as a form of reclaiming the image itself, while resituating the masks within their cosmological rather than ethnographic context by adding celestial symbols over a design representing a dance screen (Wasden 2009:29).[23] Here the Curtis film props, via the restoration project and a museum collection, influenced the creation of contemporary fine art.

After a quick trip home to Alert Bay for June Sports, an annual intertribal soccer tournament in which many of the G̱wa'wina Dancers played, the group arrived in Vancouver to find that their regalia had finally caught up with them.[24] However, a number were found to be seriously damaged, including Wasden's own Thunderbird mask. With only hours to go before the performance, the group laid out all of the items—both old personal potlatch regalia and newly carved performance props—and conducted a blessing ceremony to "brush off" the shame that had accrued to them during their time in international shipping limbo (fig. 15.13; Wasden, this volume).[25] Kevin Cranmer spent the next few hours repairing the Thunderbird so that he could dance it that evening, but Wasden said that he would have to retire it from potlatch use and commission a new one, free from the taint of this indignity, even though the damage occurred in a nonceremonial context.

As if to signal the aesthetic, theatrical, and historical articulations represented by the project, G̲wa'wina member and artist Andy Everson (the grandson of Margaret Frank, who played Naida in the film) produced a set of T-shirts featuring iron-on decals of 1914 *Head Hunters* advertizing images. He gave these shirts, a kind of informal uniform for the "2008 Head Hunters World Tour," to some of his fellow presenters in an inversion of the popular Northwest Coast souvenir apparel industry and an extension of the use of T-shirts as commemorative potlatch gifts (Glass 2008). In realms of both performance and material culture, the Curtis film is now even more deeply implicated in the indigenous production and reproduction of ceremonial as well as commercial art forms. And this is true in nonindigenous realms as well.

Productive Tensions: The Business of Curtis

Over a century after he began publishing *The North American Indian*, the business of Edward Curtis is alive and well, with each generation reinventing him and his pictures to suit changing notions of photographic representation, shifting trends in scholarship, and evolving attitudes toward indigenous peoples (Glass and Evans, this volume). Every year, new and ever-thicker coffee table books are released, most of which recycle the same well-worn images and narratives of Curtis and his various projects. During the course of our restoration project from 2006 to 2012, we became aware of numerous parallel endeavors to reexamine Curtis and his legacy in various media and in terms both celebratory and critical: a new (but hardly original) biography (*Short Nights of the Shadow Catcher: The Epic Life and Immortal Photographs of Edward Curtis* by Timothy Egan); two novels (*Shadow Catcher* by Marianne Wiggins and *To Catch the Lightening* by Alan Cheuse); a graphic novel (*The North End of the World* by Dave Hunsaker and Christopher Shy); two feature films in script development, one of which includes the making of *Head Hunters* as a central episode; a stage musical based on Curtis's work in the Pacific Northwest; numerous exhibitions, most at university art galleries; and a multimedia piece by Métis playwright Marie Clements called "The Edward Curtis Project" (Clements and Leistner 2010). In the wake of the film tour, other Kwakwa̲ka̲'wakw dance groups turned their attention to Curtis as well. For example, in 2009, the Le-La-La Dancers, a Victoria-based group, premiered a new performance entitled *Spirit Journey: Encircling Our Ancestors*, featuring sequences inspired by *Head Hunters* (see chapter 6, note 3).

Our experience managing the business of the restoration project itself reveals many of the logistical as well as conceptual tensions that underlie

Cutis's complicated legacy and current vogue—tensions between commercialism and scholarship, art and science, tradition and modernity. These ambiguities illustrate Fred Myers's characterization of museums (and other institutions of and for cultural production) as not only "significant sites of intercultural practice" (2006:528) but also sites of "fundamental dislocation between audiences, speakers, and other participants in these new global spheres of cultural translation" (510). From the beginning, Evans, Sanborn, and I decided to approach this as an educational and nonprofit endeavor even though some of our initial project partners and consultants saw the potential for high ticket prices given the unusual combination of multimedia and live performance involved. Yet for many foundations, one or more aspects of the project fell outside of their funding mandate. For some academic organizations it was not research-oriented enough, while for arts funders it was too scholarly in tone. One American regional council on the humanities deemed it insufficiently geared toward "humanities" per se, while one Canadian agency devoted to funding First Nations projects declared that U'mista was not sufficiently categorized as a "museum" to qualify for a key project grant, and that the G̲wa'wina Dancers were too "professional" already to qualify for an arts development grant.

The semiprofessional status of the G̲wa'wina Dancers and the precise nature of their presentations was a recurring challenge to define in dialogue with many of our institutional and funding partners. Traveling the group of fifteen performers from a relatively remote community to multiple venues across the United States and Canada was easily the single biggest cost incurred in the course of the project.[26] After months of project development, some of our partners balked at the initial cost estimate for bringing the dancers, primarily due to the fees earmarked for individual presenters. In some cases, the understanding that the troupe was a traditional dance group was not easily reconciled with the requirement that each member—who needed to take time off their regular employment in order to make the trip—had to be paid, beyond the token honoraria provided to the project's academic participants. As it was, the full troupe appeared only on the West Coast, where travel costs were lower.

Expectations as to what the group would provide also had to be managed. In pitching the project to potential partners, I showed DVD clips of past G̲wa'wina productions. Regardless, I think sponsors and audiences alike were unprepared for the highly refined and dramatic quality of the singing and dancing, even in Seattle and Vancouver, where many people are acquainted with regional Native performance traditions. After the precedent set on the

West Coast, some of our partners back east expressed a degree of disappointment that the few members of the visiting delegation did not reproduce the elaborate presentation that the other venues experienced. For their part, the dancers were disappointed that funds were not made available to get the whole group there.

We also repeatedly debated with our hosts and sponsors regarding how to frame the events for audiences. While some strongly encouraged Evans and me to provide some introductory words onstage before the film screening, we felt that our academic perspectives were best left to the program brochure, which provided a detailed introduction to the original film and to the restoration project. We preferred the stage to be a place for Kwakwa̱ka̱'wakw voices to speak about the film and their culture, in part to resituate authorial control as the film screening segued into the cultural presentation.[27] In fact, we actively encouraged the "indigenization" of the venues by playing Kwakwa̱ka̱'wakw music in the auditoriums as audience members were seated, while Chief Cranmer's first words of welcome were spoken in Kwak̓wala in the manner of ceremonial oratory. Even so, the issue arose of how to describe the presentation itself in publicity materials. When I suggested that we call it a "cultural performance," one project partner at the University of British Columbia responded that the word "cultural" is presumed by and thus redundant with the use of "performance" in such contexts; for this person, "cultural" registered in the colloquial, artistic sense rather than in a more specialized anthropological sense. However, for many indigenous people, the qualifier "cultural" is especially important to validate such presentations and to distinguish them from other kinds of theatrical entertainment.

The status and identity of non-Native project participants also came up for discussion, which is unsurprising for a project that set out to explore the nature of intercultural collaboration/complicity and ethnographic representation, both historically and today. The most explicit moment like this occurred for me during a public panel discussion held after the Vancouver screening event at the UBC Museum of Anthropology in order to assess and evaluate the film as well as the larger project. The evening began with short presentations by me as well as by three indigenous panelists: Barb Cranmer, a Kwakwa̱ka̱'wakw filmmaker; Dana Claxton, a Lakota media artist and educator; and Mique'l Askren, a Tsimshian art historian and leader of the Git Hayetsk Dancers. When we opened the floor to questions and comments, two young First Nations performance artists and activists confronted me by suggesting that my role in this project reiterated that of Curtis's in the film— essentially that I was guilty of parading colorful Indians while denying their modernity (one of them initiated the commentary by suggesting that I physically resemble Curtis himself). I tried to explain that this was a conscious concern of ours and that the whole project team did a number of things to help mitigate against this potential: we partnered with the Kwakwa̱ka'wakw from the start and with indigenous organizations throughout; we limited non-Native presence on the stage during events themselves; we organized symposia and public conversations around almost every event in order to provide venues for critical discussion; and we created supplementary materials such as the program brochure and photographic exhibits to provide multiple perspectives on Curtis and his work.[28] As it happened, I hardly needed to defend myself in this venue, as all three of my copanelists jumped in to point out these factors as well. Likewise, some attendees to the Seattle event took the opportunity to privately voice criticism of Bill Holm for his long history of integration with the Northwest Coast art world as well as the University of Washington art history department. However, the Kwakwa̱ka'wakw onstage clearly validated Holm's ongoing relationship with their people, and many Native scholars joined an email and electronic forum dialogue in defense of the project.

At both the University of Washington and the University of British Columbia, I heard feedback from some indigenous scholars that the project veered too close to Indian spectacle by showcasing "traditional" ceremony and regalia at the expense of educating audiences about modern Native life and concerns. While I welcome such input as an opportunity to reflect on the project, especially in relation to Curtis's filmic collaboration itself, I find aspects of such criticism perplexing, especially when coming from indigenous people in apparent defense of indigenous perspectives. For example, one of my critics at the UBC panel discussion reiterated the oft-cited instances—introduced to the literature by Christopher Lyman (1982) and endlessly and uncritically regurgitated ever since—when Edward Curtis "dressed his subjects up" in clothing and regalia that he provided and that was culturally inaccurate for some of his specific models. Moreover, he implied that the selective (re)presentation of traditional-looking Indians onstage in the Curtis project somehow reiterated the nostalgic gaze of Curtis himself, presumably at my and my (non-Native) coproducer's direction, as if we had asked the G̱wa'wina Dancers to hide their running shorts under their button blankets much as Curtis removed the famous alarm clock from the Piegan lodge (Zamir, this volume). Likewise, two other colleagues suggested to me that we missed an opportunity to foreground the fact that the participants in Curtis's film wore European clothing and drove powerboats at the time of filming (a point we actually made emphatically in the program brochure and website).[29]

While I share a sense that such points might have been more forcefully conveyed, and that stereotypes about Indians and First Nations need to be publicly challenged, there is a presumption underlying such critiques that doubly disempowers the Kwakwa̱ka'wakw who worked with Curtis on the film (or, by extension, performed at world's fairs) and with us on its restoration. To assume that Curtis wielded absolute directorial control over his photographic and filmic models is to discount their agency in having chosen to work with him, much less how and in what clothing to pose for him. To assume that a focus on "traditional" culture and regalia today reflects only non-Native criteria for authenticating Native people is to overlook the events as expressions of Kwakwa̱ka'wakw decisions as to self-presentation. Defending the cultural legitimacy and political efficacy of contemporary Aboriginal performance in nonritual settings, Howard Morphy challenges the basis of such critiques:

> While it may be the case that in the nineteenth century exhibitions were used to position indigenous peoples at the bottom of an evolutionary hierarchy, that should not deny their descendants in the twenty-first century the opportunity to present analogous cultural performances and displays as a means of asserting their autonomy and independence. Indeed, to continue to argue that such exhibitions inevitably position Indigenous societies in the past would be to implicitly accept the validity of the nineteenth-century interpretations imposed on [them]. (Morphy 2006:495)

If the G̱wa'wina Dancers choose to emphasize their cultural continuity and the survival of traditional practices in such venues, they do so in full cognizance of the range of presentational options open to them, and in contradistinction perhaps to the messages conveyed both by more self-consciously "progressive" First Nations and by more academically inclined Native intellectuals.

More to the point, our intention was to put the two collaborative, intercultural projects in direct relation in order to raise questions about indigenous agency and ethnographic representation in the first place—both then and now. Rather than argue that First Nations are "modern" only when obviously using industrial technology, getting university degrees, and wearing business or track suits—which they have been doing variably for over a century now—we hoped to reframe the question by calling attention to the fact that strategic, intercultural, public performance of something objectified as "traditional

Aaron Glass

culture" *is itself* a fundamental condition of modern self-formation for many indigenous people, a point I return to below. Critics have assumed that the decision to showcase precontact ceremonial life was Curtis's alone, but this ignores the persistence of Kwakwaka'wakw scenarios for intercultural display, which selectively reproduce the past in order to manage relations with non-Natives, and which the Gwa'wina Dancers explicitly and implicitly cited in making similar decisions today. Reasoning in the opposite temporal direction, an awareness of contemporary agency—and not just outer appearance in clothing styles and visible technology—might help us reevaluate the intentionality of Curtis's collaborators, despite the different historical and political conditions of encounter.

The complexity of this argument and its potential for misrecognition by audiences is highlighted further by discrepancies in the interest of various project partners and participants. While Evans and I were keen to explore concepts of modernity and ethnographic representation, the Kwakwaka'wakw tended to be more concerned to showcase their cultural continuity and contemporary sovereignty, although these are hardly mutually exclusive (to the contrary, I think they are fundamentally complementary and mutually constituting). Such perspectives were mapped differently across project materials—the former primarily in printed matter and extra-event forums (symposia, exhibits, the project website, this volume), and the latter on the stage itself. Although some critics were disappointed by the discursive or performative emphasis on tradition over modernity at the screening events, this is some indication of how the balance of decision making in this collaborative project played out.

In some ways, the Vancouver event most exemplifies these productive tensions. It was cosponsored by a university (celebrating its centenary), a museum (of anthropology), and a First Nations studies program; hosted by a performing arts center (whose one thousand sold-out seats held many Native people); and held on Canada's National Aboriginal Day. It was the longest event of the series, clocking in at around four hours. Here Wasden was especially careful to announce song and dance owners, and he told extended origin narratives for the privileges that come from fellow 'Namgis families in Alert Bay as well as for those that come from other villages. The Gwa'wina Dancers kept the audience late in order to recognize the descendants of the film actors onstage, to lead the audience in a Fun Dance that snaked through the aisles as eagle down wafted through the hall, and to celebrate with all of their kin in the crowd as Curtis portraits cycled on the film screen behind them (fig. 15.14). In the end, I think this extended sense of time paid off,

Fig. 15.14. The G̲wa'wina Dancers onstage with other Kwakwa̲ka'wakw at the Chan Centre for the Performing Arts, Vancouver, 2008. At center-left is Mary Everson, the daughter of Margaret Frank (who played Naida in the film). Photo by Aaron Glass.

especially for Native witnesses. Even one indigenous critic conceded that while for her the dance performance began as cultural spectacle (not unlike the film itself, which it closely followed in time and in content), it ended up ritualizing the whole venue in a manner that felt empowering rather than exploitative.

Less interested than I am in a postcolonial critique of Curtis, the G̲wa'wina Dancers preferred to emphasize genealogical ties, cultural explanations of the dances unrelated to the film itself, and current political concerns. Only in the question-and-answer periods (which the Vancouver event lacked) did the group tend to inform audiences about the modernity of the film actors in 1914, and of how traces of this are visible despite Curtis's efforts to erase them: in the high-stepping motions of the hero Motana as he gingerly ran down the rocky shore, unaccustomed to going barefoot in those years; in the obvious adjustments of the long wigs that Curtis furnished the otherwise shorn actors; in the renting of a dead whale from a commercial whaling station for the hunt scene. More important to the Kwakwa̲ka'wakw was an emphasis on the way in which the persistence of traditional culture informed the film shoot: the protocol restrictions that kept certain actors from doing certain dances;

Aaron Glass

that resulted in strategic errors and planned deviations from ritual norms; or that led to the withdrawal of the lead actress after being asked by Curtis to do something beneath her rank, even if only while acting in a movie. Similar protocols were announced to the 2008 audiences as conditions that also extended to the very event they were witnessing. In these ways, the Gwa'wina Dancers not only validated their ancestors' decisions to adapt traditional ceremonial culture to the institutions and technologies of modernity in 1914, they also established the film—and by implication other scenarios of cultural self-fashioning—as an important precedent for their own contemporary intercultural production as one crucial mode of social reproduction.

Conclusion:
The Dialectical Dance of the Native/Modern

While I have been arguing that in some important ways the two Curtis projects—the original film and its recent restoration—share similarities as intercultural encounters, especially in as much as the event series and this volume have attempted to establish this dialogue directly, the sociopolitical and historical context of the two are notably different. It is true that in 1914, the film actors were dressing in outmoded cedar-bark clothing and recreating the technologies of their ancestors, but they were also maintaining embodied cultural knowledge by rehearsing performance repertoires for the camera and for money—while under certain restrictions of both ceremonial protocol and colonial surveillance—at exactly the moment that their ceremonies were prohibited by the federal government under the potlatch prohibition. In this strategic decision, and not least by making a movie, they were expressing a fundamentally modern self-consciousness. The Gwa'wina Dancers have grown up with a relegalized potlatch, with repatriated masks in their own local cultural centers, and with cultural curricula and language education in their band-run schools. The popular discourse of the "vanishing races" is no longer operative, and in its place the dancers have witnessed the rise of local treaty and land-claim negotiations in British Columbia as well as global indigenous sovereignty movements. Aside from being discursively marked as "traditional," the donning of regalia or performing of dances today is not a mimetic simulation of the ancestral past but a crucial mode of cultural reproduction in the present, whether in the modern potlatch or in commercial or educational venues, even if the contours and parameters of those traditions are vigorously debated (Glass 2004b). Rather than approaching the legacy of such intercultural encounters and scenarios as scenes of the mere adulteration of Native culture, we ought to see them as part of larger, iterative, and ongoing tactics for resisting the forces of what Tavia Nyong'o (2010:157–65) identifies as "coercive mimeticism"—the primary colonial demand that indigenous people reproduce European culture in place of their own.

For the indigenous performers and, I assume, for audiences as well, registering both similarities to and divergences from the Curtis film itself proved highly significant in complementary ways. Where the dancers' presentations directly *mirrored* the film's ceremonial sequences and material culture, they reinforced the accuracy of the film—and thus the cultural integrity of the film's Kwakwa̱ka'wakw participants—and emphasized the persistence of Kwakwa̱ka'wakw culture over the intervening century. Thus the film and the project became mutually validating as public, "ethnographic" representations despite their unique modes and media of recontextualization. Where the current project's features *diverged* from the film, the dancers highlighted their current ability to critique and correct the errors of the past, whether we attribute the agency behind those errors to Curtis or to his indigenous collaborators. Moreover, the presentation of unique dance prerogatives that resemble (or visually rhyme with) those in the film allowed Wasden an opportunity to discuss hereditary specificity and the proprietary nature of dances, songs, and masks, as well as the continued importance of creative innovation within the constraints of inherited tradition. By keeping the two projects in dialogue with one another while avoiding strict mimicry, the Kwakwa̱ka'wakw gave audiences the opportunity to imagine the scenarios of intercultural collaboration as one context (among many possible contexts) in which thoroughly modern indigenous people might reevaluate and choose to publicly display their traditions—in the past, present, and future.

Historically speaking, one of the hallmarks—perhaps the defining feature—of modernity is the fact that tradition (or custom or "culture") is no longer taken for granted and habitually reproduced (Berman 1982; Habermas 1987). Rather, it comes under direct scrutiny and is treated accordingly—voluntarily annihilated, selectively bracketed and preserved as "heritage," or transformed as deemed appropriate—depending on various social and political factors. These are overlapping and not mutually exclusive options, and all are engaged in with a considerable degree of reflexive self-consciousness, strategic debate, and controversy (Giddens 1990:37–38). Of course, the condition of modernity need not manifest the same way everywhere (Miller 1995; Appadurai 1996; Gaonkar 2001). Most indigenous people in settler colonies had (and often continue to have) modernity foisted rather rapidly and violently upon them, especially in regions such as the north Pacific coast, which were brought under the rubric of global imperialism comparatively recently. While indigenous traditions under nineteenth-century colonial modernity ran the same gamut of historical transitions as outlined above, they did so under enormous pressure from external political, cultural, and economic forces that were heavily invested in one particular (and often contradictory) response or another. The great—and lasting—colonial paradox for indigenous peoples in particular is that they are expected to modernize (via apparent assimilation) while remaining fundamentally traditional at the same time; they are uniquely compelled toward the former as subjects of the presiding state (with its missionaries, Indian Agents, and industrialists), and uniquely rewarded and valued according to the latter (especially perhaps by anthropologists, tourists, and art markets) as the signifier of their authenticity and distinction, particularly within emergent multicultural democracies (Wolfe 1999; Povinelli 2002; Coombes 2006).

The abstract semiotic binary distinction between the traditional (or "primitive") and the modern (or "civilized") has long displaced attention from the more fundamental political opposition between indigenous peoples and immigrants under conditions of settler colonialism. Conceptually, the "Native" has historically been presented, explicitly or implicitly, as the categorical limit of the modern—the enemy always waiting on the boundary of the frontier to halt the progress of civilization (Fabian 1983; McGrane 1989; Ketchum 2005).[30] This binary logic undergirds political and geographical absorption but also ethnographic and artistic appreciation (itself a mode of appropriation) by settler states.[31] On the indigenous side, modernity in the guise of modernization of habits, technologies, and institutions is often assumed to be equivalent to—and means toward—assimilation (whether voluntary or forced), and is held to be opposed to the maintenance of tradition (which is presumed to be regressive, resistant, or reactionary). However, exposure to the tools and sensibilities of modernity is also said to unleash the creativity of Native people, to help break what Franz Boas (1974:42) called the "shackles of tradition" that hold them back, and to unleash the potential to invent new (potentially even modernist) forms with complicated relationships to previous ones (see Brody 1997; Anthes 2006).

It has been our contention in this book that the features of colonial modernity created the conditions for a transformation in Native self-consciousness that was marked by a new relationship with the traditional. This shift is best characterized as a changing sensibility and approach to self-fashioning in which "tradition"—not to mention a sense of "culture" itself—looses its status as taken-for-granted and becomes something actively preserved or abandoned, produced or reproduced, within the twin constraints and pressures of both existing cultural protocols and colonial administration. Regardless of whether beliefs and practices are maintained intact, purposefully transformed, or temporarily discarded, they survive in some form as resources—or repertoires—for current and subsequent identity formation (Mauzé 1997). The language of "traditional culture" is a discourse of value, applied variously and intentionally to contemporary cultural practices in order to validate them through strategic if selective links to the past (Glass 2004b; Dominguez 1992).

Furthermore, the reiterative scenarios of ethnographic encounter have resulted in certain material objectifications of culture, such as books, photographs, and films, which contribute to such reflexive, historical evaluation—another common experience under modernity (Giddens 1990:43, 45). Although not all may express themselves equally in every generation, the preservation and public display of cultural knowledge, material forms, and embodied practices—even under conditions of ethnographic repackaging—helps assure their potential for recuperation and reassessment in the future (Ginsburg 2002). Fred Myers (2006:532) summarizes the performative nature of contemporary indigenous identities as they are articulated in the face of (often neocolonial) institutional constraints: "The exhibitionary context cannot replicate what it represents. It necessarily recontextualizes what it shows, producing something new" (see also Kirshenblatt-Gimblett 1998; Clifford 2004). Unlike the static display of objects in museological contexts, or even the archival representation of song and dance in silent film, live performance conveys a different temporality, one that demands recognition by a spatially and historically (co)present audience of the absolute contemporaneity and embodied persistence of indigenous repertoires (Nyong'o 2010:151).

While the Kwakwa̱ka̱'wakw actively fought the potlatch ban by sending petitions to the government, hiring lawyers to argue their cause, concealing ceremonial gifts under the auspices of Christian holidays, and holding illegal ceremonies outright (introduction, this volume), they also maintained embodied cultural knowledge and practice by adapting certain elements—especially expressive forms such as visual art, music, and dance—to the intercultural contexts and venues of ethnographic display. Although the results of many of these decisions may be seen from a critical perspective to have contributed to colonialist myths and fantasies (Morris 1994; Rony 1996; Wakeham 2008), they also provided some means for Native livelihood, creative agency, and political assertions of survival (Russell 1999; Raibmon 2005; see also Phillips 2001; Roy 2002). By performing themselves for others as well as

Aaron Glass

352

for each other, the Kwakw<u>a</u>ka'wakw have long claimed the local prerogatives of ancient inheritance as well as their lasting alterity and sovereignty within the modern cosmopolitan nation.

*   *   *

At the conclusion of their Margaret Mead Film Festival programming, the Kwakw<u>a</u>ka'wakw delegation exited the American Museum of Natural History through Boas's famous Hall of Northwest Coast Indians. Setting down their rolling suitcases in an alcove dedicated to the "Kwakiutl," the group paused for a final brief visit with the ceremonial masks and cedar-bark ornaments that George Hunt and Franz Boas had collected over a century earlier. William Wasden Jr. took out a large circular hand drum, and the group began to sing a farewell song. This was a particular song composed by Tom "Mackenzie" Willie after a trip to England with the all-Native Victoria Thunderbirds soccer team, and which Wasden now sings in certain intercultural contexts. Its lyrics thank by name the people, institutions, and countries visited—the temporary hosts and the social relations forged through global circulation. The words to the song are said to be in Chinook Jargon, a hybrid language that was used all along the coast to facilitate trade, first intertribal and then intercultural. Although Wasden heard the song while studying with the elder song master as a young man, he later learned it by mining a large collection of recordings that Willie had made before passing away. I've now heard Wasden sing this song in different museums all over the world as he finishes his consultation, research, or presentation work; the group had closed their Curtis event in Vancouver with it as well. While I doubt that the gathering museum crowd appreciated it, the Kwakw<u>a</u>ka'wakw were not performing for them on this occasion; they were singing to their objects and to the ancestors who had made and used and sold and collected them, reinforcing these temporal and genealogical ties through a public form of expressive culture that demands witnesses, even if naïve ones.

The <u>G</u>wa'wina Dancers left the museum shortly thereafter to board a plane to Chicago in order to present at The Field Museum the following day, near the site where a different set of relatives had once acted in and on the world's stage at the 1893 World's Columbian Exposition. While at the Field, I walked through the Northwest Coast hall with Wasden and the others, stopping to admire the Hamaťsa diorama in which Charles Nowell once stood in 1904, interpreting Kwakw<u>a</u>ka'wakw culture to museum visitors. One can imagine the sense of uncanny animation that visitors at that time might have experienced upon seeing a museum mannequin come to life. Perhaps this parallels in some fashion what moviegoers may have thought when seeing the Curtis film a decade later—a supposedly vanishing race apparently alive and well on the silver screen. Regardless of what audiences to ethnographic spectacles made (and still make) of such exhibitions, the choice to put themselves on intercultural display has proven to be a significant and lasting strategy in the Kwakwa̱ka'wakw's ongoing effort to maintain the business of cultural survival.

This essay is based on my personal observations and participation during the Curtis project and screening series. Direct quotations not otherwise sourced were transcribed from video recordings of the public and preparatory events. Portions of the essay were earlier presented at the 2009 American Anthropological Association conference. For helpful feedback on earlier drafts, I'd like to thank Brad Evans, William Wasden Jr., Juanita Johnston, Helen Polson, Fred Myers, Charlotte Townsend-Gault, Mique'l Dangeli, and Rebecca Peabody. The perspectives, and any errors of fact, are entirely my own.

1 The Kwakwa̱ka'wakw delegation in New York and Chicago included William Cranmer, William Wasden Jr., Kevin Cranmer, Maxine Matilpi, and Dorothy "Pewi" Alfred. Fifteen singers and dancers accompanied the film at West Coast venues earlier in the year (see preface, this volume, for a full list of participating G̱wa'wina Dancers).

2 This is a famous episode in Kwakwa̱ka'wakw oral history and literature, rehearsed frequently in the communities and cited often in print (see Glass 2006a:240; Cole 1985:202; Jacknis 2002a:91; Parezo and Fowler 2007:227–30). On the photographs of Harris, see Glass (2006a:249) and Savard (2010:133).

3 I am drawing on a distinction between "modernity" as a sociohistorical condition and "modernism" as a particular set of aesthetic strategies prevalent in the nineteenth and twentieth centuries (see Frascina et al. 1993).

4 For comparative studies of the strategic indigenous deployment of recontextualized ritual for political ends, see Myers (1994); Turner (2002); and Morphy (2006).

5 By using the term "performative," I invoke something more than just the theatrical frame of song and dance. Rather, I am drawing on the linguistic "speech act" philosophy of J. L. Austin (1976) and John Searle (1969), as well as Judith Butler's (1990a, 1990b) extension of these ideas into gender studies, which focuses on the way in which certain kinds of illocutionary language constitute novel social or semiotic relations through their very enunciation or enactment (Schieffelin 1998). Two famous examples of performative speech are naming or christening, and pronouncing someone husband and wife; the illocutionary linguistic act itself changes the state of being of the people in question rather than just reflecting or referencing their preexisting identities.

6 While certain objects—especially coppers—might be held to be irreplaceable "heirlooms," in general the Kwakwa̱ka'wakw do not treat their *dɫugwe'* or "treasures" in the same manner as the Tlingit do their analogous category of valuable clan property, *at.oów*, which is generally held to be singular and inalienable (Dauenhauer 1995).

7 This is a discursive move shared by Gloria Cranmer Webster in the 1983 film *Box of Treasures*, where she situates the repatriation of objects to the U'mista Cultural Centre in terms of the ongoing struggle to regain and retain cultural and political sovereignty. Chief Cranmer also boasted onstage at Curtis events that the U'mista achieved the long-term loan of a mask from the British Museum, a rare case of the return of cultural property from this institution.

Aaron Glass

8   At the Getty symposium, Diné/Seminole/Muscogee scholar and photographer Hul-leah Tsinhnahjinnie discussed Native-made videos posted to YouTube as a kind of extension of the Northwest Coast culture of display, figuring Internet audiences as global witnesses to indigenous identity and sovereignty claims despite the lack of "liveness" (contra Phelan 1993).

9   I call such intercultural presentations "educational" as they almost always include didactic framing for audience members not familiar with Native culture. For more on the fundraiser and steamship dances, see Spradley (1969:256–58); Ostrowitz (1999:93); Jacknis (2002a:331–32); and Glass (2006a).

10 In fact, much of their commentary was focused on the 1973 soundtrack: they iden-tified speakers and singers, discussed the choice of songs, and enjoyed the audio theatrics added to the film. This is further indication that the *War Canoes* version may always be preferred by at least some Kwakwaka'wakw audiences (introduction, this volume).

11 Wayne Alfred told me an old historical narrative passed down in his family about a group of Kwagu'ł chiefs who once ambushed, killed, and beheaded a notorious Haida warrior who had tormented villages all along the coast. He suggested that his ancestors who worked on the film knew that story and would have used it to help guide the staging of the headhunting scenes, even though they lacked direct experi-ence with such activities.

12 Other discrepancies noticed by the Kwakwaka'wakw viewers include the use of woven cedar-bark rings on the Nułtsistalał or "Fire Dancer" at a stage in the dance cycle when the initiate disrupts the fire itself, which is prior to when they are typi-cally worn in ceremony.

13 See also introduction, this volume. While watching the film, Wasden suggested that the same artist added designs to both the war canoes and the house façades built for the village set, thereby repurposing existing objects to match the new ones constructed for the film. Holm and Quimby (1980:127–28) published pages from one of George Hunt's account ledgers that list many of the expenses accrued in outfitting the dancers, and that distinguishes some of the diverse sources for the film props.

14 As with any such high-profile project, the challenge of selecting participants is never free from community debate. Some Kwagu'ł people from Fort Rupert felt sidelined, as the original film had been made largely in that village, although descendants of the film actors now live in a number of other places, including Alert Bay. Even the fact that the restoration project solicited intracommunity contestations over the identity and validity of the selected performers indicates that traditional concerns about potlatch protocol and hereditary rights carry over into the realm of public presentations.

15 The sequence of Curtis and Grainger images is available as a slideshow called "Stag-ing Edward Curtis" on the project website (www.curtisfilm.rutgers.edu).

16 In addition, the dance group added the earlier or later stages of some dances as they would appear in potlatches but which were left out of the film.

17 In another nod to potlatches, this one unannounced at the public events, the singers were accompanied by a "conductor" *(ƙayudala)*, Ƙodi Nelson, who dressed a bit dif-ferently from the rest and who walked around waving two eagle-tail-feather fans, the accoutrements of his hereditary position and conducting prerogative (he keeps the singers coordinated and calls out the lyrics of the upcoming verses).

18 While there were no official indigenous hosts in Washington, DC, or Chicago, the American Museum of Natural History invited Tonya Gonnella Frichner (Onondaga) and Steve Thornton (Cherokee/Osage), two active members of New York's Native American community, to open the evening by welcoming the Kwakwaka'wakw to the city.

19　Onstage in Vancouver, Kevin Cranmer gave signed copies of his own silkscreen print to Andrea Sanborn and me, as well as to Chiefs Cranmer and Wasden for their work in leading the public presentations.

20　This resulted in a Thunderbird headdress by Wayne Alfred, a Wasp mask by Beau Dick, and a set of four Wolf headdresses by Calvin Hunt and non-Native carver John Livingston; other items were made by Donna Cranmer, Calvin Hunt, Maxine Matilpi, Don Svanvik, William Wasden Jr., and Sean Whonnock.

21　For instance, the American Museum of Natural History has a large collection of unpublished drawings collected by George Hunt for Franz Boas in the late 1890s, which depict the unique face paintings that once distinguished members of particular dance societies. I had returned copies of some of these to Kwakwaka'wakw communities in 2003, and Wasden consulted them at the museum before the New York Curtis event in 2008.

22　For example, in the 1990s a set of small versions of the *hamsaml* masks pictured by Curtis was commissioned for Kwakwaka'wakw children to use in Alert Bay's band-run school as part of their regular cultural curriculum.

23　In Kwakwaka'wakw communities, I have seen other examples of the reclamation of Curtis photographs that are specifically marked by material translation, like Wasden's use of acrylic paint. For example, this same image of the two masks was cropped and printed on compact disks of contemporary Kwakwaka'wakw music recordings; artists render Curtis portraits in graphite drawings that often hang in people's houses, sometimes those of the model's descendants; and one village used a reworked Curtis image on a printed award of merit given to other local Kwakwaka'wakw organizations. In 2010, another member of the Gwa'wina Dancers, Ian Reid, produced an artwork called *Reflections,* in which he painted over and around a Curtis photograph.

24　June Sports, which celebrated its fiftieth anniversary in 2008, is itself a perfect case study of indigenous modernities as it consolidates multiple aspects of Native response to colonial history and its contradictions (see Glass film, 2004): past missionary condemnation of intervillage warfare and its replacement by (or sublimation into) soccer; Christian blessing of the commercial fishing fleet at the opening of the salmon season; and the celebration of sporting and other nonceremonial events through public presentation of indigenous dances, some of which are included in the Gwa'wina repertoire.

25　The ceremony entailed slowly brushing the objects with cedar boughs while Wasden sang a healing chant (*k̓aƛaliƛa*). The cleansing boughs were then driven to the nearby sea and cast away, while new ones were cut from trees surrounding the Chan Centre to decorate the stage.

26　The possible exception to this may have been the technical costs involved in the film restoration itself. However, once the UCLA Film & Television Archive agreed to participate, they acquired their own funding to restore the film, so this expense did not fall to the Curtis project producers.

27　The main exception was in New York, where Peter Whiteley, curator of North American ethnology at the American Museum of Natural History, offered a short talk on the history of the museum's relationship with Franz Boas and Northwest Coast peoples, the Kwakwaka'wakw in particular.

28　The program brochure itself, as well as the two photography exhibits, are available on the project website at www.curtisfilm.rutgers.edu.

29　In fact, the Gwa'wina Dancers catered their interpretive comments and appearance to the particular audiences. If Wasden didn't bother to highlight the modern ways of the Kwakwaka'wakw to Seattle and Vancouver crowds, it may have been in part because he took for granted that regional audiences would have more experience and awareness of Native life today. In Los Angeles, he explicitly mentioned that

Aaron Glass

although their ancestors traveled in dugout canoes, today they use "cars and planes like everyone else." And although the G̲wa'wina Dancers appeared in regalia to sing and dance on the West Coast, the smaller Kwakwa̲ka'wakw delegation dressed in their everyday clothes in New York and Chicago when discussing the film.

30 One might follow Edward Said (1978), Homi Bhabha (1994), or Michael Taussig (1993) to go further by suggesting that the oppositional idea of the "primitive/indigenous" Native is necessary to the self-construction of the "civilized/modern" colonist—the temporally, spatially, culturally, and racially distanced other that is always at the heart of European expansion.

31 On the modern and colonial dynamics of ethnographic and aesthetic appreciation and/as appropriation of "the primitive," see Clifford (1988); Price (1989); Miller (1991); Hiller (1991); Rushing (1995); Thomas (1999); Jessup (2001).

AFTERWORD

Twentieth Century Fox

PAUL CHAAT SMITH

I cannot believe that thirteen years into the new century, I'm writing an essay about Edward S. Curtis. Well, God knows I need the money and everything, but even so, that guy, still, in 2013!

Let's begin with the obvious truth: nobody shaped how the world thinks about American Indians more than he did. And let's acknowledge that no single person shaped how American Indians think about American Indians more than Edward S. Curtis.

You know those annual lists of the most influential movers and shakers in politics or industry or show business? If they bothered to make such a list for Indians, which they don't, Curtis would rank first not just this year but pretty much every year.

Here's the most important thing to know about Curtis: most of his photographs were taken in the twentieth century, created to make them appear as if they are from the nineteenth. It's amazing how few people know this. Even people reasonably familiar with tiresome ESC controversies don't quite seem to get it. Those photo shoots? He drove there! In his car!

My goodness, has the world ever seen a more successful art project? Curtis transcended photography, anthropology, and even Indians. This is because he provided the winning answer to the question: WTF is it with the Indians? Who are they, what do they want, why are they here?

He answered the question with a captivating and powerful narrative. As Don Gulbrandsen (2010:ix) wrote in *Edward Sheriff Curtis: Visions of the First Americans*, "The faces stare out at you, images seemingly from an ancient time and from a place far, far away…. Yet as you gaze at the faces the humanity becomes apparent, lives filled with dignity but also sadness and loss, representatives of a world that has all but disappeared from our planet."

Ancient. Far, far away. Dignity. Sadness. Loss. (All but) disappeared.

These became the keywords that defined and still define American Indians. The Curtis narrative (and it was never his alone) became a master narrative, and those do much more than simply finish ahead of competing narratives. It obliterated them. The Curtis narrative became the frame, the natural fact, the thing everyone knows, the very definition.

And here's the really magical part: once complete, all evidence of hegemonic narratives as a project seems to disappear, leaving no fingerprints, no scaffolding, no evidence of all planning, hard work, and intent. You forget any other outcome was ever possible.

Curtis didn't disappear, of course. He's more famous than ever, a classic American rock star, yet still vastly underrated. The narrative required him to be a seeker and observer of what was, not a visionary auteur. He wasn't just a talented photographer in the right place at the right time. He dreamed of places that didn't exist, of people that never were, during a time where time didn't exist. Curtis a photographer? That's like calling Neil Armstrong a licensed pilot.

So let's agree that the Curtis archive is vast, amazing, and full of treasures still being discovered, often by Native communities who are productively mining them today. Let's agree that Indians were frequently artistic and commercial collaborators in the Curtis project. And let's agree that as an artist, Curtis was under no obligation to present an accurate view of American Indians. To argue, as I do, that his oeuvre is essentially one big fat lie, may or may not be an interesting point to make (we'll see), but has little bearing on the success of his art. Finally, let's agree that the polarized debate about Curtis needs reinvention, and this volume is part of that effort.

I am someone who knows Curtis pretty much the same way the world knows Curtis. In my case, this was as a suburban Comanche who came of age during the 1970s. Curtis was everywhere. It was the second coming of Curtis, when the US Indian world fell hard for the retraditionalization movement that still holds sway, at least rhetorically, forty years later. That movement was on board with the tenets of Edward Curtis, except for the disappearing thing. But the rest: ancient, dignified, sad, far away? Check, check, check, and check.

I believe that most Indians in the 1970s loved these images for the same reason everyone else did, and I also think there's far less difference between how we saw them and how everyone else saw them. Obviously, the reception would be different for those who recognized ancestors in the photographs, or who were from communities where Curtis spent the most time. For most of us, these Indians weren't familiar; they were exotic. They were generic old-school Indians, and old-school Indians were all the rage. We always looked good in Curtis photographs, and who doesn't like looking good?

So here's the second most important thing to know about Curtis: Indians actually loved the twentieth century. First of all, it had to be better than the last one, right? Here are scenes from the early 1900s: In Washington, Apache terrorist turned celebrity Geronimo rides in President Roosevelt's inauguration. Quanah Parker, the notorious Comanche war chief, is now a rich businessman in the new state of Oklahoma, cutting shrewd deals with ranchers and politicians. In Philadelphia, the Native leaders wearing the latest formal attire fill a ballroom and chart the future of the race. They call themselves the Society of American Indians.

The celebrity war chiefs and the Society of American Indians were not necessarily representative of the society of American Indians, but neither were the idealized Curtis Indians. What would it mean to be an American Indian in the new century? Nobody knew, which must have been thrilling. The possibilities seemed wide open, because if a war criminal like Geronimo could become a beloved American icon, who's to say what the future would bring?

The future was arriving at warp speed, and the pictures that amazed the world learned a new and even more stupendous trick: they began to move and talk. For some Indians, this must have seemed like an excellent development. If a photograph seems more true than a painting, then surely a moving photograph would be more true than a still photograph. Movies could tell the story of actual twentieth-century Indians, or at the very least make it more difficult to lie. Didn't work out that way.

Curtis made us timeless, which meant that we had no past and no future. The entire point of being Indian was about not changing.

There was nothing more or less authentically Indian about cooking with a metal pot or holding a firearm than driving a car, since metal pots and guns were also new to Indians; the stylized nineteenth century was utterly false as well. Curtis branded us. A narrow, rather weird slice of the nineteenth century defines us, even though we've been around for more than ten thousand years. This, I think, was a matter of art direction, "knowing" that Indians and horses go together; guns are okay, clocks and umbrellas are not. It was a nanosecond of the Indian experience, the horses-and-guns thing, and the vast majority of Indians even in the nineteenth century didn't have horses or guns, but it's a fabulous look.

It is revealing that the single most famous Curtis edit is a clock erased from *In a Piegen Lodge* (Zamir, this volume). No need for timepieces in a timeless world.

That's the unique element of objectification of Indians—that to be Indian we cannot be modern. Yes, there's a bit of a gray area, and in theory one can do some modern things, in moderation, and still, technically, be Indian. But at the end of the day, everyone knows that we are a pale imitation of the real thing. It's the all-encompassing definition that makes the Indian situation so different. If we change, we cease to exist.

A 1995 feature film starring Tom Berenger and Barbara Hershey proves instructive. The movie's poster reads, "An ancient tribe hidden from the modern world. Two people must risk their love and their lives to save … the *Last of the Dogmen*." This film arrived in theaters five years after *Dances with Wolves*, and the two movies have much in common. Almost everything, in fact: they are about Indians, and star white couples who seek to protect the Indians from civilization. Barbara Hershey is an anthropologist; Mary McDonnell, her counterpart in *Dances With Wolves*, is a captive. Both Berenger and actor/director Kevin Costner are tough guys who at first have no interest in Indians, but fall for their costars, who find us very interesting. The Indians (Sioux in *Wolves*, Northern Cheyenne in *Dogmen*) are virtually interchangeable. The main difference between the films is that one takes place in the 1990s, and the other takes place in the 1860s.

The dogmen are the descendents of a band of Cheyennes who disappeared into a remote stretch of Montana, around the same time that Costner's lieutenant John Dunbar was roaming the Dakotas. They live the same way their ancestors did, kill any luckless adventurers who enter their territory, have little curiosity about the jet contrails above them, or the hoard of cameras, clocks, guns, radios, and other captured items stashed away in their camp.

A key moment takes place in the camp one evening when Barbara Hershey, the anthropologist who speaks Cheyenne, is asked by the Indians about the status of their people today. The Cheyenne lean forward as she answers, and the film, in its most powerful moment, becomes silent. She speaks with a grave expression, and the camera slowly pans over the faces of the Indians, as they receive the most terrible news imaginable.

We are never told precisely what Hershey's character said, but we imagine the report tells of disease and defeat, confinement to reservations, loss of freedom and culture. That this remnant band represents the only Cheyennes left in the whole world. Not literally, of course. The movie is not stupid; its white characters know that Cheyennes still exist in 1995. But they don't exist like this; they are not true Cheyenne. So these Cheyenne, the real ones, must be protected and preserved at all costs.

Why? Cheyennes weren't doing so bad in 1995. Sure, many of them drank too much, they could have used better schools and more jobs, and they listened to the wrong kinds of country music. But in 1995 there were more Cheyenne human beings alive than at any time in the history of the world.

Cheyennes roamed the planet, enrolled in universities and prisons and corporations; one was even serving in the United States Senate. They drove cars and flew airplanes, spoke Cheyenne, practiced Cheyenne traditions, became anthropologists and filmmakers. Few would take kindly to the idea that they aren't real Cheyennes.

Fifteen years later, Louise Erdrich checked in on the condition of our condition in her tough and surprisingly funny 2009 novel *Shadow Tag*. We're in a Minneapolis kitchen, present-day: Irene America, Anishinabe, failed writer, subject and muse for her husband, Gil, a famous painter of Indians (who is also Indian, sort of). The marriage is failing; they argue a lot. This time, they're arguing about kitsch. Irene tells Gil that it's hopeless, that Indian images are kitsch. "We'll never get the franchise back," she says.

The Curtis images said that Indians and modernism were an impossible and toxic combination; a contradiction in terms, the two could never coexist. They made this definition tangible, real, visible, beautiful, and internationally famous. And they built an ideological fence that kept Indians out of the twentieth century, even in the twenty-first.

The images are indestructible, even by their creator. Curtis himself famously destroyed his original glass negatives to keep them from his wife. Nothing has stopped them so far. Irene America may well be right.

She might also be wrong. As this volume convincingly demonstrates, the Indians in front of Curtis and his camera were never simply props. True, they have been silenced, but they were never silent. Behind every still image and every moving frame is the story of a complex negotiation. Most of these stories are lost to us, but not all, and as we begin to understand the backstory to *Head Hunters*, we can see for the first time just how nuanced and complex these artificially frozen moments actually were, and how much they can teach us.

Paul Chaat Smith

APPENDIX 1

Promotional Images for
In the Land of the Head Hunters

We assume that Curtis provided photographic images to the H. C. Miner Litho Company, which produced most of the extant promotional posters. Here we have paired the posters with likely candidates for their source inspiration. Some were drawn from images later published in Curtis's book, *The Kwakiutl* (*NAI,* vol. 10, 1915). Others may have been based on snapshots taken by Edmund Schwinke on the film set, which closely correspond to scenes in the film. The artist responsible for the posters' designs may possibly be Herbert Andrew Paus, who was illustrating posters for the H. C. Miner Litho Company by 1914 and whose artistic style closely mirrors the Curtis posters' styling (Christy Hansen, Burke Museum, personal correspondence, 2012). In addition, we have included a number of advertisements placed in New York and Seattle newspapers promoting the film premiers in December 1914.

Top: Fig. A.1.1. *In the Land of the Head Hunters* billboard, 1914. 24 pieces; 8 x 20 ft. (assembled). Printed by the H. C. Miner Litho Company, New York (#17676). Private collection.

Bottom: Fig. A.1.2. Original advertising card depicting "The Bridal Party" from *In the Land of the Head Hunters,* ca. 1914. The Seattle Public Library, Photographers Scrapbooks: Asahel & Edward Curtis #180.

Top: Fig. A.1.3. Edward S. Curtis, *Tenaktak Wedding Guests*, 1914. (*NAI,* vol. 10.) Charles Deering McCormick Library of Special Collections, Northwestern University Library.

Bottom: Fig. A.1.4. Edward S. Curtis, *Coming for the Bride*, 1914. (*NAI,* portfolio 10.) Charles Deering McCormick Library of Special Collections, Northwestern University Library.

Top: Fig. A.1.5. House posts by Charlie
James on the set of *Head Hunters*, 1914.
Photo by Edmund Schwinke. Courtesy of
Mick Gidley.

Bottom: Fig. A.1.7. Edward S. Curtis, *A
Tsawatenok House-Front*, 1914. (*NAI,* vol.
10.) Charles Deering McCormick Library
of Special Collections, Northwestern
University Library.

Fig. A.1.6. Edward S. Curtis, *Tenaktak House, Harbledown Island*, 1914.
(*NAI,* vol. 10.) Charles Deering McCormick Library of Special Collections,
Northwestern University Library.

Fig. A.1.8. *In the Land of the Head Hunters* poster for the Casino Theatre featuring a Bear figure, 1914. 14 x 22 in. Private collection.

Fig. A.1.9. House post by Charlie James, from the set of *Head Hunters*, 1914. Photo by Edmund Schwinke. Courtesy of Mick Gidley.

Fig. A.1.10. *In the Land of the Head Hunters*
poster featuring a "Fire Dance," 1914.
14 x 22 in. Private collection.

Fig. A.1.11. Edward S. Curtis,
Nunhltsistalahl—Qagyuhl, 1914.
(*NAI,* vol. 10.) Charles Deering
McCormick Library of Special Collections,
Northwestern University Library.

Fig. A.1.12. *In the Land of the Head Hunters* poster featuring a Hamaťsa Dancer,
1914. 28 x 42 in. Printed by the H. C. Miner Litho Company,
New York (#17664). Private collection.

Top: Fig. A.1.13. Edward S. Curtis, *Hamatsa Emerging from the Woods—Koskimo*, 1914. (*NAI,* vol. 10.) Charles Deering McCormick Library of Special Collections, Northwestern University Library.

Bottom: Fig. A.1.14. Edward Curtis posing in front of house façade and entrance pole on the set of *Head Hunters*, 1914. Photo by Edmund Schwinke. Courtesy of Mick Gidley.

Fig. A.1.15. World Film Corporation poster featuring the battle on the cliff from *Head Hunters*, 1914. 42 x 56 in. Private collection.

Figs. A.1.16a and A.1.16b. Playbill for a screening of
Head Hunters at Carnegie Hall, February 9, 1915.
Private collection.

Fig. A.1.17. Advertisement for *Head Hunters*, December 5, 1914, *Seattle Times*.

Fig. A.1.18. Advertisement for *Head Hunters*, December 6, 1914, *Seattle Post Intelligencer*.

Fig. A.1.19. Story and advertisement for *Head Hunters*, December 6, 1914, *Seattle Post Intelligencer*.

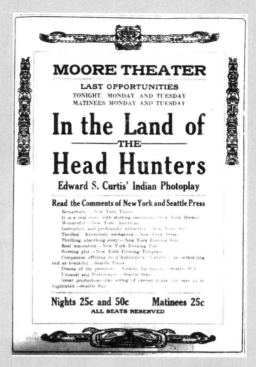

Fig. A.1.20. Advertisement for *Head Hunters*, December 7, 1914, *Seattle Times*.

Fig. A.1.22. Advertisement for *Head Hunters*, December 13, 1914, *Seattle Post Intelligencer*.

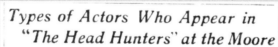

Fig. A.1.21. Advertisement for *Head Hunters*, December 13, 1914, *Seattle Post Intelligencer*.

Fig. A.1.23. Advertisement for *Head Hunters* in distribution,
February 20, 1915, *The Moving Picture World*.

APPENDIX 2

The Kwakwa̱ka'wakw Cast and Crew of *In the Land of the Head Hunters*

This list includes the known actors and crew members in the film—listed after their italicized character names, with their various aliases in Kwakwala and English, and their band affiliations (in square brackets)—as identified by elderly Kwakwa̱ka'wakw in the late 1960s. The list was compiled from multiple sources: (1) Holm and Quimby (1980:57–61, 71, 82), although we updated their orthography for writing Kwak̓wala to the system developed by the U'mista Cultural Society; (2) two documentary films containing interviews with surviving cast members: a short accompanying the release of *In the Land of the War Canoes* (1973), and T. C. McLuhans's *The Shadow Catcher* (1974); and (3) personal correspondence with William Wasden Jr. and Bill Holm. Identifying people by their Kwak̓wala names can be difficult due to a number of factors: many individuals have more than one name at any given time in their life (including everyday names, nicknames, hereditary titles, ceremonial titles, and so on) and are bestowed new names periodically; multiple individuals often carry the same Kwak̓wala name; and orthographies for spelling Kwak̓wala words have been inconsistent over the past century. As a consequence, some of the Kwak̓wala names listed here were held by the individuals at the time of filming in 1913/14, while others may have been common terms for them at the time of identification in the late 1960s.

Motana:

Stanley Hunt/Liḷalgamlilas [Kwagu'ł]

Naida:

Margaret (Maggie) Wilson Frank/U'magalis [Kwagu'ł]

Naida and a Na̱'nalalał Dancer:

Sarah Constance Smith Hunt/Ṫḷakwagilayugwa/Abaya/Mrs. David Hunt/
later Mrs. Mungo Martin [Ławitsis]

Naida and the Sorcerer's Daughter:

Mrs. George Walkus/G̱wikilayugwa [Gwa'sala]

Kenada:

Paddy 'Malid/Ḵamgidi ['Nak̓waxda'x̱w]

Waket, Yaklus, and a village-mate of Motana:

Balutsa (a Kwak̓wala-ization of the English family name "Brotchie")
['Nak̓waxda'x̱w]

Sorcerer:

Kwagwanu/Ha'etḷa'las/Long Harry [Kwagu'ł/'Nak̓waxda'x̱w]

Clam digger, captive, wedding dancer
(and prop/clothing maker):
Francine Hunt/Ṫḷaiḷa'ławidzamga/Tsak̓wani/Mrs. George Hunt
['Nak̓waxda'x̱w]

Fisherman who drops a paddle on the rocks:
Bob Wilson/I'dansu [Kwagu'ł]

Extras:

A'widi ['Nak̓waxda'x̱w]

Alfred "Skookum" Charlie/Gix̱sistalisama'yi ['Nak̓waxda'x̱w]

Jonathan (Johnny) Hunt/K̓wak̓wabalasama'yi [Kwagu'ł]

Helen Wilson Knox/Ḷalandzawik/"Nunu" [Kwagu'ł]

Emily Hunt Wilson/G̱wiḵamgi'lakw [Kwagu'ł]

Yaxyagidzamga [unknown affiliation]

APPENDIX 3

Curtis Film Props in the Collection of the Burke Museum of Natural History and Culture

This list includes all of the known props from *In the Land of the Head Hunters* currently in the collection of the Burke Museum of Natural History and Culture in Seattle, Washington. The first three masks, having been identified by Bill Holm, were purchased in 2007 from Jeffrey Myers Primitive Arts in New York (accession #2007-124). The rest of the items, along with photographic equipment not included here, were purchased by the Burke Museum (then the Washington State Museum) in 1927 from J. S. Marcusson after having been placed in storage for a number of years by the Curtis Studio and then sold for storage charges (accession #2162). While it is possible that some of these items were in use by Kwakwaka'wakw community members at the time of filming in 1913-14, the vast majority were commissioned by Curtis for the film and taken with him after its completion. Many are recorded in the account book kept by George Hunt when he was employed as Curtis's assistant during the film's production (in Holm and Quimby 1980:127–28). All objects are accompanied by their Burke Museum catalogue numbers, materials, and dimensions where recorded. Photographs of all of the objects are available in the museum's online database at http://www.burkemuseum. org/ethnology.

> *Hokhokw Mask* (2007-124/1). Cedar, paint, shredded cedar bark, and string, H: 13.5 in., W: 10 in., L: 64.25 in. (See fig. 15.11.)
>
> *Hokhokw Mask* (2007-124/2). Cedar, paint, shredded cedar bark, and string, H: 13 in., W: 10 in., L: 52.25 in. (See fig. 15.11.)
>
> *Raven Mask* (2007-124/3). Cedar, paint, shredded cedar bark, and string, H: 11.5 in., W: 9.5 in., L: 33.75 in. (See fig. 15.11.)
>
> *Head Ring* (7711). Cedar bark, diam: 23 in, H: 8 in.

Neck Ring (7712). Cedar bark, diam: 31 in, H: 20 in.

Arm Ring (7713). Cedar bark, string, and leather, H: 3 in., W: 5 in., L: 8 in.

Arm Ring (7714). Cedar bark, string, and leather, H: 3.5 in., W: 5.5 in., L: 8.5 in.

Ankle Ring (7715). Cedar bark, string, and leather, H: 5 in., W: 7.5 in., L: 10 in.

Ankle Ring (7715). Cedar bark, string, and leather, H: 4 in., W: 5.5 in., L: 10 in.

Dance Apron (7717). Cedar bark, W: 10 in., L: 17 in.

Neck Ring (7718). Cedar bark, no dimensions.

Neck Ring (7719). Cedar bark, diam: 15.75 in. (Fig. A.3.1.)

Head Ring (7720). Cedar bark, H: 4 in., W: 7.5 in., L: 9 in. (Fig. A.3.2.)

Head Ring (7721). Cedar bark, diam: 7.75 in., H: 4 in. (See fig. 15.11.)

Head Ring (7722). Cedar bark, diam: 8 in., H: 3.5 in.

Head Ring (7723). Cedar bark, cloth, and string, no dimensions.

Arm Ring (7724). Cedar bark, no dimensions.

Arm Ring (7725). Cedar bark and leather, H: 1 in., W: 4.5 in.

Cedar Bark Bundle (7726). Cedar bark, L: 31.5 in., W: 2.75 in.

Neck Ring (7727). Cedar bark and raffia, no dimensions.

Dance Apron (7728). Raffia, no dimensions.

Neck Ring (7729). Raffia, diam: 12 in.

Neck Ring (7730). Raffia, diam: 13 in.

Neck Ring (7731). Raffia, diam: 13 in.

Neck Ring (7732). Raffia, No dimensions.

Head Ring (7733). Cedar bark and raffia, H: 1.4 in., W: 9.4.00 in.

Head Ring (7734). Raffia, H: 1.3 in., W: 9.6 in.

Finger Rings (7735). Raffia, H: 0.3 in., W: 3 in.

Headband (7736). Cedar bark, dentalium, ermine, and abalone, diam: 10 in.

Head Ring Tassel (7737). Cedar bark, metal, and string, W: 5.25 in., L: 8 in.

Basketry Hat (7738). Spruce root and paint, diam: 16.5 in, H: 8 in. (See fig. 15.11.)

Basketry Hat (7739). Spruce root and paint, no dimensions. (Fig. A.3.3.)

Drum (7740). Hide and wood, no dimensions. (Fig. A.3.4.)

Whalebone Club (7741). Whalebone, no dimensions.

Whalebone Club (7742). Whalebone, no dimensions.

Whalebone Club (7743). Whalebone, H: 2.5 in., W: 4 in., L: 24.25 in. (Fig. A.3.5.)

Club (7744). Wood and paint, no dimensions.

Club (7745). Wood and paint, diam: 3.75 in., L: 14.5 in.

Club (7746). Wood and paint, W: 3.75 in., L: 14.5 in. (Fig. A.3.6)

Dagger (7747). Steel, wood, and twine, L: 23 in. (See fig. 15.11.)

Arrow Shafts (7748). Wood, feathers, and string, no dimensions.

Dunsik Boards (7749). Wood, paint, and metal,
W: 16 in., L: 31.5 in., three sections. (See fig. 15.11.)

Dunsik Boards (7750). Wood, paint, and metal,
W: 16 in., L: 31.5 in., three sections. (See fig. 15.11.)

Dunsik Boards (7751). Wood, paint, and metal,
W: 16 in., L: 31.5 in., three sections. (See fig. 15.11.)

Dunsik Boards (7752). Wood, paint, and metal,
W: 15.5 in., L: 80 in., three sections combined. (See fig. 15.11.)

Dunsik Boards (7753). Wood, paint, and metal, no dimensions. (See fig. 15.11.)

Dunsik Boards (7754). Wood, paint, and metal, no dimensions. (See fig. 15.11.)

Chest (7755). Cedar, no dimensions. (Fig. A.3.7)

Fig. A.3.1

Fig. A.3.2

CURTIS FILM PROPS

Fig. A.3.3

Fig. A.3.4

Fig. A.3.5

Fig. A.3.6

Fig. A.3.7

APPENDIX 3

APPENDIX 4

Title Cards from the 2008 Reconstruction of
In the Land of the Head Hunters

The majority of title cards present in the current reconstruction of the film, undertaken in 2008 by the UCLA Film & Television Archive, are maintained verbatim from the extant print held by The Field Museum; these are presented below without further notation. Additional titles (marked with an asterisk, or *) were taken from the newly discovered nitrate reels at the UCLA Film & Television Archive, which have been integrated with the Field footage. A number of titles (marked with a dagger, or †) were drawn from a preliminary scenario provided by the Getty Research Institute (available at www.curtisfilm.rutgers.edu) to describe extant footage that was missing title cards, or to introduce missing footage represented in the reconstruction by Library of Congress copyright frames. Additional titles were reconstructed from archival sources as indicated in endnotes. Brad Evans (1998) has published a detailed comparison of the title cards from The Field Museum's print and from the 1973 reedited version, *In the Land of the War Canoes*.

1. IN THE LAND OF THE HEAD HUNTERS has been preserved from two heavily-worn, decomposing, and incomplete prints. Missing shots have been bridged with stills and enlargements from surviving frames. Original title cards have been re-created. Text for missing titles was derived from preliminary lists found in an early synopsis of the film.[1]

2. THE WORLD FILM CORPORATION presents IN THE LAND OF THE HEAD HUNTERS A Drama of Primitive Life on the Shores of the North Pacific[2]

3. From Story Written and Picture Made by Edward S. Curtis
   Produced by The Seattle Film Co., Inc.

4. Part I: The Vigil of Motana

5. Principal characters of the play
   Kenada, Chief of Watsulis Village
   Motana, Son of Kenada
   Waket, Chief of Paas Village

Naida, Daughter of Waket

Yaklus, Warrior-Chief of Yilis Village

The Sorcerer, Brother of Yaklus

The Sorcerer's Daughter

A Young Slave

6. Kenada, Chief of Watsulis Village.[3]

7. Motana, Son of Kenada.

8. Waket, Chief of Paas Village.

9. Naida, Daughter of Waket.

10. Yaklus, Warrior-Chief of Yilis Village.

11. The Sorcerer, Brother of Yaklus.

12. The Sorcerer's Daughter.

13. Grizzly-bear Dancer.

14. Mountain-goat Dancer.

15. Wasp Dancer.

16. "Go my son, the time has come to prove your manhood. Build mountain prayer fires to call the spirits. Go far to the forest island of the dead that those of the spirit world give you power. Capture then the whale and the sea lion to prove your courage. Go my son."

17. Motana lands on an island to build his first prayer fire. In a dream appears a maid.

18. It is Naida, the maid of his dream. He gives her a love token.

19. Motana overtakes Naida, and as they walk along hand in hand they are watched by the jealous Sorcerer, to whom Naida has been promised by her father, Waket.

20. "Oh! that I might go with you walking hand in hand along that misty path of copper."

21. "It is a tribal law that in the vigil no thought may be given to women. Now I must renew my vigil. First I will visit the Island of the Dead."

22. Motana continues his vigil by journeying to the Island of the Dead.

23. Through the night he sleeps in the gruesome house of skulls.

24. With his slave he goes in quest of sea lions.

25. After weeks of preparation Motana emerges from the forest and leads a whaling expedition.

26. Awarding the portions.

27. The Sorcerer and his assistant magicians plot to destroy Motana; and they send a messenger for the Sorcerer's daughter.

28. "Get a lock of Motana's hair and with it we will make magic to destroy him."

29. For his final invocation to the gods, Motana again builds the sacred fire on the heights.

30. The Sorcerer's Daughter resolves to spare the handsome youth and make him love her.

31. "Depart! I am not thinking of women, but of the spirits!"

32. Motana discovers the theft.

APPENDIX 4

384

33. The Sorcerer determines to destroy the life of Motana by evil magic.

34. "Let Motana rot as his hair rots with these toads!"

35. Motana, after many trials and many dangers, returns triumphant to his father.

36. Motana tells of his love for Naida, and of the Sorcerer's threats and efforts to take his life.†

37. En route to ask Naida in marriage, and to take vengeance on the Sorcerer.†

38. Messengers go to demand Naida.†

39. "Naida is promised to the Sorcerer. If you want her, bring his head as a marriage offering."†

40. Kenada and his men start to Yilis, to take the head of the Sorcerer.†

41. The battle.†

42. Kenada brings the head of the Sorcerer and demands Naida.

43. The bridegroom's party starts to the wedding.

44. Approach of the bridegroom's party.†

45. The wedding.

46. Waket's dance of acceptance.

47. A rival chief's spokesman accepts a challenge to drink fish oil.

48. End of Part I

49. Part 2

50. Return of the wedding party to Watsulis.†

51. The wedding party enters Kenada's house through the Raven's mouth.†

52. Enraged by the death of his brother, the Sorcerer, Yaklus runs "Pahupaku" (*mad for blood and heads*). Now he is really Yaklus, the short life bringer.

53. By ancient custom a war party destroys whomever it meets, friend or foe. Yaklus first sights and destroys a fishing party.

54. Next they attack a party of clam-diggers and carry away the young women for slaves.

55. A band of travellers are now sighted and destroyed.

56. Yaklus, with his fiend-like warriors, attacks and destroys the village of Motana.

57. Death of Kenada.

58. The burning of Watsulis.*

59. Survivors return to the smouldering ruins.*

60. They hear Motana's cry of distress.*

61. The Medicine Man sings over Motana until consciousness returns.*

62. The Sing-Gamble game at the village of Yaklus is interrupted. The victorious war-party is sighted.

63. In honor of the victory, Yaklus gives a dance.

64. In concealment are dancers clothed as mythic animals and monsters.

65. Wind Dancer.

66. Thunderbird Dancer.⁴

67. Fire Dance. The Fire Dancer hates fire and destroys it with bare hands and feet. Attendants restrain him.

68. Bear, Wolf, Mountain Goat, Wasp, and Dog.

69. Each wreath symbolizes a captured head. *5

70. Bring in Naida.*

71. Yaklus is won by the dance of Naida. He cuts the rope from her neck and will keep her as his slave.*

72. The slave of Naida comes in with a plan of flight. She sends her love token to Motana.*

73. Naida's slave escapes from the house of Yaklus and is pursued.*

74. To avoid the trailers in the forest, he takes to the water when the day breaks.*

75. Though wounded by an arrow, he continues his flight.*6

76. "Who will help rescue my wife?"

77. Motana creeps up to the house of Yaklus.

78. Naida steals the knife of the sleeping Yaklus that she may kill her captor. The coming of Motana stays her hand.

79. Motana leads his pursuers into the roaring gorge of Hyal, where drowns the fearful Yaklus.

80. Finis.7

81. IN THE LAND OF THE HEAD HUNTERS has been restored by UCLA FILM & TELEVISION ARCHIVE in cooperation with THE FIELD MUSEUM OF NATURAL HISTORY

82. Funding provided by
THE NATIONAL FILM PRESERVATION FOUNDATION
THE STANFORD THEATRE FOUNDATION

83. Laboratory Services
THE STANFORD THEATRE FILM LABORATORY
TITLE HOUSE DIGITAL
YCM LABORATORIES

84. Special Thanks to
ERIC AIJALA
MARK ALLAN
MELISSA ANDERSON
ELIZABETH BABCOCK
JILLIAN BORDERS
THE BURKE MUSEUM OF NATURAL HISTORY AND CULTURE
DEANNA COSTANZO
RICHARD DAYTON
MELISSA ELLIOTT
ARMAND ESAI
BRAD EVANS
JAMES FRIEDMAN
THE GETTY RESEARCH INSTITUTE
DAVID GILBERT

ROBERT GITT
AARON GLASS
BRIAN GRANEY
JERE GULDIN
SEAN HEWITT

86. BILL HOLM
CHARLES HOPKINS
MARGARET KIECKHEFER
THE LIBRARY OF CONGRESS
MASIS MARKAR
MIKE MASHON
CHARLES McDONALD
ANNETTE MELVILLE
DAVID W. PACKARD
EDDIE RICHMOND

87. DAVID SHEPARD
ZORAN SINOBAD
RICHARD SMITH
KAREN STOKES
ROB STONE
ED WEYER
BARBARA WHITEHEAD
TODD WIENER
HUGO ZEITER
KATJA ZELLJADT

1   This note was added by the UCLA Film & Television Archive to contextualize the new reconstruction.

2   Both extant portions of the film are missing the opening credits. Titles 2 and 3 were reconstructed based on wording present on archival publicity material for the film (see appendix 1; Holm and Quimby 1980). The layout and logos were adapted from other World Film Corporation releases of the same period.

3   Title nos. 6 through 15, with the exception of 9, were reconstructed based on three sources. Preliminary scenarios preserved at the Getty Research Institute list character cards such as these (see www.curtisfilm.rutgers.edu). Title 9, "Naida, Daughter of Waket," followed by the portrait of her, survives in The Field Museum print, suggesting that every character had a similar introduction. Finally, there are Library of Congress copyright deposit frames of the other characters and masked figures. The template of title 9 was thus extrapolated to the remaining characters using the Library of Congress frames with the addition of new title cards identifying them.

4   Following card 66 ("Thunderbird Dancer"), The Field Museum's print has two title cards that say "End of Reel Three" and "Part Four," which were not included in the current reconstruction as they were determined not to be part of the original film.

5   It is possible that this title card and/or the footage that follows it is out of order in the current reconstruction—or was out of order in the original film—as there is also footage of the men dancing with wreaths just after the current card 63 ("In honor of the victory, Yaklus gives a dance").

6   This title card is present in The Field Museum's print, but it is out of sequence there (Evans 1998:239).

7   While missing from both extant prints, other World Film Corporation films of the period ended with a simple "Finis" card.

REFERENCES

Abel, Richard. 2006. *Americanizing the Movies and "Movie-Mad" Audiences, 1910–1914.* Berkeley: University of California Press.

Abraham, Otto, and Erich M. von Hornbostel. 1906 [1975]. "Phonographirte Indianermelodieen aus Britisch-Columbia." In *Anthropological Papers Written in Honor of Franz Boas,* 447–74. New York: Stechert. Translated by Bruno Nettl as "Indian Melodies from British Columbia Recorded on the Phonograph." In *Hornbostel Opera Omnia,* vol. 1, edited by Klaus P. Wachsmann, Dieter Christensen, and Peter Reinecke, 299–322. The Hague: EMartinus Nijhoff.

Aitken, Ian. 1990. *Film & Reform: John Grierson and the Documentary Film Movement.* London: Routledge.

Aleiss, Angela. 2005. *Making the White Man's Indian: Native Americans and Hollywood Movies.* Westport, CT: Praeger Publishers.

Allen, Graham. 2011 [2000]. *Intertextuality.* Reprint, London: Routledge.

Altman, Rick. 1996. "The Silence of the Silents." *Musical Quarterly* 80 (4): 648–718.

————. 2004. *Silent Film Sound.* New York: Columbia University Press.

Anonymous. 1927. *Who's Who in Washington State: A Compilation of Biographical Sketches of Men and Women Prominent in the Affairs of Washington State.* Seattle: Arthur H. Allen.

Anthes, Bill. 2006. *Native Moderns: American Indian Painting, 1940–1960.* Durham, NC: Duke University Press.

Appadurai, Arjun. 1996. *Modernity at Large: Cultural Dimensions of Globalization.* Minneaplis: University of Minnesota Press.

Asad, Talal. 1973. *Anthropology and the Colonial Encounter.* Reading, UK: Ithaca Press.

Askren, Mique'l. 2007. "Bringing Our History into Focus: Re-developing the Work of B. A. Haldane, 19th-Century Tsimshian Photographer." *Backflash* 24 (3): 41–47.

Austin, John L. 1976. *How to Do Things with Words.* Oxford: Oxford University Press.

Baker, Theodore. 1882 [1976]. *Über die Musik der Nordamerikanischen Wilden.* Leipzig: Breitkopf & Härtel. Translated by Ann Buckley as *On the Music of the North American Indians.* Source Materials and Studies in Ethnomusicology 9. Buren, The Netherlands: F. Knuf.

Bakhtin, M. M. 1986 [1979]. "The Problem of Speech Genres." In *Speech Genres and Other Late Essays,* edited by Caryl Emerson and Michael Holquist, 60–102. Austin: University of Texas Press.

Bauman, Richard. 2011. "'Better than Any Monument': Envisioning Museums of the Spoken Word." *Museum Anthropology Review* 5 (1–2): 1–13.

Becker, Paula. 2007. "Walla Walla Symphony Orchestra Holds Its First Concert on December 12, 1907." *HistoryLink.org Online Encyclopedia of Washington State History,* essay no. 8342. Accessed March 12, 2013. http://www.historylink.org/index.cfm?DisplayPage=output.cfm&file_id=8342.

388

Benjamin, Walter. 1980. "A Short History of Photography." In *Classic Essays on Photography,* edited by Alan Trachtenberg, 199–216. Stony Creek, CT: Leete's Island Books.

———. 1999. "Franz Kafka." In *Part 2, 1927–1934,* vol. 2 of *Selected Writings,* edited by Michael W. Jennings, Howard Eiland, and Gary Smith, 794–820. Cambridge, MA: The Belknap Press of Harvard University Press.

Ben Naftali, Michal. 2007. "The Story of a Friendship: The Archive and the Question of Palestine." In *Judeities: Questions for Jacques Derrida,* edited by Bettina Bergo, 78–110. New York: Fordam University Press.

Bennett, Tony. 1995. *The Birth of the Museum: History, Theory, Politics.* London: Routledge.

Berlin, Gabriele, and Artur Simon, eds. 2002. *Music Archiving in the World: Papers Presented at the Conference on the Occasion of the 100th Anniversary of the Berlin Phonogramm-Archiv.* Berlin: VWB (Verlag für Wissenschaft und Bildung).

Berman, Judith. 1994. "George Hunt and the Kwak̓wala Texts." *Anthropological Linguistics* 36 (4): 483–514.

———. 1996. "'The Culture as It Appears to the Indian Himself': Boas, George Hunt, and the Methods of Ethnography." In *Volksgeist as Method and Ethic: Essays on Boasian Ethnography and the German Anthropological Tradition,* edited by George W. Stocking, Jr., 215–56. Madison: University of Wisconsin Press.

Berman, Marshall. 1982. *All That Is Solid Melts into Air: The Experience of Modernity.* New York: Simon and Schuster.

Bhabha, Homi K. 1994 [1988]. *The Location of Culture.* London: Routledge.

Blackman, Margaret. 1982. "The Afterimage and the Image After: Visual Documents and the Renaissance in Northwest Coast Art." *American Indian Art Magazine* 7 (2): 30–39.

———. 1990. "Facing the Future, Envisioning the Past: Visual Literature and Contemporary Northwest Coast Masks." *Arctic Anthropology* 27 (2): 27–40.

Boas, Franz. 1897. "The Social Organization and the Secret Societies of the Kwakiutl Indians." *Report of the U.S. National Museum under the Direction of the Smithsonian Institution for the Year Ending June 30, 1895,* 311–738. Washington, DC: Government Printing Office.

———. 1921. "Ethnology of the Kwakiutl: Based on Data Collected by George Hunt." *35th Annual Report of the Bureau of American Ethnology for the Years 1913–1914,* 793–1451. Washington, DC: Government Printing Office.

———. 1966. *Kwakiutl Ethnography.* Edited by Helen Codere. Chicago: University of Chicago Press.

———. 1974. *A Franz Boas Reader: The Shaping of American Anthropology, 1883–1911.* Edited by George Stocking. Chicago: University of Chicago Press.

Bourdieu, Pierre. 1993. *The Field of Cultural Production: Essays on Art and Literature.* New York: Columbia University Press.

Bowser, Eileen. 1990. *The Transformation of Cinema, 1907–1915.* Berkeley: University of California Press.

Bracken, Christopher. 1997. *The Potlatch Papers: A Colonial Case History.* Chicago: University of Chicago Press.

Braddock, Alan C. 2009. *Thomas Eakins and the Cultures of Modernity.* Berkeley: University of California Press.

Brady, Erika. 1999. *A Spiral Way: How the Phonograph Changed Ethnography.* Jackson, MS: University Press of Mississippi.

Bramen, Carrie Tirado. 2000. *The Uses of Variety: Modern Americanism and the Quest for National Distinctiveness.* Cambridge, MA: Harvard University Press.

Briggs, Charles L., and Richard Bauman. 1992. "Genre, Intertextuality and Social Power." *Journal of Linguistic Anthropology* 2 (2): 131–72.

Brody, J. J. 1997. *Pueblo Indian Painting: Tradition and Modernism in New Mexico, 1900–1930.* Santa Fe: School of American Research Press.

REFERENCES

Browne, Colin. 1979. *Motion Picture Production in British Columbia, 1898–1940: A Brief Historical Background and Catalogue.* British Columbia Provincial Museum Heritage Record no. 6. Victoria: British Columbia Provincial Museum.

Browner, Tara. 1995. "Transposing Cultures: The Appropriation of Native American Musics, 1890–1990." PhD dissertation, University of Michigan.

Bunn-Marcuse, Kathryn. 2005. "Kwakwa̲ka'wakw on Film." In *Walking a Tightrope: Aboriginal People and Their Representations*, edited by Ute Lischke and David McNab, 305-35. Waterloo, ON: Wilfrid Laurier University Press.

Burton, Frederick R. 1908. *American Primitive Music, with Special Attention to the Songs of the Ojibways.* New York: Moffat, Yard.

Buscombe, Edward. 2006. *"Injuns!" Native Americans in the Movies.* London: Reaktion Books.

Buscombe, Edward, and Roberta E. Pearson, eds. 1998. *Back in the Saddle Again: New Essays on the Western.* London: British Film Institute.

Bush, Stephen. 1914. "'In the Land of the Head Hunters': Remarkable Motion Picture Produced by Edward S. Curtis, Famous Authority on North American Indians." *Moving Picture World* 22 (December 19): 1685.

Butler, Judith. 1990a. "Performative Acts and Gender Constitution: An Essay in Phenomenology and Feminist Theory." In *Performing Feminisms: Feminist Critical Theory and Theatre,* edited by S. E. Case, 270–82. Baltimore, MD: Johns Hopkins University Press.

———. 1990b. *Gender Trouble: Feminism and the Subversion of Identity.* New York: Routledge.

Cannizzo, Jeanne. 1983. "George Hunt and the Invention of Kwakiutl Culture." *Canadian Review of Sociology and Anthropology* 20: 44–58.

Cheuse, Alan. 2008. *To Catch the Lightning: A Novel of American Dreaming.* Naperville, IN: Sourcebooks Landmark.

Church, R. A. 1975. "Nineteenth-Century Clock Technology in Britain, the United States, and Switzerland." *Economic History Review* 28 (4): 616–30.

Clements, Marie, and Susan Leistner. 2010. *The Edward Curtis Project: A Modern Picture Story.* Vancouver, BC: Talonbooks.

Clifford, James. 1988. *The Predicament of Culture: Twentieth-Century Ethnography, Literature, and Art.* Cambridge, MA: Harvard University Press.

———. 2004. "Looking Several Ways: Anthropology and Native Heritage in Alaska." *Current Anthropology* 45 (1): 5–30.

Clifford, James, and George Marcus, eds. 1986. *Writing Culture: The Poetics and Politics of Ethnography.* Berkeley: University of California Press.

Codere, Helen. 1961. "Kwakiutl." In *Perspectives in American Indian Culture Change,* edited by Edward H. Spicer, 431–516. Chicago: University of Chicago Press.

Cohen, Norm, and Paul F. Wells. 1982. "Native American Traditions: Amerindian." In *Ethnic Recordings in America: A Neglected Heritage,* 180–84. Washington, DC: American Folklife Center, Library of Congress.

Cole, Douglas. 1985. *Captured Heritage: The Scramble for Northwest Coast Artifacts.* Seattle: University of Washington Press.

———. 1999. *Franz Boas: The Early Years, 1858–1906.* Vancouver, BC: Douglas & McIntyre.

Cole, Douglas, and Ira Chaikin. 1990. *An Iron Hand Upon the People: The Law Against the Potlatch on the Northwest Coast.* Vancouver, BC: Douglas and McIntyre.

Cole, Douglas, and Christine Mullins. 1993. "'Haida Ida': The Musical World of Ida Halpern." *BC Studies: The British Columbian Quarterly* 97: 3–37.

Coleman, A. D. 1972. "Curtis: His Work." In *Edward S. Curtis, Portraits from North American Indian Life,* edited by A. D. Coleman and T. C. McLuhan, v–vii. New York: Promontory Press.

———. 1979. *Light Readings: A Photography Critic's Writings, 1968–1978.* New York: Oxford University Press.

———. 1998. "Edward S. Curtis: The Photographer as Ethnologist." In *Depth of Field: Essays on Photography, Mass Media, and Lens Culture,* 133–58. Albuquerque: University of New Mexico Press.

Comaroff, Jean, and John Comaroff. 2009. *Ethnicity, Inc.* Chicago: University of Chicago Press.

Condon, Richard G. 1989. "The History and Development of Arctic Photography." *Arctic Anthropology* 26 (1): 46–87.

Cooke, Mervyn. 2008. *A History of Film Music.* New York: Cambridge University Press.

Coombes, Annie, ed. 2006. *Rethinking Settler Colonialism.* Manchester, UK: Manchester University Press.

Curtis, Edward S. 1907–30. *The North American Indian.* Edited by Frederick Webb Hodge. 20 vols. Cambridge, MA: University Press / and Norwood, MA: Plimpton Press.

———. 1907. "My Work in Indian Photography." *Photographic Times* 39: 195–98.

———. 1914a. "Plea for Haste in Making Documentary Records of the American Indian." *American Museum Journal* 14 (4): 163–65.

———. 1914b. *Indian Days of the Long Ago.* Yonkers-on-Hudson, NY: World Book Company.

———. 1915. *In the Land of the Head-Hunters.* Yonkers-on-Hudson, NY: World Book Company.

———. 1997. *The North American Indian: The Complete Portfolios.* Edited by Hans Christian Adam. Cologne, Germany: Taschen.

———. 2000. *Edward S. Curtis: Contemporary Prints from Original Glass Plate Negatives [in the Capitol One Collection].* Claremont, CA: Claremont Graduate University.

Dauenhauer, Nora Marks. 1995. "Tlingit *At.oów*: Traditions and Concepts." In *The Spirit Within: Northwest Coast Native Art from the John. H. Hauberg Collection,* edited by Helen Abbott, Steve Brown, Lorna Price, and Paula Thurman, 20–30. Seattle: Seattle Art Museum.

Davis, Barbara A. 1985. *Edward S. Curtis: The Life and Times of a Shadow Catcher.* San Francisco: Chronicle Books.

De Brigard, Emilie. 1995. "The History of Ethnographic Film." In *Principles of Visual Anthropology.* 2nd ed. Edited by Paul Hockings, 13–44. New York: Mouton de Gruyter.

Deloria, Philip. 1998. *Playing Indian.* New Haven, CT: Yale University Press.

———. 2004. *Indians in Unexpected Places.* Lawrence: University Press of Kansas.

Deloria, Vine, Jr. 1988 [1969]. *Custer Dies for Your Sins: An Indian Manifesto.* Reprint, Norman: University of Oklahoma Press.

Dilworth, Leah. 1996. *Imagining Indians in the Southwest: Persistent Visions of a Primitive Past.* Washington, DC: Smithsonian Institution Press.

Dippie, Brian W. 1991 [1982]. *The Vanishing American: White Attitudes and U.S. Indian Policy.* 2nd ed. Lawrence: University Press of Kansas.

Dominguez, Virginia. 1992. "Invoking Culture: The Messy Side of 'Cultural Politics.'" *South Atlantic Quarterly* 91 (1): 19–42.

Dreiser, Theodore. 2006 [1900]. *Sister Carrie.* New York: W. W. Norton Company.

Earle, William H. 1983. "November 18, 1883: The Day that Noon Showed Up on Time." *Smithsonian Magazine* (November): 193–208.

Edwards, Elizabeth. 2001. *Raw Histories: Photographs, Anthropology, and Museums.* London: Berg.

Egan, Shannon. 2006. "'Yet in a Primitive Condition:' Edward S. Curtis's *North American Indian.*" *American Art* 20 (3): 58–83.

Egan, Timothy. 2012. *Short Nights of the Shadow Catcher: The Epic Life and Immortal Photographs of Edward Curtis.* Boston: Houghton Mifflin Harcourt.

Emerson, P. H. 1980. "Hints on Art." In *Classic Essays on Photography,* edited by Alan Trachtenberg, 99–105. Stony Creek, CT: Leete's Island Books.

Erdrich, Louise. 2009. *Shadow Tag.* New York: Harper Perennial.

Etten, William J. 1926. *A Citizens' History of Grand Rapids, Michigan, with Program of the Campau Centennial.* Grand Rapids, MI: A. P. Johnson Company. Accessed July 4, 2010. http://kent.migenweb.net/etten1926/index.html.

Evans, Brad. 1998. "Commentary: Catherine Russell's Recovery of the *Head-Hunters.*" *Visual Anthropology* 11 (3): 221–41.

———. 2005. *Before Cultures: The Ethnographic Imagination in American Literature, 1865–1920.* Chicago: University of Chicago Press.

———. 2007. "Introduction: Rethinking the Disciplinary Confluence of Anthropology and Literary Studies." *Criticism* 49 (4): 429–45.

Fabian, Johannes. 2002 [1983]. *Time and the Other: How Anthropology Makes Its Object.* New York: Columbia University Press.

Faris, James. 1993. "The Navajo Photography of Edward S. Curtis." *History of Photography* 17 (4): 377–87.

———. 1996. *Navajo and Photography: A Critical History of the Representations of an American People.* Albuquerque: University of New Mexico Press.

Feaster, Patrick, and Jacob Smith. 2009. "Reconfiguring the History of Early Cinema through the Phonograph, 1877–1908." *Film History* 21 (4): 311–25.

Fienup-Riordan, Ann. 2003. *Freeze Frame: Alaska Eskimos in the Movies.* Seattle: University of Washington Press.

Fischer, Edgar S. 1908. "Note on the Indian Music." In Edward S. Curtis, *The North American Indian,* vol. 3, 142–50.

Flaherty, Robert J. 1922. "How I Filmed *Nanook of the North.*" *World's Work* (October): 632–40.

Fletcher, Alice C., and Francis LaFlesche. 1893. "A Study of Omaha Indian Music." *Archaeological and Ethnological Papers of the Peabody Museum, Harvard University* 1 (1): 233–384.

Ford, Clellan. 1941. *Smoke from Their Fires: The Life of a Kwakiutl Chief.* New Haven, CT: Yale University Press.

Franceschina, John Charles. 2003. *David Braham: The American Offenbach.* New York: Routledge.

Frascina, Francis, Tamar Garb, Nigel Blake, and Briony Fer. 1993. *Modernity and Modernism: French Painting in the Nineteenth Century.* New Haven, CT: Yale University Press.

Furst, William. 1916. "Musical Setting for the Photoplay *Let Katie Do It.*" *Triangle Plays.* New York: G. Schirmer for the Triangle Film Corporation.

Gaonkar, Dilip Parameshwar, ed. 2001. *Alternative Modernities.* Durham, NC: Duke University Press.

Gernsheim, Helmut. 1962. *Creative Photography: Aesthetic Trends, 1839–1960.* London: Faber and Faber.

Giddens, Anthony. 1990. *The Consequences of Modernity.* Stanford: Stanford University Press.

Gidley, Mick. 1994. "Three Cultural Brokers in the Context of Edward S. Curtis's *The North American Indian.*" In *Between Indian and White Worlds: The Cultural Broker,* edited by Margaret Connell Szasz, 197–215. Norman: University of Oklahoma Press.

———. 1998a. *Edward S. Curtis and the North American Indian, Incorporated.* New York: Cambridge University Press.

———. 1998b. "The Repeated Return of the Vanishing Indian." In *Americana: Essays in Memory of Marcus Cunliffe,* edited by John White and Brian Holden Reid, 209–32. Hull, England: University of Hull Press.

———. 2001. "Ways of Seeing the Curtis Project on the Plains." In Edward S. Curtis, *The Plains Photographs of Edward S. Curtis,* 39–66. Lincoln: University of Nebraska Press.

———. 2003a. "Edward S. Curtis's Photographs for *The North American Indian*: Texts and Contexts." In *Iconographies of Power: The Politics and Poetics of Visual Representation,*

REFERENCES

edited by Ulla Haseltstein, Berndt Ostendorf, and Peter Schneck, 65–85. Heidelberg: Universitätsverlag.

———, ed. 2003b. *Edward S. Curtis and the North American Indian Project in the Field.* Lincoln: University of Nebraska Press.

———. 2007. "Out West and in the Studio: Official Photographs of Indians during the Great Survey Era." In *Images of the West: Survey Photography in French Collections 1860–1880*, edited by François Brunet and Bronwyn Griffith, 32–45. Chicago: University of Chicago Press, for Musée d'Art Américain, Giverny.

Gikandi, Simon. 1996. *Maps of Englishness: Writing Identity in the Culture of Colonialism.* New York: Columbia University Press.

Gilbert, Henry F. 1921. "A Chapter of Reminiscence: Part 2." *New Music Review and Church Music Review* 20 (231): 91–94.

———. 1976 [1911]. "Note on the Indian Music." In *Selected Writings of Edward S. Curtis: Excerpts from Volumes I–XX of The North American Indian*, edited by Barry Gifford, 117–20. Berkeley: Creative Arts Book Company.

Ginsburg, Faye. 1995. "Mediating Culture: Indigenous Media, Ethnographic Film, and the Production of Identity." In *Fields of Vision: Essays in Film Studies, Visual Anthropology, and Photography*, edited by Leslie Devereaux and Roger Hillman, 256–91. Berkeley: University of California Press.

———. 2002. "Screen Memories: Resignifying the Traditional in Indigenous Media." In *Media Worlds: Anthropology on New Terrain*, edited by Faye Ginsburg, Lila Abu-Lughod, and Brian Larkin, 39–57. Berkeley: University of California Press.

Glass, Aaron. 2004a. "'The Thin Edge of the Wedge': Dancing Around the Potlatch Ban, 1922–1951." In *Right to Dance/Dancing for Rights*, edited by Naomi Jackson, 51–82. Banff, AB: Banff Centre Press.

———. 2004b. "The Intention of Tradition: Contemporary Contexts and Contests of the Hamaṱsa Dance." In *Coming to Shore: Northwest Coast Ethnology, Tradition, and Visions*, edited by Marie Mauzé, Michael Harkin, and Sergei Kan, 279–304. Lincoln: University of Nebraska Press.

———. 2006a. *Conspicuous Consumption: An Intercultural History of the Kwakwa̲ka̲'wakw Hamaṱsa.* PhD dissertation, New York University. Ann Arbor: UMI Dissertation Services/ProQuest.

———. 2006b. "From Cultural Salvage to Brokerage: The Mythologization of Mungo Martin and the Emergence of Northwest Coast Art." *Museum Anthropology* 29 (1): 20–43.

———. 2008. "Crests on Cotton: 'Souvenir' T-shirts and the Materiality of Remembrance among the Kwakwa̲ka̲'wakw of British Columbia." *Museum Anthropology* 31 (1): 1–18.

———. 2009a. "Frozen Poses: Hamaṱsa Dioramas, Recursive Representation, and the Making of a Kwakwa̲ka̲'wakw Icon." In *Photography, Anthropology, and History: Expanding the Frame*, edited by Christopher Morton and Elizabeth Edwards, 89–116. London: Ashgate Press

———. 2009b. "A Cannibal in the Archive: Performance, Materiality, and (In)visibility in Unpublished Edward Curtis Photographs of the Hamaṱsa." *Visual Anthropology Review* 25 (2): 128–49.

———. 2010. "Making Mannequins Mean: Native American Representations, Postcolonial Politics, and the Limits of Semiotic Analysis." *Museum Anthropology Review* 4 (1): 70–84.

———. 2011. "Objects of Exchange: Material Culture, Colonial Encounter, Indigenous Modernity." In *Objects of Exchange: Social and Material Transformation on the Late Nineteenth-Century Northwest Coast*, edited by Aaron Glass, 3–36. New York: Bard Graduate Center for Decorative Art, Design History, Material Culture.

———. (In press.) "Indigenous Ontologies, Digital Futures: Plural Provenances and the Kwakwa̲ka̲'wakw Collection in Berlin and Beyond." In *Museum as Process: Translat-*

ing Local and Global Knowledges, edited by Raymond Silverman. London: Routledge.

Gmelch, Sharon Bohn. 2008. *The Tlingit Encounter with Photography.* Philadelphia: University of Pennsylvania Museum of Archaeology and Anthropology.

Gomery, Douglas. 2002. "The Rise of National Theatre Chains: Balaban & Katz." In *Exhibition: The Film Reader,* edited by Ina Rae Hark, 91–106. London: Routledge.

Gorbman, Claudia. 2000. "Scoring the Indian: Music in the Liberal Western." In *Western Music and Its Others: Difference, Representation, and Appropriation in Music*, edited by Georgina Born and David Hesmondhalgh, 234–53. Berkeley: University of California Press.

Graf, Marilyn. 1991. "The Last Great Indian Council: Joseph K. Dixon's 1909 Cylinder Recordings." *Resound: A Quarterly of the Archives of Traditional Music* 10 (4): n.p.

Graybill, Florence Curtis, and Victor Boesen. 1976. *Edward Sheriff Curtis: Visions of a Vanishing Race.* New York: Crowell.

Grierson, John. 1926. "Review of *Moana.*" *New York Sun*, February 8.

———. 1966. *Grierson on Documentary.* Edited by Forsyth Hardy. London: Faber and Faber.

Griffiths, Alison. 2001. "Playing at Being Indian: Spectatorship and the Early Western." *Journal of Popular Film and Television* 29 (3): 100–111.

———. 2002. *Wondrous Difference: Cinema, Anthropology, and Turn-of-the-Century Visual Culture.* New York: Columbia University Press.

Gulbrandsen, Don. 2010 [2006]. *Edward Sheriff Curtis: Visions of the First Americans.* Edison, NJ: Chartwell Books.

Habermas, Jürgen. 1987. *The Philosophical Discourse of Modernity.* Cambridge: Polity.

Halpern, Ida. 1967. "Liner Notes." *Indian Music of the Pacific Northwest.* Folkways Records album no. FE4523. New York: Folkways Records & Service.

———. 1981. Liner notes. *Kwakiutl Indian Music of the Pacific Northwest.* Folkways Records album no. FE4122. New York: Folkways Records & Service.

Hansen, Miriam. 1999. "The Mass Production of the Senses: Classical Cinema as Vernacular Modernism." *Modernism/Modernity* 6 (2): 59–77.

Haraway, Donna. 1984/85. "Teddy Bear Patriarchy: Taxidermy in the Garden of Eden, New York City, 1908–1936." *Social Text* 11 (Winter): 20–64.

Harber, Ken, and Russell Potter. 2010. "Early Arctic Films of Nancy Columbia and Esther Eneutseak." *NIMROD: The Journal of the Ernest Shackleton Autumn School* 10. Accessed March 16, 2013. http://www.ric.edu/faculty/rpotter/temp/Harper_Potter_Nimrod.pdf.

Harrison, Klisala. 2000. "Victoria's First People's Festival: Embodying Kwakwaka'wakw History in Presentations of Music and Dance in Public Spaces." Master's Thesis, York University.

———. 2002. "The Kwagiulth Dancers: Addressing Intellectual Property Issues at Victoria's First People's Festival." *World of Music* 44 (1): 137–51.

Hart, Mickey, and K. M. Kostyal. 2003. *Songcatchers: In Search of the World's Music.* Washington, DC: National Geographic Society.

Hearne, Joanna. 2006. "Telling and Retelling in the 'Ink of Light': Documentary Cinema, Oral Narratives, and Indigenous Identities." *Screen* 47 (3): 307–26.

Hegeman, Susan. 1999. *Patterns for America: Modernism and the Concept of Culture.* Princeton: Princeton University Press.

Heider, Karl. 1976. *Ethnographic Film.* Austin: University of Texas Press.

Herle, Anita, and Sandra Rouse, eds. 1998. *Cambridge and the Torres Strait: Centenary Essays on the 1898 Anthropological Expedition.* New York: Cambridge University Press.

Herzog, George. 1936. *Research in Primitive and Folk Music in the United States.* American Council of Learned Societies, bulletin 24. Washington, DC: American Council of Learned Societies.

Hiller, Susan, ed. 1991. *The Myth of Primitivism: Perspectives on Art.* London: Routledge.

Hochstetter, F. W. 1913. "Color in Photography." *Moving Picture News*, May 3, 12–13.

Hoffman, Doré. 1913. "Méliès in New Zealand." *Motion Picture World*, February 8, 553–54.

Hofmann, Charles, ed. 1968. *Frances Densmore and American Indian Music: A Memorial Volume*. Contributions from the Museum of the American Indian, Heye Foundation 23. New York: Museum of the American Indian, Heye Foundation.

Holm, Bill. 1983a. "Book Review of Christopher Lyman *The Vanishing Race and Other Illusions*." *American Indian Art Magazine* 8 (3): 68–73.

———.1983b. *Smoky-Top: The Art and Times of Willie Seaweed*. Seattle: University of Washington Press.

Holm, Bill, and George I. Quimby. 1980. *Edward S. Curtis in the Land of the War Canoes: A Pioneer Cinematographer in the Pacific Northwest*. Seattle: University of Washington Press.

Holman, Nigel. 1996. "Photography as Social and Economic Exchange: Understanding the Challenges Posed by Photography of Zuni Religious Ceremonies." *American Indian Culture and Research Journal* 20 (3): 93–110.

Horse Capture, George P. 1993. "Forward." In *Native Nations: First Americans as Seen by Edward S. Curtis*, edited by Christopher Cardozo, 13–17. Boston: Bullfinch Press.

Hoxie, Frederick E., ed. 2001. *Talking Back to Civilization: Indian Voices from the Progressive Era*. Boston: Bedford/St. Martin's.

Huhndorf, Shari. 2001. *Going Native: Indians in the American Cultural Imagination*. Ithaca, NY: Cornell University Press.

Hungry-Wolf, Adolph. 2006. *The Blackfeet Papers*. 4 vols. Skookumchuck, BC: Good Medicine Cultural Foundation.

Hutchinson, Elizabeth. 2009. *The Indian Craze: Primitivism, Modernism, and Transculturation in American Art, 1890–1915*. Durham, NC: Duke University Press.

Hymes, Dell, ed. 1974. *Reinventing Anthropology*. New York: Vintage.

Jacknis, Ira. 1984. "Franz Boas and Photography." *Studies in Visual Communication* 10 (1): 2–60.

———. 1987. "The Picturesque and the Scientific: Franz Boas' Plan for Anthropological Filmmaking." *Visual Anthropology* 1 (1): 59–64.

———. 1991. "George Hunt, Collector of Indian Specimens." In *Chiefly Feasts: The Enduring Kwakiutl Potlatch*, edited by Aldona Jonaitis, 177–24. New York: American Museum of Natural History.

———. 1992. "George Hunt, Kwakiutl Photographer." In *Anthropology and Photography, 1860–1920*, edited by Elizabeth Edwards, 143–51. New Haven, CT: Yale University Press

———. 1996. "The Ethnographic Object and the Object of Ethnology in the Early Career of Franz Boas." In *Volksgeist as Method and Ethic: Essays on Boasian Ethnography and the German Anthropological Tradition*, edited by George W. Stocking, Jr., 185–214. History of Anthropology Series. Vol. 8. Madison: University of Wisconsin Press.

———. 2000. "Visualizing Kwakwa̲ka'wakw Tradition: The Films of William Heick, 1951–1963." *BC Studies* 125/126:99–146.

———. 2002a. *The Storage Box of Tradition: Kwakiutl Art, Anthropologists, and Museums, 1881–1981*. Washington, DC: Smithsonian Institution Press.

———. 2002b. "The First Boasian: Alfred Kroeber and Franz Boas, 1896–1905." *American Anthropologist* 104 (2): 520–32.

———. 2003a. "Franz Boas and the Music of the Northwest Coast Indians." In *Constructing Cultures Then and Now: Celebrating Franz Boas and the Jesup North Pacific Expedition*, edited by Laurel Kendall and Igor Krupnik, 105–22. Contributions to Circumpolar Anthropology, no. 4. Washington, DC: Arctic Studies Center, Smithsonian Institution.

———. 2003b. "Yahi Culture in the Wax Museum: Ishi's Sound Recordings." In *Ishi In Three Centuries*, edited by Karl Kroeber and Clifton Kroeber, 235–74. Lincoln: University of Nebraska Press.

Jacquier, Philippe, and Marion Pranal. 1996. *Gabriel Veyre, Opérateur Lumière: Autour du monde avec le Cinématographe, Correspondance (1896–1900)*. Lyons: Institut Lumière/ Actes Sud.

Jay, Gregory S. 2000. "'White Man's Book No Good': D. W. Griffith and the American Indian." *Cinema Journal* 39 (4): 3–26.

Jessup, Lynda, ed. 2001. *Antimodernism and Artistic Experience: Policing the Boundaries of Modernity*. Toronto: University of Toronto Press.

Johnson, Pauline. 1911. *Legends of Vancouver*. Vancouver, BC: David Spencer, Limited.

———. 1913. *The Shagganappii*. Toronto. The Ryerson Press.

Jojola, Ted. 2003. "Absurd Reality II: Hollywood Goes to the Indians." In *Hollywood's Indian: The Portrayal of the Native American in Film, Expanded Edition*, edited by Peter C. Rollins and John E. O'Connor, 12–26. Lexington: University Press of Kentucky.

Jonaitis, Aldona. 1999. *The Yuquot Whalers' Shrine*. Seattle: University of Washington Press.

Kafka, Franz. 1971 [1913]. "The Wish to Be a Red Indian." In *Franz Kafka: The Complete Stories*, edited by Nahum N. Glatzer, translated by Willa and Edwin Muir, 390. New York: Schocken Books.

Kahn, E. J. 1955. *The Merry Partners: The Age and Stage of Harrigan and Hart*. New York: Random House.

Kane, Joseph Nathan. 1997. *Necessity's Child: The Story of Walter Hunt, America's Forgotten Inventor*. Jefferson, NC: McFarland.

Keeling, Richard. 1991. *A Guide to Early Field Recordings (1900–1949) at the Lowie Museum of Anthropology*. Berkeley: University of California Press.

———. 1997. *North American Indian Music: A Guide to Published Sources and Selected Recordings*. New York: Garland Publishing.

———. 2001. "Voices from Siberia: Ethnomusicology of the Jesup Expedition." In *Gateways: Exploring the Legacy of the Jesup North Pacific Expedition, 1897–1902*, edited by Igor Krupnik and William W. Fitzhugh, 279–96. Contributions to Circumpolar Anthropology, no. 1. Washington, DC: Arctic Studies Center, Smithsonian Institution.

Ketchum, Shanna. 2005. "Native American Cosmopolitan Modernism(s): A Re-articulation of Presence through Time and Space." *Third Text* 19 (4): 357–64.

Kilpatrick, Neva Jacquelyn. 1999. *Celluloid Indians: Native Americans and Film*. Lincoln: University of Nebraska Press.

King, Jonathan C. H., and Henrietta Lidchi, eds. 1998. *Imaging the Arctic*. Seattle: University of Washington Press.

Kirshenblatt-Gimblett, Barbara. 1998. *Destination Culture: Tourism, Museums, and Heritage*. Berkeley: University of California Press.

Knight, Rolf. 1978. *Indians at Work: An Informal History of Native Indian Labour in British Columbia, 1858–1930*. Vancouver, BC: New Star Books.

Koszarski, Richard. 1990. *An Evening's Entertainment: The Age of the Silent Feature Picture, 1915–1928*. Berkeley: University of California Press.

Kristeva, Julia. 1980. *Desire in Language*. Translated by Leon S. Roudiez. New York: Columbia University Press.

Krouse, Susan Applegate. 1990. "Photographing the Vanishing Race." *Visual Anthropology* 3 (2–3): 213–33.

Lazecki, Casey. 1997. "Movie Houses of Greater Vancouver." In *The Greater Vancouver Book*, edited by Chuck Davis, 714. Surrey, BC: Linkman Press.

Lears, T. J. Jackson. 1981. *No Place of Grace: Antimodernism and the Transformation of American Culture, 1880–1920*. Chicago: University of Chicago Press.

Lee, Dorothy Sara. 1979. *Native North American Music and Oral Data: A Catalogue of Sound Recordings, 1893–1976*. Bloomington: Indiana University Press.

———. 1993. "Native American." In *Ethnomusicology: Historical and Regional Studies*, edited by Helen Myers, 19–36. New York: W. W. Norton.

Levine, Victoria Lindsay, ed. 2002. *Writing American Indian Music: Historic Transcriptions, Notations, and Arrangements.* Middleton, WI: Published for the American Musicological Society by A-R Editions, Inc.

Lewis, Kevin. 1987a. "A World across from Broadway: The Shuberts and the Movies." *Film History* 1, no. 1: 39–52.

———. 1987b. "A World across from Broadway II: Filmography of the World Film Corporation, 1913–1922." *Film History* 1, no. 2: 163–86.

Lindsay, Vachel. 1915. *The Art of the Moving Picture.* New York: The Macmillan Company.

Lippard, Lucy R., ed. 1992. *Partial Recall: Photographs of Native North Americans.* New York: The New Press.

——— 1997. *The Lure of the Local: Senses of Place in a Multicentered Society.* New York: The New Press.

Loo, Tina. 1992. "Dan Cranmer's Potlatch: Law as Coercion, Symbol, and Rhetoric in British Columbia, 1884–1951." *Canadian Historical Review* 73 (2): 125–65.

Lutz, John Sutton. 2008. *Makuk: A New History of Aboriginal-White Relations.* Vancouver: University of British Columbia Press.

Lyman, Christopher M. 1982. *The Vanishing Race and Other Illusions: Photographs of Indians by Edward S. Curtis.* Washington, DC: Smithsonian Institution Press.

Macdonald, Bruce. 1992. *Vancouver: A Visual History.* Vancouver, BC: Talonbooks.

MacDougal, David. 1995. "Beyond Observational Cinema." In *Principles of Visual Anthropology.* Edited by Paul Hockings, 115–32. 2nd ed. Berlin: Mouton de Gruyter.

Mackay, Isabel Ecclestone. 1913. "Pauline Johnson: A Reminiscence." *Canadian Magazine* 41: 273–78.

Maddox, Lucy. 2005. *Citizen Indians: Native American Intellectuals, Race, and Reform.* Ithaca, NY: Cornell University Press.

Mahon, Maureen. 2008. "The Visible Evidence of Cultural Producers." *Annual Review of Anthropology* 29: 467–92.

Makepeace, Anne. 2002. *Edward S. Curtis: Coming to Light.* Washington DC: National Geographic Society.

Manganaro, Marc. 2002. *Culture 1922: The Emergence of a Concept.* Princeton: Princeton University Press.

Marcus, George. 1997. "The Uses of Complicity in the Changing Mise-en-Scène of Anthropological Fieldwork." *Representations* 59 (Summer): 85–108.

Marks, Martin Miller. 1997. *Music and the Silent Film: Contexts and Case Studies, 1895–1924.* New York: Oxford University Press.

Marsh, John. 1985. "Vaudefilm: Its Contribution to a Moviegoing America." *Journal of American Culture* 18 (4): 77–84.

Marubbio, Elise. 2009. *Killing the Indian Maiden: Images of Native American Women in Film.* Lexington: University Press of Kentucky.

Matthews, Major J. S. 1937. *Early Vancouver.* Vancouver Archives.

Mauss, Marcel. 1990 [1950]. *The Gift: The Form and Reason for Exchange in Archaic Societies.* Translated by W. D. Halls. New York: W. W. Norton.

Mauzé, Marie, ed. 1997. *The Present Is Past: Some Uses of Tradition in Native Societies.* Lanham, MD: University Press of America.

McGilligan, Patrick. 2011. *Nicholas Ray: The Glorious Failure of an American Director.* New York: It Books.

McGrane, Bernard. 1989. *Beyond Anthropology: Society and the Other.* New York: Columbia University Press.

McLuhan, T. C. 1972. "Curtis: His Life." In *Portraits from North American Indian Life: Edward S. Curtis,* edited by A. D. Coleman and T. C. McLuhan, viii–xii. New York: Outerbridge and Lazard.

McNally, Michael David. 2006. "The Indian Passion Play: Contesting the Real Indian in Song of Hiawatha Pageants, 1901–1965." *American Quarterly* 58 (1): 105–36.

McNutt, James C. 1984. "John Comfort Fillmore: A Student of Indian Music Reconsidered." *American Music* 2, no. 1: 61–70.

Meany, Edmond S. 1908. "Hunting Indians with a Camera." *The World's Work* 15:10004–11.

Miller, Daniel. 1991. "Primitive Art and the Necessity of Primitivism to Art." In *The Myth of Primitivism: Perspectives on Art,* edited by Susan Hiller, 50–71. London: Routledge.

———, ed. 1995. *Worlds Apart: Modernity through the Prism of the Local.* London: Routledge.

Milner, Victor. 1923. "Fade Out and Slowly Fade In, Fourth Installment." *American Cinematographer* 4, no. 9: 9, 26.

Momaday, N. Scott. 2008 [1976]. "A First American Views His Land." In *American Earth: Environmental Writing since Thoreau,* edited by Bill McKibben, 570–81. New York: Library of America.

Moore, Paul S. 2004. "Movie Palaces on Canadian Downtown Main Streets: Montreal, Toronto, and Vancouver." *Urban History Review,* March 22, 2004. Accessed June 28, 2010. http://business.highbeam.com/4548/article-1G1-116674030/movie-palaces-canadian-downtown-main-streets-montreal.

Morphy, Howard. 2006. "Sites of Persuasion: *Yingapungapu* at the National Museum of Australia." In *Museum Frictions: Public Cultures/Global Transformations,* edited by Ivan Karp, Corrine Kratz, Lynn Szwaja, and Tomás Ybarra-Frausto, 469–99. Durham, NC: Duke University Press.

———. 2010. "'It Is Our Film': Reflections on Film and Ritual as Participatory Experiences." Unpublished manuscript.

Morris, Peter. 1978. *A History of Canadian Cinema, 1895–1939.* Montreal: McGill-Queen's University Press.

Morris, Rosalind. 1994. *New Worlds from Fragments: Film, Ethnography, and the Representation of Northwest Coast Cultures.* Boulder, CO: Westview Press.

Muhr, Adolf. 1907. "E. S. Curtis and His Work." *Photo-Era* (July): 9–13.

Myers, Fred. 1994. "Culture Making: Performing Aboriginality at the Asia Pacific Society." *American Ethnologist* 21 (4): 679–99.

———. 2002. *Painting Culture: The Making of an Aboriginal High Art.* Durham, NC: Duke University Press.

———. 2006. "The Complicity of Cultural Production: The Contingencies of Performance in Globalizing Museum Practices." In *Museum Frictions: Public Cultures/Global Transformations*, edited by Ivan Karp, Corrine Kratz, Lynn Szwaja, and Tomás Ybarra-Frausto, 504–35. Durham, NC: Duke University Press.

Myers, Helen. 1993. "Native American Music." In *Ethnomusicology: Historical and Regional Studies*, edited by Helen Myers, 404–18. New York: W. W. Norton.

National Gallery of Canada. 2006. *Emily Carr.* Ottawa: National Gallery of Canada.

Newhall, Nancy. 1978. *P. H. Emerson and the Fight for Photography as a Fine Art.* New York: Aperture.

North, Michael. 1994. *The Dialect of Modernism: Race, Language, and Twentieth-Century Literature.* New York: Oxford University Press.

Northern, Tamara, and Wendi-Starr Brown. 1993. *To Image and to See: Crow Indian Photographs by Edward S. Curtis and Richard Throssel, 1905–1910.* Hanover, NH: Hood Museum of Art, Dartmouth College.

Nyong'o, Tavia. 2010. "Out of the Archive: Performing Minority Embodiment." In *Action and Agency: Advancing the Dialogue on Native Performance Art*, edited by Nancy Blomberg, 149–79. Denver: Denver Art Museum.

O'Malley, Michael. 1990. *Keeping Watch: A History of American Time.* New York: Viking.

Ostrowitz, Judith. 1999. *Privileging the Past: Reconstructing History in Northwest Coast Art.* Seattle: University of Washington Press.

Parezo, Nancy, and Don Fowler. 2007. *Anthropology Goes to the Fair: The 1904 Louisiana Purchase Exposition.* Lincoln: University of Nebraska Press.

Peabody, Rebecca. 2012. "Documents of an Encounter: Edward Curtis and the Kwakwa̲ka'wakw First Nations." In *Visual Representations of Native Americans: Transnational Contexts and Perspectives*, edited by Karsten Fitz, 113–24. American Studies Monograph Series. Heidelberg: Universitätsverlag Winter.

Pelletier, Louis. 2007. "An Experiment in 'Historically Correct' Canadian Photoplays: Montreal's British American Film Manufacturing Co." *Film History* 19 (1): 34–48.

Petroski, Henry. 1993. *The Evolution of Useful Things*. New York: Alfred A. Knopf.

Phelan, Peggy. 1993. *Unmarked: The Politics of Performance*. London: Routledge.

Phillips, Ruth. 2001. "Performing the Native Woman: Primitivism and Mimicry in Early Twentieth-Century Visual Culture." In *Antimodernism and Artistic Experience: Policing the Boundaries of Modernity*, edited by Lynda Jessup, 26–49. Toronto: University of Toronto Press.

Pierce, David, and Dennis Doros. 1992. "Film Notes." *In the Land of the War Canoes*. Harrington Park, NJ: Milestone Film and Video.

Pisani, Michael V. 1997. "'I'm an Indian Too': Creating Native American Identities in Nineteenth- and Early Twentieth-Century Music." In *The Exotic in Western Music*, edited by Jonathan Bellman, 218–57. Boston: Northeastern University Press.

———. 2005. *Imagining Native America in Music*. New Haven, CT: Yale University Press.

Potter, Russell. 2007. *Arctic Spectacles: The Frozen North in Visual Culture, 1818–1875*. Seattle: University of Washington Press / Montreal: McGill-Queen's University Press.

Povinelli, Elizabeth. 2002. *The Cunning of Recognition: Indigenous Alterities and the Making of Australian Multiculturalism*. Durham, NC: Duke University Press.

Powell, Jay, Vickie Jensen, Vera Cranmer, and Agnes Cranmer. N.d. *Yaxwatlan's: Learning Kwak'wala Series*. Book 12. Alert Bay, BC: U'mista Cultural Society.

Price, Sally. 1989. *Primitive Art in Civilized Places*. Chicago: University of Chicago Press.

Quimby, George. 1990. "The Mystery of the First Documentary Film." *Pacific Northwest Quarterly* 81 (April): 50–53.

Raibmon, Paige. 2005. *Authentic Indians: Episodes of Encounter from the Late-Nineteenth-Century Northwest Coast*. Durham, NC: Duke University Press.

Reynolds, D. 1998. "The Dancer as Woman: Loïe Fuller and Stéphane Mallarmé." In *Impressions of French Modernity: Art and Literature in France, 1850–1900*, edited by Richard Hobbs, 155–72. Manchester: Manchester University Press.

Rhodes, Gary Don. 2007. "The Origin and Development of the American Moving Picture Poster." *Film History: An International Journal* 19 (3): 228–46.

Ricoeur, Paul. 1984 [1983]. *Time and Narrative*. Vol. 1. Translated by Kathleen McLaughlin and David Pellauer. Chicago: University of Chicago Press.

Rollins, Peter C. 2003. *Hollywood's Indian: The Portrayal of the Native American in Film*. Lexington: The University Press of Kentucky.

Rony, Fatimah Tobing. 1996. *The Third Eye: Race, Cinema, and Ethnographic Spectacle*. Durham, NC: Duke University Press.

Rosaldo, Renato. 1989. "Imperialist Nostalgia." Special issue, *Memory and Counter-Memory*. *Representations* no. 26 (Spring): 107–22.

Rosenthal, Nicolas G. 2005. "Representing Indians: Native American Actors on Hollywood's Frontier." *Western Historical Quarterly* 36 (3): 329–52.

Roy, Susan. 2002. "Performing Musqueam Culture and History at British Columbia's 1966 Centennial Celebration." *BC Studies* 135 (Autumn): 55–90.

Ruby, Jay. 2000. *Picturing Culture: Explorations of Film and Anthropology*. Chicago: University of Chicago Press.

Rushing, W. Jackson. 1995. *Native American Art and the New York Avant-Garde: A History of Cultural Primitivism*. Austin: University of Texas Press.

———. 2003. "Native Authorship in Edward Curtis's Master Prints." *American Indian Art Magazine* 29 (1): 58–63.

Russell, Catherine. 1999. *Experimental Ethnography: The Work of Film in the Age of Video.* Durham, NC: Duke University Press.

Russell, Don. 1970. *The Wild West: A History of Wild West Shows.* Austin: University of Texas Press for Amon Carter Museum.

Rydell, Robert. 1984. *All the World's a Fair: Visions of Empire at America's International Expositions, 1876–1916.* Chicago: University of Chicago Press.

Said, Edward. 1978. *Orientalism.* New York: Pantheon Books.

Saint Augustine. 2006. *Confessions.* Translated by Gary Wills. New York: Penguin Books.

Salmi, Hanna. 2003 [1998]. "The Indian of the North: Western Traditions and Finnish Indians." In *Hollywood's Indian: The Portrayal of the Native American in Film,* expanded edition, edited by Peter C. Rollins and John E. O'Connor, 39–57. Lexington: The University Press of Kentucky.

Sandweiss, Martha. 2002. *Print the Legend: Photography and the American West.* New Haven, CT: Yale University Press.

Sauer, Rodney. 1998. "Photoplay Music: A Reusable Repertory for Silent Film Scoring, 1914–1929." *American Music Research Center Journal* 8–9: 55–76.

Savard, Dan. 2010. *Images from the Likeness House.* Victoria: Royal British Columbia Museum.

Scandiffio, Theresa. 2001. "Choreographing the Past: Edward S. Curtis' *In the Land of the Head-Hunters.*" Master's thesis, York University, Ontario.

Schieffelin, Edward. 1998. "Problematizing Performance." In *Ritual, Performance, Media,* edited by Felicia Hughes-Freeland, 194–207. London: Routledge.

Searle, John R. 1969. *Speech Acts.* Cambridge: Cambridge University Press.

Seeger, Anthony, and Louise S. Spear, eds. 1987. *Early Field Recordings: A Catalogue of Cylinder Collections at the Indiana University Archives of Traditional Music.* Bloomington: Indiana University Press.

Sewid-Smith, Daisy. 1979. *Prosecution or Persecution.* Cape Mudge, BC: Nu-yum-balees Society.

Simmon, Scott. 2003. *The Invention of the Western Film: A Cultural History of the Genre's First Half-Century.* Cambridge: Cambridge University Press.

Siôn, Pwyll Ap. 2007. *The Music of Michael Nyman: Texts, Contexts, and Intertexts.* Aldershot, England: Ashgate.

Smith, Andre Brodie. 2003. *Shooting Cowboys and Indians: Silent Western Films, American Culture, and the Birth of Hollywood.* Boulder, CO: University of Colorado Press.

Smith, Linda Tuhiwai. 2000. *Decolonizing Methodologies: Research and Indigenous Peoples.* London: Zed Books / Dunedin, NZ: University of Otago Press.

Smith, Paul Chaat. 2009. *Everything You Know about Indians Is Wrong.* Minneapolis: University of Minnesota Press.

Sollors, Werner. 2008 [2002]. *Ethnic Modernism.* Cambridge, MA: Harvard University Press.

Spivak, Gayatri Chakravorty. 1988. "Can the Subaltern Speak?" In *Marxism and the Interpretation of Culture,* edited by Cary Nelson and Lawrence Grossberg, 271–313. Urbana: University of Illinois Press.

Spradley, James P. 1969. *Guests Never Leave Hungry: The Autobiography of James Sewid, a Kwakiutl Indian.* New Haven, CT: Yale University Press.

Staples, Shelly. 2001. "I Prefer the Navajo Rug: Locating an American Primitive." Accessed January 10, 2013. http://xroads.virginia.edu/~museum/armory/primitivism.html

Stephens, Carlene E. 1983. *Inventing Standard Time.* Washington, DC: National Museum of American History, Smithsonian Institution.

Sterne, Jonathan. 2003. *The Audible Past: Cultural Origins of Sound Reproduction.* Durham, NC: Duke University Press.

Stewart, Jacqueline. 2005. *Migrating to the Movies: Cinema and Black Urban Modernity.* Berkeley: University of California Press.

Stilwell, Robynn J. 2002. "Music in Films: A Critical Review of the Literature, 1980–1996." *Journal of Film Music* 1 (1): 19–61.

Strong-Boag, Veronica, and Carole Gerson. 2000. *Paddling Her Own Canoe: The Times and Texts of E. Pauline Johnson (Tekahionwake)*. Toronto: University of Toronto Press.

Talbot, Frederick. 1912. *Moving Pictures: How They Are Made and Worked*. London: William Heinemann.

Taussig, Michael. 1993. *Mimesis and Alterity: A Particular History of the Senses*. London: Routledge.

Taylor, Diana. 2003. *The Archive and the Repertoire: Performing Cultural Memory in the Americas*. Durham, NC: Duke University Press.

Taylor, John. 2007. *The Old Order and the New: P. H. Emerson and Photography, 1885–1895*. Munich: Prestel.

Taylor, Robert Lewis. 1949. "Moviemaker III: Tabu and Sabu." *The New Yorker*, June 25, 28–43.

Thomas, Nicholas. 1999. *Possessions: Indigenous Art/Colonial Culture*. London: Thames and Hudson.

Thompson, Edward H. 1932. *People of the Serpent: Life and Adventures among the Maya*. Boston: Houghton, Mifflin.

Torgovnick, Marianna. 1990. *Gone Primitive: Savage Intellects, Modern Lives*. Chicago: University of Chicago Press.

Townsend-Gault, Charlotte. 2004. "Circulating Aboriginality." *Journal of Material Culture* 9 (2): 183–202.

Trachtenberg, Alan. 2004. *Shades of Hiawatha: Staging Indians, Making Americans 1880–1930*. New York: Hill and Wang.

Traxel, David. 1980. *An American Saga: The Life and Times of Rockwell Kent*. New York: Harper & Row.

Turner, Terrence. 2002. "Representation, Politics, and Cultural Imagination in Indigenous Video: General Points and Kayapo Examples." In *Media Worlds: Anthropology on New Terrain,* edited by Faye Ginsburg, Lila Abu-Lughod, and Brian Larkin, 75–89. Berkeley: University of California Press.

Verhoeff, Nanna. 2006. *The West in Early Cinema: After the Beginning*. Amsterdam: Amsterdam University Press.

Vizenor, Gerald. 1990. *Crossbloods: Bone Courts, Bingo, and Other Reports*. Minneapolis: University of Minnesota Press.

———. 1994. *Manifest Manners: Narratives on Postindian Survivance*. Lincoln: University of Nebraska Press.

Wade, Bonnie. 2006. "A Japanese Performance of Intertextuality: From Nô to Kabuki to Film." *Colloquium: Music, Worship, Arts* 3. Accessed December 17, 2011. http://www.yale.edu/ism/colloq_journal/vol3/wade1.html.

Wakeham, Pauline. 2006. "Becoming Documentary: Edward Curtis's *In the Land of the Headhunters* and the Politics of Archival Reconstruction." *Canadian Review of American Studies* 36 (3): 293–309.

———. 2008. *Taxidermic Signs: Reconstructing Aboriginality*. Minneapolis: University of Minnesota Press.

Wasden, William. 2009. "Artist's Statement." In *Continuum: Vision and Creativity on the Northwest Coast,* 29. Vancouver, BC: Bill Reid Gallery of Northwest Coast Art.

Watkins, Marie. 1998. "The Search for the 'Real Indian': Joseph Henry Sharp and the Issue of Authenticity at the Turn of the Nineteenth Century." In *Dimensions of Native America: The Contact Zone,* edited by Jehanne Teilhet-Fisk, 96–112. Tallahassee: Museum of Fine Arts.

Webster, Gloria Cranmer. 1990. "The U'mista Cultural Centre." *Massachusetts Review* 31, no. 1/2: 132–43.

———. 1992. "From Colonization to Repatriation." In *Indigena: Contemporary Native*

Perspectives, edited by Gerald McMaster and Lee-Ann Martin, 25–37. Vancouver, BC: Douglas and McIntyre.

Weiner, Annette. 1992. *Inalienable Possessions: The Paradox of Keeping-While-Giving*. Berkeley: University of California Press.

Wells, Cheryl. 2005. *Civil War Time: Temporality and Identity in America, 1861–1865*. Athens: University of Georgia Press.

Wierzbicki, James Eugene. 2008. *Film Music: A History*. New York: Routledge.

Wiggins, Marianne. 2008. *The Shadow Catcher: A Novel*. New York: Simon and Schuster.

Williams, Carol J. 2003. *Framing the West: Race, Gender, and the Photographic Frontier in the Pacific Northwest*. Oxford: University of Oxford Press.

Williams-Davidson, Terri-Lynn, executive producer. 2009. *Songs of Haida Gwaii: Archival Anthology*. 7-CD set. Surrey, BC: Haida Gwaii Singers Society.

Winston, Brian. 1988. "Before Grierson, Before Flaherty … Was Edward S. Curtis." *Sight and Sound* 57, no. 4: 277–79.

Wolfe, Patrick. 1999. *Settler Colonialism and the Transformation of Anthropology: The Politics and Poetics of an Ethnographic Event*. London: Cassell.

Wordsworth, William. 1970 [1802]. "Preface to *Lyrical Ballads*." In *The Selected Poetry and Prose of William Wordsworth*, edited by Geoffrey H. Hartman, 410–24. New York: New American Library.

Worswick, Clark. 2001. "Edward Sheriff Curtis: An Appreciation." In *Edward S Curtis, The Master Prints*, 9–28. Santa Fe: Arena Editions.

Wulffian, Don L. 1981. *The Invention of Ordinary Things*. New York: Lothrop, Lee and Sheppard Books.

Zamir, Shamoon. 2007. "Native Agency and the Making of *The North American Indian*: Alexander B. Upshaw and Edward S. Curtis." *American Indian Quarterly* 31, no. 4: 613–53.

Filmography

Bertollini, Francesco, and Adolfo Padovan. 1911. *Dante's Inferno*. Milano Film.

Boas, Franz. 1930. Untitled film footage. Edited by Bill Holm and released in 1973 as *The Kwakiutl of British Columbia*. University of Washington.

Canada: Nova Scotia to British Columbia. 1912. British Natural Colour Kinematograph Co. / Canadian Pacific Railway Company.

Carver, H. P. 1930. *Silent Enemy: An Epic of the American Indian*. Burden-Chanler Productions. Milestone.

Conner, Linda, Patsy Asch, and Timothy Asch. 1980–81. *Jero on Jero: A Balinese Trance Seance Observed*. Documentary Education Resources.

Costner, Kevin. 1990. *Dances with Wolves*. Orion Pictures.

Crane, Frank. 1912. *The Battle of Long Sault*. British American Film Manufacturing Company.

Cranmer, Barbara. 1999. *Tłi'na: The Rendering of Wealth*. Nimpkish Wind Productions, National Film Board of Canada.

Curtis, Edward S. 1914. *In the Land of the Head Hunters*. World Film Corporation. Edited by Bill Holm and George Quimby and released in 1973 as *In the Land of the War Canoes*. Seattle: University of Washington Press / Milestone Films.

DeMille, Cecil B. 1923. *The Ten Commandments*. Paramount Pictures.

Flaherty, Robert. 1922. *Nanook of the North*. Les Frères Revillon. Criterion.

———. 1926. *Moana* or *Moana: A Romance of the Golden Age*. Famous Players-Lasky Corporation.

Glass, Aaron. 2004. *In Search of the Hamat'sa: A Tale of Headhunting*. Documentary Education Resources, Royal Anthropological Institute.

Grierson, John. 1929. *Drifters*. Empire Marketing Board/New Era Films. British Film Institute.

Griffith, D. W. 1909. *The Mended Lute*. Biograph Company.

———. 1913. *The Battle at Elderbush Gulch*. Biograph Company.

———. 1915. *The Birth of a Nation*. David W. Griffith Corporation, Epoch Producing Corporation.

———. 1916. *Intolerance*. Triangle Film Corporation.

Guazzoni, Enrico. 1913. *Quo Vadis?* Società Italiana Cines.

Kazimi, Ali. 1997. *Shooting Indians: A Journey with Jeffrey Thomas*. Peripheral Visions Film and Video, Vtape Distribution.

Kunuk, Zacharias, and Norman Cohn. 1995. *Nunavut: Our Land*. IsumaTV.

Makepeace, Anne. 2000. *Coming to Light: Edward S. Curtis and the American Indian*. Makepeace Productions.

Marker, Chris. 1983. *San Soleil*. Argos Films. Criterion Collection.

Massot, Claude. 1994. *Nanook Revisited*. IMA Productions and La Sept, Films for the Humanities & Sciences.

McLuhan, T. C. 1974. *The Shadow Catcher: Edward S. Curtis and the North American Indian*. Mystic Fire Video.

Moore, Frank E. 1913. *Hiawatha, The Indian Passion Play*.

Murphy, Tab. 1995. *Last of the Dogmen*. HBO Video.

Obomsawin, Alanis. 1993. *Kahnesatake: 270 Years of Resistance*. National Film Board of Canada.

Olin, Chuck. 1983. *Box of Treasures*. U'mista Cultural Society.

Pastrone, Giovanni. 1914. *Cabiria*. Itala Film.

Ray, Nicholas. 1955. *Rebel Without a Cause*. Warner Brothers. Warner Home Video.

———. 1960. *The Savage Innocents*. Gray Films; Joseph Janni/Appia Films; Magic Film; Play Art; Société Nouvelle Pathé Cinema.

Reeves, Daniel. 1995. *Obsessive Becoming*. Shakti Multimedia.

Rosenthal, Joseph. 1903. *Hiawatha, The Messiah of the Ojibway* or *Hiawatha, The Passion Play of America*. Charles Urban Trading Company.

Rouch, Jean, and Edgar Morin. 1960. *Chronique d'un été* [Chronicle of a Summer]. Argos Films. Criterion Collection.

Spitz, Jeff. 2001. *The Return of Navajo Boy*. Groundswell Educational Films.

Van Dyke, W. S. 1933. *Eskimo* or *Mala the Magnificent*. MGM.

Vertov, Dziga. 1928. *Man with a Movie Camera*. VUFKU. Kino-Lorber Video.

Veyre, Gabriel. 1898. *Danse indienne*. Lumière Bros.

Wheeler, Dennis. 1975. *Potlatch. . . A Strict Law Bids Us Dance*. U'mista Cultural Society.

CONTRIBUTORS

Colin Browne is a poet, filmmaker, film historian, and writer on visual art, cinema, and literature. His most recent work is *The Properties* (2012). Browne's essay "Scavengers of Paradise," which explores the history and legacy of the *surréaliste* engagement with ceremonial art of the Northwest Coast and Alaska, was published in *The Colour of My Dreams,* the book accompanying the 2011 surrealist exhibition at the Vancouver Art Gallery. He teaches in the School for the Contemporary Arts at Simon Fraser University in Vancouver, BC.

Barbara Cranmer (T̓łakwagila'ogwa), a member of the 'Namgis from the Kwakwaka'wakw Nation, lives in Alert Bay, BC, where she continues her work as a documentary filmmaker, community leader, and entrepreneur. Her films about the people and cultures of the north Pacific coast have been honored by the American Indian Film Festival, Telefilm Canada/TV Northern Canada, the Sundance Film Festival, and the Ontario Arts Council.

Brad Evans is an associate professor in the English department at Rutgers University. His publications on the historical intersection of American literature and anthropology include *Before Cultures: The Ethnographic Imagination in American Literature, 1865–1920* (2005), "Where Was Boas During the Renaissance in Harlem? Race, Diffusion, and the Culture Paradigm in the History of Anthropology" (in the History of Anthropology Series, volume 11), and "After the Cultural Turn," which introduced a special issue of the journal *Criticism* on that topic. He is currently writing a book about an international fad for modernist magazines, *Black Cats, Butterflies, and the Ephemeral Bibelots of the 1890s,* in which he is interested in the question of how art movements move.

Kate Flint is provost professor of English and art history at the University of Southern California, where she currently chairs the art history department. Her books include *The Woman Reader, 1837–1914* (1993); *The Victorians and the Visual Imagination* (2000); and *The Transatlantic Indian, 1776–1930* (2008). She is completing a study called "Flash! Photography, Writing, and Surprising Illumination," and beginning work on a cultural history of the concept of ordinariness.

Mick Gidley is professor emeritus of American literature and culture at the University of Leeds. He has published many articles and three books on Curtis, including *Edward S. Curtis and the North American Indian, Incorporated* (1998). His most recent books are *Writing with Light: Words and Photographs in American Texts* (editor, 2010), *Photography and the USA* (2011), and *Picturing Atrocity* (coeditor, 2012). He is completing a cultural history of the German-born British photographer E. O. Hoppé.

David Gilbert is music librarian at UCLA, a position he previously held at the CUNY Graduate Center and Wellesley College. He has researched the intersection of nineteenth-century

French and American musical cultures, and is currently focusing on performance practice in early silent film. Gilbert has published articles on these topics as well as critical editions of music by Hector Berlioz and Jan Ladislaus Dussek, and has served as music and book review editor for *Notes,* the quarterly journal of the Music Library Association.

Aaron Glass is assistant professor at the Bard Graduate Center in New York City, where he specializes in the anthropology of art, material culture, media, museums, and indigenous people. Among his publications focusing on the First Nations of the Northwest Coast, recent books include *The Totem Pole: An Intercultural History* (coauthored with Aldona Jonaitis, 2010) and *Objects of Exchange: Social and Material Transformation on the Late Nineteenth-Century Northwest Coast* (2011), the catalogue for an exhibition he curated at the Bard Graduate Center. Glass is currently collaborating with the Kwakwa̲ka'wakw in the use of digital media to document early museum collections and to reactivate the ethnographic archives of Franz Boas and George Hunt.

Jere Guldin is a senior film preservationist at UCLA Film & Television Archive, where he has been responsible for overseeing the preservation and restoration of hundreds of feature films and short subjects. He holds a BA in film and an MA in theatre.

Klisala Harrison, an ethnomusicologist, is research fellow at the Helsinki Collegium for Advanced Studies at the University of Helsinki, Finland. Her research focuses on indigenous music in Canada and Northern Europe, music in theatre and film, applied ethnomusicology theory and method, and music and poverty relationships. Dr. Harrison has coedited the volume *Applied Ethnomusicology: Historical and Contemporary Approaches* (2010), edited the Music and Poverty issue of the *Yearbook for Traditional Music* (2013), and authored articles in the journals *Yearbook for Traditional Music, Ethnomusicology, The World of Music,* and *MUSICultures* as well as the book *Aboriginal Music in Contemporary Canada.*

Bill Holm is curator emeritus of Northwest Coast art at the Burke Museum of Natural History and Culture, and professor emeritus of art history and anthropology at the University of Washington. In the course of his research since the early 1950s, he has enjoyed a close relationship with many Kwakwa̲ka'wakw traditionalists, some of whom were participants in Edward Curtis's film.

Dave Hunsaker is a screenwriter and playwright based in Juneau, Alaska, and in Venice, California. He was formerly artistic director of the Juneau-based Naa Kahidi Theatre, a touring company of Native Alaskan artists. Hunsaker is a fellow of the Sundance Institute, a member of the Writers Guild of America, and an adopted member of the Lukaaxadi Clan of the Tlingit Nation.

Ira Jacknis is research anthropologist at the Phoebe A. Hearst Museum of Anthropology, UC Berkeley. His research specialties include the arts and culture of Native North America, modes of ethnographic representation (photos, film, and sound recordings), museums, and the history of anthropology. He is the author of *The Storage Box of Tradition: Kwakiutl Art, Anthropologists, and Museums, 1881–1981* (2002).

Timothy Long's previous engagements have included the Utah Opera, the Boston Lyric Opera, Opera Colorado, the Wolf Trap Opera, The Juilliard School, the Brooklyn Philharmonic, the Maryland Opera Studio, and the Oregon Bach Festival. As a pianist he has performed at venues including Carnegie Hall, the Kennedy Center, Alice Tully Hall, Jordan Hall, and the Caramoor and Aspen Festivals. Mr. Long is a full-blooded Native from the Muscogee Creek (Thlopthlocco Tribal Town) and Choctaw tribes. He is a tenured associate professor at SUNY–Stony Brook and is a member of the artist faculty at the Aspen Music Festival. His former positions include associate conductor at New York City Opera, assistant conductor at the Brooklyn Philharmonic, and teaching positions at The Juilliard School and the Yale School of Music.

Laura Ortman (White Mountain Apache) received the Common Ground Award for founding the Coast Orchestra, the all-Native American orchestra that premiered to sold-out audiences in Washington, DC, and in New York City in 2008. Ortman is a multi-instrumentalist (including violin and the Apache violin) and a visual artist, and composes and performs music for art and film. She has a fine arts degree from the University of Kansas and has lived in Brooklyn since 1997.

Paul Chaat Smith is the author of *Everything You Know about Indians Is Wrong* (2009), and coauthor (with Robert Allen Warrior) of *Like a Hurricane: The Indian Movement from Alcatraz to Wounded Knee* (1996). Smith is Comanche, and serves as associate curator at the Smithsonian's National Museum of the American Indian.

Neal Stulberg is currently professor and director of orchestral studies at the UCLA Herb Alpert School of Music. He has led many of the world's leading orchestras, including the Philadelphia Orchestra; the Los Angeles Philharmonic; the Atlanta, Saint Louis, and San Francisco Symphonies; the Netherlands Radio Symphony; the West German Radio Orchestra; the St. Petersburg Symphony Orchestra; and the Moscow Chamber Orchestra. Stulberg has given premieres of works by Steve Reich, Dmitri Smirnov, Paul Chihara, Joan Tower, Peter Schat, and Peter van Onna; has led the period-instrument orchestra Philharmonia Baroque in a festival of Mozart orchestral and operatic works; and has brought to life several silent movies from the early 1900s, including the Russian classic *New Babylon*, Shostakovich's first film score.

Jeff Thomas is an Iroquois photo-based artist whose work is in the collections of numerous national and international institutions. His curatorial projects include *Where Are the Children? Healing the Legacy of the Residential Schools* (2001), and *Emergence from the Shadow: First Peoples' Photographic Perspectives* (1998).

Owen Underhill is a composer and conductor living in Vancouver, Canada. From 1987 to 2000, he was artistic director of Vancouver New Music and he is a founding co-artistic director of the Turning Point Ensemble. He has a special interest in interdisciplinary and cross-cultural projects, and is a faculty member in the School for the Contemporary Arts at Simon Fraser University.

William Hiłamas Edward Wasden Jr. (Waxawidi, "Canoes Come to Him") is a member of the 'Na̱mgis Tribe of the Kwakwa̱ka'wakw Nation. He is descended from the 'Na̱mgis and Kwagu'ł through his father William Wasden Sr. (Sibalxola, "Sound of Copper Ringing"), who also has English and Irish ancestry, and through his mother Janet Wasden, née Hunt (Pudłas, "One Who You Will Get Full From"). His ancestors include "Old" Chief Wanukw, Chief 'Nulis, and Chief K̲ixitasu (George Hunt) from the Kwagu'ł; Chiefs Tłakwudłas and Waxawidi from the 'Na̱mgis; and individuals among the Mowachaht, Nuuchahnulth, Łanget, and Hiłdzakw Nations. Of his many art and cultural teachers, Wasden recognizes the late Chief Pał'nakwalagalis Wakas (Douglas Cranmer, 'Na̱mgis), Don Yeomans (Haida and Cree Nations), the late Chief Hiwakalis (Tom "Mackenzie" Willie, Musga̱'makw Dzawada'enuxw) and his late wife and matriarch 'Ma̱lidi (Elsie, daughter of Chief Helagalis Tom Patch Wamiss, Musga̱'makw Dzawada̱'enuxw), as the primary ones who groomed him culturally.

Shamoon Zamir is associate professor of literature and visual studies at New York University Abu Dhabi. He is the author of *Dark Voices: W. E. B. Du Bois and American Thought* (1995) and *The Gift of the Face: Photography, Portraiture, and Time in Edward S. Curtis's The North American Indian* (forthcoming).

INDEX

Note: Page numbers in *italic* are citations to illustrations.

Freud, Sigmund, 186, 188n2
Friml, Rudolf, 275
Fun Dance. *See* Am'lala
futurists, 182

Gabrielino-Tonva, 335
Galsgamliła (First to Appear in the House Ceremony), 227, 294, 302, 303, 328, *331*, 337
Garcia, Harper, 275
Garden River Ojibwe, 175
Gathering Abalones—Nakoaktok (Curtis), *254*
Gaumont (film company), 176
General, Emily, 130
General, Jacob, 130
genre, 8, 9, 13, 31, 35, 44, 110, 151, 173, 182, 198, 200, 213–15, 222, 225, 227, 228, 322
Geronimo, 360
Gerson, Carole, 86
Gerth, David, xvi, 172, 212
Getty Center, xxii, 189n14, 205, 208, 301, 305, 312, 313, 335, 338, *339*
Getty Research Institute: xix, xx, xxii–xxv, 263–65, 275, 277, 278, 383, 386, 387n3; "Documents of an Encounter" (symposium) xxiii, 205, 211n12, 323, 332, 334, 335, 355n8; "Research Lab" (workshop) xxiii, 189n14, 264
Gidley, Mick, 80n4, 121
Gilbert, David, xxiii, xxv, 32, 38n26, 223, 284, 288, 289, 291, 298, 386
Gilbert, Henry F.: 53, 100, 105, 108–12, 114, 118, 120, 124–26, 181, 285n12; *Indian Sketches,* 117
Gilbert and Sullivan, 24, 212, 272, 285, 289
Gilman, Benjamin Ives, 112, 113, 123n2
Git Hayetsk Dancers, 344
Gitxsan, 196
Gixsistalisama'yi. *See* Charlie, Alfred "Skookum"
Glass, Aaron: xviii, xxiii, xxiv, 5, 32, 33, 38n35, 123, 209, 211n12, 260, 261, 287, 301, 310, 316, 340, 343, 344, 347, 348, 354, 387; collaboration and relationship with Kwakwaka'wakw, 319, 336, 345, 346, 350, 356; collaboration with conductors, 298; collaboration with other indigenous groups, 345
Goddard, Pliny, 26, 36n12
Gold Rush (Alaska), 201
Good Eagle Family (Thomas), *141*
Gounod, Charles, 275
Grainger, Sharon Eva, xxiii, xxv, 90, 311, 326, 328–31, 333, 337, 339
Grant, Chief Larry, 335
Grierson, John, 173, 182, 184, 185
Griffith, D. W., 24, 188n2, 191, 201–3, 206, 271
Griffiths, Alison, xxiv, 158, 204
Grinnell, George Bird, 101, 102, 123n1, 132
Grizzly Bear. *See* Nan
Group of Seven, 19, 96
Grouse Dancer, 302, 328
gukwdzi (Big House), xiv, xv, xvii, 24, 218, 220, 257, 304, 310, *311*, 324, 334, 336
Guldin, Jere, xxiii, xxv, 32, 207, 281, 387
Gwal'sa'las. *See* Alfred, Dorothy "Pewi."
Gwanti'lakw. *See* Harris, Mary *and* Smith, Lauren.
Gwa'sala, 378
Gwa'wina Dancers, xix, xx, xxv, xxvi, 33, *34*, 59, 166n18, 213, 227, 228, 230, 293–95, 299, 300, 302–4, 307, 310–15, *316*, 317, 319, 325, *326*, *329–31*, *333*, 335, 336, *337*, 338, *339*, 341, *341*, *342–48*, *348*, 349, 353, 354n1, 356, 357n29

Gwikamgi'lakw. *See* Wilson, Emily Hunt
Gwikilayugwa. *See* Waklus, Mrs. George

Ha'etła'las. *See* Kwagwanu
Haida, 104, 109, 111, 124n9, 126n29, 244, 245, 307, 355n11
Haida Gwaii, 171
A Haida of Massett (Curtis), 244, 245
Hairy Face, 66, 79, 80n5
Halakas'lakala (Farewell Song and Dance), 228, 332
Halpern, Ida, 123, 231n8
Hals, Frans, 44
Hamasalał (Wasp Dance), 47, 207, 224, 225, 226, 231n10, 282, 356n20, 384, 386
Hamatsa, 21, 22, 37, *112*, 113–15, 162, 188n4, 215, 218, 219, *219*, 220, 221, 225–28, 231n7, *316*, 318, 324, 327, 328, 332, *333*, *339*, 340, 353, 371. *See also* hamsamł
Hamatsa Emerging from the Woods—Koskimo (Curtis), 46, 47, 58, 372
Hamdzid, Chief, 304
Hamsamala (Dance of the hamsamł), 219
hamsamł (Hamatsa or "Cannibal Bird" mask), 22, 37n20, 218, 220, 327, 328, 338, 339, *339*, 340, 356
hamspek ("cannibal pole"), 37n21, 162
Hana'łdaxw'la, 334. *See also* Am'lala
Hansen, Miriam, 198, 199
Haraway, Donna, 159
Harrigan and Hart, 272
Harriman, Edward, 51
Harriman Expedition, 101, 151
Harrington, John P., 101
Harris, Bob, *316*, 318
Harris, Martha ('Wadzidalaga), 257
Harris, Mary (Gwanti'lakw), 257
Harris, Chief Ned (Tławudłas), 17, 257
Harry, Don, 290
Hartley, Marsden, 6, 200
Harvard University, 51, 123n2, 278
Haywahe, Kevin, 136, *136*
H. C. Miner Litho Company, 24, 37n24, 202, *203*, 363, *364*, 370
"Head Hunters" (Braham score): xix, xx, xxii, xxv, 24, 30, 32, 33, 38n26, 89, 100, 117–19, 122, 126, 185, 192, 194, 204, 209, 212, 213, 216–18, 222, 223, *223*, 225, 227, 229, 236, 260, 265, 267, 268n10, 269, 270, 273–75, *276*, 277–85, 307, 315; Kwakwaka'wakw reception, 302, 314; reception by conductors, 287–300; restoration, 288, 302
headhunting, headhunters, xvii, 11, 14, 89, 93, 155, 157–59, 165n14, 207, 355n11
Hearne, Joanna, 160
Heidegger, Martin, 68
Heiltsuk Nation, 255
Helen of Troy, 280
Hershey, Barbara, 361
Herzog, George, 119, 120, 125n16
Heye, George, 107
Hiawatha, 177, 274
Hiawatha (cantata, Burton), 279
Hiawatha, or Nanabozho: The Musical Indian Play (Armstrong), 175, 176
Hiawatha, The Indian Passion Play (Moore), 177, 178, 273, 274, 279, 285n11
Hiawatha, The Messiah of the Ojibway (Rosenthal, Bowden, and Armstrong) or *Hiawatha, The Passion Play of America,* 175
Hiawatha in the Land of the Ojibwe (Armstrong), 36n6

photography of Edward S. Curtis (*continued*)
Two Moons, 134, *134*, 135; *The Vanishing Race—Navaho*, 143, *144*, 245; *Yellow Bone Woman [Arikara Tribe]*, *141*; *A Young Kutenai*, 81n7 . *See also* Curtis (photographer, as)
Photo Secession, 43
Pick, Walter, 277, 283
pictorialism, 4, 13, 43, 48, 49, 65, 69, 183, 185
picture opera, xix, 5, *6*, 17, 31, 52, 54, 60n12, 116, 154, 181. *See also* musicale
the picturesque, 14, 44, 90, 94, 95, 147, 158, 159
Piegan, 62, *62*, 63, 64, *64*, 65–73, 75–77, 103, 124n9, 132, *132*, 345, 360
A Piegan Home (Curtis), 72, 73, 74
Pigott, Robert Stuart, 92
Pinchot, Gifford, 51
Pisani, Michael, xxiii, 118, 125n20
The Pit (Tourneur), 150, 165n3
Plains Indians, 11, 47, 49, 58, 96, 101, 103, 108, 123, 124n3, 135, 136, 176, 200, 249
Plateau, 108, 110
portraiture, *xiv*, xxv, 4, 10, 13, 43–45, *46*, 47, 58, 61, *62*, 65, 71, *72*, 77, 78, 84, 94, 129, *134*, *136*, *138*, *141*, *143*, 162, 173, 187, 200, 234, *238*, 243, 244, 248, *252*, *252*, 253, *256*, 347
postcolonial contexts, postcolonial critiques, and postcolonialism, 34, 158, 164, 348
posters, 363, *368*, *369*, *371*, *373*. *See also In the Land of the Head Hunters* (Curtis film, ephemera)
potlatch: xv–xvii, 17, 33, 88, 115, 164, 233, 304, 318–20, 322–24, 328, 334–36, 341, 342, 355; prohibition of, 10, 28, 58, 141, 157, 158, 163, 168, 197, 226, 229, 230, 235, 255, 315, 321, 324; responses to prohibition of, 16, 34, 221, 227, 318, 323, 324, 332, 349, 352. *See also* Canadian Indian Act
Potlatch … A Strict Law Bids Us Dance (Wheeler), 157, 166n18, 181, 231n9
Potter, Russell, 209, 211
powwow, 33, 136, 138, 294
A Prairie Camp—Piegan (Curtis), 73, 74
Prayer to the Mystery (Curtis), 47
pre-Columbian or precontact, 50, 93, 95, 156, 157, 183, 186, 239, 245, 247, 347
prerogatives. *See k̲ik̲esu*
prestations, 320, 324
"the primitive" and primitivism, 6, 15, 19, 45, 49, 56, 65, 83, 90, 93, 94, 118, 160, 178, 179, 187, 190–93, 199–201, 204, 209, 226, 273, 317, 351, 357n30, 379, 383
Prince Arthur, Duke of Connaught, 17, *18*
Princess Red Wing, 90
privileges. *See k̲ik̲esu*
proprietary knowledge, 33, 160, 214, 308, 321, 335, 350
protocol, 33, 308, 317, 319, 320, 324, 325, 328, 332, 334–38, 348, 349, 352, 355n14. *See also k̲ik̲esu*
Pueblo, 56, 108, 200
Pudłas. *See* Sanborn, Andrea *and* Wadhams, Maria
Pudovkin, Vsevolod I., 173

The Queen's Lace Handkerchief (Strauss), 275
Quimby, George, xvi, xviii, xxvi, 21, 25, 27–31, 38, 100, 122, 123, 156, 157, 160–62, 169–71, 174, 191, 205, 212, 217
Quinault Female Type (Curtis), 81n7
Quinn, Anthony, 174
Quo Vadis? (film), 202

racialism and racism, 8, 9, 51, 75, 158, 159, 357. *See also* colonial contexts, colonialism, and colonization
railroads and railways, 64, 85, 175, 176
Raven (housefront), 50, 385
Raven masks, 204, 309, 379
Ray, Nicholas, 174
realism and naturalism, 13, 29, 45, 49, 139, 149, 160, 175, 180, 209
Rebel Without a Cause (Ray), 174
reception and consumption, 7–10, 13, 35, 54, 78, 79, 88, 93, 95, 100, 117, 118, 150, 151, 160, 163–65, 191, 217, 287, 288, 292, 298, 318, 319, 324, 352, 353, 358
reciprocity, 67, 320, 335, 336
reclamation, 226, 229, 291, 323, 341, 356n22
Red Horn, 75
Red Indian (Thomas), *132*
Redskin (Schertzinger), 289
Reed, Hayter, 142
reenacting, reenactment, 4, 10, 12, 14, 17, 58, 89, 90, 132, 157, 164, 168, 175, 182, 228, 289, 295, 299, 300, 319, 324
Reeves, Daniel, 169
regalia, 13, 17, *18*, 22, 28, 34, 89, 157, 162, 207, 214, 215, 217–20, 225, 229, 235, 255, 303, 305, 308, 309, 312–14, 323, 324, 327, 328, 332, 335–38, 341, *341*, 345, 346, 349, 357n29
The Regatta Girl (musical), 273
Reid, Ian (Nusi), xxvi, *339*, 356n23
repatriation, 28, 157, 181, 220, 315, 323, 338, 349, 354n7
representation: 7–10, 12, 13, 28, 31, 43, 47, 65, 69, 78, 87–90, 135, 158, 164, 165n16, 168, 181, 182, 192, 194, 198, 204, 210n7, 303, 309, 344–47, 352; authenticity and, 173–75, 197, 245, 247, 251, 304, 305, 312, 319, 321, 324, 346, 350; the "Indian" in music and song, of, 222, 279; music and song, of, 32; the "other" in music and song, of, 279; photographic, 342; silent film music, in, 119; Western conventions of, 83. *See also* self-representation
residential schools, 16, 82, 141–43, 162, 241, 321
restoration and reconstruction (film), 21, 28–32, 39n36, 50, 59, 161, 167, 169–71, 185, 188n1, 192, 205–9, 227, 230n2, 260–69, 281–85, 302, 319, 323, 325, 327, 329–31, 333, 341, 342, 344, 346, 349, 355n14, 356n26, 383–87
Returning the Gaze: Black Eagle and Kevin Haywahe (Thomas), *136*
The Return of a Navajo Boy (film), 161
Rice, Edward E., 272, 273
Richmond, Eddie, 262, 387
Riis, Jacob, 247
Robinson, Henry Peach, 44
romanticism, xiii, 4, 15, 17, 19, 21, 26, 30, 33, 93, 96, 139, 146, 149, 154, 158, 159, 179, 182, 184, 222, 235, 251, 253
Romberg, Sigmund, 275
Romeo and Juliet (Shakespeare), 174, 180
Rony, Fatimah Tobing, 158, 159, 162, 211n16
Roosevelt, Theodore, 3, 44, 51, 108, 151, 154, 155, 360
Rosaldo, Renato, 199
Rosenthal, Joe, 175
Rosenthal, Nicholas G., 89
Rouch, Jean, 173
Royal BC Museum, xvi, 157, 217
Royal Commission on Aboriginal Peoples, 241

INDEX